THE COM[illegible]OK OF

PRO FOOTBALL

1991 THE COMPLETE HANDBOOK OF PRO FOOTBALL

EDITED BY

ZANDER HOLLANDER

AN ASSOCIATED FEATURES BOOK

A SIGNET BOOK

ACKNOWLEDGMENTS

Let's hear it for Bill Parcells, who went out on top. And for those who played one role or another in the 17th edition of *The Complete Handbook of Pro Football*: Contributing editor Eric Compton, the writers and Linda Spain, Kevin Mulroy, Sue Powderly, Dot Gordineer, Chris Swirnoff, Westchester Book Composition/Rainsford Type, Elias Sports Bureau, Fred Cantey, Pete Abitante, Leslie Hammond, Joe Browne, Greg Aiello, Reggie Roberts and the NFL team publicists.

Zander Hollander

PHOTO CREDITS: Cover: John McDonough/*Sports Illustrated*. Inside photos: Vernon Biever, Malcolm Emmons, George Gojkovich, Ira Golden, Pete Groh, Vic Milton, Mitch Reibel, Robert L. Smith, NBC-TV, Wide World and the NFL and college team photographers.

SIGNET
Published by the Penguin Group
Penguin Books USA Inc., 375 Hudson Street,
New York, New York 10014, U.S.A.
Penguin Books Ltd, 27 Wrights Lane,
London W8 5TZ, England
Penguin Books Australia Ltd, Ringwood,
Victoria, Australia
Penguin Books Canada Ltd, 10 Alcorn Ave.,
Toronto, Ontario, Canada M4V 3B2
Penguin Books (N.Z.) Ltd, 182-190 Wairau Road,
Auckland 10, New Zealand

Penguin Books Ltd, Registered Offices:
Harmondsworth, Middlesex, England

First Signet Printing, August, 1991
10 9 8 7 6 5 4 3 2 1

CONTENTS

Editor's Note: The material herein includes trades and rosters up to the final printing deadline.

OOPS! SUPER BOWL HALL OF SHAME

By JOE GERGEN

It was a moment of such high drama and unbearable tension that players on both teams chose not to watch. There were those among the Buffalo Bills who linked hands as a gesture of support. A group of New York Giants knelt along the sidelines in prayer.

For Scott Norwood, however, the options were few. There was no one to hold and nowhere to hide. Super Bowl XXV, the source of so much pride and an object of so much concern in light of the Persian Gulf war, was just about over.

The event had been a fascinating chess match of conflicting coaching philosophies. It also had been a crisp, thrilling and superbly played game, with four lead changes and not a single turnover. As a showcase of National Football League talent, it lacked only two components: a winner and a loser. Norwood, the placekicker for the Bills, the man standing by his lonesome in the middle of Tampa Stadium, was being asked to make the final determination.

Such a moment had not occurred in any of the previous XXIV Super Bowls. A short field goal by Jim O'Brien in the final minute of Super Bowl V had enabled the Baltimore Colts to defeat the Dallas Cowboys, 16-13, but the score was tied when the man took aim at the uprights. Joe Montana had rallied the San Francisco 49ers to a go-ahead touchdown at 14:26 of the fourth quarter in Super Bowl XXIII but the decision did not rest on the success or failure of his final pass. His game-winning pass to John Taylor

---

Joe Gergen collects bloopers but rarely makes one as an award-winning sports columnist with Newsday.

Scott Norwood bears it as Buffalo honors the losers.

occurred on 2nd-and-2 from the 10-yard line of the Cincinnati Bengals.

Never before had the championship hopes of two teams rested on the shoulders of one man with but one opportunity. The Bills trailed, 20-19, when quarterback Jim Kelly grounded the ball to stop the clock with nine seconds remaining. Buffalo was at the Giants' 29-yard line, requiring a field-goal attempt from 47 yards. "That's a tough kick under any circumstances," noted Matt Bahr, the Giants' PK whose last-gasp, 42-yard boot in San Francisco seven days earlier had lifted his team to the National Conference title. And these circumstances were unsettling even to the coolest of customers, some of whom preferred to view the scene through their fingers.

Norwood was 30, a veteran of six seasons with the Bills after playing two years in the USFL. He is the quiet, reliable type, the team's all-time leading scorer and, according to one teammate, a most meticulous man. "A neatness freak," linebacker Cornelius Bennett had called him earlier in the week. "He must comb his hair and brush his teeth five times a day."

There was time to do neither once the Bills took possession of the ball at their 10-yard line with 2:16 left. Norwood kicked a few balls into a net along the sideline, took a few deep breaths and visualized winning the Super Bowl at the end. "Positive thoughts," he said later.

Certainly, it was the chance of a lifetime. All that was required was a strong leg, tunnel vision and nerves of steel. The leg didn't fail him. Whether the other two did, only he knows. "I kicked the ball too hard," he said after his attempt sailed wide to the right. "I needed to get more follow-through, to bring the ball in. I took my best cut at the time. I don't have to tell you I'm disappointed."

And no one had to tell Norwood that his miss would not be forgotten soon. In fact, the costly failure earned him a prominent place in the Super Bowl Hall of Shame. He is, at the very least, among interesting company. Charter members include several celebrated quarterbacks, a cornerback who became a movie star, a fellow kicker who attempted (in the words of Alex Karras) to "keek a touchdown," and the current President of the United States.

Not all the individuals in this select group lost a Super Bowl game. The former kicker, Garo Yepremian, actually played for the winning team, no thanks to him. But his gaffe remains the standard by which all others are judged. And President Bush never competed in the game but his decision to attend Super Bowl XVI at Pontiac, Mich., while serving as vice president, caused chaotic conditions on the roads surrounding the Silverdome, shut off entrances to the most convenient parking lots and resulted in thousands of people walking up to a mile across ice flows in zero-degree wind chill. And the pregame and halftime snafus at Super Bowl IV did nothing to enhance Tommy Walker's reputation as football's foremost entertainment director.

Still, the majority of enshrinees played a large part in their team's defeats. Some of them threw away games, some fumbled, some simply dropped the ball at disadvantageous times. Ironically, one of the key characters at the very first Super Bowl, back before it had even acquired its name, did none of the above. Like Norwood, he suffered from an errant foot. Unlike the Bills' kicker, Fred Williamson put his in his mouth.

Williamson was a cornerback for the Kansas City Chiefs, a flamboyant figure in white shoes who billed himself as the "Hammer" in honor of the forearm blow with which he attempted to cleave the helmets of opposing receivers. In the week before the champions of the American Football League met the mighty Green

The balloon that got away at Super Bowl IV in New Orleans.

Bay Packers, Williamson enlivened the proceedings by threatening the NFL champions—and heavy favorites—with great bodily harm. His team lost badly, he was carried off the field in the fourth quarter and, in the final analysis, the publicity hurt him not a whit.

He became a success in show business, a star of so-called blaxploitation movies, after leaving football and taking a shot at architecture, his major course of study at Northwestern. In an interview conducted at the office of his Hollywood agent a few years later, he said he believed the performance he gave before that Super Bowl had prepared him for his second career. "All my acting experience," he said, "was my football shenanigans."

And what a show it was. While his teammates said they were honored to be playing with the most famous team in pro football, Williamson was impudent. "What happens," he recalled, "was that we go out there and everybody's afraid, everybody's awed. They get to L.A. and they're the we-are-glad-to-be-here group. We were there because we kicked hell out of teams. But my guys are saying things like, 'Fuzzy Thurston's a great blocker, he annihilates people.' Bull!"

So the Hammer set out to restore some of the Chiefs' swaggering confidence. He did so by describing in detail what he was personally going to do to the Packers. It didn't work. "My guys thought I was getting the Packers mad," he said, "so they got mad at me."

Green Bay won the game, 35-10, thanks largely to two touchdown receptions by Max McGee behind Willie Mitchell, the other cornerback. "They tried to blame the loss on me," Williamson said. "Not that they threw those bombs at Willie Mitchell, but that I got the Packers mad. Well, that's cool. That's all right. The Packers whooped and yelled, 'Get the Hammer,' but we had a good time afterward. Willie Wood, Herb Adderley, Thurston and me."

Williamson even claimed that he orchestrated his dramatic exit from the game, feigning the injury that drew a large howl from the crowd at the Los Angeles Coliseum. Whether or not that was the case, however, the man did earn a special niche in Super Bowl annals, not that the majority of participants would be happy to displace him. He became the first goat of a uniquely American institution.

He was followed two years later by a mild-mannered quarterback who wore black high tops, a crew-cut and a cloak of humility. Earl Morrall was a journeyman whom Baltimore acquired prior to the start of the 1968 season for insurance. As fate would have it, the Colts' star, Johnny Unitas, suffered a tear on the inside of right elbow in the final exhibition game and Morrall started the regular season.

What a season it turned out to be. The Colts dominated the NFL in 1968, winning 13 of 14 games and manhandling the Cleveland Browns, 34-0, in the NFL championship game. The 34-year-old Morrall enjoyed a stellar year. He threw 26 touchdown passes and earned Most Valuable Player honors.

But he received no respect from his opposite number in Super Bowl III. Joe Namath, the brash, controversial quarterback of the AFL champion New York Jets, announced there were at least five passers in his league superior to Morrall. In addition to himself, he listed his backup, veteran Babe Parilli, in that category.

Although his teammates and coach Don Shula expressed indignation, Morrall had no intention of being drawn into a name-calling contest. That wasn't his style. "A lot of players have opinions on other players that would send writers running for their typewriters if they expressed them," the Baltimore quarterback said. "But players keep those opinions to themselves—at least that's the way it has been. Maybe Namath represents the new breed of athletes, the kind of athletes the coming generation wants . . . I hope not."

Namath did represent a new breed. Like Williamson, he put himself squarely on the spot with his public evaluation of Morrall as well as his "guarantee" of victory a few days later. But Broadway Joe shined in the spotlight during the Jets' monumental 16-7 upset. Morrall withered.

In the first half of the game, staged at the Orange Bowl in Miami, Morrall threw three interceptions. It was the last of the trio that doomed the QB and his team. The Colts, trailing, 7-0, had the ball on the New York 42 in the final minute before intermission when Morrall handed off to Tom Matte running to his right. Matte pulled up and flipped the ball back to Morrall. The flea-flicker was such a surprise to the Jets that Jimmy Orr was wide open at the 10-yard line.

But Morrall never looked at Orr, even after the intended receiver started waving his arms to signal the QB. Instead, Morrall threw to his right in the direction of Jerry Hill. Safety Jim Hudson stepped in front of the fullback for the interception and Shula replaced Morrall with Unitas, still only 80 percent effective, after two sloppy series in the third quarter. But the damage had been done.

"As we headed for the locker room," Morrall recalled later, "Jimmy screamed, 'Didn't you see me?' I told him, 'No, Jimmy, I didn't.' I had to turn to the right in order to take the pass from

At least Earl Morrall, goat in III, got his ring in V.

Matte and when I looked up, Jimmy wasn't in my line of vision. Hill was, so I went with him."

Fortunately for Morrall, a class individual, he received a second chance in the Super Bowl two years later when Unitas, returned to the starting role, was injured late in the first half against the Dallas Cowboys. Although he didn't throw a scoring pass in the Colts' 16-13 triumph, he was honored as the winning quarterback. That game, it turned out, was the beginning of another man's identification with Super Bowl failure. In SB V, also played at the Orange Bowl, Craig Morton threw three interceptions, the last two of which led to Baltimore's tying touchdown and the winning field goal by O'Brien.

Ironically, when Morton received his next start in the big game seven years later, he found himself facing his old team, the Cowboys. By then, he was employed by the Denver Broncos, whose success in 1977 started an afflication in the Rocky Mountain region known as Orange Crush. Although the man had enjoyed an outstanding season, his nine years in Dallas had convinced his former teammates he could be rattled.

The Cowboy defenders started well before the game, with safety Cliff Harris the most outspoken. They were coming after him, Harris promised, old friend or not. They wanted Morton to worry about the blitz.

"We showed it to them," noted defensive end Harvey Martin after the game, "but we used good defensive football. We wanted to give Morton something to think about, but it was just four guys rushing the passer. It seemed as though Morton was looking at me every time he came to the line. I think he was more concerned because he thought all of us would be coming at him."

Even with a four-man rush, Dallas applied heavy pressure. And Morton responded the way the Cowboys had it figured. He threw four interceptions in the first half alone as Dallas assumed a 13-0 lead. Coach Red Miller allowed his veteran QB to start the second half but when another Morton pass was almost intercepted by Too Tall Jones, he sent in the inexperienced Norris Weese, who drove the Broncos to their lone touchdown in a 27-10 defeat.

Morton completed only four of 15 passes against Dallas and he raised his interception total to seven in two games, a Super Bowl record for dubious achievement that endures to this day. Roger Staubach, his former rival who had supplanted him as the No. 1 quarterback with the Cowboys, attempted to comfort him. "You had a great season," he told Morton afterward. "I'm sorry it ended the way it did."

That game would mark Morton's last chance at the brass ring but the Broncos would be back again and again, much to the dismay of the sporting public, under the direction of another QB. Yet, the following year it was the Cowboys' turn to provide the bozo. In fact, they supplied two.

The first was Thomas Henderson, a mouthy linebacker who had given himself the nickname of Hollywood. Much like Williamson in the first Super Bowl, he decided to goad the opponents, who happened to be the formidable Pittsburgh Steelers, as well as call attention to himself. His most memorable—and damaging—remark concerned the intellectual capacity of quarterback Terry Bradshaw. "He couldn't spell 'cat,' Henderson observed, 'if you spotted him the 'c' and the 'a.' "

As it developed, Henderson didn't have a bad game, forcing a Staubach fumble that Mike Hegman converted into a Dallas touchdown. But the quarterback was nothing short of brilliant, passing for 318 yards and four touchdowns in the Steelers' 35-31 victory. "Go and ask Henderson if I was dumb today," Bradshaw said afterward.

It wasn't necessary. Still, a characteristic Cowboys' rally might have produced a tie and forced overtime if not for a dropped pass in the end zone late in the third quarter. It was charged to Jackie Smith, who had been one of the premier tight ends in the NFL for many years with the St. Louis Cardinals before signing with Dallas at age 38 in the hope of qualifying for his first Super Bowl. He got his wish, only to see his dream of a championship flutter away.

The Steelers were leading, 21-14, when coach Tom Landry called his number in a 3rd-and-3 situation at the Pittsburgh 10-yard line. Smith was completely free over the middle and appeared to have a sure touchdown in his grasp. But his feet skidded out from under him as he slowed for the catch, he lost his balance and he couldn't hold the most significant pass of a long and proud career.

"It was a good call," Smith said. "I just missed it. I slipped a little, but still should have caught it. I've dropped passes before, but never any that was so important." On fourth down, the Cowboys settled for a Rafael Septien field goal, a subtraction of four points. The margin of their defeat would be four points.

In a reversal of Morrall's resurrection from ignominy to salvation, Joe Theismann descended from fame to shame in the course of consecutive Super Bowls. One year after throwing two touchdown passes in the Washington Redskins' 27-17 triumph over Miami, he was hounded into mistakes in a crushing 38-9 loss to the Los Angeles Raiders at Super Bowl XVIII. Although he was intercepted twice, fumbled once and was sacked six times, there was one play that typified the performance and virtually guaranteed the favorites from D.C. would not become the first repeat champions of the 1980s.

It occurred with but seconds remaining in the first half. Washington was trailing, 14-3, and backed up near its own goal line. Traditional wisdom called for the Redskins to run out the clock. Instead, coach Joe Gibbs called for his Rocket Right, Screen Left formation, sending three receivers to the right and hoping to spring scatback Joe Washington for a long gain down the left side.

The surprise was on the team with the ball. Los Angeles had replaced Matt Millen, the hard-hitting but slow inside linebacker, with Jack Squirek, an anonymous but rangy substitute, and instructed him to shadow Washington. Theismann was too busy faking to his right to even notice the reaction of the new man. He

Joe Theismann: Hero in XVII to horns in XVIII.

tossed the screen pass blindly over Lyle Alzado, the defensive end charging from his left side. "I didn't see the linebacker," the quarterback said later. "I was expecting zone coverage, but Squirek was man-to-man."

Indeed, he was. The second-year player, who hadn't been credited with a touchdown since high school when he doubled as a wide receiver, moved up to cover Washington and directly into the path of Theismann's pass. He had to run only five yards in scoring one of the more stunning TDs in Super Bowl history. "I was in shock," Squirek said. No more so than Theismann and the Redskins, who never recovered their poise.

Of course, no quarterback has suffered greater frustration in the Super Bowl than John Elway. In a span of four seasons, his team lost three championship games by ever-widening margins. And whereas the other QB with an 0-3 record—Fran Tarkenton of the Minnesota Vikings—was not singled out for criticism, Elway took the heat for Denver's failures, particularly in his most recent outing, Super Bowl XXIV.

In fact, he even was blasted before that game, by no less a personage than Bradshaw. The television analyst, whose Super Bowl record as a QB was 4-0, charged that Elway had been "babied and pampered" throughout his career, that he was only a good quarterback, "not great," and that he had to play "the

John Elway's greatest humiliation occurred in XXIV.

game of his life'' if the Broncos were going to beat the San Francisco 49ers.

An annoyed Elway suggested Bradshaw was jealous of his paycheck. ''Bradshaw's been bashing me since I was a rookie,'' the Denver QB said. ''He didn't like the money I made then and he still doesn't like the money I make. He can stick it in his ear.''

But it was Elway who was stuck, with a reputation, after the game. In a dreadful performance, he completed only 10 of 26 passes for 108 yards. More significantly, he threw two interceptions (raising his total to six for three games) and fumbled once. ''I'm definitely disappointed by the way I played,'' he said.

Among those who were not surprised was Bradshaw. He had predicted that if the Broncos didn't take an early lead, ''. . . it could be 55-3 [in favor of San Francisco].'' The final score was 55-10 but it would have been 55-3 had not a third interception of Elway, in the end zone, been nullified by a questionable pass interference call. Elway didn't even finish the game. Gary Kubiak called signals most of the fourth quarter for Denver.

Not only losers belong in the little hall of Super Bowl horrors, however. It so happens that the most entertaining pass in the history of the event was thrown by Ypremian, a left-footed kicker and part-time tie-maker from Cyprus, in Miami's 14-7 victory over Washington in No. VII. That the pass, which followed a blocked field goal, was intercepted by Mike Bass and returned for the Redskins' only touchdown only added to the interest. ''He's pretty good with his foot,'' teammate Larry Csonka said, ''but not too good with his hands.''

And Tommy Walker, the West Coast showman, earned a spot with his production of the pregame and halftime extravaganzas at Super Bowl IV in Tulane Stadium. First, a hot-air balloon representing the NFL and carrying a man in a Viking suit, was blown into a corner of the end-zone seats, scattering thousands before the game. Threatened with a careening flame-thrower, the customers responded by ripping apart the balloon.

Shortly thereafter, Pat O'Brien read the Star-Spangled Banner to the accompaniment of Doc Severinsen's blaring trumpet. Except that the public address system failed the veteran actor. Finally, during the halftime special, a reenactment of the Battle of New Orleans, Andrew Jackson's horse was frightened by the sound of a cannon and the "Americans" began a disorderly retreat to their 20-yard line, eliciting cries of "dee-fense, dee-fense" from U.S. supporters.

Bush's decision to attend the first Snow Belt Super Bowl outside Detroit in January, 1982, caused a massive traffic jam that officials had spent three years planning to prevent and confusion among bus drivers and parking attendants. Occupants of one press bus leaving NFL headquarters in Dearborn at 1:15 finally arrived inside the stadium at 4 PM, and only after skimming across an empty, ice-covered parking field. Several valuable electronic transmission machines were dropped in transit and at least one writer had his right hand, the one carrying the tool of his trade, treated for frostbite.

To these unwitting contributors to Super Bowl folklore must now be added the name of Scott Norwood. Perhaps, given the circumstances of his failure, he should be first on the list. It's a good thing for him that Buffalo fans are more forgiving than their predecessors.

Only three days before Super Bowl XXV, Bills' owner Ralph Wilson recalled the travail of placekicker Booth Lusteg after he missed a game-winning kick at old War Memorial Stadium in 1966. "On his way downtown," Wilson said, "[Lusteg] was stopped and beaten up by three young fans. When the police asked why he didn't call for help, he said, 'Because I deserved it.' "

Twenty-five years later, the city reacted positively. On the day after his miss, Norwood was cheered by a large crowd attending a Bills' rally in front of Buffalo's city hall. He had to wipe away tears before he spoke.

It was a touching moment. But, as the man noted before he left Tampa Stadium on the night of Jan. 27, 1991, "I'm certain [the miss] is something I'll never forget completely." Neither will anyone else as long as the Super Bowl is played.

THE MYSTERY OF DAVID MEGGETT

By HANK GOLA

Carl Banks and Mark Ingram thought they would be the first arrivals at the Giants' 1989 training camp. When they alighted at 6:45 AM on the campus at Fairleigh-Dickinson University in Florham Park, N.J., they came upon an apprehensive rookie poking his head out of an unpretentious blue Chevette.

"He said he was David Meggett," recalled Ingram. "He asked us, 'Can you tell me where I'm going to be living?' We told him he'd have to go get a key to the dorm and when he came back, he pulled this big old suitcase, like a trunk. He said, 'Man, I brought everything with me because I don't want to go back home.'"

It took three well-conditioned football players to get the rookie's belongings through the door.

"That's what I'll always recall about David. He knew what he was there for," Ingram said.

Not much was known or even expected of Meggett that summer. Scouts had to twist the arm of Bill Parcells to get the coach to chance a fifth-round draft pick on him. The 5-7, 175-pound back had been a phenom at Towson State, darting through Division 1-AA defenses, but this was the big-time and the Giants were a power team with a size complex. Still, Parcells had no way to measure the determination that Meggett carried with him in that ponderous foot locker.

"Entering camp, I knew it was going to be something totally

Hank Gola, at 5-6 an inch shorter than David Meggett, has covered the Giants since 1981, most recently for the New York Post. *He co-authored* Hard Nose *with former Giant nose tackle Jim Burt.*

Mighty mite Dave Meggett makes headlines one way or another.

different than I'd ever experienced,'' Meggett explained. ''So I had to set some sort of philosophy for myself about what I wanted to accomplish, something that would keep me strong through the tough times. So I brought everything I owned to training camp and I told myself, I don't plan to go home.''

In the two seasons since, Meggett has learned to travel light. Not only has he secured himself a spot on the Giants, he's changed the way the league looks at so-called undersized backs. One of the most exciting players in football, Meggett is a prototype for quickness and strength and a matchup problem for any defense. Without his contributions in the playoffs, you can make a strong case that the Giants would not be Super Bowl XXV champs.

Yet for all the sparks and flash that Meggett has produced on the field, he has kept his true personality somewhat hidden from the public. Reading Meggett, who is shy or moody, chippy or misunderstood, is like trying to grab him on the run. Newspaper headlines have added to the enigma, but they haven't touched on the drive and discipline that has taken Meggett through several turning points in his life.

''I never expect anything to go smoothly for me because nothing ever has,'' Meggett said. ''That's why I really appreciate what I have now. I started out in a not-so-great neighborhood and went to a not-so-great college. I then transferred to a not-so-big college and barely made it to a great team. None of it's been easy.''

Meggett is the youngest of seven children raised alone by his mother in a lower middle-class part of Charleston, S.C. By the time he was in high school, his four brothers and two sisters were grown and out of the house. Meggett played football at Bonds-Wilson High School, where the most famous alumnus was Hall of Famer and Raiders' coach Art Shell. He missed his entire junior season because of a freak knee injury, sustained while celebrating in the end zone after an 80-yard run on a quarterback draw in a preseason jamboree.

He returned for his senior year as an option quarterback on a team that went 5-5.

''Mostly,'' he said, ''I handed off.''

The big schools weren't intrigued and Meggett himself wasn't sure about college. He considered a military school along with several high-school teammates but instead landed with his friends at Morgan State in Baltimore, thanks to a coach who places unnoticed Charleston athletes at mostly black colleges.

Problem was, Meggett found himself a cornerback on a team that didn't win a single game his freshman or sophomore seasons. He transferred to Towson, where he redshirted a year and was

Meggett was NCAA I-AA Player of the Year at Towson State.

switched to offense because of injuries in the backfield. And that's where things finally started to come together, culminating with Meggett's selection as Division 1-AA Player of the Year in 1988.

Earl Spates said he told the people at Morgan State that Meggett had pro potential when he sent him there in 1984. Without Spates, an assistant coach at Bonds-Wilson, Meggett's football career would have been over after high school. Spates had sent several Charleston kids to Morgan and his biggest task was in getting Meggett to consider college.

"It was my opinion that David was the best athlete coming out of the area," Spates recalled. "I told the coaches at Morgan he was pro material. He could play quarterback, running back, wide receiver or defensive back. I thought if you put him on the line, he could play the line. He was the strongest kid on the team, bench-pressing over 300 in high school.

"But David's first inclination was to go into the service. His response was that he was tired of school. If we could just get some of the coaches to talk to him, I felt we could get him to school.

When David's buddies went, that's when he decided.''

Meggett said he ended up playing cornerback at Morgan State ''because that's what they needed'' but despite being named to the all-conference team as well as captain, the mounting losses got to be too much.

''We were brought there to revive the program,'' he said. ''Instead, it went in the opposite direction. I didn't want to go through that for four years.''

Towson, in the suburbs of Baltimore, was nearby and Meggett had stopped there with Spates on their way to Morgan. Towson coach Phil Albert knew of the player down the road who had been a dazzling return man—Towson had played against him for two years. But Meggett first had to sit out a season after transferring. And he had to forego his full scholarship to Morgan and accept just a half-scholarship at his new school.

It was during that offyear when Albert became impressed with Meggett. ''He'd contacted us about transferring and we told him all the right things he had to do,'' Albert said. ''Then we forgot about it for a period of time. Dave showed up in my office one day and said he was ready to transfer. We were elated about it initially because we knew he was a quality football player but as we got to know him, we more importantly found out he was a quality young man.

''Here's a kid who was ineligible for the season after transferring, yet he makes every weight-room appearance, every meeting and never misses a practice. When we're traveling, he shows up at the game out of nowhere. When the team comes out of the locker room, he's out there patting everybody on the back.

''After one year of playing for us, he was unanimously elected team captain. Here's a guy who was elected captain in two places. That tells you something about him.''

According to Albert, Towson State's allotment of full scholarships was already reached, so the best the school could do was a combination of financial aid based on need and a partial athletic grant. To finance the rest of his education, Meggett took a nighttime job at United Parcel Service, loading and unloading trucks. Good for upper body strength. Lousy for sleep.

''When I see their commercials, I know all about those brown trucks,'' Meggett said. ''I'd go to class in the morning, practice in the afternoon and work at night. I'd work about three hours, making nine dollars an hour at the time. I'd be back to my room at about 1 AM.''

Albert says that Meggett continues to give to his alma mater, through contributions and time. ''He did an autograph-signing for our university and he had a line as long as the eye can see,'' Albert recalled. ''He spent time with every person who came. Everyone else's line was going as fast as wildfire and we had guys like Johnny Unitas and Brooks Robinson. David was talking to every kid. He never forgot where he came from.''

Unfortunately for Meggett, the picture of the honest team player who wants to earn everything he gets wasn't the one that played in New York once he was drafted by the Giants.

At best uncomfortable with the press and sensitive to any criticism, Meggett began to be perceived in the media as an electrifying player with a chip on his shoulder.

''Here's a guy who never had two pennies to rub together and all of a sudden he's in the middle of more money that he's ever seen in his life in a town with tremendous media and pressure,'' Albert said. ''What might be perceived as cockiness, rudeness or arrogance is often times insecurity or shyness.''

As a fifth-round pick, Meggett was thought of more as an interesting possibility than a sure thing. When Meggett got to his first training camp, Parcells announced that if he was to make the team, he'd have to make it as a return man. ''I've already got one small back [Joe Morris],'' Parcells figured. ''What am I going to do with another one?''

And to make the team as a returner, Meggett had to unseat one of the Giants' most popular players, Phil McConkey, an overachiever who in many ways symbolized the Super Bowl XXI champs.

The two were opposite in style. McConkey never fumbled a punt but he never ran one back all the way, either. Meggett was a big-play threat—his first practices at camp showed that—but after his first preseason game, it looked as though every kick he fielded would become an adventure.

Meggett, with a flurry of moves, returned one kickoff 30 yards but he also lost two punts against the Patriots in the Foxboro Stadium lights, one that caromed off his arm for a turnover. When he got back to his room and his suitcase, he called his agent, Tony Agnone, and told him to find him another job.

In the meantime, he recoiled at any questions about the game in New England.

''That game never left me. It was a bugaboo, and I thought I'd blown it,'' he said. ''Bill got on me like he does with everybody, except I didn't know it then. To this day, I can't explain what happened that night.''

A week later, however, Meggett put on a one-man show in Kansas City. He returned the opening kickoff 47 yards, set up a

Bill Parcells counsels rookie Meggett in 1989.

TD with a 20-yard punt return, burned a KC blitz with an open-field catch he turned into a 34-yard gain and went 19 yards with a screen pass, something that had been buried deep in the Giants' playbook.

Before his rookie year was up, Meggett had done a lot of things that Giants fans weren't used to seeing.

Prior to the opening night against the Redskins at noisy RFK Stadium, Parcells said he'd probably need a cattle prod to get his overawed rookies on the field. But early in the second quarter, Meggett came out of the backfield on third down, took a short pass from Phil Simms, zipped through a couple of lunging line-backers and sprinted in for a 62-yard TD. It was clear that the Giants had never had a specialty player quite like this. As a situational third-down back, Meggett became perhaps the team's only big-play threat. His open-field ability would turn three short passes into gains of 50 yards or more, including one incredible run on an icy field in Denver.

Parcells admitted that he was wrong about Meggett. GM George Young said that the team had underestimated his "toughness." "That first year, he had to pick up the blitz 40 times and he blocked his man 39 times," Young noted. "The only time he didn't get him was a missed assignment."

That kind of tenaciousness has made Meggett one of football's most feared return specialists. Giant punter Sean Landeta knows punters whose concentration is thrown off with Meggett waiting for their kicks.

"Mike Saxon of the Cowboys said they told him not to even punt to Meggett, just to punt everything out of bounds," Landeta said. "Rohn Stark [Colts] and Rich Camarillo [Cardinals] both say that Meggett gets them nervous. The one thing about him is he's fearless. That's what makes him so dangerous."

In the 1989 regular-season finale against the Raiders, Meggett's 76-yard punt return for a TD was the first by a Giant in 12 years. The rookie was one of just two Giants voted to the Pro Bowl that year—Lawrence Taylor was the other. Meggett figured to have an immediate share of the endorsement opportunities that New York offers. The fans loved him even if he wasn't regularly quoted. Then, just four days after he returned from the Pro Bowl, his image was dealt a blow like he hadn't absorbed in an NFL game.

On Feb. 8, the back page of the *New York Post* hit the stands with bold type: **Meggett in Sex Rap**.

Meggett had been arrested in Baltimore for allegedly offering an undercover cop posing as a prostitute $40 for sex. He turned out to be in the wrong place at the wrong time. Two months later, he was acquitted after a three-day trial that he wanted to go through to clear his name. However, he paid a needless price. According to Agnone, his agent, three companies immediately backed out of promotional arrangements that cost him $10,000. Since there was a two-month lag before the trial, the charge stayed with him for some time.

"For a while, he went from being one of the all-time favorites to being labeled as a sex offender," Agnone said. "He was devastated."

When Meggett took the witness stand, he explained that he was on his way to Agnone's office when he saw the undercover cop waving. He thought he knew her, so he stopped his car. She asked him if he wanted a date. Thinking he knew her, he asked where they were going. She asked him if he had any money. He said he had 40 bucks.

"To complicate everything, the Baltimore police had a sweep out. They were looking for a drug dealer with a red sweatsuit," Agnone said. "David happened to be wearing a red sweatsuit. They thought they had their man."

Meggett's reputation has been restored and his promotional income has been steadily increasing. He once worried that the incident would stick with him. He says he's concerned with what people think of him. "It's all part of the business," Meggett said. "You've got to care about people and what people think. We're in the entertainment business."

Meggett continued to make headlines off the field last season. First, he was AWOL from practice one day, supposedly to send management a message that he was unhappy with his $90,000 base salary (the Giants say that incentives pushed his 1990 earnings close to $225,000). Meggett and his agent insisted he had the flu and the thing was forgotten after a $1,500 fine. Then late in the season, a process server approached Meggett as he stepped off the practice field in full view of the regular writers and photographers who cover the team. Agnone said the matter involved a personal debt and that it was quickly resolved.

At the same time, Meggett couldn't have been happy with what seemed to be a reduced role in the offense once the Giants drafted Rodney Hampton. When he was in the game, more teams were keying on him. Even though he led the team with 39 catches, he'd become less of a focal point. In terms of yards, Meggett accounted for 31 percent of the Giant offense, even in a part-time role in 1989. During the regular season last year, that had slipped to 24 percent.

Meggett's father, whom he hadn't seen since he was a young

child, had also reappeared in his life, adding stress and strain. As it turned out, it was not a happy reunion.

Yet by the end of the season, Meggett's play was making headlines as he ultimately bailed out the Giants following an injury to Hampton in the first playoff game.

The Giants needed something other than the inside power running of Ottis Anderson, and Meggett provided that speed to the corner, spreading defenses laterally. While Anderson was pounding the Bills during an MVP performance in Super Bowl XXV, Meggett was what Parcells called "our changeup," keeping Buffalo's defense honest with 48 yards on nine carries and 13 yards on a pair of catches.

For two games, at least, Meggett proved to be durable enough to carry a heavier load. Parcells said it's "a good question" whether Meggett could be used that much over the long haul of a regular season. Meggett says he accepts that.

"My goals have always been team-oriented," Meggett explains. "I understand what Bill did with his backs. I know it keeps me fresh. I could be carrying the ball more somewhere else but here I've got a Super Bowl ring."

Of course, when it was suggested to Meggett that the Giants were lucky to have him once Hampton was hurt in the playoffs, Meggett replied, "Absolutely."

And he did plan to test his worth when his contract came up before the 1991 season.

"Dave is restless," Agnone said. "He still doesn't think that he's had his moment in the spotlight, even with all that he's done. Maybe that never will happen on the Giants because when you think of the Giants, you think of organization, not individual players."

And when you think of Meggett?

"I hope people think of a disciplined, hard-working guy who does his job," Meggett said.

"You know," he added, "I've never felt like I had anything to prove to anybody because of my size. I've only felt that I had to prove things to myself. It's a very tough business and you have to have a lot of heart. There have been guys with all the physical talents who just didn't have the heart.

"In this league, you've got to be tough."

Meggett has learned that lesson in more ways than one.

PAUL MAGUIRE: CLOWN PRINCE ON THE TUBE

By STAN ISAACS

If John Madden is the king of pro football analysts, then Paul Maguire is the clown prince. He is the funnyman, the cutup, the guy who will do anything—well, almost anything—for a laugh. But a funny thing was happening as people began to get more acquainted with the NBC announcing pair of play-by-play man Marv Albert and analyst Maguire last year:

It became evident that there was a solid football presence in the mix as well. For many, the realization may have struck home hardest in the pair's final game assignment of last season, the Miami at Buffalo playoff game.

The Compleat Maguire was evident here. He opened the telecast with a beaut. He said the Bills were making a mistake in starting quarterback Jim Kelly coming off an injury. Kelly proceeded to have an outstanding game. That didn't faze Maguire. He kidded his own foolhardiness, saying, "Buffalo has been lying to us about Kelly. He wasn't hurt that bad."

There then came a bull's-eye that made even the football purists take notice. As Miami drove toward the Buffalo goal, Maguire suggested that the Dolphins might throw a pass to guard-eligible Roy Foster, who was inserted into the lineup near the goal line. When Dan Marino then threw a touchdown pass to Foster, Maguire cackled and Albert played the straight man.

"Get out of here, it was a lucky call," Albert said. It was part of their act. Albert knew that for once Maguire had won the moment.

Stan Isaacs, TV sports columnist for Newsday, *covered everything from big-time sports to jumping frog contests before becoming an armchair spectator.*

Analyst Paul Maguire (right) adds comedy with Marv Albert.

Albert said Maguire is deceptive as an analyst. "Because he is so light-hearted, people had gotten the idea that he doesn't work at it. People used to say he didn't prepare when he was finding his way in his early days. I have found he is one of the most prepared of all analysts. He just does it in a different way. He takes few notes. He isn't walking around with a looseleaf notebook or with things coming out of his pocket like other color commentators. But he has tremendous retention, he has an ability to react to situations and then he uses the information in his head very well."

Producer Glenn Adamo, who worked with the Albert-Maguire team last year—"and I sure hope I work with them again this

No gag, he played four years with Chargers, seven with Bills.

season''—says, ''Because Paul's always fooling around, you don't think he's serious, but when you realize how much of the field he really sees, it's scary. He picks up things. He'll say, 'Watch No. 78, he'll break free here.' And he will.''

Adamo said, ''Being with him is the closest thing to baby-sitting with my children. Because he has so much of the kid inside him.'' There are times when Maguire, an inveterate mugger with a flat face that is like a pancake with a mustache stuck on it, looks as if he might well be one of the Muppets.

Adamo remembered a play last season involving struggling Pittsburgh Steeler quarterback Bubby Brister. On a broken hook and lateral play, Albert asked Maguire, ''What happened?'' Maguire said, ''We got to see this again. Run it slow.''

He then described the play as if it were one he had seen of fans cavorting in the parking lot before the game. ''This is the guy with the hot dog and he's passing it to the other guy and now he tries to hand off to the other guy, who drops the hot dog. The guys in the parking lot didn't have helmets but they had more agility.''

Maguire kicked the longest punt (64 yards) in Bills' history.

Maguire is not a big fan of the telestrator, yet he makes it work for him. In one game last season, when a defensive lineman bumbled and stumbled trying without success to pick up a fumble, Maguire went to town on the telestrator. He drew circles around the player's hands, saying, "See, these two things are hands. That's the ball. [He circled the ball]. These hands are supposed to get the ball." He then circled the movement of the ball and the frustrated player.

"It's a game," Maguire says. "You are supposed to have fun with it. Marv and I do. My philosophy is: We are not here for a long time, we are here for a good time."

Maguire is 53. His line is "I was found by a wolf under a rock." He grew up in the Youngstown, Ohio, area, was a three-sport high-school star who ran a 4:28 mile. That's something that will surprise Albert, who blinked when he first found out that his fun-loving, almost-rotund sidekick had been an outstanding college football player at The Citadel. He led the country in receptions as an end in 1959.

Maguire says, "I had scholarship offers from 176 colleges. Al

Davis talked me into going to The Citadel. Davis is the guy where the great lie came from. He gave me all sorts of promises that were not kept. Like he said, if I do well, he'd buy me a good cheap car. I did do well, and when I went to him about the car, his tune changed to, 'I said I'd help you to buy a good cheap car.' That's Al.''

Maguire was drafted by both the Washington Redskins and the fledgling American Football League's Los Angeles Chargers. ''When I played at the Copper Bowl in Phoenix,'' he said, ''Tom Eddy of the Chargers said they'd give me $9,000 and a thousand-dollar bonus. And he put 10 one-hundred dollar bills on a bed. I would have signed in blood.''

Maguire played four years with the Chargers, who moved on to San Diego, then seven more with Buffalo where ''I played in six championship games. We won three and lost three.'' Drafted as a wide receiver, he weighed 183 pounds in college, ballooned to 225 for the pros. ''I drank up the thousand-dollar bonus,'' he said.

When he couldn't hold onto Jack Kemp's line-drive passes, he was moved to linebacker, then evolved into a punter. Over an 11-year span, he averaged 42 yards a kick and was second in the AFL in punting one season. He is proud that he is one of the 19 men who played the entire 10 seasons with the AFL before it merged with the NFL.

When his playing career ended in 1971, he hooked on with NBC, given a boost by Curt Gowdy and Bills' official Jack Horrigan. ''Chet Simmons and Scotty Connal hired me at NBC,'' Maguire recalls. ''I must have said something they liked. This was in March, I went back in June, was told they would pay me $500 a game and see me in September. I actually didn't work the first seven weeks.''

His first assignment paired him with Bill Ennis, to whom he now gives much credit as a teacher. ''Ennis told me,'' Maguire said, '' 'Talk when you have something to say. And tell the viewers why they saw what they saw.' Those have been guiding principles for me ever since.''

He said, ''Ennis taught me something else. We were in Chicago once when it was cold as a SOB. We were nearly freezing to death near the end of the game and we had a plane to catch. But Ennis made it a point to stop by the truck after the game and thank everybody for the job they did. We missed the plane, but it was more important, I learned, to appreciate the production and engineering crew. I do that every game now. They are the ones who make it possible, they make it easy—and they don't get recognized by many people."

He worked at NBC until 1979 before he was fired by Don Ohlmeyer. Some people attributed it to poor work habits and a fondness for the grape. Maguire denies that. "I never could understand it. I graded out higher than anybody at NBC. Ohlmeyer fired me because I was ugly. In those days they didn't put you on camera much, 40 seconds maximum. This face has worn out three bodies. How many people could I scare in 40 seconds?"

Maguire then worked at ESPN for six years, where for two years he was the analyst for all seasons, working the USFL in the spring and Canadian football in the fall. Larry Felser, a Buffalo columnist who is not a huge fan of Maguire's, says, "He had put things on cruise control at NBC. At ESPN, where he had to prepare, he did some of the best TV analysis I had ever heard. I heard him do a Navy-Southern Cal game and he had researched so many things that were interesting about the game, he added many things. It was a remarkable job."

Maguire went over to ESPN "fifteen minutes after I got fired at NBC. The guys who had hired me at NBC—Simmons and Connal—were now running things at ESPN. I did arm-wrestling and college golf and skateboarding. You ever tried to interview an eight-year-old? It's like being alone."

Maguire rejects any implication that he ever coasted. "Nobody works harder than I do. I really pride myself on doing the job because I was born and raised to give an honest day's work." And what would Maguire be if he hadn't had a football/broadcast career? "I never thought about that," he said. "I probably would have got a nice job in a steel mill."

He came back to NBC in 1986, worked in the studio as an analyst and prognosticator—with some outrageous picks—before returning to game analysis in the middle of the 1988 season. He hit his stride last year when he was teamed with Albert. They clicked immediately, with Albert's subtle sense of humor helping to set up Maguire and also to knock him down. Every analyst moves up a few notches by being paired with the subtly comic Albert and Maguire moved up more than anybody.

"We have a perfect mix," Albert says. "He doesn't talk all the time. We give each other space. He has a terrific timing for comedy with memorable facial expressions. He is the ideal foil. It is tough to kid with some people because they always want to get the last laugh. You have to take it, too. He can, and I don't mind his shots."

They have developed what Albert calls "a popular feature in which Paul relates to the players." One time, Maguire had Steeler

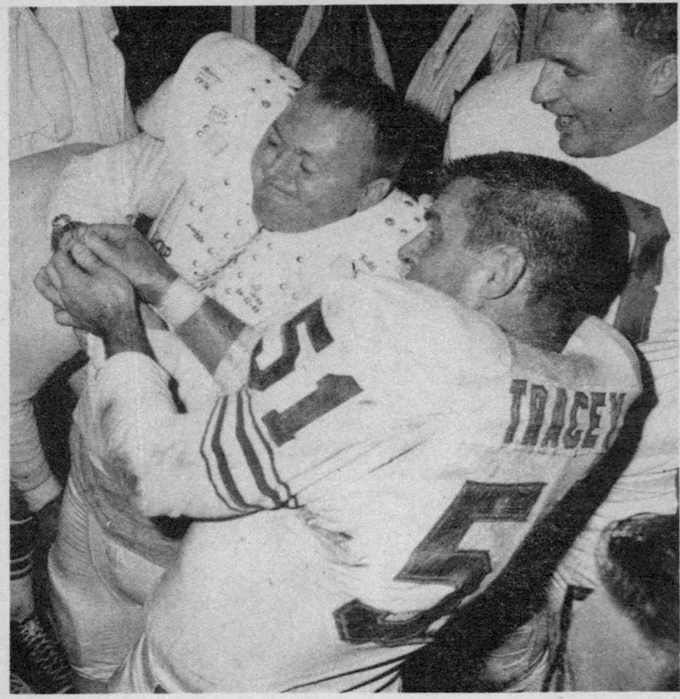

Maguire (left) uncorks with John Tracey in '64 AFL title year.

defensive lineman Keith Willis show him three things a lineman will be penalized for. Willis, prompted by somebody who will not fess up, then banged Maguire on the face mask, grabbed and pulled him and hit him some jolting head slaps. The unsuspecting Maguire, thinking Willis would go easy on him, reeled. He punched Willis, saying, "You said you would take it easy" and he smiled. It played funny on camera.

Washington lineman Joe Jacoby ripped Maguire's jacket in showing him an offensive move. And Maguire took a pratfall in the mud on a seeming investigation of a muddy field before one game. His willingness to play the buffoon fits in with his approach to football.

"It's a game, a kid's game that I played for 20 years," he said. "The worst thing about football, ask anybody, is practice.

Because it's repetitious. You hear the same lines, you look at the same films. Sunday is fun day, time to clock somebody."

Albert said, "He really has a distorted view of life. He will see the absurd in every situation, find the comedic theme in even a normal situation in a game."

To anybody who will listen, Maguire will lament that he has never had dinner with Albert before a game. Albert doesn't join their Friday night pregame work and play parties, because he is ever knee-deep in work. He usually has two or three other assignments on tap so doesn't feel he can spare the time. The joke about Albert, an ever studious long-time New York Knick announcer, is that if he were in Paris, he'd be in his room looking at Knick box scores.

Maguire says, "More than anything, I'd like to have dinner with Marv. It would be like a date. I'd like for him to give me a corsage and I'd wear it like we were at a prom."

Maguire had his moments as a prognosticator when he launched a campaign picking against the Jets in 1987, when they got off to a 10-1 start. "All year I'm picking the Jets to lose and they keep winning. One day they sent me over to the Jet camp in an armored car for protection. Joe Klecko told me, 'I hope you are picking us to lose. You are? Good.'"

Undaunted, Maguire then went on the air and pontificated that the Jets would not win another game the remainder of the season. "Bob Costas almost fell off his chair when I said that. I got hammered all over New York. Some people got a little nasty and I said, 'Sir, I am a guest in your city.'"

The Jets then proceeded to lose all their remaining regular-season games. "As they got down near the end," Maguire said, "the same guys who had been giving it to me were now saying, 'You know, you were absolutely right.'"

A man who spouts outlandish opinions, who says, however jovially, "I'm not perfect, but I have never made a mistake," is bound to have his detractors. To one keen student of TV sports, "Maguire is a personality and he has his moments, but he is also overbearing, a know-it-all, almost a smart alec in his approach."

Albert: "Some of the things he says would be more readily accepted if he were, like John Madden, a coach who had won a Super Bowl. Yet I find that he has the ability to be extremely well-liked by players even though he criticizes them. I've never seen players so drawn to a color commentator. They really get a kick out of him. He won't look to kill, but he will take his shots. If there is a bad play, particularly a lack of smarts, he'll come down on a guy. There is a lot of respect for him, and that's an

A pensive Paul finished as an active player in 1970.

aspect of him that is not generally seen."

Terry O'Neil, executive producer of NBC Sports, said he was lucky to come aboard and have Maguire in his stable. O'Neil, who has a very serious approach to the technical aspects of football, said, "Paul has a great feel for the game. He communicates with the common viewers on their terms. What is deceptive is that he knows more football than people might give him credit for. He can be funny and yet shrewd about technical aspects of the game at the same time."

Maguire is a popular figure in Buffalo with the fans, if not the local press. He hosts a cable show all-year round, "Sportsline with Paul Maguire," in which he interviews guests. He also co-hosts a Buffalo Bills' show with general manager Bill Polian which is seen as little more than a Bills' booster show by critics.

Maguire responds that the problem with Buffalo is that it has only one newspaper, the *Buffalo News*. "Their people are idiots. You can't have just one paper in a town with three major sports. When people bring the paper to my house, my dog Samantha won't even poop on that paper."

Maguire spends most of the rest of the year as a goodwill man, playing golf, for Budweiser, the sponsor of his cable television show. "My wife and I sit and watch the snow melt in January and February. We have coffee and hope we don't lose the dog in a snow bank."

Albert says, "You have to feel for his wife living with him for 25 years. Beverly keeps him in tow. She'll look at him and say, 'That's enough' and he'll stop his needling."

Beverly Maguire says, "Life is a game to him. He gets up every morning with that silly smile on his face and that's the way he is all day. What you see on the screen is the way he is at home. Being with him on the air is no different than being with him in a room."

Maguire met Beverly when he was playing in San Diego. They have raised three grown daughters in their Eden digs in the suburbs of Buffalo. "I promised him for better or worse," she says, "but not from San Diego to Buffalo."

Maguire jokes that the highlight of his broadcasting career has been working in the studio with Costas "Costas is a giant even though he's only five-feet-one. I don't know any other man who can comb his hair that much and still have that much hair."

He adds that he thinks the best is yet to come. "I would love to do a Super Bowl. With all those 55 cameras and miles of equipment, when you really come down to it, it is still a game, no different than any other game. I'd love to do it with Marv. We'd knock their asses off."

Because NBC will televise Notre Dame games this season, Dick Enberg and Bill Walsh, their No. 1 broadcasting pair, will do six Notre Dame games, opening up meatier pro football assignments for Albert and Maguire. NBC televises its next Super Bowl following the 1992 season. "We'd like to think we are running a meritocracy," says O'Neil. "If Marv and Paul are the best, they'll get it."

Jim Kelly gives it to offensive line after sack in Super Bowl.

THE GREENING OF JIM KELLY

By LARRY FELSER

It was a photograph we have seen dozens of times. A little kid, drowning in an oversize football uniform in the Punt-Pass-and-Kick competition, looks in awe as the NFL star quarterback—in this instance Terry Bradshaw—autographs a ball for him.

From the expression on the kid's face, it's easy to tell what he is dreaming. *Some day, I'll do what Terry Bradshaw has done.*

The photo is tucked in a special place in the family album back in East Brady, Pa. The dream never had to be tucked away. It came true.

The awe-struck kid in the photo was Jim Kelly, who led the Buffalo Bills to Super Bowl XXV. Now Kelly has a chance to lead them to the same sort of prominence in the '90s that Bradshaw and the Steelers enjoyed in the '70s.

Kelly came out of the same sort of Western Pennsylvania environment that produced such great quarterbacks as Joe Namath, George Blanda, Johnny Unitas, Dan Marino and Joe Montana. He and his four brothers staged an on-going round-robin tournament of football, boxing and general roughhousing when they were growing up.

Joe Paterno came to East Brady to recruit Kelly for Penn State, not as a quarterback but as a linebacker. That was understandable, since Kelly still plays quarterback with the truculence of a linebacker. The irony is that, a year later, Paterno wanted to make a linebacker out of Jeff Hostetler, who ended up the Giants' quart-

---

Larry Felser has covered the great ones in Bills' history—from O.J. Simpson to Jim Kelly—as sports columnist for the Buffalo News.

erback in their victory over Kelly and the Bills in the Super Bowl.

Despite the Paterno mystique, Kelly demurred when the invitation was offered. "I want to stay a quarterback," he explained.

Lou Saban was then the coach at the University of Miami. Needing to recruit a quarterback, Saban heard about the kid in East Brady.

"What I saw was a natural leader, one with raw toughness, but a young man who also had a great arm," explained Saban, who never got to coach Kelly. By the time Kelly arrived on campus in the fall of 1979, Saban had become head coach at West Point. His successor at Miami was Howard Schnellenberger, who had coached such quarterbacks as Bert Jones and Bob Griese in the NFL.

Even so, Schnellenberger wasn't sure what he had in Kelly.

He began to find out, strangely enough, in Rich Stadium, home of the Bills. The Syracuse Carrier Dome was still under construction, so the Orangemen were a gypsy team, playing all their home games at neutral sites. The Miami game was scheduled for Rich.

Syracuse, which had a potent offense featuring running back Joe Morris, wide receiver Art Monk and quarterback Bill Hurley, built a big lead in the first half. With the game beyond salvaging, Schnellenberger decided to allow his freshman quarterback, Kelly, to make his debut. Kelly passed his way to a couple of touchdowns to make it respectable.

Afterwards, in the Hurricane dressing room, a visitor told the Miami coach, "At last you found a quarterback."

Schnellenberger brushed aside the comment as nothing more than sympathy, but the next week, Kelly was the starting quarterback and a victorious one. The following Saturday he passed the 'Canes to one of the season's major upsets over Penn State.

As a senior, Kelly was a member of the famous Class of '83, whose quarterbacks were to dominate the NFL draft. There was John Elway at Stanford, Tony Eason at Illinois, Todd Blackledge at Penn State, Dan Marino at Pitt, a darkhorse at the University of California-Davis named Ken O'Brien, and Kelly.

As Marino moved down the prestige ladder because of a disappointing final season, Blackledge moved up. Kelly suffered a shoulder injury at midseason which ended his college career.

Just before the draft, Kelly worked out in Miami for an assembly of pro scouts. They were satisfied that he healed.

Buffalo, by circumstance, was in good draft position. In 1979, as a result of trading O.J. Simpson to San Francisco, the Bills had the 49ers' first-round pick. The Niners were in Bill Walsh's building period and had finished last, giving Buffalo the first selection in the draft. It was used on Ohio State linebacker Tom Cousineau, who signed instead with Montreal of the Canadian League.

When Cousineau came down from Canada in 1982, the Bills traded his rights to Cleveland in a deal that brought them the Browns' first-round pick in '83. This is what they used to draft Kelly.

At first, his drafting and signing seemed routine. In fact his then-agents, Greg Lustig and A.J. Faigin, were in the office of the late Pat McGroder, the Bills' vice president, discussing the timing of the press conference to announce the signing when McGroder's secretary opened the door.

"There is a telephone call for Mr. Faigin," she said. "It's a Mr. Bruce Allen."

McGroder's face turned ashen. Bruce Allen was the son of George Allen, who was coaching the Arizona team in the rival USFL at the time. Kelly's contract with the Bills had not actually been signed yet.

Faigin rushed outside, took the call and was told by Allen, "Don't sign anything. We'll put Jim with any USFL team he wants."

The agents left quickly and within days Kelly was a Houston Gambler. In the next three seasons, without their quarterback of the future, Buffalo won just 12 of their 48 games.

Meanwhile, Kelly thrived. Jack Pardee, head coach of the Gamblers, turned over the offense to Mouse Davis, the run-'n-shoot guru. In two USFL seasons under Davis, Kelly passed for 83 touchdowns and almost 10,000 yards. He was the league's Most Valuable Player in his rookie season.

When the USFL folded in the summer of '86, the route from the airport to the Bills' offices was lined with fans greeting Kelly on his way to sign his Buffalo contract—at last.

In that first season in the NFL, Kelly broke the Bills' records for pass completions, 285, and for completion percentage, 59.4, but the team won only four games. Despite his coming, it was another season of turmoil for Buffalo. But early in November, the groundwork for serious change was laid when Marv Levy was hired to replace Hank Bullough as head coach.

When Levy set about to construct his own coaching staff in January 1987, he was careful about filling the sensitive position of passing coordinator. He seemed to have the perfect man to guide Kelly with the hiring of Bobby Ross, who had just resigned as head coach at the University of Maryland. Ross, formerly Levy's special teams coach at Kansas City, had dominated the

Atlantic Coast Conference during his Terrapin days.

Then, just days after he agreed to come to Buffalo, Ross abruptly backed out to take the head coaching job at Georgia Tech.

Levy had to start over in a handicapped position to fill a vital job. Most of the available coaches had been hired. It seemed that it came down to "settling for" Ted Marchibroda. Once the successful head coach of the Baltimore Colts, Marchibroda was out of a job. The consensus around the NFL was that the game might have passed him by.

As it turned out, Marchibroda's reputation would be redeemed in Buffalo and Kelly would be the beneficiary.

The turnaround came after the players' strike early in the '87 season. The turnaround game was against Denver in Rich Stadium, when Kelly out-dueled Elway in a 21-14 Bills' victory. From that point, Buffalo went 4-2 over a six week stretch and the outlook for the entire franchise changed.

Buffalo was the surprise team of 1988, winning 11 of its first 12 games as Kelly established a reputation for bringing his colleagues from behind. At New England, he completed 12 passes in a row to ignite a winning rally in the second half. Indianapolis led, 17-0, at halftime, but Kelly exploded in the second half on his way to a three-touchdown pass, 315-yard day and a 37-24 victory.

"We have to believe," said linebacker Ray Bentley. "No matter how down we are, Jim can bring us back."

It was a sentiment that had been missing from the Bills' locker room for most of the decade.

Buffalo won its first division championship in nine seasons, beat Houston in the opening round of the playoffs, but then lost to Cincinnati in the AFC championship.

Nevetheless, the Bills wore a new label: "Next year's champions."

It didn't happen. The 1989 season was the Year of the Bickering Bills. Kelly played a key role.

The season began sensationally. In the opening game, against Miami, he rallied the Bills from a 24-13 deficit with less than four minutes to play. He scored the winning touchdown himself with no time left.

Two weeks later Kelly won a classic shootout from Houston's Warren Moon, passing 28 yards to Andre Reed for an overtime touchdown to give Buffalo a 47-40 victory. It was Kelly's fifth touchdown pass of the game. He had a total of 363 yards.

Then, the day after the season's fifth game, trouble erupted. Kelly suffered a separated shoulder in the third quarter of a

Kelly celebrates the first TD of Super Bowl XXV.

37-14 loss to Indianapolis. Speaking to the press more than 24 hours after the fact, the quarterback blamed a missed block by Howard Ballard, a young offensive tackle, for his injury. He repeated the charge for the television cameras.

There was fierce backlash. Kelly was criticized in the media. There was harsher criticism from within the Bills, especially since Ballard, a quiet, hard-working youngster who since has become a rising star, is popular with his teammates.

The fracas acerbated when Kelly was attacked on local TV shows, first by running back Robb Riddick and then by Thurman Thomas, whose own prestige in Buffalo rivals Kelly's.

Kelly's popularity wasn't helped as the Bills won all three games during his absence under the direction of backup quarterback Frank Reich. When Kelly returned, the Bills faltered, losing five of their next seven games, including losses to Atlanta, New England and Seattle.

The healing took place in Cleveland, when the Bills met the Browns in a memorable playoff game.

Marchibroda concocted a brilliant offensive plan, featuring a short passing attack with Thomas as Kelly's central collaborator. "It caught us by surprise," admitted Bud Carson, then the Browns' head coach. Kelly passed for 405 yards and four touchdowns. Of course, 150 yards and two touchdown passes went to Thomas, his former critic.

What propelled the Bills into their magic season of 1990, however, was the drive that failed.

With 2 minutes, 41 seconds left to play, Kelly started a drive that took the Bills to the Browns' 11. He converted two fourth-down plays and a third-and-10.

There were 14 seconds left when Kelly seemed about to complete his odyssey. Along the sidelines, the once-Bickering Bills held hands with one another. Kelly dropped into the protective pocket, threw a perfect pass to Ronnie Harmon, open in the corner of the end zone. Harmon dropped the ball. On the next play, Cleveland linebacker Clay Matthews intercepted Kelly and Buffalo's season was over.

The maturing of Kelly, however, had just begun.

A few weeks later, Kelly signed a six-year contract that paid him $3.3 million last season and henceforth guarantees him at least $1.4 million in base salary. He also had a variety of television, radio, and regional and national commercial contracts that add significantly to his yearly income.

At the time of the signing, Kelly, who had just turned 30, suggested that he had changed. "Everybody has to grow up sometime," he philosophized.

Despite his fast-lane lifestyle as an enthusiastic bachelor, he has always had decent inclinations. Three of his brothers live with him. One now serves as his agent. He bought a home and a large recreational vehicle for his mother and father, a retired steelworker who still lives in East Brady.

Kelly runs a summer football camp at nearby St. Bonaventure

University. Last year there was a local contest which offered free board and tuition at the camp for the winner. The lucky number was held by a young boy who suffered from Down's Syndrome. The boy's father called Kelly to explain the handicap. Kelly told him not to worry about a thing, just to bring his son to the camp.

Wherever Kelly went, the boy went with him. As the quarterback wheeled from group to group to offer instruction, his little buddy sat next to him in his golf cart.

"It was the best thing that ever happened to my son," said the father.

When the 1990 football season arrived, it was a time of renewal for Kelly. In the back of his mind, he had always yearned for an offense on the scale of the Run-'n-Shoot in which he was so effective in the USFL. Marchibroda, who had watched him fly so successfully by the seat of his pants whenever the Bills used their two-minute offense, reasoned that the same efficiency could happen for most of a game.

That is how the Bills' No-Huddle offense came into being.

It put Kelly in his comfort zone. It also made him the first NFL quarterback to call his own plays since Jim Plunkett's salad days with the Raiders. For the Bills' attack, it was a scorched-earth policy. Their 428 points led the NFL. Their 13 victories set a franchise record.

Yet, when Kelly suffered strained ligaments in his knee in a victory over the Giants in early December, it seemed as if he might miss the playoffs and Buffalo's Super Bowl dream might evaporate.

"I'll be back for the playoffs," he promised.

Kelly came back with a vengeance against the Miami Dolphins, who had chased the Bills all season in quest of the AFC East title. He started the game with a 20-yard pass to Thomas. He threw his second pass to Reed for a 40-yard touchdown. By the time he finished, he had 339 yards, three touchdowns and a 44-34 victory.

A week later, Kelly was nearly unstoppable as the Bills scored the most one-sided postseason victory since the 1941 Chicago Bears beat Washington, 73-0. Kelly even turned a fumble into a touchdown, snatching the ball on the bounce, then throwing a scoring pass to James Lofton as the Bills rolled, 51-3, over the Raiders.

Had Scott Norwood's 47-yard field goal attempt hooked 20 inches right, Kelly would still be taking bows for engineering Buffalo's final drive in the Super Bowl.

INSIDE THE NFC

By PHIL ANASTASIA

PREDICTED ORDER OF FINISH

EAST	CENTRAL	WEST
Washington	Chicago	San Francisco
N.Y. Giants	Minnesota	Atlanta
Philadelphia	Tampa Bay	New Orleans
Dallas	Green Bay	Los Angeles
Phoenix	Detroit	

NFC Champion: Washington

Three teams have won nine of the last 10 NFC championships. San Francisco, Washington and the New York Giants have dominated the last decade.

Change is coming. It's in the wind. It's inevitable. But 1991 still looks like a last hurrah for the 49ers, Redskins and Giants.

Who can break their grip on the conference? How about Chicago, the only other team to win the title since 1980? The Bears have refurbished their roster and look like the class of the Central.

Philadelphia? The Eagles, who won the title back in 1980, are young and talented and they have a new coach, Rich Kotite.

The Giants, defending NFC and Super Bowl champions, will face strong challenges in the East from the Redskins, Eagles and upstart Cowboys. The Giants have a new coach, Ray Handley, and an unsettled quarterback situation, age concerns on defense and a history of trouble following a Super Bowl triumph. They went 6-9 in 1987 after winning it all in 1986.

Phil Anastasia gets his kicks covering the Eagles and the NFL for the Camden (N.J.) Courier-Post.

Still, the Giants have a formula for success. Power football works for New York and they figure to bring the same simple, solid system into the playoffs in 1991. The tough part for New York will be repeating as division champions. Washington and Philadelphia are established powers and Dallas and Phoenix are on the rise.

The Redskins have rebuilt their defense. The offensive line still is strong, the running game is potent and there's "The Posse" of wide receivers. If quarterback Mark Rypien can cut down on the mistakes, the Redskins will surpass the Giants.

The Eagles have talent, and quarterback Randall Cunningham might be the game's most exciting player. Watch out for Dallas. The Cowboys almost landed Notre Dame's Rocket Ismail, but he fled to Canada for $26 million and a chance to play on a wider field.

Chicago bounced back from a disastrous 1989 to win the Central Division in 1990. The Bears are solid enough to defend their division crown but lack the tools to power through the playoffs.

Minnesota has talent but no chemistry. The Vikings' time may have passed. Tampa Bay has a fresh approach under new coach Richard Williamson, who has some good young defenders but still needs consistency from quarterback Vinny Testaverde.

The health of quarterback Don Majkowski is just one of many questions for Green Bay. Detroit looks doomed to an up-and-down year as the Lions adjust their offensive philosophy.

San Francisco was proven to be mortal in a loss to the Giants in the NFC title game last year. They also lost veterans Ronnie Lott and Roger Craig to the Raiders in Plan B. The 49ers still have Joe Montana, Jerry Rice and an underrated defense. That ought to be enough to win the West, but look for Washington—with the home-field advantage this time—to extract some revenge in the playoffs.

Atlanta has a ton of talent, a mean attitude under Jerry Glanville and may be ready to grab a wild-card berth. New Orleans, while solid, lacks flash and dash. The Rams have a new defense, but many of the same old problems.

The road to the Super Bowl will run through RFK Stadium, where the Redskins rarely lose. The Giants, Eagles, Bears, 49ers and Falcons will fill out the field. It'll be the 49ers and Redskins in the title game. Two teams that combined for seven crowns in the previous 10 years will fight for the top spot one last time.

It will end an era. The balance of power will shift. Maybe next year.

ATLANTA FALCONS

TEAM DIRECTORY: Chairman: Rankin Smith Sr.; Pres.: Taylor Smith; VP-Player Personnel: Ken Herock; Dir. Pub. Rel.: Charlie Taylor; Head Coach: Jerry Glanville. Home field: Atlanta Stadium (59,643). Colors: Black, red, silver and white.

SCOUTING REPORT

OFFENSE: Thanks to some key offseason additions and the continued improvement of quarterback Chris Miller, the Falcons jumped from 24th in the NFL in offense in 1989 to 10th in 1990. They have the talent to fly even higher.

If Miller could stay healthy for an entire season, he could put some big, big numbers on the board. He has a strong arm and a nice feel for the game. More important, he's got some quality targets.

Wide receiver Andre Rison arrived from Indianapolis in the Jeff George trade and set a team record for catches with 82. Three other wide receivers—Shawn Collins, Floyd Dixon and Michael Haynes—flourished in the Falcons' wide-open offense and combined for 103 catches.

The Falcons need to get better at running the football. Mike Rozier came on late in the season but is entering the twilight of his career. Rookie Steve Broussard showed flashes of ability but was inconsistent.

The offensive line is strong. Guard Bill Fralic and tackle Chris Hinton, another addition in the George trade, are among the best at their positions in the NFL.

DEFENSE: The Falcons won't contend for a playoff berth unless they improve on this side of the football. Specifically, they need to play better pass defense.

A better pass rush from their defensive line is a must. Tim Green has found a home at end after years as a mediocre linebacker, but the Falcons need more production from the rest of their linemen.

Darion Conner could be the pass-rushing linebacker the Falcons need to make their 3-4 defense work. Former No. 1 overall draft pick Aundray Bruce has been a disappointment. Inside linebackers Jessie Tuggle and John Rade are solid against the run but the Falcons are looking for more big plays from this group.

The secondary needs work. The cornerbacks at the end of 1990

Collarbone healed, Chris Miller is at the trigger again.

were Deion Sanders, who has a world of ability but has yet to put everything together, and aging Bobby Butler. They'll get help from Tim McKyer, acquired from Miami. The safeties were journeymen Scott Case and Brian Jordan.

SPECIAL TEAMS: The Falcons have an excellent return man in Sanders, who brought a punt back 79 yards for a TD in 1990 and also brings back kickoffs. The Falcons also have a knack for blocking punts and their coverage teams are excellent.

Punter Scott Fulhage had a good year, but placekicker Greg Davis was inconsistent. He made his first five field-goal attempts and was just 17-for-28 the rest of the year.

FALCONS VETERAN ROSTER

HEAD COACH—Jerry Glanville. Assistant Coaches—Bobby April, Jimmy Carr, June Jones, Tim Jorgensen, Bill Kollar, Jimmy Robinson, Keith Rowen, Doug Shively, Ollie Wilson.

No.	Name	Pos.	Ht.	Wt.	NFL Exp.	College
72	Barnett, Oliver	DT	6-3	285	2	Kentucky
83	Bartlewski, Rich	TE	6-5	255	1	Fresno State
1	Borgognone, Dirk	PK	6-2	220	1	Pacific
65	Bingham, Guy	C	6-3	260	12	Montana
63	Brinkley, Lester	DE	6-6	255	2	Mississippi
34	Broussard, Steve	RB	5-7	201	2	Washington State
93	Bruce, Aundray	LB	6-5	250	4	Auburn
77	Bryan, Rick	DE	6-4	265	8	Oklahoma
23	Butler, Bobby	CB	5-11	175	11	Florida State
20	Carey, Richard	CB	5-9	185	3	Idaho
25	Case, Scott	S	6-1	188	8	Oklahoma
75	Casillas, Tony	NT	6-3	280	6	Oklahoma
28	Chaffey, Pat	FB	6-1	218	1	Oregon State
85	Collins, Shawn	WR	6-2	207	3	Northern Arizona
56	Conner, Darion	LB	6-2	256	2	Jackson State
86	Dixon, Floyd	WR	5-9	170	6	Stephen F. Austin
42	Donaldson, Jeff	S	6-0	188	8	Colorado
64	Dukes, Jamie	C	6-1	285	6	Florida State
32	Eaton, Tracey	S	6-1	195	4	Portland State
74	Epps, Tory	NT	6-0	270	2	Memphis State
27	Evers, William	CB	5-10	175	1	Florida A&M
28	Fishback, Joe	S	5-11	198	1	Carson-Newman
79	Fralic, Bill	G	6-5	280	7	Pittsburgh
17	Fulhage, Scott	P	6-0	193	5	Kansas State
76	Gann, Mike	DE	6-5	270	7	Notre Dame
99	Green, Tim	DE	6-2	255	6	Syracuse
81	Haynes, Michael	WR	6-0	180	4	Northern Arizona
71	Hinton, Chris	T	6-4	300	9	Northwestern
69	Hoover, Houston	G	6-2	295	4	Jackson State
68	Hunter, John	T	6-8	300	3	Brigham Young
98	Jackson, Jacque	LB	6-2	228	1	Jackson State
26	Jackson, Pat	WR	5-8	165	1	Stephen F. Austin
3	Johnson, Tracy	RB	6-0	230	3	Clemson
38	Jones, Keith	RB	6-1	210	3	Illinois
40	Jordan, Brian	S	6-1	205	3	Richmond
3	Karlis, Rich	K	6-0	180	10	Cincinnati
78	Kenn, Mike	T	6-7	280	14	Michigan
88	Le Bel, Harper	TE	6-4	245	3	Colo. State
54	Lyles, Robert	LB	6-1	230	8	Texas Christian
22	McKyer, Tim	CB	6-0	174	6	Texas-Arlington
96	Miles, Eddie	LB	6-1	233	1	Minnesota
12	Miller, Chris	QB	6-2	195	6	Oregon
97	Phillips, Jason	WR	5-7	168	3	Houston
24	Pringle, Mike	RB	5-8	186	2	Cal-Fullerton
51	Pritchett, Wes	LB	6-4	234	1	Notre Dame
59	Rade, John	LB	6-1	240	9	Boise State
70	Redding, Reggie	T	6-3	290	1	Cal-Fullerton
95	Reid, Michael	LB	6-2	235	6	Wisconsin
14	Renfroe, Gilbert	QB	6-1	195	2	Tennessee State
7	Rhodes, Mike	QB	6-7	230	1	Georgia Tech
80	Rison, Andre	WR	6-0	190	3	Michigan State
92	Roland, Benji	DL	6-3	260	2	Auburn
30	Rozier, Mike	RB	5-10	212	7	Nebraska
55	Ruether, Mike	C	6-4	286	6	Texas
21	Sanders, Deion	CB	6-0	187	3	Florida State
61	Scully, John	G	6-6	275	10	Notre Dame
37	Shelley, Elbert	S	5-11	185	5	Arkansas State
89	Thomas, George	WR	5-9	169	3	Nevada-Las Vegas
52	Tippins, Ken	LB	6-1	230	3	Mid. Tenn. State
58	Tuggle, Jessie	LB	5-11	230	5	Valdosta State
87	Wilkins, Gary	TE	6-2	248	6	Georgia Tech
90	Williams, Mike	WR	5-10	177	1	Northeastern
94	Worthen, Naz	WR	5-8	177	2	North Carolina State

TOP DRAFT CHOICES

Rd.	Name	Sel. No.	Pos.	Ht.	Wt.	College
1	Pickens, Bruce	3	CB	5-10	193	Nebraska
1	Pritchard, Mike	13	WR	5-10	182	Colorado
2	Favre, Brett	33	QB	6-2	220	Southern Mississippi
4	Gardner, Moe	87	NT	6-2	254	Illinois
5	Goode, James	114	LB	6-3	242	Oklahoma

THE ROOKIES: Coach Jerry Glanville bragged after the draft that the Falcons had become the fastest team in the NFL. Atlanta added pure speed in cornerback Bruce Pickens from Nebraska and wide receiver Mike Pritchard from Colorado. The Falcons also might have found their quarterback of the future in Southern Mississippi's Brett Favre.

OUTLOOK: Glanville's Falcons went from 3-13 in 1989 to 5-11 last year. They have the talent to make the jump to .500 but still lack experience and consistency. They'll be dangerous every week but they still look like the fourth-best team in a four-team division.

FALCON PROFILES

CHRIS MILLER 26 6-2 195 **Quarterback**

Passed for career-best 17 TDs despite missing final three games with broken collarbone . . . Threw for 2,735 yards . . . Must avoid nagging injuries to reach his potential . . . Key to Red Gun offense Falcons employed at times under new coach Jerry Glanville . . . Threw for career-best 366 yards in victory over New Orleans . . . Had three TD passes against San Francisco . . . Did not throw an interception in six games, including streaks of 110 and 77 passes without a pick . . . Threw for career-high 3,459 yards in 1989 . . . As a baseball shortstop, he was drafted by Toronto and Seattle . . . Falcons' No. 1 pick in 1987 draft out of Oregon . . . Oregon record-holder in most passing categories . . . Born Aug. 9, 1965, in Pomona, Cal. . . . 1990 base salary: $550,000.

ANDRE RISON 24 6-0 190 **Wide Receiver**

Burst on Atlanta scene with club-record 90 receptions . . . Generated 1,208 yards and 10 TDs . . . Named NFC Offensive Player of Month for October (26 catches, 501 yards, 6 TDs) . . . Caught 11 passes against San Francisco . . . Six catches, 100 yards—all in fourth quarter against Cleveland . . . Confident, talkative player . . . Acquired by Atlanta from Indianapolis in draft-day deal that sent No. 1 overall pick (Jeff George) to Colts . . . Caught 52 passes for 820 yards as a rookie for Indianapolis . . . Colts' No. 1 pick out of Michigan State in 1989 . . . Was all-state in basketball playing on same high school team as Glen Rice of NBA's Miami Heat . . . Born March 18, 1967, in Muncie, Ind. . . . Earned $275,000 in 1990.

DEION SANDERS 24 6-0 187 — Cornerback

Led Falcons with 1,254 total yards—851 in kickoff returns, 250 in punt returns, 153 in interception returns . . . Returned an interception 82 yards for TD against Houston and another 61 yards for TD against Dallas . . . Returned a punt 79 yards for TD against Cincinnati . . . Brash, cocky player who hasn't always backed up his boasts . . . Called "a coward" by former Eagles' coach Buddy Ryan, who said Sanders never hit anybody on defense . . . Needs to be more consistent in pass defense and as a tackler . . . Also a baseball prospect who signed with Atlanta Braves after being released by the Yankees . . . Nicknames include "Neon Deion," "Money" and "Prime Time" . . . Falcons' No. 1 pick in 1989 out of Florida State . . . Legendary athlete at Florida State, he arrived for final college home game in a limousine, wearing a tuxedo . . . Born Aug. 9, 1967, in Ft. Myers, Fla. . . . 1990 base salary: $550,000.

MIKE ROZIER 30 5-10 212 — Running Back

Led Falcons in rushing with 675 yards despite starting just five games . . . Claimed on waivers from Houston Oct. 3 . . . Reunited with Falcons' coach Jerry Glanville, who was his coach in Houston . . . Ran for 100 or more yards in three of final five games . . . Gained 157 yards, including 67-yard run, in season finale against Dallas . . . Ran for 115 against Tampa Bay and for 100 against Rams . . . Glanville said Rozier brings the "toughness" the coach is trying to establish with his new team . . . Contract problems, minor injuries and presence of other talented halfbacks led to his release by Oilers . . . Ran for 1,002 yards and 11 TDs for Houston in 1988 . . . Joined Oilers from USFL in 1985 . . . Played two seasons for Jacksonville Bulls after winning Heisman Trophy at Nebraska . . . Born March 1, 1961, in Camden, N.J. . . . 1990 base salary: $650,000.

BILL FRALIC 28 6-5 280 **Guard**

Considered one of top guards in NFL . . . Started all 16 games . . . Was called for just one holding penalty all season . . . Unfortunately, that wiped out crucial first down late in one-point loss to Philadelphia . . . Perennial Pro Bowl selection . . . Respected around league for outspoken stance against steroid use . . . Missed first game in 1989 after protracted contract holdout . . . A starter since rookie season . . . Falcons' No. 1 pick out of Pittsburgh in 1985 . . . His dad, Bill Sr., once put up a sign in family front yard: "Forget the dog, beware of owner" . . . Weighed 170 pounds at age nine . . . Born Oct. 31, 1962, in Pittsburgh . . . 1990 base salary: $725,000.

CHRIS HINTON 30 6-4 300 **Tackle**

Key to blockbuster draft-day 1990 trade was Falcons' acquisition of Hinton from Indianapolis . . . Perennial Pro Bowl selection who is regarded as one of the best tackles in NFL . . . Has great strength and excellent blocking technique . . . His presence helped Falcons improve in total offense from 24th in 1989 to 10th in 1990 . . . In seven seasons with Colts, he made Pro Bowl six times . . . First rookie offensive lineman to make Pro Bowl . . . Fourth pick in 1983 draft, Hinton was traded to Colts in a deal that sent John Elway to Denver . . . Played just one season of tackle at Northwestern . . . Played linebacker and tight end earlier in college career . . . Born July 31, 1961, in Chicago . . . 1990 base salary: $725,000.

TIM GREEN 27 6-2 255 **Defensive End**

Flourished at defensive end after four so-so seasons at linebacker . . . Led Falcons in sacks with six and quarterback pressures with 37 . . . Also registered career-high 121 tackles . . . Forced four fumbles . . . Started all 16 games . . . Slowed by injuries early in career . . . Hit his stride in 1989, with 111 tackles and five sacks as outside linebacker . . . Started just 11 games in first three seasons . . . Falcons' No. 1 pick in 1987 out of Syracuse . . . Rhodes Scholar nominee in 1985 and 1986 . . . Studying for law degree . . . Born Dec. 16, 1963, in Syracuse . . . 1990 base salary: $350,000.

STEVE BROUSSARD 24 5-7 201 **Running Back**

Falcons' No. 1 pick was slowed by injuries and made limited impact as a rookie . . . Rushed for 454 yards and caught 24 passes for 160 yards . . . Quick scatback was thought to be perfect for Falcons' wide-open Red Gun offense . . . Best game came in Week Two when he collected 114 total yards (86 rushing, 26 receiving) against Detroit . . . Also broke loose for 50-yard TD run in upset of Cincinnati . . . Started 10 games but was on bench behind Mike Rozier at season's end . . . The 21st overall pick in 1990 draft, out of Washington State . . . Holds school record with 41 career TDs . . . Led Pac-10 in receptions with 59 as a sophomore . . . Won Los Angeles 100-meter track title as a senior at Manuel High School . . . Born Feb. 22, 1967, in Los Angeles . . . 1990 base salary: $250,000.

SHAWN COLLINS 24 6-2 207 **Wide Receiver**

Overshadowed by newcomer Andre Rison on Falcons' receiving corps . . . Caught 38 passes in 1990—a 20-catch dropoff from his total as a rookie in 1989 . . . One of four Falcon wide receivers (Rison, Floyd Dixon and Michael Haynes are the others) to catch more than 30 passes . . . Caught 61-yard pass against San Francisco . . . Played in all 16 games, starting six . . . Had started all 16 games in 1989, when he was consensus all-rookie selection . . . His 58 catches tied Redskins' Art Monk for most by a rookie wide receiver in the 1980s . . . Falcons' second No. 1 pick (Deion Sanders was the first) in 1989 out of Northern Arizona . . . Played some tight end in college . . . Born Feb. 27, 1967, in San Diego . . . 1990 base salary: $236,000.

DARION CONNER 23 6-2 256 **Linebacker**

Second to Washington's Andre Collins among NFL rookie linebackers with 83 tackles . . . Strong impact in second half of season after learning system and role . . . Credited with six quarterback pressures against Rams . . . Has size, speed and demeanor to be a big-play man in Falcons' aggressive defense . . . Called a "borderline trained killer" by Jerry Glanville . . . Falcons' second-round pick in 1990 out of Jackson State . . .

Tragedy struck six days before draft when his brother, Casey, and two other Jackson State teammates were killed in car accident . . . One of 10 children . . . Born Sept. 28, 1967, in Prairie Point, Miss. . . . 1990 base salary: $200,000.

COACH JERRY GLANVILLE: The Man in Black rekindled

interest in Falcons' football . . . Led team to 5-11 record (an improvement from 3-13 mark in 1989) in first season with Atlanta . . . Colorful, quotable, controversial character . . . Loved by some players and fans, despised by others . . . His teams are regarded as tough and aggressive by some, nasty and dirty by others . . . Falcons improved from 28th to third in rush defense and from 24th to 10th in total offense . . . Led Falcons to 47-27 victory over Oilers, his old team, in season-opener . . . Falcons' 5-3 home record was best since 1980 . . . Falcons sold out six of eight home games . . . Team slumped badly in midseason with seven consecutive losses before winning last two . . . Return to Atlanta was homecoming of sorts for former Falcons' assistant . . . Led Oilers to three playoff berths in four seasons as head coach but his controversial style led to his dismissal . . . Known for leaving tickets for Elvis Presley and other luminaries, real and fictional, dead and alive . . . Career record as head coach is 38-43 . . . Served as assistant in Buffalo, Detroit and Atlanta before joining Oilers as a defensive coordinator in 1984 . . . Played linebacker at Northern Michigan . . . Born Oct. 14, 1941, in Detroit.

GREATEST PUNTER

A football team undergoes a drastic number of changes over the course of a decade. But through the 10 seasons from 1972 through 1981, one constant for the Falcons was punter John James.

A free agent from the University of Florida, James set Falcons' records for most punts in a career (873), a season (109 in 1978) and a game (12 vs. Washington in 1978). He also uncorked the two longest punts in team history—a 75-yarder against Oakland in 1975 and a 72-yarder against New Orleans in 1973.

James averaged 40.8 yards over his long career. His best season was his first as he averaged 42.7 yards in 1972. Four years later, James also set a team record with 28 punts downed inside the 20.

INDIVIDUAL FALCON RECORDS

Rushing

Most Yards Game:	202	Gerald Riggs, vs New Orleans, 1984
Season:	1,719	Gerald Riggs, 1985
Career:	6,631	Gerald Riggs, 1982-88

Passing

Most TD Passes Game:	4	3 times, most recently Steve Bartkowski, 1981
Season:	31	Steve Bartkowski, 1980
Career:	149	Steve Bartkowski, 1975-85

Receiving

Most TD Passes Game:	3	6 times, most recently Gerald Riggs, vs L.A. Rams, 1985
Season:	13	Alfred Jenkins, 1981
Career:	40	Alfred Jenkins, 1975-83

Scoring

Most Points Game:	18	6 times, most recently Gerald Riggs, vs L.A. Rams, 1985
Season:	114	Mick Luckhurst, 1981
Career:	558	Mick Luckhurst, 1981-87
Most TDs Game:	3	4 times, most recently Gerald Riggs, vs L.A. Rams, 1985
Season:	13	Alfred Jenkins, 1981
	13	Gerald Riggs, 1984
Career:	48	Gerald Riggs, 1982-88

CHICAGO BEARS

TEAM DIRECTORY: Chairman: Edward B. McCaskey; Pres.: Michael B. McCaskey; VP-Player Personnel: Bill Tobin; Dir. Adm.: Tim LeFevour; Dir. Finance: Ted Phillips; Dir. Marketing and Communications: Ken Valdiserri; Pub. Rel. Dir.: Bryan Harlan; Head Coach: Mike Ditka. Home field: Soldier Field (66,946). Colors: Navy blue, orange and white.

SCOUTING REPORT

OFFENSE: The Bears (11-5 last year) have a safe, simple and successful formula: Run the football. With a powerful offensive

Neal Anderson's offense makes him a most dangerous Bear.

line and a pair of skilled running backs, the Bears control the clock, limit their mistakes and rest their defense.

The key is Neal Anderson, one of the NFL's most versatile, productive running backs. Fullback Brad Muster came into his own last year.

Jim Harbaugh became a full-time starter at quarterback in 1990. He's not flashy but he's tough. He can run and he avoids mistakes.

The passing game is subpar by NFL standards. Wendall Davis and Ron Morris are average wide receivers and tight end James Thornton is better as a blocker than a catcher.

The offensive line is solid and durable. Age is a concern, though, since all five starters will be over 30 this season. Top pick Stan Thomas of Texas should help out at tackle.

DEFENSE: With the emergence of several good young players, the Bears put the bite back in their defense last year. Rookie Mark Carrier was a revelation at free safety. Trace Armstrong developed into a strong end, and John Roper and Ron Cox looked like promising outside linebackers.

But the line is showing signs of age. Dan Hampton has retired and Steve McMichael and Richard Dent are in their 30s. The Bears traded with Miami for Eric Kumerow.

Middle linebacker Mike Singletary remains the heart of the Bears' defense, but Roper and Cox have potential as big-play men. Carrier led the NFL in interceptions with 10. The top cornerback is Donnell Woolford, but the Bears could use more speed and depth in the secondary.

SPECIAL TEAMS: The Bears are known for their solid special teams. Kicker Kevin Butler is one of the game's best. He was a little inconsistent in 1990 but showed his leg strength by making four field goals from 50 yards and beyond. The punter is Maury Buford, who averaged a respectable 40.4 yards but had two kicks blocked.

The Bears have good coverage teams. Rookie Johnny Bailey was a find as a kick-returner and set a team record with a 95-yard punt return for a TD.

THE ROOKIES: The Bears added youth and depth to both of their lines. Thomas is a strong run-blocker. Notre Dame defensive tackle Chris Zorich is a Chicago native who is a little undersized but tenacious and productive. Clemson's Chris Gardocki, a placekicker and punter, might get a chance at both chores.

BEARS VETERAN ROSTER

HEAD COACH—Mike Ditka. Assistant Coaches—Steve Kazor, Greg Landry, John Levra, David McGinnis, Vic Rapp, Johnny Roland, Dick Stanfel, Vince Tobin, Zaven Yaralian.

No.	Name	Pos.	Ht.	Wt.	NFL Exp.	College
35	Anderson, Neal	RB	5-11	210	6	Florida
93	Armstrong, Trace	DE	6-4	270	3	Florida
22	Bailey, Johnny	RB	5-8	180	2	Texas A&I
79	Becker, Kurt	G	6-5	269	10	Michigan
62	Bortz, Mark	G	6-6	270	9	Iowa
86	Boso, Cap	TE	6-4	240	5	Illinois
8	Buford, Maury	P	6-0	198	10	Texas Tech
6	Butler, Kevin	K	6-1	190	7	Georgia
20	Carrier, Mark	S	6-1	180	2	Southern California
89	Coley, James	TE	6-3	270	2	Clemson
74	Covert, Jim	T	6-4	278	9	Pittsburgh
54	Cox, Ron	LB	6-2	242	2	Fresno State
82	Davis, Wendell	WR	5-11	188	4	Louisiana State
95	Dent, Richard	DE	6-5	260	9	Tennessee State
37	Douglass, Maurice	CB	5-11	200	6	Kentucky
67	Fontenot, Jerry	C	6-3	272	3	Texas A&M
23	Gayle, Shaun	S	5-11	194	8	Ohio State
29	Gentry, Dennis	WR	5-8	180	10	Baylor
31	Green, Mark	RB	5-11	195	3	Notre Dame
4	Harbaugh, Jim	QB	6-3	220	5	Michigan
63	Hilgenberg, Jay	C	6-3	265	11	Iowa
53	Jones, Dante	LB	6-1	236	4	Oklahoma
88	Kozlowski, Glen	WR	6-1	205	5	Brigham Young
70	Kumerow, Eric	DE	6-7	260	4	Ohio State
46	Lott, James	CB	5-9	181	1	Clemson
75	Matusz, Roman	T	6-4	270	1	Pittsburgh
26	Mangum, John	CB	5-10	173	2	Alabama
76	McMichael, Steve	DT	6-2	268	12	Texas
84	Morris, Ron	WR	6-1	195	5	Southern Methodist
51	Morrissey, Jim	LB	6-3	227	7	Michigan State
25	Muster, Brad	FB	6-3	232	4	Stanford
36	Paul, Markus	S	6-2	199	3	Syracuse
72	Perry, William	DT	6-2	325	7	Clemson
52	Pruitt, Mickey	LB	6-1	215	4	Colorado
59	Rivera, Ron	LB	6-3	240	8	California
55	Roper, John	LB	6-1	228	3	Texas A&M
30	Rouse, James	FB	6-0	220	2	Arkansas
96	Ryan, Tim	DT	6-4	268	2	Southern California
50	Singletary, Mike	LB	6-0	228	11	Baylor
85	Smith, Quintin	WR	5-10	172	2	Kansas
12	Snyder, Brent	QB	6-3	230	[illegible]	Utah State
32	Stinson, Lemuel	CB	5-9	159	4	Texas Tech
49	Tate, David	S	6-0	177	4	Colorado
57	Thayer, Tom	G	6-4	270	7	Notre Dame
80	Thornton, James	TE	6-2	242	4	Cal-Fullerton
78	Van Horne, Keith	T	6-6	283	11	Southern California
87	Waddle, Tom	WR	6-0	181	3	Boston College
10	Willis, Peter Tom	QB	6-2	188	2	Florida State
73	Wojciechowski, John	G	6-4	270	5	Michigan State
21	Woolford, Donnell	CB	5-9	188	3	Clemson

TOP DRAFT CHOICES

Rd.	Name	Sel. No.	Pos.	Ht.	Wt.	College
1	Thomas, Stan	22	OT	6-5	302	Texas
2	Zorich, Chris	49	DT	6-3	267	Notre Dame
3	Gardocki, Chris	78	P-K	6-2	193	Clemson
4	Johnson, Joe	105	DB	5-9	186	North Carolina State
5	Morgan, Anthony	134	WR	6-0	195	Tennessee

OUTLOOK: Mike Ditka's team, the most consistent in the NFC Central, has done a nice job of replenishing their roster with young players. They aren't flashy, but they have a formula for success. They also have enough talent to defend their division title.

BEAR PROFILES

NEAL ANDERSON 27 5-11 210 — Running Back

Perhaps the NFL's best all-around running back . . . Rushed for 1,078 yards and caught 42 passes for 484 yards in 1990 . . . Scored 13 TDs . . . Named to the Pro Bowl for third year in a row . . . Caught 50-yard TD pass to beat Lions in overtime . . . Ran for 102 yards in playoff victory over New Orleans . . . Great speed, vision, moves . . . Has run for more than 1,000 yards in each of last three seasons . . . Ran for 1,275 yards in 1989 and 1,106 in 1988 . . . Has emerged from long shadow cast by former teammate Walter Payton, the NFL's all-time leading rusher . . . Bears' No. 1 pick in 1986 out of Florida . . . Has degree in public relations . . . Born Aug. 14, 1964, in Graceville, Fla. . . . 1990 base salary: $2.2 million.

JIM HARBAUGH 27 6-3 220 — Quarterback

Finally emerged as Bears' starting quarterback in fourth season . . . Started first 14 games before suffering shoulder separation . . . Led Bears to 10-4 record . . . Passed for 2,178 yards with 10 TDs and six interceptions . . . Conservative passer tends to avoid both big plays and mistakes . . . Went a team-record 173 passes without an interception . . . Career completion percentage of 57.9 is another team record . . . Decent scrambler, ran for 321 yards in 1990 . . . Started just seven games in first three seasons . . . Backup to both Jim McMahon and Mike Tomczak . . . Bears' No. 1 pick in 1987 out of Michigan . . . First player in Michigan history to pass for more than 2,000 yards in a season . . . Born Dec. 23, 1963, in Ann Arbor, Mich. . . . 1990 base salary: $320,000.

TRACE ARMSTRONG 25 6-4 270 Defensive End

Emerged as one of the best young defensive ends in football . . . Finished second on the team with 10 sacks . . . Also made 82 tackles and recovered three fumbles . . . NFC Defensive Player of Month in September with five sacks and two forced fumbles . . . Solid run-defender has 163 tackles in first two seasons . . . Led all NFC rookies in sacks with five in 1989 . . . Bears' second No. 1 pick in 1989 (Donnell Woolford was first) . . . Bears acquired the draft choice used to pick Armstrong from Washington as compensation for Redskins signing Wilber Marshall . . . All-American selection at Florida . . . Earned degree in psychology . . . Born Oct. 5, 1965, in Birmingham, Ala. . . . 1990 base salary: $240,000.

MIKE SINGLETARY 32 6-0 228 Linebacker

Heart and soul of Bears' defense . . . Made Pro Bowl for eighth year in a row . . . Led the team in tackles with 151 . . . Ninth year in a row he was either first or second on team in tackles . . . Set a personal record with 20 tackles in overtime victory over Broncos . . . Vocal, spirited player . . . Often the focus of TV cameras because of his intense stare . . . Renowned for film study and preparation . . . Two-time NFL Defensive Player of Year (1985 and 1988) . . . Bears' second-round pick in 1981 out of Baylor . . . Legendary Southwest Conference player supposedly broke 18 helmets in his college career . . . Born Oct. 9, 1958, in Houston . . . 1990 base salary: $200,000.

RICHARD DENT 30 6-5 260 Defensive End

Big-play man in Bears' defense . . . Named to the Pro Bowl for third time . . . Led team in sacks with 12 . . . Also had three interceptions (as many as starting cornerback Donnell Woolford) and returned a fumble 45 yards for a TD . . . Excellent speed and agility . . . Has terrorized offensive tackles for years with outside rush . . . Has 91 sacks since 1984 . . . Can be vulnerable against the run . . . Led NFL in sacks with 17 in 1985 . . . MVP of Super Bowl XX as Bears annihilated New England, 46-10 . . . Bears' eighth-round pick in 1983 out of Tennessee State

. . . Lowly regarded by pro scouts because he was underweight for defensive end . . . Born Dec. 13, 1960, in Atlanta . . . 1990 base salary: $1.2 million.

MARK CARRIER 23 6-1 180 Safety

NFL Defensive Rookie of the Year . . . Led NFL with team-record 10 interceptions . . . Made Pro Bowl . . . Finished third on team in tackles with 122 . . . Led Bears with five forced fumbles . . . Picked off three passes in game against Washington . . . Smart, crafty player with excellent feel for his position . . . A starter from Day One . . . Entered draft after junior season at USC . . . Selected by Bears with sixth overall pick . . . All-American at USC . . . Born April 28, 1968, in Lake Charles, La. . . . 1990 base salary: $300,000.

DONNELL WOOLFORD 25 5-9 188 Cornerback

Emerged from coach Mike Ditka's doghouse with solid second NFL season . . . Finished with 70 tackles, 13 passes defended and three interceptions . . . Good man-to-man coverage skills . . . Usually is assigned opponent's best wide receiver . . . Struggled with injuries and inconsistency as a rookie . . . Also earned wrath of Ditka, who complained, "This guy can't cover anybody." . . . Bears' No. 1 pick in 1989 out of Clemson . . . Bears acquired choice from Raiders for Willie Gault . . . Born Jan. 6, 1966, in Fayetteville, N.C. . . . 1990 base salary: $250,000.

MARK BORTZ 30 6-6 270 Guard

A starter in the Pro Bowl after his best season . . . His run-blocking is key to the Bears' powerful ground game . . . Helped Bears rank second in NFL in rushing with 2,436 yards . . . Bears were first in time of possession (33:06), a testament to strong offensive line . . . A Pro Bowl alternate in 1988 and 1989 . . . No-nonsense, hard worker . . . Emerged as a starter in second NFL season (1984) . . . Bears' sixth-round pick out of Iowa in 1983 . . . Born Feb. 12, 1961, in Pardeeville, Wisc. . . . 1990 base salary: $410,000.

JAY HILGENBERG 31 6-3 265 **Center**

One of the great free-agent finds of all time . . . Named to the Pro Bowl for the sixth year in a row . . . Played entire season despite elbow injury that required offseason surgery . . . The Bears have produced a 1,000-yard rusher in every non-strike season in which he has been the team's center . . . Relies on technique rather than power to make blocks . . . Highly regarded around league for discipline, knowledge of the game . . . A two-time All-Big Ten selection at Iowa, he still was ignored in 1981 draft . . . Signed by Bears as a free agent two weeks after 1981 draft . . . Born March 21, 1960, in Iowa City, Iowa . . . 1990 base salary: $540,000.

BRAD MUSTER 26 6-4 232 **Fullback**

Versatile fullback is an ideal complement to halfback Neal Anderson . . . Had best season as an NFL player in 1990, with career-high 664 rushing yards and team-high 47 catches . . . Combined for 143 yards (50 rushing, 93 receiving) against Tampa Bay . . . Rushed for 99 yards against Phoenix . . . Caught a pass in 17 of 18 games . . . Ran for six TDs . . . Good blocker . . . Scored eight TDs in 1989 . . . Had little impact as a rookie in 1988 . . . No starts and just 197 rushing yards his first season . . . Bears' No. 1 pick out of Stanford . . . Pac-10 Offensive Player of the Year as a junior . . . Born April 11, 1965, in San Marin, Cal. . . . 1990 base salary: $260,000.

COACH MIKE DITKA: Directed one of the turnaround teams

of 1990 . . . After going 6-10 in 1989, the Bears went 11-5 in 1990 and won NFC Central title . . . It was his sixth NFC Central crown in nine seasons . . . Seems to have mellowed some after frustrating 1989 season . . . Still has reputation as volatile, tough, uncompromising, emotional coach . . . Nickname: "Iron Mike" . . . Heavily critical of younger players as team unraveled in 1989 . . . Survived heart attack in 1988, returning to coach at end of season . . . Led Bears to only Super Bowl in 1985 . . . That team went 18-1 and is regarded as one of best in NFL history . . . Career record is 97-52, including playoffs . . . Has 48-19 record against NFC Central teams . . . Served nine years as Cowboys' assistant under Tom Landry before taking Bears' job in 1982 . . . A Hall of Fame tight end in playing career with Bears, Eagles, Cowboys . . . Caught 427 passes, scored 43 TDs . . . All-American at Pitt . . . Born Oct. 13, 1939, in Carnegie, Pa.

GREATEST PUNTER

Given the usual turnover at the position, the top two punters in Bears' history are remarkable for their longevity as well as their accomplishments.

From 1962 through 1983, the Bears had just two punters—Bobby Joe Green and Bob Parsons. They combined for more than 69,000 yards in punts.

Green was the Bears' punter from 1962 through 1973. He is the team's all-time leader with 35,057 yards and ranks second in career average with 42.1. He also has the top two single-season averages with 46.5 in 1963 and 44.5 in 1964.

Parsons played for the Bears from 1972 through 1983. He ranks second in total yards with 34,180 and tops in single-season yardage with 4,531 in 1981. Parsons also holds the team record with 158 career punts downed inside the 20-yard line.

INDIVIDUAL BEAR RECORDS

Rushing

Most Yards Game:	275	Walter Payton, vs Minnesota, 1977
Season:	1,852	Walter Payton, 1977
Career:	16,726	Walter Payton, 1975-87

Passing:

Most TD Passes Game:	7	Sid Luckman, vs N.Y. Giants, 1943
Season:	28	Sid Luckman, 1943
Career:	137	Sid Luckman, 1939-50

Receiving

Most TD Passes Game:	4	2 times, most recently Mike Ditka, vs L.A. Rams, 1963
Season:	13	2 times, most recently Dick Gordon, 1970
Career:	50	Ken Kavanaugh, 1940-41, 1945-50

Scoring

Most Points Game:	36	Gale Sayers, vs San Francisco, 1965
Season:	144	Kevin Butler, 1985
Career:	750	Walter Payton, 1975-87
Most TDs Game:	6	Gale Sayers, vs San Francisco, 1965
Season:	22	Gale Sayers, 1965
Career:	125	Walter Payton, 1975-87

Trace Armstrong looms large at defensive end.

DALLAS COWBOYS

TEAM DIRECTORY: Owner/Pres./GM: Jerry Jones; VP-Pro Personnel: Bob Ackles; Pub. Rel. Dir.: Rich Dalrymple; Head Coach: Jimmy Johnson. Home field: Texas Stadium (65,024). Colors: Royal blue, metallic blue and white.

SCOUTING REPORT

OFFENSE: The Cowboys have found the running back to complement quarterback Troy Aikman. Now they need to improve the offensive line and wide-receiving corps.

Emmitt Smith led all NFL rookies with 937 rushing yards and 11 TDs. His presence takes a lot of pressure off Aikman, who is emerging as one of the best young quarterbacks in the NFL.

Kelvin Martin is a solid wide receiver and Jay Novacek led all NFC tight ends in receptions, but Aikman needs more targets. The Cowboys need more game-breakers at the other end of Aikman's passes. Wide receiver Mike Irvin showed signs last year of rebounding from a devastating knee injury and the team remains hopeful that speedster Alex Wright will develop.

Keeping Aikman healthy is the job of the offensive line. This group has a good young player in center Mark Stepnoski but has to do better.

DEFENSE: Improvement on this side of the football was the main reason the Cowboys improved from 1-15 to 7-9. Rookie tackle Jimmie Jones and end Daniel Stubbs, acquired in a trade, gave the Cowboys new life along the defensive line. Veterans Jim Jeffcoat and Danny Noonan are solid but the team needs more impact players in this area. Top pick Russell Maryland could be one big answer.

Outside linebacker Ken Norton Jr. is a good young player and they could use more like him. Eugene Lockhart was left unprotected in Plan B and Jack Del Rio is a journeyman.

Cornerback Issiac Holt was a steal in the Herschel Walker trade. He's a big-play man. The Cowboys would like to upgrade at safety, where retreads Ray Horton and James Washington are stop-gap measures.

SPECIAL TEAMS: Most good teams have solid special teams; the Cowboys need to improve in this area to become a good team.

Young Troy Aikman had best season and should get better.

COWBOYS VETERAN ROSTER

HEAD COACH—Jimmy Johnson. Assistant Coaches—Hubbard Alexander, Joe Avezzano, Joe Brodsky, Dave Campo, Butch Davis, Robert Ford, Steve Hoffman, Ron Meeks, Norv Turner, Dave Wannstedt, Tony Wise, Mike Woicik.

No.	Name	Pos.	Ht.	Wt.	NFL Exp.	College
34	Agee, Tommie	FB	6-0	223	4	Auburn
8	Aikman, Troy	QB	6-3	220	3	UCLA
36	Albritton, Vince	S	6-2	212	8	Washington
89	Awalt, Rob	TE	6-5	238	5	San Diego State
40	Bates, Bill	S	6-1	204	9	Tennessee
44	Brooks, Michael	DB	6-0	195	2	North Carolina State
79	Broughton, Willie	DT	6-5	280	5	Miami (Fla.)
65	Childress, Freddie	G	6-4	333	1	Arkansas
90	Crockett, Wills	LB	6-3	234	2	Georgia Tech
55	Del Rio, Jack	LB	6-4	232	7	Southern California
21	Dixon, James	RB	5-10	184	3	Houston
85	Folsom, Steve	TE	6-5	240	6	Utah
29	Gant, Kenneth	CB	5-11	181	2	Albany State
63	Gesek, John	G	6-5	283	5	Cal-Sacramento
49	Gicewicz, Rich	TE	6-4	245	1	Michigan State
66	Gogan, Kevin	G-T	6-7	311	5	Washington
78	Hamel, Dean	DT	6-3	271	7	Tulsa
50	Harper, David	LB	6-1	220	2	Humboldt State
25	Harris, Odie	CB-S	6-0	190	4	Sam Houston State
70	Hellestrae, Dale	G-C	6-5	275	5	Southern Methodist
45	Hendrix, Manny	CB	5-10	185	6	Utah
32	Highsmith, Alonzo	FB	6-1	234	5	Miami (Fla.)
30	Holt, Issiac	CB	6-2	202	7	Alcorn State
20	Horton, Ray	S	5-11	186	9	Washington
82	Hudson, Craig	TE	6-3	245	1	Wisconsin
88	Irvin, Michael	WR	6-2	202	4	Miami (Fla.)
19	Javis, John	WR	5-10	181	1	Howard
77	Jeffcoat, Jim	DE	6-5	263	9	Arizona State
48	Johnston, Daryl	RB	6-2	238	3	Syracuse
97	Jones, Jimmie	DT	6-4	272	2	Miami (Fla.)
26	Jones, Keith	RB	5-10	180	2	Nebraska
15	Laufenberg, Babe	QB	6-3	214	7	Indiana
83	Martin, Kelvin	WR	5-9	163	5	Boston College
61	Newton, Nate	T	6-3	322	6	Florida A&M
73	Noonan, Danny	DT	6-4	270	5	Nebraska
51	Norton, Ken	LB	6-3	237	4	UCLA
84	Novacek, Jay	TE	6-4	235	7	Wyoming
86	Roberts, Alfredo	TE	6-3	246	4	Miami (Fla.)
4	Saxon, Mike	P	6-3	200	7	San Diego State
87	Shepard, Derrick	WR	5-10	181	4	Oklahoma
42	Smagala, Stan	S	5-10	184	2	Notre Dame
22	Smith, Emmitt	RB	5-9	199	2	Florida
57	Smith, Vinson	LB	6-2	225	3	East Carolina
54	Solomon, Jesse	LB	6-0	235	6	Florida State
53	Stepnoski, Mark	C-G	6-2	266	3	Pittsburgh
18	Stoudt, Cliff	QB	6-4	222	12	Youngstown State
96	Stubbs, Daniel	DE	6-4	264	4	Miami (Fla.)
92	Tolbert, Tony	DE	6-6	254	3	Texas-El Paso
71	Tuinei, Mark	T	6-5	293	9	Hawaii
75	Veingrad, Alan	T	6-5	277	5	East Texas State
35	Warnsley, Reginald	FB	5-10	215	1	Southern Mississippi
37	Washington, James	S	6-1	195	4	UCLA
23	Williams, Robert	CB	5-10	186	5	Baylor
1	Willis, Ken	K	5-11	189	2	Kentucky
81	Wright, Alexander	WR	5-11	184	2	Auburn
76	Zimmerman, Jeff	OL	6-3	332	5	Florida

TOP DRAFT CHOICES

Rd.	Name	Sel. No.	Pos.	Ht.	Wt.	College
1	Maryland, Russell	1	DT	6-0	274	Miami (Fla.)
1	Harper, Alvin	12	WR	6-3	206	Tennessee
2	Edwards, Dixon	37	LB	6-0	220	Michigan State
3	Myles, Godfrey	62	LB	6-1	242	Florida
3	Richards, James	64	G	6-4	289	California

Ken Willis has potential as a kicker. He was 18-for-25 in field goals as a rookie. Punter Mike Saxon had a good year with a 43.2 average.

The coverage teams are spotty, though, and the Cowboys don't have a dependable punt-returner. James Dixon showed some flashes as a kick-returner.

THE ROOKIES: Wheeling and dealing on draft day, the Cowboys continued to stockpile young players. Maryland is a strong, quick addition. Tennessee's Alvin Harper is a smooth, all-around wide receiver. Michigan State's Dixon Edwards and Florida's Godfrey Myles add youth and depth to the linebacking corps.

OUTLOOK: Jimmy Johnson's Cowboys went from atrocious in 1989 to OK in 1990. The next step, to legitimate contender, is a big one. Aikman and Smith are great young players, but there are still too many journeymen on the roster for a sustained run at the division title.

COWBOY PROFILES

TROY AIKMAN 24 6-3 220 — Quarterback

Established himself as one of best young quarterbacks in NFL . . . Led Cowboys into playoff race but team faded from contention after he sustained separated shoulder in first series of Week 15 loss to Philadelphia . . . Passed for 2,579 yards and 11 TDs . . . Needs to cut down on interceptions (18 in both 1989 and 1990) . . . Good scrambler . . . Led Dallas to come-from-behind victories four times in 1990 . . . Went 11-for-11 in second half of victory over New Orleans . . . Completed 21 of 26 passes (81 percent) in loss to Giants . . . Set NFL rookie record with 379 passing yards in game against Cardinals in 1989 . . . First player selected in 1989 draft, out of UCLA . . . Ranks third on all-time NCAA passing list . . . Began collegiate career at Oklahoma but transferred to UCLA . . . Born Nov. 21, 1966, in Cerritos, Cal. . . . 1990 base salary: $865,000.

EMMITT SMITH 22 5-9 199 **Running Back**

Consensus NFL Offensive Rookie of Year . . . Finished fifth in NFC in rushing with 937 yards . . . Ranked fifth in NFL in rushing TDs with 11 . . . Cowboys were 5-0 in games in which he rushed 20 times or more . . . Ran for four TDs against Phoenix Dec. 16 . . . Ran for 132 yards in upset of Washington Nov. 22 . . . First rookie to start at halfback for Dallas since Ron Springs in 1979 . . . Cowboys' No. 1 pick in 1990 . . . Entered draft after junior season at Florida . . . Has brothers named Erik, Emory and Emil . . . Born May 15, 1969, in Pensacola, Fla. . . . 1990 base salary: $200,000.

ISSIAC HOLT 28 6-2 202 **Cornerback**

Emerged as the leader of the Cowboys' rebuilt secondary . . . Named second-team All-NFC by UPI . . . Led Cowboys in passes defended with 18 and tied for team lead in interceptions with three . . . Physical defender who excels in bump-and-run coverage . . . Blocked two punts, setting up two TDs . . . Returned interception 64 yards for TD in fourth quarter of comeback victory over Tampa Bay . . . Acquired by Cowboys from Minnesota Oct. 12, 1989, as part of the Herschel Walker trade . . . Vikings' second-round draft pick out of Alcorn State in 1985 . . . Set NCAA Division 1-AA career record with 24 interceptions . . . Born Oct. 4, 1962, in Birmingham, Ala. . . . 1990 base salary: $290,000.

MIKE IRVIN 25 6-2 202 **Wide Receiver**

Battled back from severe knee injury in 1989 to reach full speed by midpoint of 1990 season . . . Finished with 20 receptions for 413 yards (20.7 average) and 5 TDs . . . Led team in yards-per-catch and registered longest reception with 61-yarder against Rams . . . Was on pace for 1,000-yard season in 1989 when he sustained torn ligament in right knee . . . Rehabilitation took almost entire year . . . Cowboys' No. 1 pick out of Miami in 1988 . . . Caught 32 passes for 654 yards and 5 TDs as a rookie . . . Holds University of Miami career records for catches

(143), receiving yards (2,423) and TD receptions (26) . . . Comes from family of 17 children . . . Born March 5, 1966, in Fort Lauderdale, Fla. . . . 1990 base salary: $250,000.

JAY NOVACEK 28 6-4 235 — Tight End

Led NFL tight ends in receptions with 59 . . . Named first-team All-Pro by *Football Digest* and *Pro Football Weekly* . . . Generated 105 receiving yards in game against Philadelphia . . . Set career-high with nine catches in game against Giants . . . Smart, crafty receiver who was a quarterback in high school . . . Signed by Cowboys in 1990 as a Plan B free agent from Phoenix . . . Played five seasons for Cardinals, catching 83 passes . . . Cardinals' sixth-round pick out of Wyoming in 1985 . . . Won Western Athletic Conference decathlon championship in 1984 . . . Born Oct. 24, 1962, in Gothenburg, Neb. . . . 1990 base salary: $325,000.

ALEX WRIGHT 24 5-11 184 — Wide Receiver

Missed most of training camp in contract holdout . . . Contributed mostly on special teams but is projected as impact wide receiver in the future . . . Returned a kickoff 90 yards for TD against Giants . . . Caught 11 passes . . . Blazing speed . . . Track star as well as football standout at Auburn . . . Won Southeastern Conference titles in 55-meter dash and 200-meter dash in 1988 . . . Set school record with 263 receiving yards and TDs covering 78, 73, 60 and 41 yards in a game against Pacific . . . Cowboys' second-round pick in 1990 . . . First wide receiver selected in 1990 draft . . . Born July 19, 1967, in Albany, Ga. . . . 1990 base salary: $210,000.

ALONZO HIGHSMITH 26 6-1 234 — Fullback

Sat out final eight games with knee injury . . . Expected back at full strength by training camp . . . Powerful blocker with excellent moves and hands for a big man . . . Acquired by Cowboys in 1990 trade with Houston . . . Reunited with college coach Jimmy Johnson . . . Led Oilers in rushing in 1989 with 531 yards and also scored five TDs . . . Houston's No. 1 pick (third overall) in 1987 . . . Starter for most of three seasons in Houston . . . All-American selection as a senior at University of Miami . . . Born Feb. 26, 1965, in Bartow, Fla. . . . 1990 base salary: $500,000.

JIM JEFFCOAT 30 6-5 263 **Defensive End**

Has started (104) and played (124) more games than any current Cowboy . . . Finished 1990 with 65 tackles and 3½ sacks . . . Veteran on young, inexperienced defensive line . . . Has 64 career sacks . . . Best pass-rushing season was 1986, with 14 sacks . . . Has scored four TDs in career . . . Cowboys' No. 1 pick in 1983 out of Arizona State . . . Has degree in communications and is working toward masters in business . . . Born April 1, 1961, in Cliffwood, N.J. . . . 1990 base salary: $340,000.

DANNY NOONAN 26 6-4 270 **Defensive Tackle**

Led all Dallas defensive linemen with career-high 85 tackles . . . Also registered 4½ sacks . . . Healthy in 1990 after being slowed by nagging injuries for much of career . . . His 85 tackles matched his combined total from 1987, 1988 and 1989 seasons . . . Hard worker who is solid in run defense . . . Accounted for eight points (returned interception for TD, tackled Chris Miller for a safety) in 1988 game against Atlanta . . . Cowboys' No. 1 pick out of Nebraska in 1987 . . . Consensus All-American as a senior . . . Born July 1, 1965, in Lincoln, Neb.

KEN NORTON 24 6-2 237 **Linebacker**

Emerged as solid player in his third season . . . Finished second on team in tackles with career-high 119 . . . Led in solo tackles with 79 . . . Forced three fumbles and recovered two . . . Tops among Dallas linebackers in sacks with 3½ . . . Slowed by injuries early in career . . . Missed most of rookie season in 1988 with broken thumb and part of 1989 with injured knee . . . Cowboys' second pick in 1988, out of UCLA . . . Son of former heavyweight boxer Ken Norton . . . Born Sept. 29, 1966, in Los Angeles . . . 1990 base salary: $350,000.

COACH JIMMY JOHNSON: Named NFL Coach of the Year

by AP . . . UPI's NFC Coach of the Year . . . Took team that won one game in 1989 to brink of a playoff berth in 1990 . . . Cowboys won four in a row to even record at 7-7 but lost last two after quarterback Troy Aikman went out with a separated shoulder . . . Has turned over roster since succeeding Tom Landry on Feb. 25, 1989 . . . Just the second head coach in Cowboys' history . . . Suffered through 1-15 season in 1989 . . . Unlike many NFL coaches, he has authority over personnel decisions . . . Close friend and former college roommate of Cowboys' owner Jerry Jones . . . Compiled 52-9 record in five seasons at University of Miami . . . Won national title in 1987 . . . His Miami teams were regarded as "bad boys" of college football . . . Was 29-25-3 in five seasons at Oklahoma State . . . Played defensive tackle on Arkansas' 1964 national championship team . . . Began coaching career as an assistant at Louisiana Tech in 1965 . . . Born July 16, 1942, in Port Arthur, Tex.

GREATEST PUNTER

Danny White holds the Cowboys' career passing records for completions, touchdowns and completion percentage. But White also was the greatest punter in Dallas history.

White spent his first four seasons as the backup quarterback to Roger Staubach. He was also the Cowboys' regular punter from his rookie season of 1976 until he was replaced by current Cowboy Mike Saxon in 1985.

White holds Dallas career records for punts (612) and yardage (24,571). He averaged 40.1 yards, the second-highest mark in team history, during his career.

White's best season was 1979, when he ranked fourth in the NFL with a 41.7 average and unleashed a 73-yard punt, his career-best.

INDIVIDUAL COWBOY RECORDS

Rushing

Most Yards Game:	206	Tony Dorsett, vs Philadelphia, 1978
Season:	1,646	Tony Dorsett, 1981
Career:	12,036	Tony Dorsett, 1977-87

Passing

Most TD Passes Game:	5	7 times, most recently Danny White, vs N.Y. Giants, 1983
Season:	29	Danny White, 1983
Career:	154	Danny White, 1976-87

Receiving

Most TD Passes Game:	4	Bob Hayes, vs Houston, 1970
Season:	14	Frank Clarke, 1962
Career:	71	Bob Hayes, 1965-74

Scoring

Most Points Game:	24	4 times, most recently Duane Thomas, vs St. Louis, 1971
Season:	123	Rafael Septien, 1983
Career:	874	Rafael Septien, 1978-86
Most TDs Game:	4	4 times, most recently Duane Thomas, vs St. Louis, 1971
Season:	16	Dan Reeves, 1966
Career:	86	Tony Dorsett, 1977-87

DETROIT LIONS

TEAM DIRECTORY: Pres.: William Clay Ford; Exec. VP/CEO: Charles Schmidt; Dir. Player Personnel: Ron Hughes; Dir. Marketing, Broadcasting and Communication: Bill Keenist; Media Rel. Coordinator: Mike Murray; Head Coach: Wayne Fontes. Home field: Pontiac Silverdome (80,500). Colors: Honolulu blue and silver.

Barry Sanders led NFC rushers for second year in a row.

SCOUTING REPORT

OFFENSE: The Lions are in transition. Turmoil might be a better word. The plan is to use their Run-n'-Shoot offense on a part-time basis and return to normal formations on other occasions.

Rodney Peete ended 1990 as the starting quarterback. But the Lions have Andre Ware, their No. 1 pick in 1990, in the wings. The situation needs to be settled.

A bright spot is running back Barry Sanders. He led the NFL in rushing yards (1,304) in 1990. He might be even better with a fullback and tight end to block for him.

The Lions' top wide receiver in 1990, Richard Johnson, signed with Houston in Plan B. Robert Clark returns but this is an area in need of improvement. That explains why the Lions' made Virginia's Herman Moore their first draft pick.

The line is a strong point. Tackle Lomas Brown and center Kevin Glover are anchors of a solid, durable group.

DEFENSE: If they can avoid injuries, the Lions have the makings of a good defense.

Nose tackle Jerry Ball is an excellent player and the Lions have high hopes for young ends Dan Owens and Marc Spindler. Linebacking is a strong suit, with heavy-hitter Chris Spielman and pass-rusher Mike Cofer. Dennis Gibson is underrated.

The secondary is led by powerful safety Bennie Blades.

SPECIAL TEAMS: The Lions have some of the best special teams in the NFL. Placekicker Eddie Murray and punter Jim Arnold are proven veterans. Return-specialist Mel Gray is a Pro Bowler.

The coverage teams are solid, too. The Lions allowed just 8.1 yards on punt returns and 17.6 on kickoff returns in 1990.

THE ROOKIES: The Lions wanted big, strong wide receivers and got two good ones in Moore and UTEP's Reggie Barrett. Looking for more size and strength on the other side of the football, the Lions traded with Dallas to acquire defensive lineman Kelvin Pritchett, a No. 1 pick from Mississippi.

OUTLOOK: The pressure is on coach Wayne Fontes and the Lions. They teased their fans with a surge at the end of 1989, when they wound up at 7-9. But they fell to 6-10 in 1990. In the tight NFC Central, they are one of four teams that could finish as

LIONS VETERAN ROSTER

HEAD COACH—Wayne Fontes. Assistant Coaches—Raymond Berry, Don Clemons, Len Fontes, Frank Gansz, Bert Hill Lamar Leachman, Dave Levy, Billie Matthews, Herb Paterra, Charlie Sanders, Jerry Wampfier, Woody Widenhofer.

No.	Name	Pos.	Ht.	Wt.	NFL Exp.	College
32	Alexander, Bruce	CB	5-9	169	3	Stephen F. Austin
65	Andolsek, Eric	G	6-2	286	4	Louisiana State
6	Arnold, Jim	P	6-3	211	9	Vanderbilt
93	Ball, Jerry	NT	6-1	296	5	Southern Methodist
36	Blades, Bennie	S	6-1	221	4	Miami (Fla.)
66	Bouwens, Shawn	OG	6-4	280	2	Nebraska-Wesleyan
75	Brown, Lomas	T	6-4	275	7	Florida
52	Brown, Mark	LB	6-2	240	9	Purdue
87	Campbell, Jeff	WR	5-8	167	2	Colorado
50	Caston, Toby	ILB	6-1	243	5	Louisiana State
59	Chesley, Delmar	ILB	6-2	235	1	Southern California
80	Claiborne, Robert	WR	5-10	175	2	San Diego State
82	Clark, Robert	WR	5-11	173	4	North Carolina Central
55	Cofer, Michael	OLB	6-5	245	9	Tennessee
39	Crockett, Ray	CB	5-9	181	3	Baylor
67	Dallafior, Ken	G-C	6-4	279	7	Minnesota
91	Duckens, Mark	DE	6-4	270	3	Arizona State
81	Farr, Mike	WR	5-10	192	2	UCLA
77	Ferguson, Keith	DE	6-5	276	11	Ohio State
69	Fortin, Roman	T	6-5	270	1	San Diego State
40	Futrell, Bobby	DB	5-11	185	5	Elizabeth State
98	Gibson, Dennis	ILB	6-2	243	5	Iowa State
53	Glover, Kevin	C	6-2	282	1	Maryland
23	Gray, Mel	WR-KR	5-9	166	6	Purdue
74	Graybill, Michael	OT	6-7	280	3	Boston University
86	Green, Willie	WR	6-2	179	1	Mississippi
89	Greer, Terry	WR	6-1	192	6	Alabama State
71	Hadd, Gary	DE	6-4	278	3	Minnesota
99	Hayworth, Tracy	LB	6-3	250	2	Tennessee
95	Hinckley, Rob	OLB	6-4	241	1	Stanford
97	Hunter, Jeff	DE	6-5	285	2	Albany State
58	Jamison, George	LB	6-1	228	5	Cincinnati
24	Jenkins, Melvin	CB	5-10	173	5	Cincinnati
57	Jones, Victor	ILB	6-2	240	4	Virginia Tech
12	Kramer, Erik	QB	6-1	195	1	North Carolina State
83	Matthews, Aubrey	WR	5-7	165	6	Delta State
29	McNorton, Bruce	CB	5-11	175	10	Georgetown
3	Murray, Eddie	K	5-10	180	12	Tulane
51	Noga, Niko	LB	6-1	235	8	Hawaii
28	Oldham, Chris	CB	5-9	183	2	Oregon
33	Overton, Don	RB	6-0	221	2	Fairmont State
90	Owens, Dan	DE	6-3	268	2	Southern California
9	Peete, Rodney	QB	6-0	195	3	Southern California
96	Pete, Lawrence	NT	6-0	282	3	Nebraska
4	Pillow, Frank	WR	5-11	170	4	Tennessee State
44	Riley, Eugene	TE	6-3	238	2	Ball State
73	Salem, Harvey	T-G	6-6	289	9	California
20	Sanders, Barry	SB	5-8	203	3	Oklahoma State
64	Sanders, Eric	T-G	6-7	286	11	Nevada-Reno
54	Spielman, Chris	ILB	6-0	247	4	Ohio State
92	Spindler, Marc	DL	6-5	277	2	Pittsburgh
46	Tennell, Derek	TE	6-5	250	4	UCLA
60	Utley, Mike	G-T	6-6	279	3	Washington State
26	Van Horse, Sean	CB	5-10	180	1	Howard
11	Ware, Andre	QB	6-2	205	2	Houston
27	Welch, Herb	S	5-11	180	6	UCLA
25	White, Sheldon	CB	5-11	188	4	Miami (Ohio)
35	White, William	DB	5-10	191	4	Ohio State
34	Wilder, James	SB	6-3	225	11	Missouri

TOP DRAFT CHOICES

Rd.	Name	Sel. No.	Pos.	Ht.	Wt.	College
1	Moore, Herman	10	WR	6-4	205	Virginia
1	Pritchett, Kelvin	20	DT	6-3	281	Mississippi
3	Barrett, Reggie	58	WR	6-3	215	Texas-El Paso
4	Scott, Kevin	91	CB	5-9	175	Stanford
5	Conover, Scott	118	G	6-4	276	Purdue

high as second and as low as fifth. The change in offensive philosophy points to the latter.

LION PROFILES

BARRY SANDERS 23 5-8 203 **Running Back**

Perhaps the most exciting running back in football . . . Followed up sensational rookie season with impressive second year . . . Led NFL with 1,304 rushing yards and averaged 5.1 yards per carry . . . Also caught 35 passes for 462 yards . . . Great speed, quickness, change of direction . . . Benefits from room created by Lions' four-wide-receiver offense . . . Earned second straight Pro Bowl berth . . . NFC Rookie of Year and first-team All-Pro in 1989 . . . Broke Billy Sims' team record with 1,437 rushing yards . . . Quiet, humble athlete known for handing football to referee after scoring TDs . . . Lions' No. 1 pick (third overall selection) after winning Heisman Trophy at Oklahoma State . . . Set 13 NCAA single-season records in 1988, including TDs (39) and rushing yards (2,628) . . . Entered NFL draft after junior season . . . Born July 16, 1968, in Wichita, Kan. . . . 1990 base salary: $500,000.

BENNIE BLADES 25 6-1 221 **Safety**

A linebacker in safety's clothing . . . Big hitter makes Detroit secondary a dangerous place for opposing wide receivers . . . Third on team in tackles with 83 despite missing four games with injury . . . Also snared two interceptions . . . Switched from strong safety to free safety midway in 1989 season . . . Made 100 tackles in 1989 after getting 102 as a rookie in 1988 . . . Lions' No. 1 pick in 1988 out of Miami . . . Co-winner of Jim Thorpe Award as nation's outstanding defensive back as a senior . . . Brother, Brian, plays wide receiver for Seattle . . . Born Sept. 3, 1966, in Fort Lauderdale, Fla. . . . 1990 base salary: $250,000.

CHRIS SPIELMAN 25 6-1 247 **Linebacker**

Natural linebacker has the instincts and demeanor for the position . . . Has led Lions in tackles in each of his three seasons . . . Produced 108 tackles in 1990 despite missing four games with an injury . . . Also credited with two sacks and two fumble recoveries . . . Made 15 tackles against Atlanta . . . Made 125 tackles and earned Pro Bowl berth in 1989 . . . Broke team record with 153 tackles as a rookie . . . Lions' second-round pick in 1988 out of Ohio State . . . Lombardi Award winner as nation's best linebacker as a senior . . . Hall-of-Fame career would mean a return home for this Ohio native . . . Born Oct. 11, 1965, in Canton, Ohio (home of the Hall of Fame) . . . 1990 base salary: $220,000.

JERRY BALL 26 6-1 296 **Nose Tackle**

Recognition finally has arrived for this natural nose tackle . . . Made Pro Bowl for second year in a row following 1990 season . . . Recorded 50 tackles and two sacks . . . Excellent run-defender . . . His consistent pass-rush pressure up the middle creates opportunities for teammates . . . Named Lions' defensive MVP in 1989 . . . Produced 79 tackles and nine sacks and made first Pro Bowl after three solid seasons . . . Pro Bowl alternate in 1988 . . . Started 59 consecutive games before sitting out 1990 season finale . . . Lions' third-round pick out of SMU in 1987 . . . All-American selection . . . Born Dec. 15, 1964, in Beaumont, Tex . . . 1990 base salary: $375,000.

RODNEY PEETE 25 6-0 195 **Quarterback**

Lions' starting quarterback at end of 1990 season will face a strong challenge from highly-touted Andre Ware . . . Peete started final five games of promising but inconsistent season . . . Passed for 1,974 yards and 13 TDs . . . Threw just eight interceptions . . . Went 122 passes in a row without an interception . . . Ran for 365 yards (7.6 average) and six TDs . . . Passed for 316 yards and four TDs in victory over Chicago . . . Slowed by injuries and erratic play . . . Started eight games as a rookie . . . Passed for 1,479 yards and five TDs but threw nine interceptions . . . Lions' sixth-round pick in 1989 out of USC . . . Second in Heisman Trophy balloting to future teammate Barry Sanders . . . Lightly regarded by some scouts because of size, limited arm strength . . . His father, Willie, is an assistant coach with the Packers . . . Born March 16, 1966, in Tuscon, Ariz. . . . 1990 base salary: $90,000.

ANDRE WARE 22 6-2 205 Quarterback

Struggled through frustrating rookie season in 1990 . . . Future wasn't now for Lions' promising young quarterback . . . Played in just four games, starting one . . . Completed 13 of 30 passes for 164 yards and one TD, with two interceptions . . . Only start came in Week 9 against Minnesota . . . Went 5-for-11 for 48 yards and was yanked at halftime . . . Expected to challenge Rodney Peete for starting job in training camp . . . Lions' No. 1 pick in 1990 out of Houston . . . Trigger man for Houston's explosive Run-n'-Shoot offense . . . Passed for NCAA-record 4,699 yards in 1989 . . . Also threw for 46 TDs . . . Entered NFL draft after junior season . . . Born July 31, 1969, in Dickinson, Tex. . . . 1990 base salary: $250,000.

MEL GRAY 30 5-9 166 Wide Receiver

USFL refugee has found new life as return specialist in NFL . . . Earned first Pro Bowl berth after another electrifying season in 1990 . . . Among NFL leaders in both kickoff-return average (22.9) and punt-return average (10.6) . . . His 939 kickoff-return yards were second-most in Lions' history . . . Broke off 65-yard kickoff return against Buccaneers and 39-yard punt return against Vikings . . . Lions got him as a Plan B free agent from New Orleans in 1989 . . . Led NFC in kickoff returns that season with 26.7-yard average . . . Played three seasons for Saints . . . Started pro career as running back for USFL's Los Angeles Express . . . Led Purdue in rushing his final two seasons . . . Born March 16, 1961, in Williamsburg, Va. . . . 1990 base salary: $300,000.

LOMAS BROWN 28 6-4 275 **Tackle**

Pro Bowl recognition was a long time coming to this consummate professional . . . Finally made Pro Bowl in sixth NFL season . . . Durable, dependable player has started 58 consecutive games, longest streak on team . . . Has missed just one start in career . . . Run-blocking helped pave way for Barry Sanders to run for more than 2,700 yards last two seasons . . . Also regarded as excellent pass-blocker . . . Pro Bowl alternate after 1987 and 1988 seasons . . . Lions' No. 1 pick in 1985 out of Florida . . . Two-time All-American . . . Born March 30, 1963, in Miami . . . 1990 base salary: $425,000.

MICHAEL COFER 31 6-5 245 **Linebacker**

Big-play man led the Lions in sacks for the fourth year in a row . . . His 10 sacks in 1990 brought his eight-year total to 60 . . . Started all 16 games in bouncing back from injury-marred 1989 season . . . Speed, size and agility make him one of the NFL's best pass-rushing linebackers . . . Pro Bowler in 1988, when he recorded a career-high 12 sacks . . . Frustrating season in 1989, when he missed nine starts with injuries . . . Still led the team with 9½ sacks . . . Lions' third-round draft choice in 1983 out of Tennessee . . . Started career at defensive end, switched to linebacker in 1985 . . . Born April 7, 1960, in Knoxville, Tenn. . . . 1990 base salary: $500,000.

KEVIN GLOVER 28 6-2 282 **Center**

Underrated player who has developed into one of the NFL's best centers . . . Has started every game for the Lions the last three years . . . Strong run-blocking has helped Barry Sanders rack up more than 2,700 rushing yards in last two seasons . . . Drafted as a center, he played guard early in his career . . . Good athlete for his position, he once returned a kickoff 19 yards against the Rams . . . Knee injuries kept him sidelined for much of his first two seasons . . . Lions' second-round pick in 1985 out of Maryland . . . First-team All-American as a senior, as picked by *The Sporting News* . . . Born June 17, 1963, in Largo, Md. . . . 1990 base salary: $264,000.

COACH WAYNE FONTES: Tried to look at bright side of frustrating second season . . . After Lions won seven of final nine games in 1989, hopes were high in 1990 . . . Lions' 6-10 record left Fontes under considerable pressure . . . Two of Lions' losses were in overtime . . . Heavily criticized by disgruntled former linebacker Jimmy Williams . . . Feels team is ready to move into contention for NFC Central title . . . Has assembled impressive array of young offensive talent . . . Lions' Silver Stretch offense set team record with 46 TDs in 1990 . . . Became interim coach following firing of Darryl Rogers midway in 1988 season . . . Enthusiastic, popular with most of the players . . . Spent four years as Lions' defensive coordinator before becoming head coach . . . Served nine years as an assistant coach at Tampa Bay . . . A defensive back with the AFL Jets in 1962 . . . Returned an interception 83 yards for TD, a Jets' record until Erik McMillan went 93 yards for TD in 1989 . . . College assistant coach at Dayton, Iowa and USC . . . Played college football at Michigan State . . . Born Feb. 2, 1940, in Canton, Ohio.

GREATEST PUNTER

Yale Lary was a nine-time Pro Bowl defensive back for the Lions in the 1950s and 1960s. He made the Hall of Fame in large part because of his 50 career interceptions and outstanding defensive play.

But Lary also was the best punter in Detroit history. He holds team records for career punts (503) and career punting average (44.3), and his 48.9 average in 1948 is tops in team history.

Moving into Lary's class as a punter is current Lion Jim Arnold, a perennial Pro Bowler. Since arriving from Kansas City in 1986, Arnold has averaged better than 42 yards per punt.

INDIVIDUAL LION RECORDS

Rushing

Most Yards Game:	198	Bob Hoernschemeyer, vs N.Y. Yanks, 1950
Season:	1,470	Barry Sanders, 1989
Career:	5,106	Billy Sims, 1980-84

Passing

Most TD Passes Game:	5	Gary Danielson, vs Minnesota, 1978
Season:	26	Bobby Layne, 1951
Career:	118	Bobby Layne, 1950-58

Receiving

Most TD Passes Game:	4	Cloyce Box, vs Baltimore, 1950
Season:	15	Cloyce Box, 1952
Career:	35	Terry Barr, 1957-65

Scoring

Most Points Game:	24	Cloyce Box, vs Baltimore, 1950
Season:	128	Doak Walker, 1950
Career:	1,016	Eddie Murray, 1980-90
Most TDs Game:	4	Cloyce Box, vs Baltimore, 1950
Season:	16	Billy Sims, 1980
Career:	47	Billy Sims, 1980-84

GREEN BAY PACKERS

TEAM DIRECTORY: Chairman: Judge Robert J. Parins; Pres.: Bob Harlan; Sec.: Peter Platten III; Exec. VP-Football Operations: Tom Braatz; Exec. Dir. Pub. Rel.: Lee Remmel; Head Coach: Lindy Infante. Home fields: Lambeau Field (59,543) and County Stadium, Milwaukee (56,051). Colors: Green and gold.

Another Sterling effort landed Sharpe in the Pro Bowl.

SCOUTING REPORT

OFFENSE: A disappointing 1990 season (6-10) began with quarterback Don Majkowski's contract holdout and ended with his injury. His health is a major concern.

The Packers signed former Bears' quarterback Mike Tomczak as a Plan B free agent. He'll be the starting quarterback if Majkowski doesn't recover from shoulder surgery.

The wide receivers are set with Pro Bowler Sterling Sharpe and Perry Kemp. The Packers are looking for more production from running back Darrell Thompson, a No. 1 pick in 1990.

The line was a disaster area in 1990. Holdouts, injuries and incompetence contributed to a league-high 62 sacks allowed. Right tackle Tony Mandarich is looking more and more like a big bust.

DEFENSE: There is some hope here, but the Packers need to get better at rushing the passer and creating big plays.

The line needs improvement. End Shawn Patterson still is working his way back from knee surgery but has potential.

The linebackers are solid. Tim Harris is a quality pass-rusher, although he was inconsistent in 1990. Tony Bennett, another No. 1 pick in 1990, could become a big-play man.

Age is a problem in the secondary. Cornerback LeRoy Butler and safety Chuck Cecil are good young players, but the Packers need more like them. Coach Lindy Infante has high hopes for Vincent Clark, a rookie defensive back from Ohio State.

SPECIAL TEAMS: A mixed bag. Placekicker Chris Jacke is consistent and the return teams are OK. But punter Don Bracken was nothing special in 1990 and the Packers need to improve their coverage teams.

THE ROOKIES: The Packers traded down in the first round and picked up an extra No. 1 pick for 1992. They took Clark to inject some youth and speed to their suspect secondary. Oregon State's Esera Tuaolo and Wisconsin's Don Davey were added to the defensive line.

OUTLOOK: From 10-6 in 1989 to 6-10 in 1990, the Packers seem to be moving in the wrong direction. They need to stop the slide before they can contemplate playoff contention. Majkowski's return to health would be a big step forward. But this still looks like a sub-.500 team.

PACKERS VETERAN ROSTER

HEAD COACH—Lindy Infante. Assistant Coaches—Hank Bullough, Greg Blache, Joe Clark, Charlie Davis, Buddy Geis, Dick Jauron, Virgil Knight, Dick Moseley, Willie Peete, Russ Riederer, Tip Tippett.

No.	Name	Pos.	Ht.	Wt.	NFL Exp.	College
82	Affholter, Erik	WR	6-0	182	1	Southern California
74	Archambeau, Lester	DE	6-4	270	2	Stanford
67	Ard, Billy	G	6-3	273	11	Wake Forest
90	Bennett, Tony	LB	6-2	233	2	Mississippi
83	Bland, Carl	WR	5-11	179	8	Virginia Union
17	Bracken, Don	P	6-1	218	7	Michigan
62	Brock, Matt	DE-NT	6-5	285	3	Oregon
93	Brown, Robert	DE	6-3	270	10	Virginia Tech
51	Bush, Blair	C	6-3	273	14	Washington
36	Butler, LeRoy	CB	6-0	192	2	Florida State
63	Campen, James	C	6-2	275	5	Tulane
26	Cecil, Chuck	S	6-0	188	4	Arizona
78	Cheek, Louis	G-T	6-6	295	4	Texas A&M
55	Clark, Greg	LB	6-0	232	4	Arizona State
56	Dent, Burnell	LB	6-1	234	6	Tulane
60	Derby, Glenn	T-G	6-6	290	3	Wisconsin
8	Dilweg, Anthony	QB	6-3	198	3	Duke
27	Fontenot, Herman	RB	6-0	205	7	Louisiana State
23	Greene, Tiger	S	6-0	192	7	Western Carolina
33	Haddix, Michael	FB	6-1	230	9	Mississippi State
65	Hallstrom, Ron	G	6-6	297	10	Iowa
80	Harris, Jackie	TE	6-3	240	2	NE Louisiana
97	Harris, Tim	LB	6-6	245	6	Memphis State
89	Harris, William	TE	6-5	255	4	Bishop College
24	Hauck, Tim	S	5-11	185	2	Montana
50	Holland, Johnny	LB	6-1	233	5	Texas A&M
44	Holmes, Jerry	CB	6-1	176	10	West Virginia
13	Jacke, Chris	K	6-0	197	3	Texas-El Paso
71	Jones, Scott	T	6-5	282	3	Washington
81	Kemp, Perry	WR	5-11	170	5	California (Pa.)
10	Kiel, Blair	QB	6-0	203	7	Notre Dame
48	Kinchen, Brian	TE	6-2	232	4	Louisiana State
38	Labbe, Rico	S	6-0	210	1	Boston College
59	Larson, Kurt	LB	6-4	244	3	Michigan State
22	Lee, Mark	CB	6-0	195	12	Washington
7	Majkowski, Don	QB	6-2	207	5	Virginia
77	Mandarich, Tony	T	6-5	315	3	Michigan State
47	Mitchell, Roland	CB	5-11	180	5	Texas Tech
57	Moran, Rich	G	6-2	283	7	San Diego State
37	Murphy, Mark	S	6-2	203	10	West Liberty State
79	Nelson, Bob	NT	6-4	275	5	Miami (Fla.)
43	Neubert, Keith	TE	6-6	250	2	Nebraska
91	Noble, Brian	LB	6-4	243	7	Arizona State
96	Patterson, Shawn	DE	6-4	270	4	Arizona State
95	Paup, Bryce	LB	6-5	245	2	Northern Iowa
28	Pitts, Ron	CB	5-10	183	6	UCLA
85	Query, Jeff	WR	6-0	167	3	Millikin
31	Rice, Allen	RB	5-10	206	8	Baylor
75	Ruettgers, Ken	T	6-5	288	7	Southern California
84	Sharpe, Sterling	WR	5-11	202	4	South Carolina
45	Sikahema, Vai	RB-KR	5-9	191	6	Brigham Young
56	Stephen, Scott	LB	6-2	243	5	Arizona State
39	Thompson, Darrell	FB	6-0	215	2	Minnesota
18	Tomczak, Mike	QB	6-1	195	7	Ohio State
70	Uecker, Keith	G-T	6-5	295	8	Auburn
87	Weathers, Clarence	WR	5-8	182	9	Delaware State
52	Weddington, Mike	LB	6-3	243	6	Oklahoma
86	West, Ed	TE	6-1	240	8	Auburn
88	Wilson, Charles	WR	5-9	174	2	Memphis State
68	Winter, Blaise	DE	6-4	282	7	Syracuse
29	Woods, Jerry	S	5-8	193	2	Northern Michigan
33	Woodside, Keith	RB	6-0	200	4	Texas A&M
46	Workman, Vince	RB	5-10	195	3	Ohio State

TOP DRAFT CHOICES

Rd.	Name	Sel. No.	Pos.	Ht.	Wt.	College
1	Clark, Vinnie	19	DB	6-0	189	Ohio State
2	Tuaolo, Esera	35	NT	6-2	280	Oregon State
3	Davey, Don	67	DE	6-3	269	Wisconsin
3	Webb, Chuck	81	RB	5-9	209	Tennessee
5	Fite, Jeff	135	P	6-1	206	Memphis State

PACKER PROFILES

DON MAJKOWSKI 27 6-2 207 **Quarterback**

The majik ran out for Green Bay quarterback in 1990 . . . Frustrating season ended with career in balance following severe shoulder injury . . . Played in just nine games, passing for 1,925 yards with more interceptions (12) than TDs (10) . . . Missed first game of season after lengthy contract squabble . . . Passed for 355 yards against Tampa Bay but threw five interceptions . . . Suffered right shoulder injury in Week 10 game at Phoenix . . . Missed rest of season . . . Looked like one of NFL's best young quarterbacks in 1989 . . . Passed for 4,381 yards and 27 TDs in first full season as starter . . . Made the Pro Bowl . . . Nicknamed "The Majik Man" . . . Packers' 10th-round pick in 1988 out of Virginia . . . Born Feb. 25, 1964, in Depew, N.Y. . . . 1990 base salary: $1.5 million.

STERLING SHARPE 26 5-11 202 **Wide Receiver**

Inconsistency at quarterback hurt this talented wide receiver . . . Pro Bowl berth was evidence of respect around league . . . Caught 67 passes for 1,106 yards and six TDs . . . But that was a drop from his 1989 numbers: 90 catches, 1,423 yards, 12 TDs . . . Caught 10 passes for 157 yards against Buccaneers . . . Reached 200 receptions faster than any player in Packers' history . . . Enters 1991 with receptions in 39 consecutive games . . . Caught 55 passes for 791 yards as a rookie in 1988 . . . Packers' No. 1 pick in 1988 out of South Carolina . . . Born April 6, 1965, in Glenville, Ga. . . . 1990 base salary: $300,000.

TIM HARRIS 26 6-6 245 **Linebacker**

Big talker wasn't able to back up his words in 1990 . . . Respectable total of seven sacks was huge drop from his 19½ in 1989 . . . Still led team in sacks for fifth year in a row . . . Credited with 90 tackles . . . Considered one of the brashest, loudest players in the league . . . His reputation didn't stop him from making Pro Bowl in 1989 . . . Has 55 sacks in his five-year career . . . Great pass-rusher needs to be more consistent against the run

. . . Would benefit from stronger supporting cast on defense . . . Packers' fourth-round pick in 1986 out of Memphis State . . . Born Sept. 10, 1964, in Birmingham, Ala. . . . 1990 base salary: $600,000.

KEN RUETTGERS 29 6-5 288 **Tackle**

Slowed by contract holdout and injuries in 1990 just as he was emerging as one of NFL's best tackles . . . Missed five games with leg injuries and was hampered in others . . . Hard worker renowned for countless hours of film study . . . Best season was 1987, when he allowed just 3½ sacks . . . Started 44 consecutive games before missing 1988 season opener with shoulder injury . . . Pass-blocking helped Packers develop explosive air attack in 1989 . . . Packers' No. 1 pick in 1985 out of USC . . . Born Aug. 20, 1962, in Bakersfield, Cal. . . . 1990 base salary: $625,000.

TONY MANDARICH 25 6-5 315 **Tackle**

Packers still are waiting for this highly-touted player to approach his potential . . . Started all 16 games at right tackle but was far from dominant . . . Manhandled by Reggie White in 31-0 loss to Eagles . . . One of the most heralded offensive linemen to enter NFL in recent history . . . A flop as a rookie in 1989 . . . Had zero starts after extended training-camp holdout . . . Had threatened to quit football and fight heavyweight boxer Mike Tyson . . . Has great speed for size but has yet to adapt to NFL game . . . Consensus All-American at Michigan State . . . Second pick in 1989 draft (one ahead of Barry Sanders) . . . Born Sept. 23, 1966, in Ontario, Canada . . . 1990 base salary: $400,000.

PERRY KEMP 30 5-11 170 **Wide Receiver**

Smooth, smart receiver is perfect for Packers' sophisticated passing game . . . Second on the team in receptions with 44 . . . Caught five passes for 83 yards against Minnesota . . . Showed a willingness to cross middle . . . Caught 48 passes in both 1988 and 1989 . . . USFL refugee . . . Played for Packers' coach Lindy Infante with Jacksonville Bulls . . .

Signed with Packers as a free agent in 1988 . . . Played three games for Cleveland in 1987 after being out of football in 1986 . . . Born Jan. 31, 1961, in Westland, Pa. . . . Played for tiny California (Pa.) University . . . Selected by Bulls in 11th round of 1984 USFL draft . . . 1990 base salary: $325,000.

DARRELL THOMPSON 23 6-0 215 — Running Back

Slow start for Packers' No. 1 pick in 1990 . . . Rushed for 264 yards on 76 carries (3.5 average) . . . Best game was last: six carries, 63 yards against Broncos . . . Returned kickoff 76 yards for TD against Detroit . . . Had just nine carries for 18 yards in first six NFL games . . . Ripped off 37-yard run against Buccaneers . . . All-time leading rusher at Minnesota with 4,518 yards . . . Great speed for size, timed in 4.42 seconds in 40-yard dash . . . Born Nov. 23, 1967, in Rochester, Minn. . . . 1990 base salary: $250,000.

SHAWN PATTERSON 27 6-4 270 — Defensive End

Battled back from devastating knee injury to finish second on team in sacks with four in 1990 . . . Showed big-play ability with interception return for TD in victory over Vikings . . . Also knocked down three passes . . . Rounded into shape late in season after finishing rehabilitation of knee injury suffered in sixth game of 1989 season . . . Produced five sacks as a rookie in 1988 . . . Hard worker is regarded as an intense competitor . . . Packers' second-round pick in 1988 out of Arizona State . . . Born June 13, 1964, in Tempe, Ariz. . . . 1990 base salary: $205,000.

BRIAN NOBLE 28 6-4 243 — Linebacker

Hard hitter is the heart of Packers' defense . . . Finished second on team in tackles with 113 despite missing two games with injuries . . . Also defended five passes . . . Has averaged better than 100 tackles per season in six-year career . . . Vocal team leader . . . Career-best 138 tackles in 1989 . . . Has been a starter since rookie season of 1985 . . . Packers' fifth-round pick in 1985 out of Arizona State . . . Enjoys shark fishing . . . Born Sept. 6, 1962, in Anaheim, Cal. . . . 1990 base salary: $550,000.

LeROY BUTLER 23 6-0 192 **Defensive Back**

Talented rookie made big impact with Packers in 1990 . . . Tied for team lead in interceptions with three and passes defended with 11 . . . Backup to veteran cornerbacks Jerry Holmes and Mark Lee . . . Also team's third-ranked special-teams player . . . Versatile performer can handle both cornerback and safety positions . . . Played cornerback as a senior at Florida State after spending most of career at free safety . . . Intercepted seven passes as a senior . . . Born July 19, 1968, in Jacksonville, Fla. . . . 1990 base salary: $170,000.

COACH LINDY INFANTE: Frustrating season ended with a 6-10 record and a seriously injured quarterback . . . Packers lost four games by a TD or less . . . Season was especially difficult since Packers went 10-6 in 1989 . . . That season was regarded as one of the great turnarounds in recent NFL history . . . Infante's first Packer team, in 1988, went 4-12 . . . Regarded as one of the sharpest offensive minds in the NFL . . . Has installed sophisticated passing attack . . . Suffered last season because of problems encountered by quarterback Don Majkowski . . . Joined Packers after two seasons as offensive coordinator in Cleveland . . . Head coach of Jacksonville Bulls of USFL . . . College assistant at Florida, Memphis State and Tulane . . . Also an assistant with Charlotte in old World Football League . . . NFL assistant with Giants and Bengals before becoming head coach in Jacksonville in 1984 . . . An All-SEC defensive back at Florida . . . Played for Hamilton in CFL . . . Born May 27, 1940, in Miami.

GREATEST PUNTER

Dick Deschaine was the Packers' punter for just three seasons (1955-57), but his performance was so consistently outstanding that he ranks as the best in the club's storied history.

Deschaine never averaged less than 42 yards per punt in his

career. He ranked second in the NFL in punting with averages of 43.2 in 1955 and 42.7 in 1956. In balloting of Green Bay fans in 29 states, Deschaine was named the best punter in the Packers' modern era.

Special mention goes to Don Chandler, who was better known as the Packers' placekicker in the mid-1960s. On Oct. 10, 1965, in a game against San Francisco, Chandler set a team record with a 90-yard punt—the fourth-longest in NFL history.

INDIVIDUAL PACKER RECORDS

Rushing

Most Yards Game:	186	Jim Taylor, vs N.Y. Giants, 1961
Season:	1,474	Jim Taylor, 1962
Career:	8,207	Jim Taylor, 1958-66

Passing

Most TD Passes Game:	5	4 times, most recently Lynn Dickey, vs Houston, 1983
Season:	32	Lynn Dickey, 1983
Career:	152	Bart Starr, 1956-71

Receiving

Most TD Passes Game:	4	Don Hutson, vs Detroit, 1945
Season:	17	Don Hutson, 1943
Career:	99	Don Hutson, 1935-45

Scoring

Most Points Game:	33	Paul Hornung, vs Baltimore, 1961
Season:	176	Paul Hornung, 1960
Career:	823	Don Hutson, 1935-45
Most TDs Game:	5	Paul Hornung, vs Baltimore, 1961
Season:	19	Jim Taylor, 1962
Career:	105	Don Hutson, 1935-45

LOS ANGELES RAMS

TEAM DIRECTORY: Pres.: Georgia Frontiere; Exec. VP: John Shaw; VP-Media and Community Rel.: Marshall Klein; Dir. Operations: Dick Beam; Adm. Football Operations: Jack Faulkner; Dir. Player Personnel: John Math; Dir. Marketing: Pete Donovan; Dir. Pub. Rel.: John Oswald; Head Coach: John Robinson. Home field: Anaheim Stadium (69,008). Colors: Royal blue, gold and white.

SCOUTING REPORT

OFFENSE: Although the defense was even more disappointing, the offense must share the blame for the Rams' disastrous 5-11 season. Look for this group to bounce back in a big way.

Quarterback Jim Everett still is one of the best in the business, but he needs to handle pass-rush pressure a little better. Still, Everett is accomplished enough to have passed for 3,989 yards and 23 TDs in a bad year.

The wide receivers are excellent. Records are starting to fall every time Henry Ellard gets his hands on the football. Willie Anderson has averaged more yards per catch than anybody in the NFL over the last two seasons. A replacement must be found for dependable H-back Pete Holohan, who signed with Kansas City as a Plan B free agent.

The keys to the running game have been turned over to Cleveland Gary. He ran for 14 TDs in 1990 but must kick his habit of fumbling. Buford McGee is a versatile fullback.

The offensive line is showing some age. Doug Smith, Irv Pankey and Jackie Slater all are past 33. The Rams want to phase in 1990 No. 1 pick Bern Brostek and maybe some other young players as well.

DEFENSE: A disaster area. John Robinson fired defensive coordinator Fritz Shurmur and his assistants after the team allowed 412 points.

New defensive coordinator Jeff Fisher arrives from Philadelphia with orders to rebuild the Rams in the image of the Eagles. That means a four-man line, with lots of blitzing and man-to-man pass coverage.

The line needs to be overhauled. Former high draft picks Bill Hawkins and Brian Smith will get a long look. Veterans Mike

Henry Ellard was second to Jerry Rice in receiving yards.

Piel, Doug Reed and Alvin Wright will compete with what is expected to be an influx of rookies.

Kevin Greene and Frank Stams are solid at linebacker. Veterans Mike Wilcher, Fred Strickland and Larry Kelm also figure in the mix.

Guess what? The secondary needs to be rebuilt, too. Cornerback Jerry Gray, a four-time Pro Bowler, was hindered by injuries

RAMS VETERAN ROSTER

HEAD COACH—John Robinson. Assistant Coaches—Tom Bettis, Garrett Giemont, Jeff Fisher, Marv Goux, Gil Haskell, Hudson Houck, Ronnie Jones, Jimmy Raye, John Teerlinck, Clarence Shelmon, Ernie Zampese.

No.	Name	Pos.	Ht.	Wt.	NFL Exp.	College
83	Anderson, Willie	WR	6-0	172	4	UCLA
82	Bailey, Stacey	WR	6-1	163	10	San Jose State
42	Berry, Latin	CB	5-10	196	2	Oregon
57	Bethune, George	LB	6-4	240	3	Alabama
61	Brostek, Bern	G-C	6-3	300	2	Washington
59	Butcher, Paul	LB	6-0	230	6	Wayne State
98	Carr, Derrick	DE	6-6	270	1	Bowling Green
88	Carter, Pat	TE	6-3	255	4	Florida State
84	Cox, Aaron	WR	5-10	178	4	Arizona State
72	Cox, Robert	T	6-5	285	6	UCLA
81	Delaney, Jarrod	WR	6-5	196	1	Texas Christian
39	Delpino, Robert	FB	6-0	205	4	Missouri
22	Dupree, Marcus	RB	6-2	225	2	Southern Mississippi
80	Ellard, Henry	WR	5-11	180	9	Fresno State
29	Emanuel, Aaron	RB	6-2	235	1	USC
8	English, Keith	P	6-3	220	2	Colorado
11	Everett, Jim	QB	6-5	214	6	Purdue
89	Faison, Derrick	WR	6-4	200	2	Howard
51	Faryniarz, Brett	LB	6-3	232	4	San Diego State
43	Gary, Cleveland	RB	6-0	226	3	Miami (Fla.)
79	Goldberg, Bill	DT	6-3	266	1	Georgia
25	Gray, Jerry	CB	6-0	185	7	Texas
91	Greene, Kevin	DE	6-3	238	7	Auburn
19	Harris, Greg	WR	5-9	155	1	Troy State
5	Hatcher, Dale	P	6-2	220	7	Clemson
70	Hawkins, Bill	DE	6-6	266	3	Miami (Fla.)
20	Henley, Darryl	CB	5-9	172	3	UCLA
31	Jackson, Alfred	CB	6-0	180	2	San Diego State
86	Johnson, Damone	TE	6-4	250	7	Cal Poly SLO
52	Kelm, Larry	LB	6-4	240	5	Texas A&M
27	Lilly, Sammy	CB	5-9	178	3	Georgia Tech
63	Lindsey, Michael	LB	6-2	243	1	Southern
16	Long, Chuck	QB	6-4	221	6	Iowa
67	Love, Duval	G	6-3	287	7	UCLA
24	McGee, Buford	FB	6-0	210	8	Mississippi
71	Milinichik, Joe	G	6-5	275	5	North Carolina State
66	Newberry, Tom	C-G	6-2	285	6	Wisconsin-LaCrosse
26	Newman, Anthony	S	6-0	199	4	Oregon
75	Pankey, Irv	T	6-5	292	12	Penn State
60	Perry, Gerald	T	6-6	305	4	Southern University
95	Piel, Mike	DT	6-4	270	3	Illinois
87	Price, Jim	TE	6-4	247	1	Stanford
93	Reed, Doug	DT	6-3	265	9	San Diego State
97	Robinson, Gerald	DE	6-3	262	4	Auburn
55	Sanders, Glenell	LB	6-0	224	2	Louisiana Tech
78	Slater, Jackie	T	6-4	287	16	Jackson State
96	Smith, Brian	DT	6-6	268	3	Auburn
56	Smith, Doug	C	6-3	275	14	Bowling Green
50	Stams, Frank	LB	6-2	240	3	Notre Dame
23	Stewart, Michael	S	6-0	199	5	Fresno State
53	Strickland, Fred	LB	6-2	250	4	Purdue
30	Tatupu, Mosi	FB	6-0	227	14	USC
37	Terrell, Pat	S	6-0	195	2	Notre Dame
94	Thomas, Ben	DE	6-3	275	5	Auburn
21	Thomas, Rodney	CB	5-10	190	4	Brigham Young
54	Wilcher, Mike	LB	6-3	245	9	North Carolina
77	Wilson, Karl	DE	6-4	275	5	Louisiana State
99	Wright, Alvin	DT	6-2	285	6	Jacksonville State
10	Zendejas, Tony	K	5-8	165	7	Nevada-Reno

TOP DRAFT CHOICES

Rd.	Name	Sel. No.	Pos.	Ht.	Wt.	College
1	Lyght, Todd	5	CB	6-0	186	Notre Dame
2	Phifer, Roman	31	LB	6-2	217	UCLA
4	Bailey, Robert	107	DB	6-1	187	Miami
5	Young, Robert	116	DE	6-6	267	Mississippi State
6	Fort, Neal	143	T	6-5	279	Brigham Young

last year and the Rams expect to shore up this sector with Notre Dame's Todd Lyght, the fifth pick in the draft.

SPECIAL TEAMS: Another unsettled area. The Rams lost kicker Mike Lansford to Cleveland in Plan B and signed Houston's erratic Tony Zendejas during the same period. Punter Keith English averaged 39.2 yards.

Darryl Henley is OK on punt returns. The Rams need to improve their coverage teams.

THE ROOKIES: The Rams went for defense with their first four picks. Top choice Lyght was considered the nation's best college cornerback. Outside linebacker Roman Phifer from UCLA should fit in well in the 4-3 defensive system. The Rams didn't address their aging offensive line until the sixth round, when they took BYU tackle Neal Fort.

OUTLOOK: The Rams still have a lot of offensive talent, but the defense is a mess. It will take time to learn Fisher's system and to bring in the right players. Look for a lot of high-scoring games and a slight improvement back to around the .500 mark.

RAM PROFILES

JIM EVERETT 28 6-5 214 **Quarterback**

Quarterback's season mirrored the Rams' in 1990 . . . On the verge of greatness, the player and team fell back into the pack . . . Posted impressive statistics but was unable to pull the team out of its tailspin . . . His 3,989 passing yards led the NFC . . . Threw 23 TD passes, with 17 interceptions . . . Threw four TD passes in victories over Tampa Bay and Cleveland . . . Flip side was his play against the Giants (zero TDs, three interceptions) and Falcons (13-for-40, two interceptions) . . . Looked like NFL's best young quarterback in 1989 . . . Passed for team-record 4,310 yards and also threw 29 TD passes . . . Led Rams to playoff victories over Eagles and Giants . . . Rams got him in 1986 trade with Houston for DE William Fuller, G Kent Hill, two No. 1 draft picks and a fifth-rounder . . . Three-year starter at Purdue

. . . Born Jan. 3, 1963, in Emporia, Kan. . . . 1990 base salary: $2 million.

HENRY ELLARD 30 5-11 180 **Wide Receiver**

Speedy, smart wide receiver ranks at top of Rams' all-time list in catches (421) and yards (7,037) . . . Led Rams in 1990 with 76 catches and 1,294 yards . . . Posted six 100-yard receiving games . . . Has caught a pass in 64 straight regular-season games, four shy of team record . . . Has caught more than 50 passes in each of last four seasons . . . Led NFL in receiving yards in 1988 with 1,414 . . . Has gone to Pro Bowl twice as wide receiver and once as a punt-returner . . . Rams' second-round pick in 1983 out of Fresno State . . . Born July 21, 1961, in Fresno, Cal. . . . 1990 base salary: $800,000.

JERRY GRAY 28 6-0 185 **Defensive Back**

Injuries and the team's woes made for a frustrating season for this four-time Pro Bowler . . . Failed to intercept a pass for the first time since rookie season of 1981 . . . Missed first three games after suffering knee injury in exhibition finale . . . Finished with just 31 tackles . . . Missed another game in midseason with a bruised knee . . . Picked off 19 passes between 1986-89 and made annual trip to Pro Bowl . . . MVP of 1989 Pro Bowl after returning interception 51 yards for TD . . . Might be moved to safety, the position he played in college . . . Consensus two-time All-American at Texas . . . Born Dec. 16, 1962, in Lubbock, Tex. . . . 1990 base salary: $500,000.

CLEVELAND GARY 25 6-0 226 **Running Back**

Fumbles marred an otherwise impressive 1990 season . . . Led Rams in rushing with 808 yards . . . Tied for second in NFL with 15 TDs . . . Ran for 102 yards against Atlanta, 103 against Dallas . . . Scored three TDs in upset of San Francisco . . . Fumbled 12 times, losing seven . . . Has the size and moves to be the Rams' feature back . . . Played in just eight games in 1989, all in reserve role . . . Baseball prospect who has played in Expos' farm system . . . Rams' first-round pick in 1989 out of

Miami . . . Set Miami record with 57 catches as a senior . . . Born May 4, 1966, in Indiantown, Fla. . . . 1990 base salary: $250,000.

DAMONE JOHNSON 29 6-4 250 Tight End

Contract problems and injuries combined to make for a difficult 1990 season for this talented tight end . . . Missed all of training camp and season opener in contract dispute . . . Missed two more games and slowed in others because of hamstring injury . . . Finished with just 12 catches, his low since becoming a starter in 1987 . . . His good blocking is key to Rams' running game . . . Best season was 1988 with 42 receptions, six TDs . . . Caught TD pass in playoff victory over Eagles in 1989 . . . Rams' sixth-round pick out of Cal Poly in 1985 . . . Born March 2, 1962, in Santa Monica, Cal. . . . 1990 base salary: $325,000.

WILLIE ANDERSON 26 6-0 172 Wide Receiver

Big-play man makes the most of his receptions . . . Led NFL in yards-per-catch for second year in a row with 21.5 . . . Caught 51 passes for 1,097 yards . . . Caught eight passes for 149 yards in upset of 49ers . . . Surpassed 1,000 receiving yards for second year in a row . . . Has great deep speed and decent moves . . . Burst on scene in 1989 with 1,146 yards and a remarkable 26.0 average . . . Set NFL record with 336 receiving yards against Saints . . . Caught two TD passes, including game-winner in overtime, in playoff victory over Giants . . . Nicknamed "Flipper" by grandmother, who said his cry as a baby sounded like TV dolphin . . . Rams' second-round pick in 1988 out of UCLA . . . Born March 7, 1965, in Paulsboro, N.J. . . . 1990 base salary: $200,000.

BUFORD McGEE 31 6-0 210 Fullback

Versatile running back put together his best season in 1990 . . . Set career highs in rushing yards (234) and receptions (47) . . . Averaged 5.3 yards per carry . . . Scored four TDs . . . Suffered fractured bone in the forearm in season finale but is expected to be fully recovered . . . Smart, shifty receiver is frequent safety valve for quarterback Jim Everett . . . Acquired by the

Rams from Chargers in 1987 in exchange for running back Barry Redden . . . Chargers' 11th-round pick in 1984 out of Mississippi . . . Born July 16, 1960, in Durant, Miss. . . . 1990 base salary: $300,000.

TOM NEWBERRY 28 6-2 285 **Guard**

Two streaks were broken in 1990 for this highly regarded offensive lineman . . . Missed Pro Bowl after two consecutive appearances . . . String of 73 consecutive starts was snapped when he missed regular-season finale with an ankle sprain . . . Great athletic ability for a man of his size . . . Runs 40-yard dash in 4.7 seconds and has 34-inch vertical leap . . . Might be moved to center in 1991 to make room for Bern Brostek at guard . . . In 1986, became first pure rookie since Eric Dickerson to start for the Rams . . . Rams' second-round pick out of Wisconsin-La Crosse . . . NCAA Division III shot-put and discus champion in 1984 and 1985 . . . Born Oct. 20, 1962, in Onalaska, Wisc. . . . 1990 base salary: $350,000.

KEVIN GREENE 29 6-3 238 **Linebacker**

Led Rams in sacks for third consecutive year with 13 . . . Started slowly after lengthy contract dispute . . . Ten of his sacks came in final eight games . . . Has 46 sacks in last three seasons . . . Recognition as one of NFL's best outside linebackers was slow to come . . . Finally made Pro Bowl in 1989 after second consecutive 16½-sack season . . . Also registered three sacks in 1989 playoffs . . . Spent three seasons as a backup before becoming starter in 1988 . . . A walk-on at Auburn . . . Rams' fifth-round draft choice in 1985 . . . Born July 31, 1962, in Granite City, Ill.

FRANK STAMS 26 6-2 240 **Linebacker**

Emerged as solid inside linebacker in second season . . . Finished second on team in tackles with 78 despite missing final two-plus games with knee injury . . . Had career-high 11 tackles against Giants . . . Hard hitter excels against run but needs to improve pass-defense . . . Started three games and made 27 tackles as a rookie . . . Rams' second-round pick in 1989 out of

Notre Dame . . . Associated Press first-team All-American . . . Defensive MVP of Fiesta Bowl victory over West Virginia that clinched national championship . . . Born July 17, 1965, in Akron, Ohio . . . 1990 base salary: $185,000.

COACH JOHN ROBINSON: Losing seasons are unfamiliar to this highly-successful coach . . . Suffered through perhaps the most frustrating season of his career in 1990 . . . Rams' 5-11 record was his worst as a head coach . . . Only second losing season in his 15 years as head coach at USC and Rams . . . Dogged by rumors of his possible firing and also that he might leave for another team . . . Signed contract extension late in season and vowed to return Rams to past glory . . . Dismissed six assistants, including defensive coordinator Fritz Shurmur, after the season . . . Hired former Eagles' defensive coordinator Jeff Fisher, who played for Robinson at USC . . . Career record with Rams is 76-61 . . . Has led Rams to six playoff berths in eight seasons . . . His best teams lost in NFC championship games in 1985 (to Chicago) and 1989 (to San Francisco) . . . Has knack for developing strong running game . . . Joined Rams in 1983 after going 67-14-2 and winning three Rose Bowls at USC . . . Boyhood friend of John Madden, under whom he worked as an assistant with the Raiders . . . College assistant at Oregon, where he played end, and USC . . . Born July 25, 1935, in Daly City, Cal.

GREATEST PUNTER

Norm Van Brocklin and Bobby Waterfield were two of the best passers in Rams' history. They handled the team's punting chores with distinction as well.

Waterfield, a triple threat who also did the team's placekicking, holds the Rams' record for longest punt with an 88-yarder in 1948. He also unleashed an 86-yarder in 1947. Waterfield's total of 315 punts ranks third in team history.

Van Brocklin, who is second in team history to Roman Gabriel in passing yards and TD passes, was the Rams' punter from 1951 through 1957. His 72-yard punt in 1956 is the third-longest in team history.

INDIVIDUAL RAM RECORDS

Rushing

Most Yards Game:	248	Eric Dickerson, vs Dallas, 1985
Season:	2,105	Eric Dickerson, 1984
Career:	7,245	Eric Dickerson, 1983-87

Passing

Most TD Passes Game:	5	7 times, most recently Jim Everett, vs N.Y. Giants, 1988
Season:	31	Jim Everett, 1988
Career:	154	Roman Gabriel, 1962-72

Receiving

Most TD Passes Game:	4	3 times, most recently Harold Jackson, vs Dallas, 1973
Season:	17	Elroy Hirsch, 1951
Career:	53	Elroy Hirsch, 1949-57

Scoring

Most Points Game:	24	3 times, most recently Harold Jackson, vs Dallas, 1973
Season:	130	David Ray, 1973
Career:	789	Mike Lansford, 1982-90
Most TDs Game:	4	3 times, most recently Harold Jackson, vs Dallas, 1973
Season:	20	Eric Dickerson, 1983
Career:	58	Eric Dickerson, 1983-87

MINNESOTA VIKINGS

TEAM DIRECTORY: Chairman: John Skoglund; Pres. and CEO: Roger Headrick; VP/Asst. GM/Finance and Adm.: Jeff Diamond; Dir. Football Oper.: Jerry Reichow; Pub. Rel. Dir.: Merrill Swanson; Head Coach: Jerry Burns. Home field: Hubert H. Humphrey Metrodome (63,000). Colors: Purple, white and gold.

Anthony Carter seeks fourth-straight 1,000-yard season.

SCOUTING REPORT

OFFENSE: The Vikings have talent galore, but they can't seem to get things together. Coach Jerry Burns has to settle the quarterback situation and decide on a fitting role for running back Herschel Walker.

Quarterback Wade Wilson is 32 and coming off an injury-marred season. His extended absence opened the door for Rich Gannon, who showed some ability but was inconsistent. The Vikings mortgaged their future for Walker but he still doesn't fit into their offense. They need to get him the football—or admit they made a mistake in acquiring him.

Wide receiver is a bright spot with Anthony Carter, and tight end Steve Jordan is a Pro Bowler.

The offensive line is a team strength. The best of the bunch are left tackle Gary Zimmerman and left guard Randall McDaniel.

DEFENSE: The Vikings were No. 1 in overall defense in 1988 and 1989. But they dropped to 13th last year.

Injuries were a problem, as defensive tackle Keith Millard, the NFL's Defensive Player of the Year in 1989, missed most of the season following knee surgery. He's expected back.

The line is strong, with Millard and end Chris Doleman among the game's best pass-rushers. Tackle Henry Thomas is underrated. Ray Berry is expected to replace the retired Scott Studwell at middle linebacker. Outside linebacker Mike Merriweather is a big-play man.

Safety Joey Browner and cornerback Carl Lee are Pro Bowlers.

SPECIAL TEAMS: Another area of concern. The Vikings need to improve at covering kicks and returning them.

Kicker Donald Igwebuike was 14-for-16 on field goals in his half-season with the team. He was charged—and later acquitted—of smuggling heroin. His replacement, Fuad Reveiz, was 11-for-12 and made his last 10. Punter Harry Newsome was a Plan B find from Pittsburgh. He averaged 42.3 yards.

Walker struggled as a kickoff-returner and the Vikings are looking for a dependable punt-returner.

THE ROOKIES: The Vikings continue to pay for the Walker trade. They waited until the third round, then took Michigan State linebacker Carlos Jenkins and Grambling wide receiver Jake Reed.

VIKINGS VETERAN ROSTER

HEAD COACH—Jerry Burns. Assistant Coaches—Tom Batta, Maxie Baughan, Jerry Brown, John Michels, Tom Moore, Dick Rehbein, Marc Trestman, Paul Wiggin.

No.	Name	Pos.	Ht.	Wt.	NFL Exp.	College
21	Allen, Terry	RB	5-10	210	1	Clemson
46	Anderson, Alfred	RB	6-1	214	8	Baylor
50	Berry, Ray	LB	6-2	226	5	Baylor
47	Browner, Joey	S	6-2	228	9	USC
81	Carter, Anthony	WR	5-11	175	7	Michigan
80	Carter, Cris	WR	6-3	200	5	Ohio State
71	Clarke, Ken	DT	6-2	280	14	Syracuse
56	Doleman, Chris	DE	6-5	250	7	Pittsburgh
42	Dozier, D.J.	RB	6-0	205	5	Penn State
59	Dusbabek, Mark	LB	6-3	230	3	Minnesota
24	Eilers, Pat	S	5-11	195	2	Notre Dame
31	Fenney, Rick	RB	6-1	231	5	Washington
62	Foote, Chris	C	6-4	266	9	USC
29	Fullington, Darrell	S	6-1	195	4	Miami (Fla.)
16	Gannon, Rich	QB	6-3	202	5	Delaware
74	Habib, Brian	T	6-7	288	3	Washington
77	Hammerstein, Mike	DT	6-4	272	5	Michigan
25	Hampton, Alonzo	CB	5-10	191	2	Pittsburgh
4	Igwebuike, Donald	K	5-9	184	7	Clemson
76	Irwin, Tim	T	6-7	295	11	Tennessee
84	Jones, Hassan	WR	6-0	198	6	Florida State
82	Jones, Mike	TE	6-3	255	2	Texas A&M
83	Jordan, Steve	TE	6-4	240	10	Brown
69	Kalis, Todd	G	6-5	286	4	Arizona State
52	Kirksey, William	LB	6-2	221	2	Southern Mississippi
39	Lee, Carl	CB	5-11	184	9	Marshall
87	Lewis, Leo	WR	5-8	166	11	Missouri
63	Lowdermilk, Kirk	C	6-3	263	7	Ohio State
91	Manusky, Greg	LB	6-1	242	4	Colgate
64	McDaniel, Randall	G	6-4	275	4	Arizona State
26	McMillian, Audray	CB	6-0	189	6	Houston
57	Merriweather, Mike	LB	6-2	219	9	Pacific
75	Millard, Keith	DT	6-5	262	7	Washington State
23	Mims, Carl	CB	5-10	180	1	Sam Houston State
18	Newsome, Harry	P	6-0	188	7	Wake Forest
99	Noga, Al	DE	6-1	248	4	Hawaii
85	Novoselsky, Brent	TE	6-2	238	4	Pennsylvania
17	Obee, Terry	WR	5-10	182	1	Oregon
86	Pruitt, James	WR	6-3	201	6	Cal-Fullerton
93	Randle, John	DE	6-1	248	2	Texas A&I
7	Reveiz, Fuad	K	5-11	216	7	Tennessee
48	Rutland, Reggie	CB	6-1	192	5	Georgia Tech
12	Salisbury, Sean	QB	6-5	208	4	Southern California
60	Schreiber, Adam	C-G	6-4	288	8	Texas
30	Smith, Cedric	RB	5-10	223	2	Florida
27	Stills, Ken	S	5-10	186	7	Wisconsin
94	Strauthers, Thomas	DE	6-4	262	8	Jackson State
97	Thomas, Henry	NT	6-2	268	5	Louisiana State
54	Vanderbeek, Matt	LB	6-3	246	2	Michigan State
34	Walker, Herschel	RB	6-1	223	6	Georgia
89	Walker, Wayne	WR	5-8	162	2	Texas Tech
92	Westbrooks, David	DT	6-4	252	1	Howard
41	Wilcots, Solomon	S	5-11	195	5	Colorado
58	Williams, Jimmy	LB	6-3	225	10	Nebraska
11	Wilson, Wade	QB	6-3	210	11	East Texas State
73	Wolfley, Craig	G	6-1	277	12	Syracuse
22	Wright, Felix	S	6-2	195	7	Drake
65	Zimmerman, Gary	T	6-6	284	6	Oregon

TOP DRAFT CHOICES

Rd.	Name	Sel. No.	Pos.	Ht.	Wt.	College
3	Jenkins, Carlos	65	LB	6-3	222	Michigan State
3	Reed, Jake	68	WR	6-3	215	Grambling
4	Baldwin, Randy	92	RB	5-11	216	Mississippi
5	Thome, Chris	119	C	6-4	278	Minnesota
6	Scott, Todd	163	DB	5-10	204	SW Louisiana

Jenkins is a versatile player who should help on special teams. Reed is a big, strong receiver with decent speed.

OUTLOOK: Was last year's 6-10 mark an aberration, or the beginning of the end for a team with lots of talent but no consistency?

If they can settle things at quarterback, tap Walker, avoid injuries and develop a winning attitude, the Vikings can challenge the Bears. It might be too much to ask.

VIKING PROFILES

CHRIS DOLEMAN 29 6-5 250 Defensive End

Despite drop in statistics, he was voted to the Pro Bowl for fourth year in a row . . . Led Vikings in sacks with 11 . . . That was 10 fewer than his league-leading 21 in 1989 . . . Production was hurt by absence of defensive tackle Keith Millard, who missed most of season with knee injury . . . Has started every game (58) since end of 1987 players' strike . . . Forced four fumbles . . . Has 54 sacks in six-year career . . . Explosive combination of strength and speed . . . His sensational 1989 season included five forced fumbles and five fumble recoveries . . . A so-so player at linebacker in first two NFL seasons . . . Burst onto scene after switch to defensive end in 1987 . . . Vikings' No. 1 pick in 1985 out of Pittsburgh . . . Born Oct. 16, 1961, in Indianapolis . . . 1990 base salary: $330,000.

KEITH MILLARD 29 6-5 262 Defensive Tackle

Devastating knee injury ended his 1990 season in late September . . . Projected to make recovery in time for 1991 . . . Had 12 tackles and two sacks in four games . . . Associated Press Defensive Player of the Year in 1989 . . . His 18 sacks tied a league record for sacks by a tackle . . . Two-time Pro Bowler . . . Scored TD on eight-yard fumble recovery in 1989 Pro Bowl . . . Relentless pass-rusher also excels against the run . . . Repeated problems with drinking and driving . . . Drafted by Vikings out of Washington State in 1984 but spent season with Jacksonville Bulls of USFL . . . Joined Vikings in 1985 . . . Born March 28, 1962, in Pleasonton, Cal. . . . 1990 base salary: $850,000.

ANTHONY CARTER 30 5-11 175 Wide Receiver

Speedy, crafty wide receiver is the Vikings' big-play man . . . Led team in 1990 with 70 catches, 1,008 receiving yards and eight TDs . . . Diving, juggling TD catch against Green Bay was a highlight-film special . . . Has surpassed 1,000 yards in each of last three seasons . . . Needs just 673 yards to eclipse Sammy White's team record of 6,400 career receiving yards . . . Holds team record with 18 100-yard receiving games . . . Best season was 1988 with 72 catches, 1,225 yards . . . Broke NFL playoff records in 1987 with most receiving yards in game (227 against 49ers) and most punt-return yards in game (143 against Saints) . . . Spent three seasons with Michigan Panthers and Oakland Invaders of USFL . . . Vikings acquired his NFL rights in trade with Miami . . . Three-time All-American at University of Michigan . . . Born Sept. 17, 1960, in Riviera Beach, Fla. . . . 1990 base salary: $750,000.

HERSCHEL WALKER 29 6-1 223 Running Back

Vikings might need years to recover from the decision to acquire this disappointing running back . . . Arrived from Dallas in 12-for-1 deal midway in 1989 . . . Heralded as final piece to Super Bowl puzzle . . . Has yet to make impact with Vikings and some suggest his presence has hurt the team . . . Running style seems ill-suited for Vikings' offensive scheme . . . Ran for 770 yards and caught 35 passes in 1990 . . . Plagued by fumbles . . . Blamed embarrassing performance in Monday night game against Eagles on a "cold" . . . Seemed at times more interested in bobsledding than football . . . Vikings gave up five players and seven draft picks to get him from Dallas . . . Led NFC in rushing in 1988 with 1,502 yards . . . Joined Cowboys in 1986 after three seasons with New Jersey Generals of USFL . . . Heisman Trophy winner at Georgia . . . Born March 3, 1962, in Wrightsville, Ga. . . . 1990 base salary: $2.25 million.

STEVE JORDAN 30 6-4 230 — Tight End

One of the top tight ends in football . . . Named to the Pro Bowl for fifth consecutive season in 1990 . . . Caught 45 passes for 636 yards and three TDs . . . Third on team's all-time reception list with 354 . . . Best season was 1985, with 68 receptions . . . Caught six TD passes in 1986 . . . Vikings' seventh-round draft choice in 1982 out of Brown . . . Earned degree in civil engineering . . . Tennis star in high school . . . Born Jan. 10, 1961, in Phoenix . . . 1990 base salary: $600,000.

HASSAN JONES 27 6-0 198 — Wide Receiver

Emerging from Anthony Carter's shadow as quality wide receiver in his own right . . . Set career highs with 51 catches, 810 receiving yards and seven TDs in 1990 . . . Compiled big numbers despite missing one game and five starts with nagging injuries . . . Fast, physical receiver . . . Caught 40 passes in 1988 and 42 in 1989 . . . Vikings' fifth-round pick in 1985 out of Florida State . . . Earned degree in criminology . . . Born July 2, 1964, in Clearwater, Fla. . . . 1990 base salary: $250,000.

GARY ZIMMERMAN 29 6-6 284 — Tackle

Vikings' disappointing season might have cost this talented player another Pro Bowl berth . . . Snubbed in Pro Bowl voting after making it three years in a row . . . Dependable, durable player has started 76 consecutive non-strike games . . . Starting streak is third-longest in team history (Jim Marshall 270, Mick Tinglehoff 240) . . . Excellent pass-blocker . . . Named to second team of NFL's All-1980s Team . . . Played two seasons with Los Angeles Express of USFL . . . Giants made him the third overall pick in the 1984 supplemental draft . . . Vikings acquired his rights for two No. 2 picks in 1986 trade with Giants . . . Three-year starter at Oregon . . . Born Dec. 13, 1961, in Fullerton, Cal. . . . 1990 base salary: $400,000.

RANDALL McDANIEL 26 6-4 275 — Guard

Combination of strength and athletic ability has turned this young player into one of the best guards in football . . . Named to the Pro Bowl in 1990 for the second year in a row . . . Started all 16 games . . . Excels at both pass-blocking and run-blocking . . . Ability to handle his man enables Vikings to double-team other defenders . . . A starter since the second game of his rookie season . . . Vikings' No. 1 pick in 1988 out of Arizona State . . . Can dunk basketball wearing full football uniform . . . Competitive weightlifter . . . Holds NCAA record with 620-pound deadlift . . . Born Dec. 19, 1964, in Phoenix . . . 1990 base salary: $260,000.

MIKE MERRIWEATHER 30 6-2 219 — Linebacker

Versatile linebacker is growing more and more comfortable in Vikings' defense . . . Enjoyed best season with Vikings in 1990, with team-high 153 tackles . . . Also registered 2½ sacks, forced three fumbles and recovered four . . . His three interceptions tied a career high . . . Vikings acquired him in exchange for No. 1 pick in draft day, 1989 trade with Pittsburgh . . . Sat out entire 1988 in contract dispute with the Steelers . . . Three-time Pro Bowler in Pittsburgh . . . Best season was 1984, with 15 sacks . . . Steelers' third-round pick in 1982 out of College of the Pacific . . . Born Nov. 26, 1960, in Albans, N.Y. . . . 1990 base salary: $500,000.

JOEY BROWNER 31 6-2 228 — Safety

Six Pro Bowl berths in a row for this talented defensive back . . . Set a career high with seven interceptions in 1990 . . . Now has 32 career interceptions . . . Ranked second in team in tackles with 120 . . . Has not missed a start in six seasons . . . Big hitter with excellent instincts for his position . . . Picked off three passes in 1988 playoffs . . . Has 27 interceptions in last five seasons . . . Vikings' No. 1 pick in 1983 out of USC . . . Brothers Ross, Jim and Keith all played in NFL . . . Black belt in martial arts . . . Born May 15, 1960, in Warren, Ohio . . . 1990 base salary: $850,000.

COACH JERRY BURNS: Difficult fifth season for this popular coach . . . Considered retirement at one point but has vowed to get Vikings back on winning track before he walks away . . . Vikings' 6-10 record marked the first losing season of his career . . . Held team together after 1-6 start and Vikings rallied to win five in a row and even record at 6-6 . . . Losses in final four games sealed frustrating season . . . Career record is 44-35, with 3-3 mark in playoffs . . . First four Vikings' teams went 38-25 and three made the playoffs . . . Criticized for inability to get most from talent-laden team . . . Struggled to find comfortable role for heralded running back Herschel Walker . . . Longtime assistant is popular with the players . . . Served as Vikings' offensive coordinator from 1968-1985 . . . Got his first NFL head coaching job at age of 59 in 1986 . . . Oldest coach in NFL . . . Head coach at Iowa (1961-65) and an assistant at Hawaii and Whittier . . . Played quarterback at Michigan . . . Born Jan. 24, 1927, in Detroit.

GREATEST PUNTER

In terms of longevity, no punter in Vikings' history compares to Greg Coleman. For individual brilliance, none compares to Bobby Walden.

Coleman's career with Minnesota spanned 10 seasons, from 1978 to 1987. No other Minnesota punter has lasted more than four seasons. Coleman holds team career records for punts in a game (12), a season (91 in 1981) and a career (721). He has more than twice as many career yards (29,391) than any other Viking and his 40.8 career average is third on the team's all-time list.

Walden punted for the Vikings for just four seasons but made his mark. His 46.4 average in 1964 is an all-time team record. He never averaged less than 41 yards in a season and his 42.9 career average is tops in Vikings' history.

INDIVIDUAL VIKING RECORDS

Rushing

Most Yards Game:	200	Chuck Foreman, vs Philadelphia, 1976
Season:	1,155	Chuck Foreman, 1975
Career:	5,879	Chuck Foreman, 1973-79

Passing

Most TD Passes Game:	7	Joe Kapp, vs Baltimore, 1969
Season:	26	Tommy Kramer, 1981
Career:	239	Francis Tarkenton, 1961-66, 1972-78

Receiving

Most TD Passes Game:	4	Ahmad Rashad, vs San Francisco, 1979
Season:	11	Jerry Reichow, 1961
Career:	50	Sammy White, 1976-85

Scoring

Most Points Game:	24	2 times, most recently Ahmad Rashad, vs San Francisco, 1979
Season:	132	Chuck Foreman, 1975
Career:	1,365	Fred Cox, 1963-77
Most TDs Game:	4	2 times, most recently Ahmad Rashad, vs San Francisco, 1979
Season:	22	Chuck Foreman, 1975
Career:	76	Bill Brown, 1962-74

NEW ORLEANS SAINTS

TEAM DIRECTORY: Owner: Tom Benson; Pres./GM: Jim Finks; VP-Administration: Jim Miller; Bus. Mgr./Controller: Bruce Broussard; Dir. Media Rel.: Rusty Kasmiersky; Head Coach: Jim Mora. Home field: Superdome (69,065). Colors: Old gold, black and white.

SCOUTING REPORT

OFFENSE: It all starts with Steve Walsh. The Saints gave up a lot for the former Cowboy quarterback and he needs to justify their faith in him. Walsh lacks a big arm but he has a nice touch on the ball and a good feel for the game. He should fit in the Saints' short-passing system.

He could use better receivers. Eric Martin is a good wide receiver but the Saints still are waiting for big things from Brett Perriman and Lonzell Hill. Tight end Hoby Brenner is more blocker than receiver.

The team has a good ground game. Former No. 1 pick Craig Heyward showed flashes of his vast potential at fullback and Dalton Hilliard and Rueben Mayes are a quality combination at halfback.

The offensive line is big, durable and dependable. The best of the bunch is left guard Jim Dombrowski.

DEFENSE: The strength of the team. A strong, solid group with a couple young players on the verge of stardom.

The Saints have concentrated on their defensive line in recent drafts, and former No. 1 picks Wayne Martin and Renaldo Turnbull might be ready for big things.

The linebacker corps is among the best in the business. Inside are Vaughan Johnson and Sam Mills. Outside are Pat Swilling, one of the game's best young players, and veteran Rickey Jackson.

The Saints need more big plays from their defensive backs. Robert Massey and Vince Buck have lots of potential at cornerback. The safeties are Brett Maxie and Gene Atkins.

SPECIAL TEAMS: The Saints have one of the best kickers in NFL history in Morten Andersen and a solid punter in Tommy Barnhardt. There are no problems there.

The coverage teams are strong. Buck handled punt returns as a rookie and Gil Fenerty and Atkins were an effective duo on kickoff returns.

Pat Swilling sacked his way to second straight Pro Bowl.

THE ROOKIES: The Saints had no first- or third-round picks because of the Walsh trade. They added a target for Walsh in the second round in Miami wide receiver Wesley Carroll. Defensive back Reggie Jones of Memphis State could make some impact in the secondary.

OUTLOOK: The Saints, 8-8 last year, will begin to find out this season if Walsh is the answer at quarterback. If he is, Jim Mora's team has enough talent to challenge for the division title and return to the playoffs.

SAINTS VETERAN ROSTER

HEAD COACH—Jim Mora. Assistant Coaches—Paul Boudreau, Dom Capers, Vic Fangio, Joe Marciano, Russell Paternostro, John Pease, Steve Sidwell, Jim Skipper, Carl Smith, Steve Walters.

No.	Name	Pos.	Ht.	Wt.	NFL Exp.	College
45	Aeilts, Rick	TE	6-4	245	1	SE Missouri State
86	Alphin, Gerald	WR	6-3	220	2	Kansas State
7	Andersen, Morten	K	6-2	221	10	Michigan State
28	Atkins, Gene	FS	6-1	200	5	Florida A&M
6	Barnhardt, Tommy	P	6-2	207	5	North Carolina
85	Brenner, Hoby	TE	6-5	245	11	USC
67	Brock, Stan	T	6-6	278	12	Colorado
59	Brockman, Lonnie	LB	6-3	230	1	West Virginia
16	Buck, Mike	QB	6-3	227	2	Maine
26	Buck, Vince	CB	6-0	198	2	Central State (Ohio)
98	Cole, Leon	DE	6-4	285	1	Texas A&M
41	Cook, Toi	CB	5-11	188	5	Stanford
71	Cooper, Richard	T	6-5	290	2	Tennessee
72	Dombrowski, Jim	G-T	6-5	298	6	Virginia
89	Early, Quinn	WR	6-0	190	4	Iowa
22	Fenerty, Gill	RB	6-0	205	2	Holy Cross
52	Forde, Brian	LB	6-3	225	4	Washington State
11	Fourcade, John	QB	6-1	215	5	Mississippi
91	Goff, Robert	NT	6-3	270	4	Auburn
66	Griffith, Brent	T	6-6	300	1	Minnesota-Duluth
74	Haverdink, Kevin	T	6-5	285	3	Western Michigan
34	Heyward, Craig	FB	5-11	260	4	Pittsburgh
61	Hilgenberg, Joel	C-G	6-2	252	8	Iowa
87	Hill, Lonzell	WR	5-11	189	5	Washington
21	Hilliard, Dalton	RB	5-8	204	6	Louisiana State
57	Jackson, Rickey	LB	6-2	239	11	Pittsburgh
53	Johnson, Vaughan	LB	6-3	239	6	North Carolina State
23	Jordan, Buford	FB	6-0	223	6	McNeese State
62	Leggett, Brad	C	6-4	270	1	Southern California
24	Mack, Milton	CB	5-11	182	6	Alcorn State
42	Manoa, Tim	FB	6-1	245	4	Penn State
84	Martin, Eric	WR	6-1	195	7	Louisiana State
93	Martin, Wayne	DE	6-5	275	3	Arkansas
40	Massey, Robert	CB	5-10	182	3	North Carolina Central
39	Maxie, Brett	SS	6-2	194	7	Texas Southern
36	Mayes, Rueben	RB	5-11	200	5	Washington State
69	Miller, Les	DE	6-7	293	5	Ft. Hays State
51	Mills, Sam	LB	5-9	225	6	Montclair State
35	Morse, Bobby	FB	5-10	213	4	Michigan State
15	Newman, Patrick	WR	5-11	189	1	Utah State
38	Nicholson, Calvin	CB	5-9	183	1	Oregon State
80	Perriman, Brett	WR	5-9	180	4	Miami (Fla.)
70	Port, Chris	G	6-5	290	1	Duke
83	Scales, Greg	TE	6-4	253	4	Wake Forest
63	Sign, Bobby	G-C	6-2	285	1	Baylor
17	Simien, Kerry	WR	5-10	185	1	Texas A&I
96	Simmons, Michael	DE	6-4	269	2	Mississippi State
99	Smeenge, Joel	DE	6-5	250	2	Western Michigan
33	Spears, Ernest	FS	5-11	192	2	Southern California
56	Swilling, Pat	LB	6-3	242	6	Georgia Tech
37	Thompson, Bennie	SS	6-0	200	2	Grambling State
82	Tice, John	TE	6-5	249	9	Maryland
65	Trapilo, Steve	G	6-5	281	5	Boston College
97	Turnbull, Renaldo	DE	6-4	248	2	West Virginia
88	Turner, Floyd	WR	5-11	188	3	NW Louisiana
64	Vines, Kenny	G-C	6-4	285	1	Central State (Ohio)
4	Walsh, Steve	QB	6-3	195	3	Miami (Fla.)
50	Wheeler, Todd	C	6-4	269	1	Georgia
94	Wilks, Jim	DE	6-5	275	11	San Diego State
90	Williams, James	LB	6-0	230	2	Mississippi State
20	Williams, Reggie	WR	6-1	194	1	Pittsburgh
92	Winston, DeMond	LB	6-2	239	2	Vanderbilt

TOP DRAFT CHOICES

Rd.	Name	Sel. No.	Pos.	Ht.	Wt.	College
2	Carroll, Wesley	42	WR	6-0	176	Miami
5	Jones, Reginald	126	DB	6-0	198	Memphis State
6	McAfee, Fred	154	RB	5-10	193	Mississippi College
7	Haynes, Hayward	182	G	6-2	290	Florida State
8	Wainright, Frank	210	TE	6-3	236	Northern Colorado

SAINT PROFILES

STEVE WALSH 24 6-3 195 **Quarterback**

Saints have hitched their hopes to this talented young quarterback . . . Started 11 games after arriving from Dallas in blockbuster trade three weeks into the 1990 season . . . Price was steep: Saints surrendered first- and third-round draft picks in 1991, plus a conditional second-rounder in 1992 . . . Passed for 1,970 yards and 12 TDs, with 13 interceptions . . . Erratic play was attributed to lack of experience with Saints' offense . . . Passed for three TDs in victory over Browns . . . Dallas picked him in the first round of 1989 supplemental draft . . . Stuck behind Troy Aikman on Cowboys' depth chart . . . Started five games as a rookie when Aikman broke his finger . . . Had a 23-1 record as a starter at University of Miami . . . Born Dec. 1, 1966, in St. Paul, Minn. . . . 1990 base salary: $800,000.

PAT SWILLING 26 6-3 242 **Linebacker**

Has emerged as one of the NFL's premier outside linebackers . . . Earned second consecutive trip to the Pro Bowl . . . Led Saints in sacks with 11 . . . Named second-team All-Pro by Associated Press . . . Combines speed and power, like Lawrence Taylor . . . Set a team record in 1989 with 16½ sacks, all in the final 12 games . . . Also forced five fumbles . . . Has 49 sacks in five NFL seasons . . . Saints' third-round pick in 1986 out of Georgia Tech . . . Played defensive end in college . . . Born Oct. 25, 1964, in Toccoa, Ga. . . . 1990 base salary: $700,000.

DALTON HILLIARD 27 5-8 204 **Running Back**

Last year was a frustrating follow-up to his breakthrough 1989 season . . . Missed 10 games with a knee injury . . . Finished with just 284 rushing yards and 14 receptions . . . Scored just one TD, a huge drop from previous season . . . Emerged as one of the NFL's most versatile, productive running backs in 1989 . . . Rushed for 1,262 yards and caught 52 passes for another 514 yards . . . Led the NFL with 18 TDs (13 rushing, five receiving) . . . First non-kicker in team history to score more than

100 points (108) . . . Lack of height doesn't diminish his power or willingness to run inside . . . Finished LSU career as No. 3 rusher in SEC history (behind Herschel Walker and Bo Jackson) . . . New Orleans' second-round pick in 1986 . . . Born Jan. 21, 1964, in Patterson, La. . . . 1990 base salary: $535,000.

RICKEY JACKSON 33 6-2 239 **Linebacker**

The wily veteran of one of the NFL's best linebacking corps . . . Kept rolling along in 1990 with another solid season . . . Set a team record with seven fumble recoveries . . . Recorded six sacks to up his team record to 85½ for his career . . . Had nine or more sacks for five consecutive seasons from 1983-87 . . . Durable player has started all 148 games in which he's appeared . . . Pro Bowler four years in a row from 1983-86 . . . Played defensive end at Pitt . . . New Orleans' second-round pick in 1981 . . . Passing his name along to son Rickeem and daughter Rickeyah . . . Born March 20, 1958, in Pahokee, Fla. . . . 1990 base salary: $775,000.

VAUGHAN JOHNSON 29 6-3 245 **Linebacker**

Recognition was a long time coming for this USFL refugee . . . Has established himself as one of the NFL's best inside linebackers . . . Made Pro Bowl in 1990 for second year in a row . . . Hard hitter who is regarded as excellent run-defender . . . Had Saints' second-high total with 13 tackles against Vikings . . . Led Saints in tackles in 1987 and 1988 but was little known outside of New Orleans . . . Played two seasons for Jacksonville Bulls of USFL . . . Signed with Saints in 1986 . . . Attended North Carolina State . . . Born March 4, 1962, in Morehead City, N.C. . . . 1990 base salary: $400,000.

SAM MILLS 32 5-9 225 **Linebacker**

Little man continues to make big impact in center of Saints' defense . . . Leader of one of the NFL's best linebacking quartets . . . Led team in tackles with 88 . . . Shortest linebacker in the league but regarded as one of the best . . . Pro Bowl starter in 1988 . . . Began career in USFL, where he played under Saints' coach Jim Mora . . . Played college ball at tiny Montclair (N.J.)

State . . . Scouts weren't impressed with 5-9 linebacker from a Division III school . . . Signed with Cleveland as a free agent but was cut in training camp . . . Taught school before joining Philadelphia Stars of USFL . . . Born June 3, 1959, in Neptune, N.J. . . . 1990 base salary: $229,200.

RENALDO TURNBULL 25 6-4 248 — Defensive End

Led all NFC rookies in sacks with nine . . . Started just six games but saw considerable action as situational pass-rusher . . . Projected as every-down player in the future . . . Tied Rickey Jackson's team record for sacks by a rookie . . . Recorded two sacks in playoff loss to Bears . . . Great speed and quickness for his size . . . Recorded 20 sacks in final two seasons at West Virginia . . . New Orleans' No. 1 pick in 1990 . . . MVP of Senior Bowl . . . Originally recruited to West Virginia to play basketball . . . Born Jan. 5, 1966, in St. Thomas, Virgin Islands . . . 1990 base salary: $250,000.

JIM DOMBROWSKI 27 6-5 298 — Guard

Big man is the cornerstone of the Saints' offensive line . . . Has started last 59 games . . . Did not miss a down in 1990 . . . Big reason the Saints allowed just 20 sacks in 1990 . . . Started career as a left tackle and made smooth switch to left guard midway in 1989 season . . . Became full-time starter following players' strike in 1987 . . . Missed most of 1986 season with broken foot . . . The first player drafted by the Saints' new braintrust of president Jim Finks and coach Jim Mora in 1986 . . . Consensus All-American at Virginia . . . Has degree in biology and plans career as orthopedic surgeon . . . Born Oct. 19, 1963, in Williamsville, N.Y. . . . 1990 base salary: $575,000.

ERIC MARTIN 29 6-1 195 — Wide Receiver

Led Saints in receptions for fourth year in a row with 63 . . . Generated 912 yards and five TDs . . . Caught 10 passes for 131 yards against Redskins . . . Holds team records for career receptions (332) and yardage (5,060) . . . Has caught a pass in 57 consecutive games . . . Smooth, shifty receiver with great concentration . . . Broke 1,000 yards in receiving in both

1989 (1,090) and 1988 (1,083) . . . Set SEC career record for receiving yards at LSU but was downgraded by scouts because of lack of blazing speed . . . New Orleans got him in the seventh round in 1985 . . . Born Nov. 8, 1961, in Van Vleck, Tex. . . . 1990 base salary: $475,000.

MORTEN ANDERSEN 31 6-2 221 — Placekicker

Bounced back from subpar 1989 season . . . Returned to the Pro Bowl for a team-record fifth time . . . Converted 21 Of 27 field-goal attempts and all 29 of his PATs . . . Led Saints in scoring with 92 points but it was the first time in six seasons he didn't reach 100 . . . Enters 1991 as the NFL's third-most accurate kicker of all time . . . Career percentage of 77.1 places him behind Kansas City's Nick Lowery (79 percent) and Pittsburgh's Gary Anderson (77.2 percent) . . . Saints' all-time leader in points (852) and field goals (192) . . . A fourth-round pick in 1982 out of Michigan State . . . Came to America from Denmark as exchange student in 1977 . . . Born Aug. 19, 1960, in Struer, Denmark . . . 1990 base salary: $500,000.

COACH JIM MORA: Led Saints to the second playoff in their history . . . Saints' 8-8 record was their worst since 1986 but good enough for third wild-card berth . . . Held team together after difficult 2-5 start . . . Has turned one of the NFL's worst franchises into a perennial playoff contender . . . NFL Coach of the Year in 1987 after Saints went 12-3 and qualified for playoffs for the first time . . . His first Saints' team went 7-9 in 1986—his only losing record . . . Has 46-38 record with the Saints, by far the best in team history . . . Phenomenal success in USFL . . . Led Philadelphia/Baltimore Stars to three consecutive berths in USFL title games . . . Won USFL title in 1984 and 1985 . . . NFL assistant at Seattle and New England . . . College assistant at Colorado, Stanford, Washington and UCLA . . . Spent three years as head coach of Occidental (Calif.) College . . . Played tight end at Occidental and roomed with future NFL quarterback and U.S. Senator Jack Kemp . . . Born May 24, 1935, in Glendale, Cal.

GREATEST PUNTER

Their first three years of existence were a dark time for the Saints, who won just 12 games from 1967 through 1969. One bright spot, however, was punter Tom McNeill.

The first punter in Saints' history probably was the best. A free agent from Stephen F. Austin College, McNeill holds the team record for career punting average with a 42.3 mark.

McNeill also set the Saints' record for longest punt with an 81-yarder against Dallas on Sept. 28, 1969.

INDIVIDUAL SAINT RECORDS

Rushing

Most Yards Game:	206	George Rogers, vs St. Louis, 1983
Season:	1,674	George Rogers, 1981
Career:	4,267	George Rogers, 1981-84

Passing

Most TD Passes Game:	6	Billy Kilmer, vs St. Louis, 1969
Season:	23	Archie Manning, 1980
Career:	155	Archie Manning, 1971-81

Receiving

Most TD Passes Game:	3	Dan Abramowicz, vs San Francisco, 1971
Season:	9	Henry Childs, 1977
Career:	37	Dan Abramowicz, 1967-72

Scoring

Most Points Game:	18	8 times, most recently Reuben Mayes, vs Phoenix, 1990
Season:	121	Morten Andersen, 1987
Career:	852	Morten Andersen, 1982-90
Most TDs Game:	3	8 times, most recently Reuben Mayes, vs Phoenix, 1990
Season:	18	Dalton Hilliard, 1989
Career:	38	Dalton Hilliard, 1986-90

NEW YORK GIANTS

TEAM DIRECTORY: Pres.: Wellington Mara; Chairman: Bob Tisch; VP/GM: George Young; Dir. Pro Personnel: Tom Boisture; Dir. Pub. Rel.: Ed Croke; Head Coach: Ray Handley. Home field: Giants Stadium (77,311). Colors: Blue, red and white.

SCOUTING REPORT

OFFENSE: Bill Parcells, who stunned the football world when he resigned as coach, won't have to make the big decision on who will play quarterback. That rests with his replacement, Ray Handley, who knows an unsettled quarterback situation is a concern for any team, even defending Super Bowl champions.

Jeff Hostetler, a career backup, led the Giants to five consecutive victories and the Super Bowl title. Will he keep the top spot? Phil Simms has been No. 1 for a long time, but he's 35 and coming off a foot injury.

The ground game is a source of comfort. Old reliable Ottis Anderson is the ideal runner for the Giants' power formations and at times Rodney Hampton looked like a future star as a rookie in 1990. First pick Jarrod Bunch will get some time at fullback.

The Giants are glad they drafted offensive linemen in the early rounds in recent years. This group, led by tackle Jumbo Elliott and guard Eric Moore, is big, talented and just hitting its stride.

DEFENSE: Defensive coordinator Bill Belichick got the head-coaching job in Cleveland, so Al Groh takes over as the new maestro of a unit whose waning star, at 32, is Lawrence Taylor.

Taylor is part of a linebacking corps that no longer dominates games. Pepper Johnson had emerged as a star but Carl Banks has battled injuries and Gary Reasons and Steve DeOssie are largely one-dimensional players.

The defensive line lacks a dominant player now that end Leonard Marshall is past his prime. Nose tackle Erik Howard and end Eric Dorsey are solid and the Giants have high hopes for Mike Fox.

Smart, steady secondary play is a key to the Giants' defense. Cornerback Mark Collins is underrated. Young safeties Myron Guyton and Greg Jackson are developing into one of the NFL's best tandems. Veteran cornerback Everson Walls and veteran safety Dave Duerson were reborn in the Giants' disciplined system.

Ottis Anderson hurtles to MVP honors in Super Bowl XXV.

SPECIAL TEAMS: The Giants love to play for field position and depend heavily on their special teams.

Punter Sean Landeta is a Pro Bowler who gets good hang time on his kicks. Matt Bahr is a veteran who made a lot of important field goals in the playoffs last year.

The coverage teams, led by reserve cornerback Reyna Thompson, are excellent. David Meggett is one of the NFL's best return men.

THE ROOKIES: Power football is the Giants' way and they got a big, strong fullback in Michigan's Bunch. Their second pick, Colorado linebacker Kanavis McGhee, is another physical player.

GIANTS VETERAN ROSTER

HEAD COACH—Ray Handley. Assistant Coaches—Fred Bruney, Romeo Crennel, Ron Erhardt, Jim Fassel, Al Groh, Fred Hoaglin, Johnny Parker, Mike Pope, Bob Trott, George Sefcik, Mike Sweatman, Charlie Weis.

No.	Name	Pos.	Ht.	Wt.	NFL Exp.	College
51	Abrams, Bobby	LB	6-3	230	2	Michigan
24	Anderson, Ottis	RB	6-2	225	13	Miami (Fla.)
—	Ashe, Richard	TE	6-5	252	1	Humboldt State
9	Bahr, Matt	K	5-10	175	14	Penn State
85	Baker, Stephen	WR	5-8	160	5	Fresno State
58	Banks, Carl	LB	6-4	235	8	Michigan State
89	Bavaro, Mark	TE	6-4	245	7	Notre Dame
46	Brown, Roger	CB	6-0	196	2	Virginia Tech
44	Carthon, Maurice	RB	6-1	225	7	Arkansas State
6	Cavanaugh, Matt	QB	6-2	210	14	Pittsburgh
25	Collins, Mark	CB	5-10	190	6	Cal-Fullerton
98	Cooks, Johnie	LB	6-4	251	10	Mississippi State
87	Cross, Howard	TE	6-5	245	3	Alabama
99	DeOssie, Steve	LB	6-2	248	8	Boston College
77	Dorsey, Eric	DE	6-5	280	6	Notre Dame
92	Downing, Tim	DE	6-5	260	2	Washington State
26	Duerson, Dave	S	6-1	208	9	Notre Dame
76	Elliott, John	T	6-7	305	4	Michigan
93	Fox, Mike	DE	6-6	275	2	West Virginia
29	Guyton, Myron	DB	6-1	205	3	Eastern Kentucky
27	Hampton, Rodney	RB	5-11	215	2	Georgia
15	Hostetler, Jeff	QB	6-3	212	8	West Virginia
74	Howard, Erik	NT	6-4	268	6	Washington State
82	Ingram, Mark	WR	5-10	188	5	Michigan State
47	Jackson, Greg	S	6-1	200	3	Louisiana State
79	James, Clint	DE	6-6	270	2	Louisiana State
52	Johnson, Pepper	LB	6-3	248	6	Ohio State
—	Kaumeyer, Thom	S	5-11	190	4	Oregon
61	Kratch, Bob	G	6-3	288	3	Iowa
5	Landeta, Sean	P	6-0	200	7	Towson State
70	Marshall, Leonard	DE	6-3	285	9	Louisiana State
57	McGrew, Lawrence	LB	6-6	250	11	Southern California
30	Meggett, David	RB	5-7	180	3	Towson State
—	Milling, James	WR	5-9	156	4	Maryland
60	Moore, Eric	T	6-5	290	4	Indiana
80	Mrosko, Robert	TE	6-5	270	4	Penn State
65	Oates, Bart	C	6-3	265	7	Brigham Young
55	Reasons, Gary	LB	6-4	234	8	NW Louisiana State
64	Rehder, Tom	G-T	6-7	290	4	Notre Dame
72	Riesenberg, Doug	T	6-5	275	5	California
66	Roberts, William	T	6-5	280	7	Ohio State
81	Robinson, Stacy	WR	5-11	186	7	North Dakota State
11	Simms, Phil	QB	6-3	214	13	Morehead State
56	Taylor, Lawrence	LB	6-3	243	11	North Carolina
21	Thompson, Reyna	CB	6-0	193	6	Baylor
34	Tillman, Lewis	RB	6-0	195	3	Jackson State
28	Walls, Everson	CB	6-1	194	11	Grambling
73	Washington, John	DE	6-4	275	6	Oklahoma State
59	Williams, Brian	C-G	6-5	300	3	Minnesota
23	Williams, Perry	CB	6-2	203	7	North Carolina State
36	White, Adrian	S	6-0	200	5	Florida

TOP DRAFT CHOICES

Rd.	Name	Sel. No.	Pos.	Ht.	Wt.	College
1	Bunch, Jarrod	27	FB	6-2	248	Michigan
2	McGhee, Kanavis	55	LB	6-4	257	Colorado
3	McCaffrey, Ed	83	WR	6-5	210	Stanford
4	Jones, Clarence	111	OT	6-5	273	Maryland
5	Moss, Anthony	139	LB	6-3	233	Florida State

The Giants also might have uncovered a third-down receiver in Stanford's lanky, athletic Ed McCaffrey.

OUTLOOK: The Giants don't look like a dynasty, so repeating as Super Bowl champions seems unlikely. The last time the Giants won it all, 1986, they went 6-9 the next year.

Still, they are the class of the NFC East until proven otherwise. If their veterans can hold out for one more season, Bill Parcells' Giants can defend their division title and take their chances in the playoffs.

GIANT PROFILES

LAWRENCE TAYLOR 32 6-3 243 Linebacker

Greatest outside linebacker in NFL history appears to be slowing down . . . Played with less abandon and freedom in 1990 . . . Still highly effective player with occasional flashes of brilliance . . . Led Giants in sacks with 10½ but just 7½ of them came after first game of season . . . Voted to the Pro Bowl an unprecedented 10th time in a row . . . Leads all NFL players in career sacks with 124½ . . . Held out all of 1990 training camp and signed new contract three days before season opener . . . Suspended for four games in 1988 for violating NFL's drug policy . . . Unanimous selection to NFL's Team of Decade for 1980s . . . Second selection (behind George Rogers) in 1981 draft, out of North Carolina . . . An avid golfer . . . Born Feb. 4, 1959, in Williamsburg, Va. . . . 1990 base salary: $1.55 million.

PEPPER JOHNSON 27 6-3 248 Linebacker

Emerged as Pro Bowl player in fifth NFL season . . . Led Giants in tackles with 119 . . . Also recovered three fumbles and had 3½ sacks . . . Vocal, emotional player . . . Overshadowed for much of his career by teammates Lawrence Taylor and Carl Banks . . . Led Giants in tackles with 93 in 1988 . . . Slowed in 1989 after lengthy contract holdout . . . Best man at wedding of Eagles' running back Keith Byars, his roommate at Ohio State . . . Giants' second-round pick in 1986 . . . Real first name is Thomas . . . Earned nickname from aunt who saw him sprinkle pepper on cereal . . . Born June 29, 1964, in Detroit . . . 1990 base salary: $350,000.

JUMBO ELLIOTT 26 6-7 305 **Tackle**

Cornerstone of Giants' rebuilt offensive line . . . Excellent run-blocker is the key to the Giants' powerful ground game . . . Has improved as pass-blocker . . . Still vulnerable at times to speedy pass-rushers . . . Great game against Chicago's Richard Dent as Giants ran for 194 yards in 31-3 playoff whipping of Bears . . . Slowed by injuries early in career . . . Started 11 games in 1989 and five in 1988 . . . Giants' second-round pick in 1988 out of Michigan . . . Born April 1, 1965, in Lake Ronkonkoma, N.Y. . . . 1990 base salary: $262,000.

PHIL SIMMS 35 6-3 214 **Quarterback**

Enters 1991 as question mark after injury ended his 1990 season . . . Was en route to his best regular season ever when he suffered a foot injury in Week 14 loss to Buffalo . . . Sat out last two regular-season games and all three postseason games . . . His long-time backup, Jeff Hostetler, led Giants to five consecutive victories, including Super Bowl triumph . . . Completed 59.2 percent of his passes for 2,284 yards and 15 TDs, with just four interceptions . . . Led Giants to 10-0 start . . . Plagued by injuries early in career, he became one of NFL's top quarterbacks in mid-1980s . . . Record-setting performance in Super Bowl XXI included 22 completions in 25 attempts in Giants' victory over Denver . . . Giants' No. 1 pick in 1979 out of Morehead (Ky.) State . . . Born Nov. 3, 1955, in Springfield, Ky. . . . 1990 base salary: $1.4 million.

JEFF HOSTETLER 30 6-3 212 **Quarterback**

Long-time backup got his chance late in 1990 and led Giants to their second Super Bowl title . . . Replaced the injured Phil Simms at quarterback in Week 15 and led Giants to five consecutive victories . . . Played virtually mistake-free football in playoffs . . . His scrambling was key to playoff victories over Chicago and San Francisco . . . Spent most of career as dependable, seldom-used backup to Simms . . . Did not throw a pass in NFL game until 1988, his fifth season . . . Led Giants to back-to-back victories in 1989 after Simms was sidelined with ankle injury . . . Giants' third-round pick in 1984 out of West Virginia . . . Married to former Vicky Nehlen, daughter of West Virginia coach Don Nehlen . . . Born April 22, 1961, in Johnstown, Pa. . . . 1990 base salary: $425,000.

OTTIS ANDERSON 33 6-2 225 **Running Back**

Was named MVP of Super Bowl to complete one of great comeback stories in NFL history . . . Thought to be finished after he rushed for just 932 yards from 1985-88 . . . Reborn in 1989 with 1,023 yards and 14 TDs . . . Followed up with 784 yards and 11 TDs in 1990 . . . Strong, smart runner is ideal for Giants' power formations . . . Was speed back with great moves early in his career with St. Louis Cardinals . . . Cardinals' first-round pick in 1979 out of University of Miami . . . Gained 1,000 yards in five of first six NFL seasons . . . Acquired by Giants early in 1986 season for second- and seventh-round picks in 1987 draft . . . Left unprotected by Giants in Plan B following 1988, 1989 and 1990 seasons . . . Born Nov. 19, 1957, in West Palm Beach, Fla. . . . 1990 base salary: $450,000.

DAVID MEGGETT 25 5-7 180 **Running Back**

Led Giants in all-purpose yards with 1,533 . . . It broke down this way: 492 in kickoff returns, 467 in punt returns, 410 receiving, 164 rushing . . . Also led Giants in receptions with 39 . . . Favorite target of Giants' quarterbacks on third down . . . Returned punt 68 yards for TD in season-opener against Philadelphia . . . Considered one of the best open-field runners in NFL . . . Regarded as steal of 1989 draft after he made the Pro Bowl as a rookie . . . Accounted for 1,806 all-purpose yards and the team's three longest TDs of the season . . . His 76-yard punt return for TD was first by a Giant since 1978 . . . Rookie season was marred somewhat by fumbles . . . Giants' fifth-round pick in 1989 out of tiny Towson (Md.) State . . . Born April 30, 1966, in Charleston, S.C. . . . 1990 base salary: $90,000.

MARK INGRAM 26 5-10 188 Wide Receiver

Former No. 1 pick has been slow to meet Giants' expectations . . . Caught 26 passes for 499 yards and five TDs in 1990 . . . Production has been hurt somewhat by Giants' ball-control philosophy . . . Made big catch-and-run for first down on crucial third-down play in Super Bowl . . . Burned Eagles for 40-yard TD that sealed important victory in season opener . . . Caught a total of just 32 passes in first three seasons . . . Giants' No. 1 pick out of Michigan State in 1987 . . . Born Aug. 23, 1965, in Rockford, Ill. . . . 1990 base salary: $250,000.

RODNEY HAMPTON 22 5-11 215 Running Back

Giants' back of the future offered a glimpse of his potential in 1990 . . . Second on team in rushing with 455 yards . . . Third in receptions with 32 . . . Scored four TDs . . . Speed and moves offered a change of pace when he replaced power back Ottis Anderson . . . Expected to emerge this season as Giants' feature back . . . Sustained fractured fibula in playoff victory over Chicago, but expected to be recovered by 1991 training camp . . . Giants' No. 1 pick in 1990 out of Georgia . . . One of the NFL's youngest players last season at age 21 . . . Entered NFL draft after junior season at Georgia . . . Ran for 1,059 yards and 12 TDs in final collegiate season . . . Born April 3, 1969, in Houston . . . 1990 base salary: $250,000.

LEONARD MARSHALL 29 6-3 285 Defensive End

Finished just 13th on team in tackles in 1990 with 41 . . . His total of 4½ sacks was less than half of his 1989 total of 9½ . . . Played in all 16 regular-season games but started just six . . . Slowed by protracted contract holdout . . . Needs to regain consistency that marked the middle of his career . . . Best season was 1985 with 15½ sacks . . . Was named NFC's Defensive Lineman of Year by NFLPA that year . . . Two-time Pro Bowl selection . . . Giants' second-round pick in 1983 out of LSU . . . Born Oct. 22, 1961, in Franklin, La. . . . 1990 base salary: $467,500.

CARL BANKS 29 6-4 235 **Linebacker**

Slowed by injury during regular season, Banks picked up the pace in playoffs . . . Heavy hitter keyed Giants' defensive excellence in postseason victories over Chicago, San Francisco and Buffalo . . . Missed seven games in midseason with wrist injury . . . Finished with 51 tackles and just one sack . . . Forced team-record six fumbles in 1989 . . . Suffered through subpar season in 1988 after lengthy contract holdout . . . Led Giants in tackles in 1986 and 1987 . . . Pro Bowler after 1987 season . . . Giants' No. 1 pick in 1984 out of Michigan State . . . Born Aug. 29, 1962, in Flint, Mich. . . . 1990 base salary: $900,000.

COACH RAY HANDLEY: It's his biggest challenge, taking over for two-time Super Bowl winner Bill Parcells . . . Contrasted with the fiery Parcells, Handley is a low-key pragmatist who says, "Bill's more of a barker . . . I'm more of a mathematician." . . . In fact, he taught high-school math in Sparks, Nev., where he had his only previous head-coaching job . . . His background has been offense all the way (unlike Parcells) . . . Coached Giants' running backs for seven years before being named offensive coordinator early this year . . Was assistant coach at Stanford, West Point and Air Force Academy . . . Born Oct. 8, 1944, in Artesia, N.M., he starred as a running back at Stanford, where he set many school running marks . . . Met Parcells when they were assistants at West Point . . . Never played in the pros . . . Was planning to leave the Giants this year to enter law school at George Washington, but Parcells convinced him to remain . . . Little did he know that on May 15, 1991, he would take over as coach of the defending champions.

GREATEST PUNTER

Year by year, Sean Landeta continues to distinguish himself as one of the best punters in the NFL and one of the best in Giants' history. For now, though, the top spot belongs to Dave Jennings.

A free agent from little St. Lawrence College, Jennings

joined the Giants in 1974. He lasted for 12 seasons and set just about every team punting record.

Jennings holds team records for total punts (931) and yardage (38,792). He owns the five highest single-season totals in number of punts and punting yardage in Giants' history.

Landeta has spent six seasons with the Giants and punted for two Super Bowl champions. Joining the Giants after three seasons in the USFL, Landeta has an NFL career average of better than 42 yards per punt and a Pro Bowl appearance on his resume.

INDIVIDUAL GIANT RECORDS

Rushing

Most Yards Game:	218	Gene Roberts, vs Chicago Cardinals, 1950
Season:	1,516	Joe Morris, 1986
Career:	5,296	Joe Morris, 1982-89

Passing

Most TD Passes Game:	7	Y. A. Tittle, vs Washington, 1962
Season:	36	Y. A. Tittle, 1963
Career:	173	Charlie Conerly, 1948-61

Receiving

Most TD Passes Game:	4	Earnest Gray, vs St. Louis, 1980
Season:	13	Homer Jones, 1967
Career:	48	Kyle Rote, 1951-61

Scoring

Most Points Game:	24	2 times, most recently Earnest Gray, vs St. Louis, 1980
Season:	127	Ali Haji-Sheikh, 1983
Career:	646	Pete Gogolak, 1966-74
Most TDs Game:	4	2 times, most recently Earnest Gray, vs St. Louis, 1980
Season:	21	Joe Morris, 1985
Career:	78	Frank Gifford, 1952-60, 1962-64

PHILADELPHIA EAGLES

TEAM DIRECTORY: Owner: Norman Braman; Pres./CEO: Harry Gamble; VP-Finance: Mimi Box; VP: Susan Braman; VP-Marketing: Decker Uhlhorn; Dir. Player Personnel: Joe Woolley; Dir. Pub. Rel.: Ron Howard; Head Coach: Rich Kotite. Home field: Veterans Stadium (65,356). Colors: Kelly green, white and silver.

SCOUTING REPORT

OFFENSE: No team appears to rely as heavily on one player as the Eagles do on Randall Cunningham. The quarterback passed

Scramblin', passin' Randall Cunningham can't do it alone.

for 30 TDs last year and ran for 942 yards. But as the Redskins proved in the playoffs: Stop Cunningham and you stop the Eagles.

Cunningham has some good young wide receivers in Fred Barnett and Calvin Williams, who combined for 17 TD catches as rookies in 1990. Tight end Keith Jackson has been in the Pro Bowl after each of his first three seasons and Keith Byars has more receptions over the last three years than any other running back in the NFL.

The ground game is a concern. Take away Cunningham's improvised scrambles, and the Eagles lack punch in their rushing attack. Byars catches, blocks and sometimes throws, but rarely runs. Heath Sherman looked good at times last year but was prone to fumbling.

The offensive line lacks size, durability and that one outstanding player. He could be rookie Antone Davis.

DEFENSE: Subtle changes are expected with the arrival of new defensive coordinator Bud Carson. Look for more zone pass coverage and fewer blitzes in the wake of the dismissal of former coach Buddy Ryan.

When healthy, the defensive line is awesome. But end Clyde Simmons and tackle Jerome Brown have been slowed by nagging injuries. Brown also needs to get his weight under control. Tackle Mike Pitts is 30 and coming off knee surgery. End Reggie White still ranks among the league's best but is not as dominating as he once was.

Underrated Seth Joyner is the class of the linebacking corps. Byron Evans hits hard but sometimes gets caught out of position and Jessie Small still is adjusting to the NFL.

Cornerbacks Eric Allen and Ben Smith are solid. Safeties Wes Hopkins and Andre Waters are hard hitters but lack speed and range.

SPECIAL TEAMS: An area in need of improvement. Kicker Roger Ruzek and punter Jeff Feagles are OK, but the return and coverage teams rank among the league's worst.

New coach Rich Kotite has vowed to use starters on special teams, a no-no under Ryan. That should improve the return and coverage teams. The Eagles think they found a quality return man in Rod Harris, claimed on waivers from Dallas late last year.

THE ROOKIES: The Eagles wanted a big, talented offensive tackle. They paid heavily—this year's No. 1 pick, plus their No. 1 pick in 1992—for Tennessee's 327-pound Davis. North Carolina

EAGLES VETERAN ROSTER

HEAD COACH—Rich Kotite. Assistant Coaches—Bud Carson, Zeke Bratkowski, Lew Carpenter, Peter Guinta, Dale Haupt, Dan Neal, Jim Vechiarella, Bill Walsh, Jim Williams, Richard Wood.

No.	Name	Pos.	Ht.	Wt.	NFL Exp.	College
72	Alexander, David	C	6-3	282	5	Tulsa
21	Allen, Eric	CB	5-10	180	4	Arizona State
86	Barnett, Fred	WR	6-0	199	2	Arkansas State
81	Bellamy, Mike	WR	6-0	195	2	Illinois
42	Booty, John	CB	6-0	180	4	Texas Christian
99	Brown, Jerome	DT	6-2	295	5	Miami
41	Byars, Keith	RB	6-1	238	6	Ohio State
97	Chapura, Dick	DT	6-3	277	5	Missouri
69	Collie, Bruce	G	6-6	270	7	Texas-Arlington
12	Cunningham, Randall	QB	6-4	205	7	Nevada-Las Vegas
78	Darwin, Matt	T	6-4	275	5	Texas A&M
36	Drummond, Robert	RB	6-1	205	3	Syracuse
56	Evans, Byron	LB	6-2	235	5	Arizona
5	Feagles, Jeff	P	6-1	205	4	Miami
90	Golic, Mike	DT	6-5	275	6	Notre Dame
71	Gray, Cecil	G	6-4	275	2	North Carolina
54	Hager, Britt	LB	6-1	225	3	Texas
80	Harris, Rod	WR	5-10	185	3	Texas A&M
73	Heller, Ron	T	6-6	280	8	Penn State
48	Hopkins, Wes	FS	6-1	215	8	Southern Methodist
76	Hudson, John	G-C	6-2	275	1	Auburn
88	Jackson, Keith	TE	6-2	250	4	Oklahoma
83	Jackson, Kenny	WR	6-0	180	8	Penn State
46	Jenkins, Izel	CB	5-10	190	4	North Carolina State
87	Johnson, Maurice	TE	6-2	243	1	Temple
59	Joyner, Seth	LB	6-2	240	6	Texas-El Paso
94	Kaufusi, Steve	DE	6-4	257	3	Brigham Young
62	McKnight, Dennis	C-G	6-3	280	9	Drake
9	McMahon, Jim	QB	6-1	195	10	Brigham Young
1	McPherson, Don	QB	6-1	190	1	Syracuse
47	Moten, Ron	LB	6-1	232	1	Florida
74	Pitts, Mike	DT	6-5	280	9	Alabama
82	Quick, Mike	WR	6-2	195	10	North Carolina State
55	Rose, Ken	LB	6-1	215	5	Nevada-Las Vegas
7	Ruzek, Roger	K	6-1	200	5	Weber State
45	Sanders, Thomas	RB	5-11	202	7	Texas A&M
79	Schad, Mike	G	6-5	290	4	Queens (Canada)
23	Sherman, Heath	RB	6-0	205	3	Texas A&I
85	Shuler, Mickey	TE	6-3	230	14	Penn State
96	Simmons, Clyde	DE	6-6	275	6	Western Carolina
68	Singletary, Reggie	T	6-3	285	5	North Carolina State
52	Small, Jessie	LB	6-3	240	3	Eastern Kentucky
26	Smith, Ben	CB-S	5-11	185	2	Georgia
63	Smith, Daryle	T	6-5	276	4	Tennessee
30	Smith, Otis	CB	5-11	184	1	Missouri
66	Solt, Ron	G	6-3	275	7	Maryland
61	Tamburello, Ben	C-G	6-3	270	4	Auburn
10	Teltschik, John	P	6-2	215	5	Texas
25	Toney, Anthony	RB	6-0	230	6	Texas A&M
43	Vick, Roger	RB	6-3	235	5	Texas A&M
20	Waters, Andre	SS	5-11	200	8	Cheyney
92	White, Reggie	DE	6-5	285	7	Tennessee
89	Williams, Calvin	WR	5-11	181	2	Purdue

TOP DRAFT CHOICES

Rd.	Name	Sel. No.	Pos.	Ht.	Wt.	College
1	Davis, Antone	8	OT	6-5	327	Tennessee
2	Campbell, Jesse	48	DB	6-2	212	North Carolina State
3	Selby, Rob	75	OT	6-4	291	Auburn
4	Thomas, William	104	LB	6-3	207	Texas A&M
5	Erickson, Craig	131	QB	6-2	195	Miami

State's Jesse Campbell is a big, physical safety. The Eagles might have found their quarterback of the future in Miami's Craig Erickson, who has to recover from knee surgery.

OUTLOOK: Everything depends on the team's adjustment to life after five fascinating seasons of Ryan. The talent is there for another 10-win season and return to the playoffs but this team might be looking at a step backward before it moves forward again.

EAGLE PROFILES

RANDALL CUNNINGHAM 28 6-4 205 Quarterback

Put together best regular season of his six-year career in 1990 . . . Completed 271 of 465 passes (58.3 percent) for 3,466 yards and career-high 30 touchdowns . . . Threw just 13 interceptions . . . Passing rating of 91.6 was highest in his career . . . Rushed for career-high 942 yards, just 26 shy of Bobby Douglass' NFL quarterback single-season rushing record . . . One of just two NFL quarterbacks (Miami's Dan Marino is the other) to start every game since end of 1987 players' strike . . . First quarterback in modern era to lead team in rushing four years in a row . . . Has struggled in playoff games with no TD passes and five interceptions in losses to Chicago (1988), Rams (1989) and Washington (1990) . . . 1988 Pro Bowl MVP . . . Has made Pro Bowl three years in a row . . . Second-round pick out of Nevada-Las Vegas in 1985 . . . All-American punter in college . . . Born March 27, 1963, in Santa Barbara, Cal. . . . 1990 base salary: $1.275 million.

REGGIE WHITE 29 6-5 285 Defensive End

Led Eagles in sacks with 15 . . . Named as starter to the Pro Bowl for fifth season in a row . . . Since entering NFL in 1985, has compiled more sacks (96) than any other player . . . Recorded first interception of career and returned it 33 yards to set up TD against Washington . . . Also led team with 56 quarterback hurries despite double- and triple-team blocking . . .

Was critical of management after dismissal of coach Buddy Ryan . . . A licensed Baptist minister, his nickname is "The Minister of Defense" . . . MVP of 1987 Pro Bowl . . . Played two seasons for Memphis Showboats of USFL after All-American career at the University of Tennessee . . . Claimed by the Eagles in the first round of the 1984 supplemental draft . . . Born Dec. 19, 1961, in Chattanooga, Tenn. . . . 1990 base salary: $1.35 million.

KEITH BYARS 27 6-1 238 Running Back

Led all NFL running backs with 81 receptions and 819 receiving yards . . . Went 4-for-4 for 53 yards and four TDs as a passer . . . Excellent blocker . . . Has developed into versatile all-purpose back who lines up as fullback, half-back, tight end and wide receiver in different formations . . . Just 37 rushing attempts for 141 yards (both career lows) in 1990 . . . Ranks fifth in the NFL (tops among running backs) with 221 receptions over last three seasons . . . Left-handed . . . Second-leading rusher in Ohio State history . . . His wife, gospel singer Margaret Bell Byars, sang national anthem before two Eagles' games . . . Best man at wedding was Giants' linebacker Pepper Johnson, Byars' college roommate . . . Eagles' No. 1 draft pick in 1986, the first selection made by former coach Buddy Ryan . . . Born Oct. 14, 1963, in Dayton, Ohio . . . 1990 base salary: $625,000.

KEITH JACKSON 26 6-2 250 Tight End

Named starter in Pro Bowl after each of his first three seasons . . . Ranked second on team in receptions with 50 despite missing first two games . . . Boycotted training camp and first two games in contract dispute . . . Returned to team after 50-day holdout . . . Six TD receptions tied career high set as rookie in 1988 . . . His 194 receptions since 1988 is tops among NFL tight ends . . . NFC Rookie of Year in 1988 . . . Had more receptions in first NFL season (81) than during entire career at Oklahoma (62) . . . Produced a rap video featuring former coach Buddy Ryan and 25 teammates during 1990 offseason . . . Plays the cello . . . Received degree in communications in 3½ years . . . Born April 19, 1965, in Little Rock, Ark. . . . 1990 base salary: $300,000.

DAVID ALEXANDER 27 6-3 282 — Center

Eagles' offensive co-captain, along with quarterback Randall Cunningham . . . Has started last 44 regular-season games . . . Has graded out as team's top offensive lineman last two seasons . . . Versatility has allowed him to play guard and tackle as well as center in his career . . . Twice named offensive player of game by Eagles' coaches . . . Snaps on placekicks . . . Suffered severe knee injury in regular-season finale against Phoenix . . . Entered playoff game against Washington in third quarter but lasted just three plays before knee gave out . . . Underwent knee surgery Jan. 16 . . . Eagles' fifth-round draft pick in 1987 . . . Earned business degree from Tulsa . . . Born July 28, 1964, in Silver Spring, Md. . . . 1990 base salary: $375,000.

CALVIN WILLIAMS 24 5-11 181 — Wide Receiver

Set team record for touchdown receptions by a rookie with nine . . . Trailed only San Francisco's Jerry Rice (13) and Atlanta's Andre Rison (10) in TD receptions in the NFL . . . Smart receiver who runs precise routes . . . Emerged as starter during first minicamp of rookie season . . . Along with Fred Barnett, formed rookie starting wide-receiver combination . . . Fifth-round pick from Purdue . . . Team MVP as a senior . . . Earned B.S. degree in hotel and restaurant management . . . Born March 3, 1967, in Baltimore . . . 1990 base salary: $84,500.

FRED BARNETT 25 6-0 203 — Wide Receiver

Emerged as big-play man as a rookie, with eight TD receptions and a 20-yard average . . . Great speed, strength and leaping ability . . . Along with Calvin Williams, formed NFL's only starting rookie wide-receiver combination . . . Produced 100-yard receiving games against Minnesota, Buffalo and Green Bay . . . Caught 95-yard TD pass from Randall Cunningham against Buffalo . . . Third-round draft pick from Arkansas State . . . Set school records for catches (95) and receiving yards (1,571) . . . Did not play football until senior season at Rosedale (Miss.) High School because his mother, Earlean, thought it was too dangerous . . . Born June 17, 1966, in Shelby, Miss. . . . 1990 base salary: $135,000.

JEROME BROWN 26 6-2 295 **Defensive Tackle**

Made Pro Bowl despite severe drop in statistics . . . Recorded just one sack (after producing 10½ in 1989) but excelled in run defense . . . Credited with 99 tackles . . . Has been slowed by nagging injuries through much of his career . . . Suffered slight tear of right rotator cuff in regular-season finale in Phoenix but still played in playoff game against Washington . . . Underwent offseason shoulder surgery . . . Needs to keep weight under control to reach his potential . . . Best season was 1989 with 10½ sacks, 132 tackles and 46 quarterback hurries . . . Consensus All-American selection at University of Miami . . . Eagles' No. 1 draft pick in 1987 . . . Preferred baseball to football as a youngster . . . Hit .385 with 24 stolen bases as a senior right fielder at Hernando High in Brooksville, Fla. . . . Born Feb. 4, 1965, in Brooksville, Fla. . . . 1990 base salary: $330,000.

CLYDE SIMMONS 27 6-6 275 **Defensive End**

Recorded 7½ sacks in 1990, less than half of his 1989 total of 15½ . . . Slowed by Achilles injury for much of season . . . Quiet, unsung hero of Eagles' powerful defensive line . . . Came on late in season to record 6½ of his sacks in last eight games . . . Credited with 97 tackles . . . Has burned Giants with two touchdowns (15-yard return of blocked field goal, 60-yard return of interception) in his career . . . Eagles' ninth-round draft pick from Western Carolina in 1986 . . . Babe Ruth League teammate of Michael Jordan's and played high school basketball against the Chicago Bulls' star . . . Born Aug. 4, 1964, in Lane, S.C. . . . 1990 base salary: $380,000.

SETH JOYNER 26 6-2 240 **Linebacker**

Named Eagles' defensive MVP by teammates after recording 127 tackles . . . Also notched career-high 7½ sacks . . . Only linebacker Eagles keep on field in passing situations . . . Underrated by many observers because of solid, unspectacular all-around play . . . Named All-Pro for 1990 by *Sports Illustrated* . . . Intense competitor prides himself on hard work and preparation . . . Became starter midway in rookie season of 1986

. . . Eighth-round draft pick by the Eagles . . . Released on final cut as rookie but re-signed by Eagles two weeks later . . . Played at Texas-El Paso . . . Future plans include becoming sports cameraman . . . Born Nov. 18, 1964, in Spring Valley, N.Y. . . . 1990 base salary: $380,000.

COACH RICH KOTITE: Promoted from offensive coordinator on Jan. 8, 1991—the same day Buddy Ryan was dismissed as Eagles' head coach . . . First head-coaching job in NFL . . . Spent just one year with the Eagles as offensive coordinator and quarterbacks coach . . . Directed impressive offense that set team record and finished second in NFL with 396 points . . . Established good rapport with quarterback Randall Cunningham . . . Spent previous seven seasons with Jets as receivers coach (1983-84) and offensive coordinator (1985-89) . . . Hired four former Jet assistants (Bud Carson, Jim Vechiarella, Zeke Bratkowski, Jimmy Williams) after he got the Eagles' job . . . Also served as an assistant coach in New Orleans (1977) and Cleveland (1978-82) . . . Little All-American as a tight end at Wagner College in Staten Island, N.Y. . . . Began collegiate career at University of Miami, where he was school's heavyweight boxing champ and served as a sparring partner for Muhammad Ali . . . Born Oct. 13, 1942, in Brooklyn, N.Y.

GREATEST PUNTER

In the late 1940s, the Eagles reached the NFL title game three times in a row. They won the championship in 1948 and 1949. Those teams were led by future Hall of Famers Steve Van Buren and Alex Wojiechowicz. And by coach Greasy Neale, who also would end up in the Hall of Fame. And by Joe Muha. Joe Muha?

Muha played five seasons for the Eagles, from 1946 through 1950. He holds the team record for best punt average in a career (42.9) and in a season (47.2 in 1948).

Muha also owned the longest punt in Eagle history—an 82-yarder against the Giants in 1948—until Randall Cunningham unleashed a 91-yarder in 1989.

Cunningham, the Eagles' current quarterback, deserves special mention. An All-American punter in college, Cunningham has punted just nine times in the NFL. But he has averaged 54 yards per punt and his 91-yarder against the Giants in the Meadowlands ranks the third-longest in NFL history.

INDIVIDUAL EAGLE RECORDS

Rushing

Most Yards Game:	205	Steve Van Buren, vs Pittsburgh, 1949
Season:	1,512	Wilbert Montgomery 1979
Career:	6,538	Wilbert Montgomery, 1977-84

Passing

Most TD Passes Game:	7	Adrian Burk, vs Washington, 1954
Season:	32	Sonny Jurgensen, 1961
Career:	167	Ron Jaworski, 1977-85

Receiving

Most TD Passes Game:	4	2 times, most recently Ben Hawkins, vs Pittsburgh, 1969
Season:	13	3 times, most recently Mike Quick, 1983
Career:	79	Harold Carmichael, 1971-83

Scoring

Most Points Game:	25	Bobby Walston, vs Washington, 1954
Season:	116	Paul McFadden, 1984
Career:	881	Bobby Walston, 1951-62
Most TDs Game:	4	6 times, most recently Wilbert Montgomery, vs Washington, 1979
Season:	18	Steve Van Buren, 1945
Career:	79	Harold Carmichael, 1971-83

PHOENIX CARDINALS

TEAM DIRECTORY: Pres.: William V. Bidwill; Exec. VP: Joe Rhein; VP-Adm.: Curt Mosher; VP-Communications: Terry Bledsoe; Dir. Pro Personnel: Erik Widmark; Dir. Pub. Rel.: Paul Jensen; Head Coach: Joe Bugel. Home field: Sun Devil Stadium (74,724). Colors: Cardinal red, white and black.

SCOUTING REPORT

OFFENSE: The Cardinals answered a lot of questions in 1990. Timm Rosenbach emerged at quarterback and Johnny Johnson made the Pro Bowl as a rookie at running back.

Rosenbach is an exciting, gutsy player. He needs to be more consistent but should get better with experience. Johnson was a revelation as a seventh-round draft pick. He is backed up by another young player with star potential, Anthony Thompson.

The Cardinals' aging wide-receiver corps got a boost from rookie Ricky Proehl. But Roy Green and J.T. Smith both lost a step and the Cardinals need another big-play man.

The offensive line is huge, durable and experienced. But they need to be more consistent as a group for the Cardinals, 5-11 in 1990, to emerge from the division basement.

DEFENSE: The Cardinals found the solution to some of their offensive problems. Now they need to get better on defense.

Frustrated by their shortage of defensive linemen, the Cardinals switched from a 4-3 to a 3-4 formation midway through the season. But no matter how they line up, they need more muscle and talent along the defensive front.

They picked up former Redskin lineman Dexter Manley late in the season. He might give them some pass rush to complement end Freddie Joe Nunn. Top pick Eric Swann has the size, if not the experience.

The Cardinals have first-rate linebackers. Ken Harvey is a good pass-rusher and Eric Hill and Anthony Bell are heavy hitters. Safeties Tim McDonald and Lonnie Young are solid. The Cardinals have high hopes for young cornerback Jay Taylor, but this is another area in need of improvement.

SPECIAL TEAMS: For years, the Cardinals were a team with solid return teams and questionable kickers. Now, the reverse might be true.

Quarterback Timm Rosenbach adds a plus with his running.

CARDINALS VETERAN ROSTER

HEAD COACH—Joe Bugel. Assistant Coaches—Ted Cottrell, Bobby Hammond, Jim Johnson, Tom Lovat, Mike Murphy, Ted Plumb, Joe Pascale, Jerry Rhome, Pete Rodriguez, Bob Rogucki, Fritz Shurmur.

No.	Name	Pos.	Ht.	Wt.	NFL Exp.	College
55	Bell, Anthony	OLB	6-3	235	6	Michigan State
54	Braxton, David	OLB	6-1	232	3	Wake Forest
16	Camarillo, Rich	P	5-11	193	11	Washington
37	Centers, Larry	RB	5-10	203	2	Stephen F. Austin
79	Clasby, Bob	NT	6-5	276	5	Notre Dame
93	Coleman, Sidney	ILB	6-2	250	4	Southern Mississippi
5	Davis, Greg	K	5-11	197	5	Citadel
17	Del Greco, Al	K	5-10	195	8	Auburn
21	Edwards, Anthony	WR	5-11	185	3	New Mexico Highlands
94	Faulkner, Jeff	DE	6-3	305	2	Southern
26	Field, Amod	WR	5-11	181	1	Montclair State
32	Flagler, Terence	RB	6-0	200	5	Clemson
20	Flutie, Darren	WR	5-10	187	3	Boston College
81	Green, Roy	WR	6-0	195	13	Henderson State
56	Harvey, Ken	OLB	6-2	225	4	California
18	Hill, Derek	WR	6-1	193	3	Arizona
58	Hill, Eric	ILB	6-1	248	3	Louisiana State
83	Holmes, Don	WR	5-10	182	6	Mesa
80	Jackson, John	WR	5-10	175	2	Southern California
53	Jax, Garth	ILB	6-2	236	6	Florida State
39	Johnson, Johnny	R-B	6-2	216	2	San Jose State
86	Jones, Ernie	WR	5-11	196	4	Indiana
85	Jorden, Tim	TE	6-2	220	2	Indiana
57	Kauahi, Kani	C	6-2	274	9	Hawaii
70	Kennard, Derek	G	6-3	319	6	Nevada-Reno
7	Kupp, Craig	QB	6-4	215	1	Pacific Lutheran
51	Lewis, Bill	C	6-7	278	6	Nebraska
30	Little, David	TE	6-2	226	8	Middle Tennessee State
22	Lomack, Tony	WR	5-8	180	2	Florida
29	Lynch, Lorenzo	CB	5-9	200	5	Cal-Sacramento
47	Mack, Cedric	CB	6-0	185	9	Baylor
92	Manley, Dexter	DE	6-3	257	11	Oklahoma State
46	McDonald, Tim	SS	6-2	207	5	Southern California
78	Nunn, Freddie Joe	OLB	6-4	255	6	Mississippi
90	Osborne, Eldonta	OLB	6-0	226	2	Louisiana Tech
76	Patterson, Craig	NT	6-5	310	2	Brigham Young
87	Proehl, Ricky	WR	5-10	181	2	Wake Forest
89	Reeves, Walter	TE	6-3	262	3	Auburn
63	Robbins, Tootie	T	6-5	322	10	East Carolina
3	Rosenbach, Timm	QB	6-2	215	3	Washington State
72	Saddler, Rod	DE	6-5	280	5	Texas A&M
67	Sharpe, Luis	T	6-4	260	10	UCLA
61	Smith, Lance	G	6-2	285	7	Louisiana State
69	Smith, Vernice	G-T	6-2	289	2	Florida A&M
91	Stowe, Tyronne	ILB	6-1	236	5	Rutgers
27	Taylor, Jay	CB	5-9	175	3	San Jose State
34	Thompson, Anthony	RB	5-11	207	2	Indiana
19	Tupa, Tom	QB-P	6-4	225	4	Ohio State
23	Turner, Marcus	DB	6-0	187	3	UCLA
66	Wahler, Jim	NT	6-3	276	3	UCLA
60	Walker, Jeff	G-T	6-4	286	4	Memphis State
82	Williams, Willie	T	6-5	296	1	Louisiana State
68	Wolf, Joe	T	6-5	283	3	Boston College
24	Wolfley, Ron	RB	6-0	222	7	West Virginia
43	Young, Lonnie	FS	6-1	191	7	Michigan State
38	Zordich, Michael	FS	5-11	200	5	Penn State

TOP DRAFT CHOICES

Rd.	Name	Sel. No.	Pos.	Ht.	Wt.	College
1	Swann, Eric	6	DE	6-4	311	None
2	Jones, Mike	32	DE	6-3	274	North Carolina State
3	Williams, Aeneas	59	DB	5-10	187	Southern
4	Davis, Dexter	86	DB	5-9	175	Clemson
5	Hammond, Vance	117	DT	6-6	300	Clemson

Vai Sikahema, who holds nearly all of the Cardinals' return records, signed with Green Bay as a Plan B free agent. He leaves a huge void on both kickoff returns and punt returns. On the plus side, the Cardinals have a dependable duo in kicker Al Del Greco and punter Rich Camarillo.

THE ROOKIES: The Cardinals took a first-round gamble on defensive lineman Eric Swann, an imposing 311-pounder who never played college football. The defense got more attention with the additions of end Mike Jones of North Carolina State and cornerbacks Aeneas Williams of Southern and Dexter Davis of Clemson.

OUTLOOK: Still a cut below the top three teams in the division, Joe Bugel's Cardinals once again will battle the Cowboys in an effort to stay out of the NFC East dungeon. But like the Cowboys, the Cardinals have some good young players and they have closed the gap on the Giants, Redskins and Eagles. If one or more of the top three falter, they could find themselves in the race for a playoff berth.

CARDINAL PROFILES

TIMM ROSENBACH 24 6-2 215 — Quarterback

Came on strong late in season to finish with 3,098 passing yards . . . Started all 16 games in 1990 after appearing in just two games as a rookie in 1989 . . . Mobility and toughness make him one of NFL's best young quarterbacks . . . Nine of his 17 interceptions came in first three games . . . First two 300-yard performances of career came in last two games of season . . . Threw for 381 yards against Giants and 301 against Eagles . . . Also rushed for 470 yards, second only to Randall Cunningham among NFL quarterbacks . . . Struggled in limited action as a rookie . . . Selected by Cardinals in first round of 1989 supplemental draft . . . Passed for 5,995 yards in three seasons at Washington State . . . Won Montana state javelin championship with throw of 231 feet . . . Born Oct. 27, 1966, in Everett, Wash. . . . 1990 base salary: $700,000.

TIM McDONALD 26 6-2 207 **Safety**

Led Cardinals in tackles for third year in a row with 132 . . . Also led team with four interceptions . . . Missed Pro Bowl after making it for first time in 1989 . . . Heavy hitter with excellent range and instincts . . . Second in NFC in interceptions with seven in 1989 . . . Also led NFC with 170 interception-return yards . . . Moved into starting lineup in 1988 after missing most of 1987 with broken ankle . . . Cardinals' second-round pick out of USC in 1987 . . . Born Jan. 6, 1965, in Fresno, Cal. . . . 1990 base salary: $700,000.

JOHNNY JOHNSON 23 6-2 216 **Running Back**

The steal of the 1990 draft . . . A seventh-round draft pick, Johnson made the Pro Bowl after rushing for 926 yards and catching 25 passes . . . Led all NFL rookies in total yards from scrimmage with 1,167 . . . Missed most of three games in midseason with ankle injury . . . Ran for 120 yards against Cowboys, 110 against Giants, 103 against Packers . . . Running style has been compared to Eric Dickerson's . . . Left San Jose State after five games of senior season following dispute with coach . . . As a junior, became first player in NCAA history to rush for more than 1,200 yards and catch 60 passes . . . Born June 11, 1968, in Santa Clara, Cal. . . . 1990 base salary: $80,000.

LUIS SHARPE 31 6-4 260 **Tackle**

Missed Pro Bowl in 1990 after making it three years in a row . . . Regarded as one of the game's best pass-blockers . . . Started all 16 games . . . Strong blocking helped Cardinals establish running game under new coach Joe Bugel . . . "Iron Man" act in 1984-85 included playing in 44 games in 16-month period . . . Started 16 games for Cardinals in 1984, then 12 games with Memphis Showboats of USFL in spring of 1985, then 16 more for Cardinals in fall of 1985 . . . Has been starter since rookie season of 1982 . . . Cardinals' No. 1 pick in 1982 out of UCLA . . . Born June 16, 1960, in Havana, Cuba . . . Moved to Detroit at age six . . . 1990 base salary: $640,000.

KEN HARVEY 26 6-2 225 **Linebacker**

Has developed into one of the NFL's best pass-rushing outside linebackers . . . Great speed, strength and agility . . . Led Cardinals with 10 sacks in 1990 . . . Registered three sacks in game against Atlanta . . . Finished with 99 tackles and 24 quarterback hurries . . . Six sacks as a rookie in 1988, seven more in 1989 . . . Needs to improve run-defense . . . Set weight-lifting record at University of California . . . Cardinals' No. 1 pick in 1988 . . . Dropped out of high school and worked at McDonald's but got degree and enrolled at Laney (Tex.) Junior College . . . Born May 6, 1965, in Austin, Tex. . . . 1990 base salary: $250,000.

ERIC HILL 24 6-1 248 **Linebacker**

Big hitter in middle of Cardinals' defense . . . Started all 16 games—four at middle linebacker, 12 at right inside linebacker after switch to 3-4 defense . . . Finished fourth on team in tackles with 96 . . . Started 14 games as a rookie in 1989 . . . Consensus all-rookie selection after making 91 tackles . . . Cardinals' first-round pick in 1989 out of LSU . . . Born Nov. 14, 1966, in Galveston, Tex. . . . 1990 base salary: $350,000.

ROY GREEN 34 6-0 195 **Wide Receiver**

Kept rolling along in 12th NFL season with 53 catches for 797 yards . . . Became Cardinals' all-time leader in receptions (522) and receiving yardage (8,497) . . . Also is team's all-time leader in TDs with 69 . . . Started all 16 games . . . Caught eight passes for 147 yards in Week 15 against Giants . . . A Pro Bowler in 1983 and 1984 . . . Nicknamed "The Jet Stream" . . . Started career at defensive back . . . Caught a TD pass and made an interception in same game against Washington in 1981 . . . Cardinals' fourth-round pick in 1979 out of Henderson (Ark.) State . . . Born June 30, 1957, in Magnolia, Ark. . . . 1990 base salary: $750,000.

LONNIE YOUNG 28 6-1 191 **Safety**

Bounced back from injury-marred 1989 season to finish second on team in tackles with 111 in 1990 . . . Also intercepted two passes and recovered two fumbles . . . Smart, steady player serves as quarterback of Cardinals' secondary . . . Has exceeded expectations since joining Cardinals' as 12th-round draft pick out of Michigan State in 1985 . . . Chosen 325th out of 336 players in 1985 draft . . . Played cornerback in college . . . Became starter at safety midway in first season and was consensus all-rookie team selection . . . Childhood friend of Giants' linebacker Carl Banks; they went to same elementary school, same high school, same college . . . Born July 18, 1963, in Flint, Mich. . . . 1990 base salary: $410,000.

RICKY PROEHL 23 5-10 181 **Wide Receiver**

Led all NFL rookie wide receivers in catches with 56 . . . First rookie to lead Cardinals in catches in 40 years . . . Generated 802 yards and four TDs . . . Smart, crafty receiver with good moves and great hands . . . Used mostly as third wide receiver on passing downs . . . Started just two games, both at H-back . . . Caught seven passes for 132 yards in season finale against Philadelphia . . . Caught six passes for 102 yards against Atlanta . . . Cardinals' third-round pick in 1990 out of Wake Forest . . . His 188 receptions, 2,949 yards and 25 TDs are Wake Forest records . . . Born March 7, 1968, in Belle Mead, N.J. . . . 1990 base salary: $155,000.

FREDDIE JOE NUNN 29 6-4 255 **Defensive End**

Battled back from disruptive 1989 season to register nine sacks in 1990 . . . Also credited with 57 tackles and 16 quarterback hurries . . . Considered one of better pass-rushing defensive ends in NFL . . . Suspended for four games in 1989 for violating league's substance-abuse policy . . . Managed just five sacks in 1989 after collecting 14 in 1988 and 11 in 1987 . . . Switched to defensive end from linebacker in 1987 . . . Added 30 pounds to gain strength but retained much of his quickness . . .

Cardinals' first-round pick in 1985 out of Mississippi . . . Cousin is boxer Michael Nunn . . . Born April 9, 1962, in Noxubee, Miss. . . . 1990 base salary: $500,000.

COACH JOE BUGEL: Upbeat, enthusiastic coach appears to have Cardinals on right track . . . Although 5-11 record in his first season was same as team's 1989 mark, the Cardinals look to be moving in right direction . . . Team improved in several important categories (run-offense, run-defense) and reflected Bugel's enthusiasm . . . Secured first victory as NFL head coach in Week Two upset at Philadelphia . . . Led Cardinals to three-game winning streak in midseason . . . Installed one-back offense that helped Cardinals rush for 1,912 yards . . . Spent nine seasons as assistant coach with Washington . . . Developed "Hogs" of offensive line that helped produce two Super Bowl titles . . . An assistant in Detroit (1975-76) and Houston (1977-80) before joining Redskins' staff . . . Assistant coach at Ohio State, Iowa State, Navy and Western Kentucky . . . Roommate of Atlanta coach Jerry Glanville when both were assistants at Western Kentucky . . . Played guard at Western Kentucky . . . Earned masters in counseling . . . Born March 10, 1940, in Pittsburgh.

GREATEST PUNTER

Change has been a constant among Cardinals' punters.

The team record for punts in a career is held by Carl Birdsong, who had 360 from 1981 through 1985. No other player has punted as many as 250 times for the Cardinals.

A free agent from Southwest Oklahoma State, Birdsong was among the NFL's best punters in the early 1980s. He punted 85 times in both 1983 and 1985 and averaged 41.5 and 41.7 yards, respectively.

Jerry Norton punted for the Cardinals for just three years (1959-61) but probably was the most productive player at the position in team history. His season averages of 45.5, 44.9 and 44.7 yards are the top three in Cardinal history.

INDIVIDUAL CARDINAL RECORDS

Rushing

Most Yards Game:	203	John David Crow, vs Pittsburgh, 1960
Season:	1,605	Ottis Anderson, 1979
Career:	7,999	Ottis Anderson, 1979-86

Passing

Most TD Passes Game:	6	3 times, most recently Charley Johnson, vs New Orleans, 1969
Season:	28	2 times, most recently Neil Lomax, 1984
Career:	205	Jim Hart, 1966-82

Receiving

Most TD Passes Game:	5	Bob Shaw, vs Baltimore, 1950
Season:	15	Sonny Randle, 1960
Career:	66	Roy Green, 1979-1990

Scoring

Most Points Game:	40	Ernie Nevers, vs Chicago, 1929
Season:	117	2 times, most recently Neil O'Donoghue, 1984
Career:	1,380	Jim Bakken, 1962-78
Most TDs Game:	6	Ernie Nevers, vs Chicago, 1929
Season:	17	John David Crow, 1962
Career:	69	Roy Green, 1979-1990

SAN FRANCISCO 49ERS

TEAM DIRECTORY: Owner: Edward J. DeBartolo Jr.; Pres.: Carmen Policy; VP-Football Adm.: John McVay; Dir. Pub. Rel.: Jerry Walker; Head Coach: George Seifert. Home field: Candlestick Park (66,445). Colors: 49er gold and scarlet.

SCOUTING REPORT

OFFENSE: For a team that scored 353 points in a 14-2 regular season and came within a last-second field goal of making a third

Charles Haley's 16 sacks were the most in the NFC.

consecutive appearance in the Super Bowl, the 49ers have a lot of questions on offense.

The line is set and the receivers are excellent, but what about the running game? More importantly, what about the quarterback?

Joe Montana put together another superb season in 1990, but now he's 35 and one year closer to enshrinement in the Hall of Fame. Can he still perform up to his own lofty standards?

Running back is another concern. Roger Craig signed with the Raiders as a Plan B free agent. Dexter Carter has ability but might not be an every-down back such as Craig. The good news: Jerry Rice still is around. So are John Taylor and Brent Jones. Rice just gets better and better. Taylor is an emerging star and Jones is a complete tight end.

The offensive line is OK, too. Guards Guy McIntyre and Harris Barton anchor a solid, seasoned group.

DEFENSE: Suddenly, the defense is the most settled part of the franchise and is finally getting the credit it deserves.

The line is deep and talented. The 49ers get excellent production from ends Kevin Fagan and Pierce Holt. Nose tackles Michael Carter and Jim Burt still stand out against the run, and the team has high hopes for young end Dennis Brown.

Linebacker Charles Haley is the big-play man; he led the NFC in sacks with 16. Bill Romanowski is an underrated outside linebacker. Keith DeLong and Michael Walter are solid against the run.

The secondary will miss safety Ronnie Lott, who also signed with the Raiders during Plan B. Johnny Jackson and Chet Brooks have to step up. The cornerbacks are solid, with starters Darryl Pollard and Don Griffin and promising youngster Eric Davis.

SPECIAL TEAMS: Stronger special-teams play will help the 49ers avoid slipping back into the pack. Kicker Mike Cofer struggled a bit from distance but was dependable from inside the 40. He made 17-of-19 field-goal attempts from there. Punter Barry Helton averaged just 36.8 yards; that's not good enough.

The coverage teams are good, but the 49ers need to improve on returns. Carter has speed and moves but never got loose on kickoff returns. Taylor is a proven punt-returner coming off a so-so season.

THE ROOKIES: The 49ers felt Louisville defensive tackle Ted Washington was too talented to pass up. If he stays motivated and keep his weight under control, he's a great addition to an already

49ERS VETERAN ROSTER

HEAD COACH—George Seifert. Assistant Coaches—Jerry Attaway, Dwaine Board, Tommy Hart, Sherman Lewis, John Marshall, Bobb McKittrick, Ray Rhodes, Ray Sherman, Lynn Stiles, Bob Zeman.

No.	Name	Pos.	Ht.	Wt.	NFL Exp.	College
79	Barton, Harris	T	6-4	280	5	North Carolina
86	Beach, Sanjay	WR	6-1	190	1	Colorado State
20	Blair, Stanley	CB	6-0	188	2	SE Oklahoma State
13	Bono, Steve	QB	6-4	215	7	UCLA
22	Bowles, Todd	S	6-2	205	6	Temple
96	Brown, Dennis	DE	6-4	290	3	Washington
32	Brown, Steve	CB	6-0	187	9	Oregon
64	Burt, Jim	NT	6-1	270	11	Miami (Fla.)
52	Caliguire, Dean	C	6-2	282	1	Pittsburgh
35	Carter, Dexter	RB	5-9	170	2	Florida State
95	Carter, Michael	NT	6-2	285	8	Southern Methodist
6	Cofer, Mike	K	6-1	160	4	North Carolina State
38	Cox, Greg	S-LB	6-0	217	4	San Jose State
25	Davis, Eric	CB	5-11	178	2	Jacksonville State
59	DeLong, Keith	LB	6-2	235	3	Tennessee
22	DuBose, Doug	RB	6-0	205	3	Nebraska
50	Etienne, LeRoy	LB	6-2	245	2	Nebraska
75	Fagan, Kevin	DE	6-3	260	5	Miami (Fla.)
67	Foster, Roy	G	6-4	290	10	Southern California
98	Goss, Antonio	LB	6-4	228	3	North Carolina
18	Green, Anthony	WR	6-0	188	1	Western Kentucky
29	Griffin, Don	CB	6-0	176	6	Middle Tennessee State
94	Haley, Charles	LB-DE	6-5	230	6	James Madison
56	Harrison, Martin	LB-DE	6-5	240	1	Washington
60	Harvey, Stacey	LB	6-3	250	2	Arizona State
9	Helton, Barry	P	6-3	205	4	Colorado
30	Henderson, Keith	FB	6-1	220	4	Georgia
77	Hodge, Milford	DE	6-3	278	5	Washington State
78	Holt, Pierce	DE	6-4	280	4	Angelo State
90	Ingram, Darryl	TE	6-3	240	2	California
40	Jackson, Johnny	S	6-1	204	3	Houston
84	Jones, Brent	TE	6-4	230	5	Santa Clara
90	Jordan, Darin	LB	6-2	245	2	Northeastern
45	Lewis, Kevin	CB	5-11	173	2	NW Louisiana
83	Lewis, Ronald	WR	5-11	173	2	Florida State
17	Mandley, Pete	WR	5-10	192	7	Northern Arizona
62	McIntyre, Guy	G	6-3	265	8	Georgia
71	Mitz, Alonzo	DE	6-4	278	5	Florida
4	Mojsiejenko, Ralf	P	6-3	212	7	Michigan State
16	Montana, Joe	QB	6-1	195	13	Notre Dame
69	Neville, Tom	G	6-5	298	4	Fresno State
77	Paris, Bubba	T	6-6	299	9	Michigan
28	Plummer, Bruce	S	6-0	198	5	Mississippi State
72	Pollack, Frank	T-G	6-5	285	2	Northern Arizona
26	Pollard, Darryl	CB	5-11	187	5	Weber State
55	Radloff, Wayne	C	6-5	277	6	Georgia
44	Rathman, Tom	FB	6-1	232	6	Nebraska
80	Rice, Jerry	WR	6-2	200	7	Miss. Valley State
91	Roberts, Larry	DE	6-3	275	6	Alabama
57	Robinson, Jeroy	LB	6-2	245	2	Texas A&M
53	Romanowski, Bill	LB	6-4	231	4	Boston College
61	Sapolu, Jesse	C	6-4	260	6	Hawaii
88	Sherrard, Mike	WR	6-2	187	3	UCLA
63	Siglar, Ricky	G-T	6-7	296	2	San Jose State
72	Smith, Sean	DE	6-4	272	4	Grambling
24	Sydney, Harry	FB	6-0	217	5	Kansas
82	Taylor, John	WR	6-1	185	5	Delaware State
60	Thomas, Chuck	C	6-3	280	6	Oklahoma
23	Tillman, Spencer	RB	5-11	206	5	Oklahoma
74	Wallace, Steve	T	6-5	276	6	Auburn
89	Walls, Wesley	TE	6-5	246	3	Mississippi
99	Walter, Michael	LB	6-3	238	9	Oregon
51	Washington, Chris	LB	6-4	240	7	Iowa State
43	Waymer, Dave	S	6-1	188	12	Notre Dame
93	Wells, Kent	NT	6-4	295	2	Nebraska
41	Whitmore, David	S	6-0	235	2	Stephen F. Austin
81	Williams, Jamie	TE	6-4	245	9	Nebraska
8	Young, Steve	QB	6-2	200	7	Brigham Young

TOP DRAFT CHOICES

Rd.	Name	Sel. No.	Pos.	Ht.	Wt.	College
1	Washington, Ted	25	DT	6-4	303	Louisville
2	Watters, Ricky	45	RB	6-1	212	Notre Dame
2	Johnson, John	53	LB	6-3	230	Clemson
4	Donahue, Mitch	95	LB	6-2	233	Wyoming
5	Hanks, Merton	122	DB	6-1	177	Iowa

strong defensive front. Running back Ricky Watters from Notre Dame has the skill and size to inherit Craig's role in the offense.

OUTLOOK: This is a great team in transition. The loss of Lott and Craig will hurt off the field as well as on, and it will be interesting to see how George Seifert's 49ers react to missing the Super Bowl for the first time in three years.

The key is Montana. If he's healthy and back near his previous level of play, the 49ers have the other offensive weapons and the defense to repeat as division champs and make a run for the Super Bowl.

49ER PROFILES

JOE MONTANA 35 6-1 195 **Quarterback**

Only an injury and a loss in the NFC championship game marred another remarkable season for Montana . . . Selected to the Pro Bowl for the seventh time . . . Set a team record with 3,944 passing yards . . . Also threw for 26 TDs, bringing his career total to 242 . . . Eclipsed John Brodie for first place on the 49ers' all-time passing yardage list with 34,998 . . . Set personal bests with 476 yards and six TDs in game against Atlanta . . . Injuries in final game (finger, concussion) and his age cast some doubt on his future . . . But he has defied the odds before, battling back from 1987 back surgery that some thought would end his career . . . He and Terry Bradshaw are only quarterbacks to lead team to four Super Bowl titles . . . Only three-time Super Bowl MVP . . . 49ers' third-round pick in 1979 out of Notre Dame . . . Born June 11, 1956, in New Eagle, Pa. . . . 1990 base salary: $4 million.

JERRY RICE 28 6-2 200 **Wide Receiver**

Some say this big-play man will finish his career as the greatest wide receiver of all time . . . Led the NFL in catches (100), receiving yards (1,502) and TD catches (13) in 1990 . . . Named to the Pro Bowl for the fifth year in a row . . . On pace after six seasons to break most NFL career receiving records . . . Already has 446 catches, 7,866 yards and an astounding 79 TDs

. . . Set personal bests in 1990 game against Falcons with 13 catches, 225 yards and five TDs . . . Super Bowl MVP in 1988 . . . NFL MVP in strike-shortened 1987 season after catching 22 TD passes in just 12 games . . . Uncanny knack for turning short pass into long gain . . . San Francisco's No. 1 pick in 1985 out of Mississippi Valley State . . . Set 18 Division 1-AA records in college . . . Born Oct. 13, 1962, in Starkville, Miss. . . . 1990 base salary: $900,000.

JOHN TAYLOR 29 6-1 185 **Wide Receiver**

This talented wide receiver toils in the shadow of Jerry Rice . . . Caught 49 passes for 748 yards and seven TDs . . . Caught 61-yard TD pass in playoff loss to the Giants . . . Two-time Pro Bowler, once as a returner and once as a receiver . . . Best season was 1989, with 60 catches, 1,077 yards, 10 TDs . . . Caught 11 passes for 286 yards in game against Rams . . . Returned from four-game suspension for substance abuse in 1988 to catch winning TD in final seconds of Super Bowl XXIII . . . Led NFL in punt returns in 1988 . . . San Francisco's third-round pick in 1986 out of Delaware State . . . Born March 31, 1962, in Pennsauken, N.J. . . . 1990 base salary: $400,000.

HARRIS BARTON 27 6-4 280 **Center-Guard**

Versatile offensive lineman made switch to center/guard in 1990 . . . Spent first three seasons at tackle, with emergency work at guard . . . Named first-team All-Pro by *Football News* and second-team All-NFL by *The National* . . . Smart player who compensates for lack of overpowering strength with know-how and technique . . . Started all 16 regular-season games, plus playoffs, in 1989 despite two operations on thumb . . . Named NFL Lineman of Year by CBS radio . . . Moved into starting lineup in fifth game of rookie season and has been there ever since . . . San Francisco's No. 1 pick in 1987 out of North Carolina . . . Started at center as a sophomore and at tackle his last two seasons . . . Born April 19, 1964, in Atlanta . . . 1990 base salary: $530,000.

CHARLES HALEY 27 6-5 230 — Linebacker

Back in the Pro Bowl after strong 1990 season . . . The big-play man in the 49ers' disciplined defense . . . Led NFC with 16 sacks . . . Ranked sixth on team in tackles with 58 . . . Has 56 sacks in five-year career . . . Great pass-rusher with speed, agility, relentless attitude . . . Pro Bowler in 1988 . . . Led team with 12 sacks as a rookie in 1986 . . . A steal in the 1986 draft, the 49ers got him in the fourth round out of James Madison . . . Four-year starter never missed a snap in college . . . Born Jan. 6, 1964, in Gladys, Va. . . . 1990 base salary: $750,000.

TOM RATHMAN 28 6-1 232 — Fullback

The perfect fullback for the 49ers' offensive system . . . Terrific blocker and exceptional pass-receiver . . . Caught 48 passes in 1990 . . . Also rushed for 318 yards and seven TDs . . . Led all NFL running backs in receptions in 1989 with 73 . . . Scored two TDs in Super Bowl XXIV . . . His toughness is a key ingredient for the 49ers, who sometimes are regarded as a finesse team . . . San Francisco's third-round pick in 1986 out of Nebraska . . . Used almost exclusively as blocking back in college . . . Caught just five passes as a collegian . . . Born Oct. 7, 1962, in Grand Island, Neb. . . . 1990 base salary: $540,000.

DEXTER CARTER 23 5-9 170 — Running Back

This swift, elusive runner is expected to emerge as the 49ers' feature back following the departure of Plan B free agent Roger Craig . . . Led 49ers in all-purpose yards as a rookie in 1990 with 1,460 . . . They broke down this way: team-high 460 rushing yards, 217 receiving yards, team-high 783 kickoff-return yards . . . Caught 25 passes . . . Shook loose for 74-yard TD run from scrimmage . . . Diminutive size makes his durability as an every-down back a question . . . San Francisco's No. 1 pick in 1990 out of Florida State . . . Emerged as starter as a senior after serving as backup to Sammie Smith, Dolphins' No. 1 pick in 1989 . . . Born Sept. 15, 1967, in Baxley, Ga. . . . 1990 base salary: $225,000.

GUY McINTYRE 30 6-3 265 **Guard**

Slow, steady development has led to Pro Bowl stature for this talented offensive lineman . . . Selected to Pro Bowl for second year in a row in 1990 . . . Combines speed and strength with knowledge of the game . . . Paid his dues, serving as backup in first four NFL seasons . . . Finally became starter in 1988 and promptly helped 49ers to two consecutive Super Bowl titles . . . Worked some as blocking back in 1984 playoffs . . . That move helped inspire the Bears to use William "The Refrigerator" Perry in same role the next season . . . San Francisco's third-round pick in 1984 out of Georgia . . . Born Feb. 17, 1961, in Thomasville, Ga. . . . 1990 base salary: $415,000.

KEVIN FAGAN 28 6-3 260 **Defensive End**

Continues to reward 49ers' faith in his ability to come back from devastating knee injury . . . Set career-high with 9½ sacks in 1990 . . . Also recorded career-high 63 tackles . . . Named first-team All-NFL by *The National* . . . His sack and tackle totals have improved in each of his four NFL seasons . . . Has more tackles (158) in last three seasons than any other 49ers' defensive lineman . . . Collected three sacks in 1989 playoffs . . . San Francisco's fourth-round pick in 1986 out of Miami . . . Had been projected as a No. 1 pick but suffered severe knee injury in Sugar Bowl . . . Spent entire 1986 season on injured-reserve list . . . Born April 25, 1963, in Lake Worth, Fla. . . . 1990 base salary: $625,000.

DON GRIFFIN 27 6-0 176 **Cornerback**

Steady defensive back is regarded as best coverage man in 49ers' secondary . . . Led team in passes defended in 1990 with 19 and tied for second in interceptions with three . . . Named second-team All-NFC by United Press International . . . Has been starter since the first game of his rookie season . . . Doubles as an occasional punt-returner . . . Has averaged better than nine yards per return in his career and broke off a 76-

yarder for a TD as a rookie in 1986 . . . San Francisco's sixth-round pick in 1986 out of Middle Tennessee State . . . Four-year letterman at free safety . . . Played just one game (high-school all-star game) at cornerback in his life prior to joining 49ers . . . Born March 17, 1964, in Pelham, Ga. . . . 1990 base salary: $540,000.

COACH GEORGE SEIFERT: Smooth, steadying influence

who kept the 49ers on the winning track in his second season . . . Named NFL Coach of the Year by *Football News*, Touchdown Club of Washington, D.C., *The National* and the *Boston Globe* . . . Led 49ers to best regular-season record in NFL for second year in a row . . . His two-year record, including playoffs, is 32-5 . . . Praised by players for creating warmer, closer atmosphere following retirement of former coach Bill Walsh . . . Spent nine years with the 49ers before getting his chance at the helm . . . Defensive assistant on first three 49ers' Super Bowl-winning teams . . . Credited with molding 49ers' disciplined defense as coordinator since 1983 . . . Spent 15 years in college ranks . . . Head coach at Westminster College (Utah) and Cornell . . . Won just three games in two seasons at Cornell in mid-1970s . . . An assistant at Iowa, Oregon and Stanford . . . Played end and guard at Utah . . . As a schoolboy, he served as an usher at 49ers' games at Kezar Stadium . . . Born Jan. 22, 1940, in San Francisco.

GREATEST PUNTER

Tommy Davis was one of the last of the two-way kickers. He was both placekicker and punter for the 49ers through the 1960s. Davis ranks second to Ray Wersching in most team placekicking categories, but is far and away the top punter in San Francisco history.

Davis holds team records for career punts (511), punt yardage (22,841) and average (44.7). He also produced two punts that covered more than 80 yards—an 82-yarder against Minnesota in 1962 and an 81-yarder against St. Louis the same year.

INDIVIDUAL 49ER RECORDS

Rushing

Most Yards Game:	194	Delvin Williams, vs St. Louis, 1976
Season:	1,502	Roger Craig, 1988
Career:	7,344	Joe Perry, 1948-60, 1963

Passing

Most TD Passes Game:	6	Joe Montana, vs Atlanta, 1990
Season:	31	Joe Montana, 1987
Career:	242	Joe Montana, 1979-90

Receiving

Most TD Passes Game:	5	Jerry Rice, vs Atlanta, 1990
Season:	22	Jerry Rice, 1987
Career:	79	Jerry Rice, 1985-90

Scoring

Most Points Game:	30	Jerry Rice, vs Atlanta, 1990
Season:	138	Jerry Rice, 1987
Career:	896	Ray Wersching, 1977-86
Most TDs Game:	5	Jerry Rice, vs Atlanta, 1990
Season:	23	Jerry Rice, 1987
Career:	83	Jerry Rice, 1985-90

TAMPA BAY BUCCANEERS

TEAM DIRECTORY: Owner: Hugh Culverhouse; Pres.: Gary Culverhouse; GM: Phil Krueger; Dir. Player Personnel: Jerry Angelo; Dir. Pro Personnel: Ruston Webster; Dir. Pub. Rel.: Rick Odioso; Head Coach: Richard Williamson. Home field: Tampa Stadium (74,296). Colors: Florida orange, white and red.

SCOUTING REPORT

OFFENSE: The wait continues for Vinny Testaverde. Sometimes he seems on the verge of becoming an excellent quarterback. Sometimes not. His inconsistency tortures the Bucs.

Testaverde has good wide receivers in Mark Carrier and Bruce Hill. Ron Hall is a talented but underrated tight end.

The running game got a boost in 1990 from Gary Anderson, who was acquired in a trade with San Diego. Fullback Reggie Cobb has some big-play ability.

Left tackle Paul Gruber is an outstanding offensive lineman and center Randy Grimes is the best of a mediocre group. Tennessee tackle Charles McRae, the Bucs' first draft pick, should be a plus.

DEFENSE: If the Bucs hope to challenge for a playoff berth, they need to get better on this side of the football.

The line needs significant improvement. End Reuben Davis is a solid player but the Bucs must get bigger, stronger and more productive.

The linebackers are a source of hope. The outside guys are Broderick Thomas and Keith McCants, a pair of former high No. 1 picks. The top inside linebacker is Winston Moss, a heavy hitter.

The secondary is another area of concern even though cornerback Wayne Haddix made the Pro Bowl after returning three interceptions for TDs. William Frizzell, a Plan B find from Philadelphia, could help at safety.

SPECIAL TEAMS: The Bucs have a pair of talented young specialists in placekicker Steve Christie and punter Mark Royals. Christie was 23-for-27 in field goals, including 6-for-7 from 40 yards and beyond. Royals averaged 40.3 yards on punts.

Willie Drewery and Danny Peebles are solid as returners. The Bucs need to tighten up their kickoff-coverage after allowing a league-high 24.1 yards per return.

Vinny Testaverde led NFC in yards per passing attempt.

THE ROOKIES: The Bucs wanted to improve their defense, but their first three draft picks were offensive players. McRae, the first offensive lineman selected in the draft, is a smooth pass-blocker. Florida State's Lawrence Dawsey is a talented wide receiver and Texas A&M's Robert Wilson is a big, blocking fullback.

OUTLOOK: The talent is there for this team, 6-10 in 1990, to go .500 under new coach Richard Williamson. It all comes back to Testaverde. If he can be consistently good, he won't be the leader of a losing team for the fifth year in a row.

BUCCANEERS VETERAN ROSTER

HEAD COACH—Richard Williamson. Assistant Coaches—Jeff Fitzgerald, Ray Hamilton, Tim Harkness, Kent Johnston, Hank Kuhlmann, Dale Lindsey, Alan Lowry, Carl Mauck, Floyd Peters, Tom Schertz, Steve Shafer, Morris Watts, Richard Wood.

No.	Name	Pos.	Ht.	Wt.	NFL Exp.	College
40	Anderson, Gary	RB	6-1	190	6	Arkansas
89	Anderson, Jesse	TE	6-2	245	2	Mississippi State
56	Anno, Sam	LB	6-2	235	5	Southern California
85	Anthony, Terry	WR	6-0	200	1	Florida State
75	Bax, Carl	OL	6-4	290	3	Missouri
62	Beckles, Ian	OG	6-1	295	2	Indiana
69	Bruhin, John	OG	6-3	285	4	Tennessee
7	Carlson, Jeff	QB	6-3	215	2	Weber State
88	Carrier, Mark	WR	6-0	182	5	Nicholls State
17	Chandler, Chris	QB	6-4	220	4	Washington
2	Christie, Steve	K	6-0	185	2	William & Mary
33	Cobb, Reggie	RB	6-0	225	2	Tennessee
79	Davis, Reuben	DE	6-4	285	4	North Carolina
76	Dill, Scott	OT	6-5	285	4	Memphis State
87	Drewrey, Willie	WR	5-7	170	7	West Virginia
42	Everett, Eric	DB	5-10	170	4	Texas Tech
81	Ford, Chris	WR	6-1	185	1	Lamar
37	Frizzell, William	DB	6-3	205	8	North Carolina Central
60	Grimes, Randy	C	6-4	275	9	Baylor
74	Gruber, Paul	OT	6-5	290	4	Wisconsin
45	Haddix, Wayne	DB	6-1	200	4	Liberty
82	Hall, Ron	TE	6-4	245	5	Hawaii
39	Hamilton, Harry	DB	6-0	195	8	Penn State
18	Harkness, Chris	WR	6-0	185	1	Ashland
26	Harvey, John	RB	5-11	185	2	Texas-El Paso
84	Hill, Bruce	WR	6-0	180	5	Arizona State
97	Jones, Marlon	DE	6-4	270	5	Central State
38	Lawson, Jamie	RB	5-10	240	3	Nicholls State
99	Marve, Eugene	LB	6-2	240	10	Saginaw Valley
61	Mayberry, Tony	C	6-4	285	2	Wake Forest
52	McCants, Keith	LB	6-3	255	2	Alabama
73	McHale, Tom	OG	6-4	280	5	Cornell
19	Moss, Tony	WR	5-7	170	1	Louisiana State
59	Murphy, Kevin	LB	6-2	235	6	Oklahoma
96	Newton, Tim	NT	6-0	275	7	Florida
83	Peebles, Danny	WR	5-11	180	3	North Carolina State
32	Perkins, Bruce	RB	6-2	230	2	Arizona State
54	Randle, Ervin	LB	6-1	250	7	Baylor
27	Reed, Daryl	DB	6-1	186	1	Oregon
29	Reynolds, Ricky	DB	5-11	190	5	Washington State
31	Rice, Rodney	DB	5-8	180	3	Brigham Young
90	Robertson, Derrell	DE	6-7	245	2	Mississippi State
30	Robinson, Mark	DB	5-11	200	8	Penn St.
3	Royals, Mark	P	6-5	215	2	Appalachian State
98	Seals, Ray	DE	6-3	270	2	None
71	Skow, Jim	DE	6-3	250	6	Nebraska
72	Taylor, Rob	OT	6-6	290	6	Northwestern
14	Testaverde, Vinny	QB	6-5	218	5	Miami
51	Thomas, Broderick	LB	6-4	245	3	Nebraska
86	Thomas, Ed	TE	6-3	235	2	Houston
50	Vargo, Ron	C	6-2	290	1	Indiana
91	White, Robb	DE	6-5	280	4	South Dakota

TOP DRAFT CHOICES

Rd.	Name	Sel. No.	Pos.	Ht.	Wt.	College
1	McRae, Charles	7	OT	6-7	290	Tennessee
3	Dawsey, Lawrence	66	WR	6-0	192	Florida State
3	Wilson, Robert	80	RB	6-0	240	Texas A&M
4	Covington, Tony	93	DB	5-10	189	Virginia
5	Bagsby, Terry	120	LB	6-0	235	East Texas State

BUCCANEER PROFILES

VINNY TESTAVERDE 27 6-5 218 Quarterback

Interceptions continue to plague this talented but erratic quarterback . . . Threw 18 interceptions in 1990 to give him 81 in four-year career . . . Threw just 55 TD passes in game span . . . Showed signs of improvement in 1990 and is still young enough to emerge as a quality quarterback . . . Passed for 2,818 yards and 17 TDs . . . Ran for career-high 280 yards, including 48-yard TD . . . Ranks second on Bucs' all-time list with 10,272 passing yards . . . Needs 2,376 to pass Doug Williams' club record . . . Set team record with 20 TD passes in 1989 . . . Threw an atrocious 35 interceptions in 1988 . . . Blamed much of his troubles on "color blindness" . . . Bucs' No. 1 pick (first overall) in 1987 out of Miami . . . 1986 Heisman Trophy winner . . . Born Nov. 13, 1963, in Brooklyn, N.Y. . . . 1990 base salary: $1.2 million.

BRODERICK THOMAS 24 6-4 245 Linebacker

Highly-touted linebacker began to make impact in 1990 . . . Set team record for linebackers with 7½ sacks . . . Also led team with 33 quarterback pressures . . . Made 72 tackles, including five for losses . . . Vastly improved in 1990 after disappointing rookie season . . . Sixth overall pick in the draft made little contribution to the Bucs in 1989 . . . Slowed by contract holdout and difficult adjustment to NFL game . . . No starts as a rookie . . . Made 27 tackles and two sacks . . . Consensus All-American at Nebraska . . . Nephew of Bears' linebacker Mike Singletary . . . Born Feb. 20, 1967, in Houston . . . 1990 base salary: $400,000.

KEITH McCANTS 22 6-3 255 Linebacker

Buccaneers expect big second season from this talented, inconsistent player . . . Started final four games as a rookie and began to display some of his potential . . . Finished with 44 tackles . . . Credited with two sacks and two forced fumbles . . . Combines with Broderick Thomas to give Bucs imposing pair of young outside linebackers . . . Pass-rushing potential has been likened to Lawrence Taylor and Derrick Thomas . . . Entered NFL draft after junior season at Alabama . . . Considered by many to be top collegiate defensive player in 1989 . . . Bucs made him the fourth overall pick in the draft . . . Born Nov. 19, 1968, in Mobile, Ala. . . . 1990 base salary: $450,000.

PAUL GRUBER 26 6-5 290 **Tackle**

Recognition is long overdue for this underrated player . . . Still looking for first Pro Bowl berth . . . Has started all 48 games of his three-year career . . . Cornerstone of Bucs' offensive line . . . Awards might start coming his way if Bucs ever start winning some games . . . Excels at both pass- and run-blocking . . . Was not penalized for holding during entire 1989 season (1,025 offensive plays) . . . All-rookie selection in 1988 . . . First lineman selected in 1988 draft (fourth overall pick) . . . Consensus All-American at Wisconsin . . . Born Feb. 24, 1965, in Madison, Wisc. . . . 1990 base salary: $475,000.

WAYNE HADDIX 26 6-1 200 **Defensive Back**

Capped remarkable 1990 season with Pro Bowl berth . . . Signed by the Bucs as a free agent after sitting out 1989 season . . . Released by the Giants on final cut in 1989 . . . Started all 16 games in 1990 for Bucs and led the team in interceptions with seven . . . Returned three interceptions for TDs, a team record . . . His 231 yards in interception returns was another team record . . . Never started a game in two seasons with the Giants . . . Used mostly on special teams . . . Undrafted after four-year career at Liberty Baptist . . . Division II All-American . . . Born July 23, 1965, in Bolivar, Tenn. . . . 1990 base salary: $90,000.

GARY ANDERSON 30 6-1 190 **Running Back**

Homecoming of sorts was a success for Anderson . . . Returned to Tampa, where he was a star in the USFL, and made big impact with Bucs in 1990 . . . Led team with 1,235 total yards . . . Scored five TDs . . . Ran for team-high 646 yards and caught 38 passes for another 464 yards . . . Also contributed 123 yards in kickoff-returns . . . Acquired by Bucs from San Diego in exchange for No. 3 draft pick in 1990 and conditional pick in 1991 . . . Sat out 1989 in contract dispute with Chargers

. . . Voted Chargers' MVP by teammates after rushing for 1,119 yards . . . Ran for career-high 219 yards in 1988 finale vs. Kansas City . . . Pro Bowler in 1986 . . . Rushed for 2,731 yards in three seasons with Tampa Bay Bandits of USFL . . . MVP of three bowl games at Arkansas . . . Born April 18, 1961, in Columbia, Mo. . . . 1990 base salary: $600,000.

REUBEN DAVIS 26 6-4 285 — Defensive End

Low-round draft pick continues to produce high marks for the Bucs . . . Set career high with 62 tackles in 1990 . . . Good run-defender is solid but unspectacular pass-rusher . . . Has started 44 of possible 48 games in his career . . . Identical totals of 61 tackles and three sacks in both 1988 and 1989 . . . A ninth-round find by the Bucs in 1988 out of North Carolina . . . Four-year starter was downgraded by pro scouts . . . Has degree in journalism . . . Born May 7, 1965, in Greensboro, N.C. . . . 1990 base salary: $300,000.

RON HALL 27 6-4 245 — Tight End

Gradually gaining notice as one of the NFL's better tight ends . . . Caught 31 passes for 464 yards and two TDs in 1990 . . . His 15-yard-per-catch average was impressive for a tight end . . . Also regarded as an outstanding blocker . . . Named All-Pro by *Sports Illustrated* . . . Nicknamed "Ironman" for mental and physical toughness . . . A starter since 1988 . . . An even 100 receptions in last three seasons . . . Bucs' fourth-round pick in 1987 out of Hawaii . . . Walked on "hot coals" to improve concentration in college, not once but three times . . . Born March 15, 1964, in Ft. Huachuca, Ariz. . . . 1990 base salary: $275,000.

BRUCE HILL 27 6-0 180 — Wide Receiver

Smooth receiver led the Bucs with five TD catches in 1990 . . . Ranked second on team in total catches with 42 and receiving yards with 641 . . . Teams with Mark Carrier to form potent wide-receiver combination . . . Best season was 1988 with 58 receptions, 1,040 yards and nine TDs . . . Caught 50 passes for 673 yards and five TDs in 1989 . . . Bucs' fourth-round pick in 1987 out of Arizona State . . . Born on leap day, he has celebrated just six actual "birthdays," with the latest in 1988 . . . Degree in criminal justice . . . Born Feb. 29, 1964, in Fort Dix, N.J. . . . 1990 base salary: $350,000.

MARK CARRIER 25 6-0 182 **Wide Receiver**

Bucs are looking for his talented wide receiver to regain his 1989 form . . . Severe drop in production in 1990 . . . Still led team with 49 catches, 813 receiving yards . . . Statistics paled compared to his production in 1989, when he set team records for catches (86) and yards (1,422) . . . Named to Pro Bowl in 1989 . . . Ranks third on Bucs' all-time list in receiving yards with 3,628 and is fifth in catches with 218 . . . Caught 57 passes for 970 yards in 1988 . . . Bucs' third-round pick in 1987 out of Nicholls State . . . Distant cousin of Bears' safety Mark Carrier . . . Born Oct. 28, 1965, in Lafayette, La. . . . 1990 base salary: $650,000.

COACH RICHARD WILLIAMSON: Replaced the fired

Ray Perkins and served as interim coach for final three games of 1990 season . . . Appointed head coach Feb. 4, 1991 . . . Team went 1-2 under his direction in final three games . . . Spent four seasons as Buccaneers' receivers coach . . . Popular with players, his positive approach will be a dramatic change from the grim Perkins . . . Previous head-coaching experience with Memphis State from 1975-80 . . . Went 31-35 in six years with the Tigers . . . An NFL assistant in Kansas City (1983-86) before joining Buccaneers . . . Flip-flopped between Alabama (1963-67, 1970-71) and Arkansas (1968-69, 1972-74) in 12 years as college assistant coach . . . Played wide receiver and defensive back under Bear Bryant at Alabama . . . Played on 1961 national championship team . . . Spent two years in early 1980s as executive director of Bluebonnet Bowl . . . Born April 13, 1941, in Ft. Deposit, Ala.

GREATEST PUNTER

The mid-1980s was a difficult time for the Buccaneers, but one source of solace was the consistency of punter Frank Garcia. Garcia punted for Tampa Bay from 1983 through 1987. The Buccaneers won just 16 games in those five seasons and never produced a winning record.

Garcia was a bright spot, though. He led the NFC with a 42.2 average in 1983 and his career average of 41.3 yards is a team record.

Garcia also holds Buccaneer records for total punts (379) and yardage (15,588).

INDIVIDUAL BUCCANEER RECORDS

Rushing

Most Yards Game:	219	James Wilder, vs Minnesota, 1983
Season:	1,544	James Wilder, 1984
Career:	5,957	James Wilder, 1981-89

Passing

Most TD Passes Game:	5	Steve DeBerg, vs Atlanta, 1987
Season:	20	2 times, most recently Vinny Testaverde, 1989
Career:	73	Doug Williams, 1978-82

Receiving

Most TD Passes Game:	4	Jimmie Giles, vs Miami, 1985
Season:	9	3 times, most recently Mark Carrier, 1989
Career:	34	Jimmie Giles, 1978-86

Scoring

Most Points Game:	24	Jimmie Giles, vs Miami, 1985
Season:	99	Donald Igwebuike, 1989
Career:	416	Donald Igwebuike, 1985-89
Most TDs Game:	4	Jimmie Giles, vs Miami, 1985
Season:	13	James Wilder, 1984
Career:	43	James Wilder, 1981-89

WASHINGTON REDSKINS

TEAM DIRECTORY: Chairman/CEO: Jack Kent Cooke; Exec. VP: John Kent Cooke; GM: Charley Casserly; Asst. GM: Bobby Mitchell; Dir. Pro Scouting: Joe Mack; Dir. Pro Player Personnel: Kirk Mee; Dir. College Scouting: George Saimes; VP-Communications: Charlie Dayton; Dir. Information: Jamie Crittenberger; Dir. Media Rel.: Mike McCall; Head Coach: Joe Gibbs. Home field: Robert F. Kennedy Stadium (55,672). Colors: Burgundy and gold.

SCOUTING REPORT

OFFENSE: Inconsistency is quarterback Mark Rypien's biggest problem. When he's hot, he's one of the NFL's best. When he's not, he's a turnover waiting to happen.

Coach Joe Gibbs tries to ease the pressure on Rypien with a big, burly offensive line and increased emphasis on the ground game. Sometimes, it works. Sometimes, a quarterback has to make plays.

Rypien has plenty of targets in wide receivers Art Monk, Gary Clark and Ricky Sanders. They might not be as productive as they once were, but "The Posse" still ranks among the toughest trios in football.

Earnest Byner emerged as the 10-6 Redskins' feature running back last year. He can run, block and catch. Gerald Riggs is an excellent reserve, ideally suited for the Redskins' power formations.

The offensive line came together late in the year. Age is a concern but the Redskins have a star in his prime in tackle Jim Lachey and a potential star in Mohammed Elewonibi.

DEFENSE: An unselfish, disciplined defense was the key to the Redskins' return to the playoffs in 1990. They could be even better this year.

Washington has a deep, versatile defensive line. End Charles Mann is the closest thing to a star. Tackles Eric Williams and Tim Johnson were acquired last year and made a difference. Tackles Darryl Grant, Tracy Rocker and James Geathers and ends Fred Stokes and Markus Koch are solid situational players.

Outside linebacker Wilber Marshall has finally adjusted to the Redskins' system. Andre Collins started every game as a rookie.

Kurt Gouveia is the incumbent at middle linebacker but Plan B free agent Matt Millen is expected to make an impact.

Darrell Green remains one of the NFL's best cornerbacks. Alvin Walton is a hitter at strong safety but the Redskins are looking for a change at free safety and could turn to Plan B free agent Terry Hoage.

Earnest Byner's 1,000-yard season led to first Pro Bowl.

REDSKINS VETERAN ROSTER

HEAD COACH—Joe Gibbs. Assistant Coaches—Don Breau, Jack Burns, Bobby DePaul, Rod Dowhower, Jim Hanifan, Larry Peccatiello, Richie Petitbon, Dan Riley, Wayne Sevier, Rennie Simmons, Charlie Taylor, Emmitt Thomas, Torgy Torgeson, Steve Wetzel.

No.	Name	Pos.	Ht.	Wt.	NFL Exp.	College
61	Adickes, Mark	G	6-4	275	6	Baylor
53	Bostic, Jeff	C	6-2	260	12	Clemson
82	Brandes, John	TE	6-2	250	5	Cameron (Okla.)
67	Brown, Ray	T	6-5	280	5	Arkansas State
21	Byner, Earnest	RB	5-10	215	8	East Carolina
50	Caldwell, Ravin	LB	6-3	229	5	Arkansas
84	Clark, Gary	WR	5-9	173	7	James Madison
51	Coleman, Monte	LB	6-2	230	13	Central Arkansas
55	Collins, Andre	LB	6-1	230	2	Penn State
12	Conklin, Cary	QB	6-4	215	1	Washington
26	Copeland, Danny	SS	6-2	210	3	Eastern Kentucky
27	Edwards, Brad	FS	6-2	196	4	South Carolina
64	Elewonibi, Mo	T	6-4	282	1	Brigham Young
97	Geathers, James	DT	6-7	290	7	Wichita State
2	Goodburn, Kelly	P	6-2	202	5	Emporia State
54	Gouveia, Kurt	LB	6-1	227	5	Brigham Young
77	Grant, Darryl	DT	6-1	275	11	Rice
28	Green, Darrell	CB	5-8	170	9	Texas A&I
68	Grimm, Russ	G	6-3	275	11	Pittsburgh
90	Harry, Carl	WR	5-9	170	1	Utah
34	Hoage, Terry	FS	6-2	201	8	Georgia
86	Hobbs, Stephen	WR	5-11	195	2	North Alabama
80	Howard, Joe	WR	5-8	170	3	Notre Dame
16	Humphries, Stan	QB	6-2	223	3	NE Louisiana
66	Jacoby, Joe	G	6-7	310	11	Louisville
47	Johnson, AJ	CB	5-8	176	3	SW Texas State
88	Johnson, Jimmie	TE	6-2	246	3	Howard
45	Johnson, Sidney	CB	5-9	175	3	California
78	Johnson, Tim	DT	6-3	261	5	Penn State
74	Koch, Markus	DE	6-5	275	6	Boise State
79	Lachey, Jim	T	6-6	290	7	Ohio State
56	Leverenz, Jon	LB	6-2	230	1	Minnesota
8	Lohmiller, Chip	K	6-3	213	4	Minnesota
71	Mann, Charles	DE	6-6	270	9	Nevada-Reno
58	Marshall, Wilber	LB	6-1	230	8	Florida
35	Mayhew, Martin	CB	5-8	172	3	Florida State
20	Mays, Alvoid	CB	5-9	180	2	West Virginia
63	McKenzie, Raleigh	C-G	6-2	270	7	Tennessee
87	Middleton, Ron	TE	6-2	255	6	Auburn
57	Millen, Matt	LB	6-2	245	12	Penn State
30	Mitchell, Brian	RB	5-10	195	2	SW Louisiana
81	Monk, Art	WR	6-3	209	12	Syracuse
92	Rayam, Thomas	DE	6-6	285	1	Alabama
37	Riggs, Gerald	RB	6-1	232	10	Arizona State
99	Rocker, Tracy	DT	6-3	288	3	Auburn
10	Rutledge, Jeff	QB	6-1	195	13	Alabama
11	Rypien, Mark	QB	6-4	234	5	Washington State
83	Sanders, Ricky	WR	5-11	180	6	SW Texas State
69	Schlereth, Mark	G	6-3	285	3	Idaho
23	Settle, John	RB	5-9	210	5	Appalachian State
76	Simmons, Ed	T	6-5	300	6	E. Washington
89	Stanley, Walter	WR	5-9	180	7	Mesa
60	Stokes, Fred	DE	6-3	262	5	Georgia Southern
31	Vaughn, Clarence	SS	6-0	200	4	Northern Illinois
40	Walton, Alvin	SS	6-0	180	6	Kansas
85	Warren, Don	TE	6-4	242	13	San Diego State
48	Whisenhunt, Ken	TE	6-3	240	5	Georgia Tech
75	Williams, Eric	DT	6-4	286	8	Washington State

TOP DRAFT CHOICES

Rd.	Name	Sel. No.	Pos.	Ht.	Wt.	College
1	Wilson, Bobby	17	DT	6-2	276	Michigan State
3	Ervins, Ricky	76	RB	5-7	200	Southern California
6	Ransom, Dennis	159	TE	6-3	248	Texas A&M
7	Cash, Keith	188	TE	6-4	215	Texas
8	Spencer, Jimmy	215	DB	5-9	180	Florida

SPECIAL TEAMS: Kicker Chip Lohmiller is one of the NFL's best. He made his final nine field-goal attempts in the regular season and his final 20 attempts from inside 50 yards. Punting is a concern. Kelly Goodburn replaced Ralf Mojsiejenko at midseason and averaged just 36.8 yards. Improvement is needed.

The coverage teams are solid, but the Redskins would like more production from return men Walter Stanley and Joe Howard.

THE ROOKIES: A No. 1 pick was something new for the Redskins. They used their first since 1983 to select Michigan State defensive tackle Bobby Wilson, an all-out hustler who is a punishing inside charger. Southern Cal's Ricky Ervins adds depth at running back.

OUTLOOK: The Redskins have passed the Eagles and rank as the NFC East's second-best team, behind the Giants. They have the talent and coaching to win the division. but they need to find a way to finally beat the Giants in head-to-head matchups.

REDSKIN PROFILES

DARRELL GREEN 31 5-8 170 — Cornerback

Key man in Redskins' disciplined defense . . . Plays man-to-man coverage against opponent's best receiver . . . Bounced back from injury-shortened 1989 season to lead Redskins in passes defended (17) and rank second in interceptions (4) in 1990 . . . Excelled in playoff victory over Philadelphia as Redskins held Eagles' wide receivers to a total of one catch for nine yards . . . Has twice won "NFL's Fastest Man" competition . . . Used occasionally as a punt-returner, he has a career average of better than 11 yards and clinched a 1987 playoff victory over Chicago with a 52-yard return for TD . . . Has been a starter since first game of rookie season . . . Redskins' No. 1 draft pick from tiny Texas A&I in 1983 . . . Born Feb. 15, 1960, in Houston . . . 1990 base salary: $725,000.

WILBER MARSHALL 29 6-1 230 **Linebacker**

Big-play man continued to grow more comfortable in Redskins' defensive scheme . . . Ranked third on team in tackles with 106 and fourth in sacks with five . . . Also forced three fumbles . . . Heralded free agent signed by the Redskins in March 1988, at the cost of two No. 1 draft picks, after spending four seasons in Chicago . . . Impact limited by demands of Redskins' disciplined defense . . . Made Pro Bowl twice with the Bears . . . Chicago's No. 1 pick out of Florida in 1984 . . . One of 12 children . . . Born April 18, 1962, in Titusville, Fla. . . . 1990 base salary: $1.1 million.

EARNEST BYNER 28 5-10 215 **Running Back**

Ranked fourth in NFL with career-high 1,219 rushing yards . . . Named to first Pro Bowl . . . Became Redskins' workhorse back in his second season with the team . . . Terrific down the stretch with five 100-yard rushing performances in final seven games . . . Also caught 31 passes . . . Acquired by Redskins from Cleveland in exchange for running back Mike Oliphant April 22, 1989 . . . Rushed for 1,002 yards and caught 45 passes for the Browns in 1985 . . . Browns' 10th-round draft pick in 1984 out of East Carolina . . . Born Sept. 15, 1962, in Milledgeville, Ga. . . . 1990 base salary: $535,000.

RALEIGH McKENZIE 28 6-2 270 **Guard**

Versatile performer has played four offensive-line positions for Redskins . . . Settled in at left guard last season . . . Helped Redskins reestablish strong running game . . . Has quickness and agility to pull and handle defender in Redskins' famous counter-gap play . . . In the first eight weeks of 1989, filled in for four different former Pro Bowl players at four different spots . . . Played guard and center in 1988 . . . Only Redskins' offensive lineman to play every play in 1987 . . . Made the team as an unheralded 11th-round draft pick from Tennessee in 1985 . . . Twin brother Reggie is a linebacker for the Cardinals . . . Graduated third in high-school class . . . Born Feb. 8, 1963, in Knoxville, Tenn. . . . 1990 base salary: $325,000.

MARK RYPIEN 28 6-4 234 **Quarterback**

Missed six games with leg injuries . . . Redskins went 7-3 in regular-season games he started and scored impressive playoff victory at Philadelphia . . . Avoided mistakes and threw two TD passes in playoff victory over Eagles . . . Passed for 2,070 yards and 16 TDs in regular season . . . Was sacked just six times . . . Slumped briefly upon return from injury but bounced back at end of season . . . Distributed football well, as three Redskins' wide receivers combined for 199 catches . . . Redskins' sixth-round pick in 1986 out of Washington State . . . Spent first two years on injured-reserve list . . . Excellent golfer . . . Born Oct. 2, 1962, in Calgary, Alberta . . . 1990 base salary: $275,000.

JIM LACHEY 28 6-6 290 **Offensive Tackle**

Key man on Redskins' dominating offensive line . . . Handles NFL's best pass-rushers . . . Strong blocking enabled Redskins to re-establish running game in 1990 . . . Started all 16 games and both playoff games . . . Named to Pro Bowl . . . Acquired by Redskins from Raiders in exchange for Jay Schroeder on Sept. 3, 1988 . . . Spent only six weeks with Raiders, who acquired him from San Diego in a trade just before 1988 training camp . . . San Diego's No. 1 pick out of Ohio State in 1985 . . . Best man at wedding was quarterback Mike Tomczak, a teammate at Ohio State . . . Born June 4, 1963, in St. Henry, Ohio . . . 1990 base salary: $725,000.

ART MONK 33 6-3 209 **Wide Receiver**

The old man of Redskins' receiving corps kept rolling along with 68 receptions in 1990 . . . Moved into third place on NFL's all-time list with 730 career receptions . . . Needs 20 to pass Charlie Joiner for second place and 87 to pass Steve Largent for top spot . . . Has caught a pass in 116 consecutive regular-season games . . . Started all 16 games in 1990 . . . Caught TD pass in playoff victory over Philadelphia . . . Quiet player who tends to avoid interviews . . . Set NFL single-season record with 106 receptions in 1984 . . . Redskins' No. 1 pick out of Syracuse in 1980 . . . Born Dec. 5, 1957, in White Plains, N.Y. . . . 1990 base salary: $900,000.

GARY CLARK 29 5-9 173 **Wide Receiver**

Led Redskins in receptions (75), receiving yards (1,112) and TD catches (8) in 1990 . . . Topped 1,000-yard mark for fourth time in six-year NFL career . . . Excels at catching ball over middle despite diminutive stature . . . Never has caught fewer than 56 passes in NFL season . . . Has 415 receptions in career . . . A regular on the "All-Madden Team" . . . Played two years for Jacksonville Bulls of USFL . . . Signed by Redskins as a free agent on May 13, 1985 . . . All-time leading receiver at James Madison University . . . Born May 1, 1962, in Dublin, Va. . . . 1990 base salary: $650,000.

RICKY SANDERS 29 5-11 180 **Wide Receiver**

Production dropped off to 56 catches after making 80 in 1989 . . . Also failed to crack 1,000-yard barrier for first time since 1987 . . . Still generated 727 yards and three TDs . . . Big-play man in Redskins' posse of three excellent wide receivers . . . Named team MVP in 1988 after catching 73 passes for 1,148 yards and 12 TDs . . . Caught nine passes for 193 yards and two TDs in Super Bowl XXII . . . Played for Houston Gamblers of USFL . . . Caught 104 passes for Gamblers in 1984 . . . Redskins acquired his rights from New England in exchange for third-round pick in 1987 . . . Signed with Washington on Aug. 11, 1986 . . . A running back at Southwest Texas State . . . Born Aug. 30, 1962, in Temple, Tex. . . . 1990 base salary: $650,000.

MATT MILLEN 33 6-2 245 **Linebacker**

Vocal, emotional player is expected to step into the Redskins' starting lineup as middle linebacker . . . Signed as Plan B free agent in March after two seasons with San Francisco . . . Ranked fourth on 49ers in tackles in 1990 with 62 . . . Great run-defender . . . Long-time leader of the Oakland/Los Angeles Raiders defense . . . Spent nine seasons with the Raiders . . . Pro Bowler in 1988 . . . Drafted by Raiders in the second round in 1980 out of Penn State . . . Four-year starter for Nittany Lions . . . Born March 12, 1958, in Hokendauqua, Pa.

CHARLES MANN 30 6-6 270 **Defensive End**

Regarded as one of best defensive ends in football . . . Perennial Pro Bowler . . . Registered 5½ sacks in 1990 and led Redskins with 23 quarterback hurries . . . All-around player who defends run as well as rushing passer . . . Has 65½ sacks in eight seasons . . . Hosted his own local radio show in offseason . . . Redskins' third-round draft choice out of Nevada-Reno in 1983 . . . Born April 12, 1961, in Sacramento, Cal. . . . 1990 base salary: $800,000.

COACH JOE GIBBS: Led Redskins into the playoffs for the sixth time in his 10 seasons . . . Owns a 101-51 regular-season record . . . His 12-4 playoff record is tops among all active coaches and third on all-time list . . . The fourth-winningest active NFL coach, behind only Don Shula, Chuck Noll and Chuck Knox . . . Intense competitor prides himself on hard work and preparation . . . Frequently sleeps in his office during the season . . . Has led Redskins to two Super Bowl titles and three NFC championships . . . Played tight end at San Diego State, where he began coaching career under Don Coryell . . . NFL assistant at St. Louis, Tampa Bay and San Diego before being named Redskins' head coach in 1981 . . . National champion racquetball player (35-and-over) in 1976 . . . Born Nov. 25, 1940, in Mocksville, N.C.

GREATEST PUNTER

The player who might have been the greatest passer in Redskins' history also might have been the team's greatest punter.

"Slingin" Sammy Baugh was better known for his arm. He holds the team record for career TD passes (187) and once completed 70.3 percent of his passes in a season (1945). But Baugh made his mark with his leg, too. In 1940, Baugh averaged an NFL-record 51.4 yards per punt. He averaged 48.7 the next year.

His 45.1 average over a 16-year career is tops in Redskin history.

Baugh also set a still-standing Redskin record with an 85-yard punt against the Eagles in 1940.

INDIVIDUAL REDSKIN RECORDS

Rushing

Most Yards Game:	221	Gerald Riggs, vs Philadelphia, 1989
Season:	1,347	John Riggins, 1983
Career:	7,472	John Riggins, 1976-79, 1981-85

Passing

Most TD Passes Game:	6	2 times, most recently Sammy Baugh, vs St. Louis, 1947
Season:	31	Sonny Jurgensen, 1967
Career:	187	Sammy Baugh, 1937-52

Receiving

Most TD Passes Game:	3	14 times, most recently Art Monk, vs Indianapolis, 1984
Season:	12	4 times, most recently Ricky Sanders, 1988
Career:	79	Charley Taylor, 1964-77

Scoring

Most Points Game:	24	2 times, most recently Larry Brown, vs Philadelphia, 1973
Season:	161	Mark Moseley, 1983
Career:	1,176	Mark Moseley, 1974-85
Most TDs Game:	4	2 times, most recently Larry Brown, vs Philadelphia, 1973
Season:	24	John Riggins, 1983
Career:	90	Charley Taylor, 1964-77

Speedy Darrell Green burns the receivers.

INSIDE THE AFC

By KEVIN MANNIX and JOHN CLAYTON

PREDICTED ORDER OF FINISH

EAST	CENTRAL	WEST
Buffalo	Houston	L.A. Raiders
Miami	Cincinnati	Kansas City
N.Y. Jets	Pittsburgh	Denver
Indianapolis	Cleveland	Seattle
New England		San Diego

AFC Champion: Buffalo

Potential gave way to productivity for the Bills in 1990. Instead of being a "talented but troubled" team, Buffalo turned from bickering with each other to bashing opponents and wound up winning the AFC title.

Even their Super Bowl loss to the Giants provided reason for hope in 1991. They took the best the Giants could offer and came within a missed last-second field goal of winning it all.

Some teams, like the Patriots in 1985, get to the Super Bowl and then disappear. Others, like the Broncos and Bengals, use losing Super Bowls as springboards to future appearances. So what if they didn't win the big one? They got there again. The Bills should follow their lead this year. They've always had the talent. Now they have become the AFC's preeminent team.

Miami should again provide the Bills with their biggest challenge in the East. The Dolphins' defense rested against the Bills

---

Kevin Mannix of the Boston Herald *follows the Patriots and John Clayton of the* Seattle Morning News Tribune *has the Seahawk beat. Mannix wrote the AFC East and the introduction after consultation with Clayton, who did the Central and the West.*

in the playoffs, but prior to that had an unexpectedly successful season. And with Dan Marino throwing to the Marks Brothers and rookie Randal Hill and Sammie Smith running behind Richmond Webb et al, the offense will again do its share.

The Jets still have a shaky offensive line but they have some big-play people who will allow them to win more than they lose.

In Indianapolis, the Colts have their first two-dimensional offense. Like the Jets, however, they have an offensive line that could make Jeff George old before his time. Eric Dickerson and Albert Bentley will be used together more this year than in the past and if Dickerson still wants to play, the Colts could surprise.

New England has a new coach in Dick MacPherson but the same old problems—no established quarterback and no chemistry. They'll win more than one game but it's hard to see them winning more than five.

If the Bills do stumble, look for the Oilers to be the AFC representative. They adapted to Jack Pardee's version of the Run-n'-Shoot very well at the end of last year. If Warren Moon hadn't broken the thumb on his throwing hand late in the year, they would have been a legitimate contender.

Cincinnati has Boomer Esiason and Brooksie and Munoz and Brown. It also has familiar defensive problems. Besides, the Bengals are not getting any younger.

The Steelers are also one-dimensional. Their defense was the best in the league last year but the offense languished at the bottom of the standings. The key is Bubby Brister.

Cleveland is the Central's version of the Patriots, an old team that has developed a penchant for losing. Bill Belichick will instill some Bill Parcells-style discipline and defense but the Browns are woefully weak up front.

The Raiders caught the Chiefs at the end of the 1990 season to win the AFC West. Art Shell taught them how to win again and maybe Plan B vets Ronnie Lott and Roger Craig can instill some of the 49er touch to get them to the next step.

The Chiefs relied on the running of Barry Word and Christian Okoye, the big plays of Steve DeBerg, the NFL's oldest quarterback, and an NFL-best giveaway-takeaway ratio (plus-26) to get to the playoffs. The defense will probably be at least as good this year but can the Chiefs catch the Raiders?

Denver, Seattle and San Diego are similar teams on a lower level than the Raiders and Chiefs. But if one team could surprise people, it could be Denver.

The real surprise, however, will be if Buffalo doesn't shuffle to the Super Bowl again.

BUFFALO BILLS

TEAM DIRECTORY: Pres.: Ralph Wilson; GM/VP-Administration: Bill Polian; Dir. Pro Personnel: Bob Ferguson; Mgr. Media Rel.: Scott Berchtold; Dir. Pub. and Community Rel.: Denny Lynch; Head Coach: Marv Levy. Home field: Rich Stadium (80,290). Colors: Scarlet red, royal blue and white.

SCOUTING REPORT

OFFENSE: The dynasty has begun. By the end of the season, the Bills had become a monster offensively, thanks to Jim Kelly's

Thurman Thomas had most NFL yardage (1,829) in 1990.

play in the no-huddle offense. They finished the season with a league-high 428 points, won the AFC championship and came within a missed field goal in the final seconds of winning the Super Bowl.

This is clearly the team to beat in the AFC. They've got the quarterback/leader. They've got the elusive running back in Thurman Thomas, arguably the best all-purpose back in the league. Fullback Jamie Mueller is a throwback to football of the 50s, an excellent lead blocker for Thomas.

The offensive line is as good as it is unheralded, dominating the line of scrimmage and protecting Kelly. Kent Hull is the NFL's best center and both Will Wolford and Howard Ballard are Pro Bowl-quality tackles. Second-year man John Davis provided unexpected strength at guard.

The receivers, led by Andre Reed and James Lofton, give Kelly the sure-handed, fleet targets he needs to make the no-hurry effective. Tight end Keith McKeller is an exceptional receiver, even on deeper patterns.

DEFENSE: Surprisingly, the one area where the Bills could use some improvement is on the defensive line. The champion Giants were able to neutralize the Bills' offense by keeping them on the sidelines via a dominating ground game that pushed the Bills' defensive line around. Bruce Smith holds his ground, but the rest of the three-man front needs to get bigger and more physical.

With Darryl Talley, Shane Conlan and Cornelius Bennett, the Bills have as good a corps of linebackers as there is in the league.

In the secondary, cornerbacks Nate Odomes and J.D Williams are solid but strong safety Leonard Smith is a liability in pass-coverage. The Bills hoped to remedy that with their first draft pick, Illinois safety Henry Jones.

SPECIAL TEAMS: Scott Norwood is coming back, looking to make amends for his missed field goal at the end of the Super Bowl. But his place on the roster is not secure, and not just because of his miss. Norwood ranked last among AFC field-goal kickers in terms of length of misses and conversions. His field goals averaged 34.2 yards. Rick Tuten was also at the lower echelon among AFC punters, so that area has to be improved.

Al Edwards is a strong kick-returner but after him there is a deep drop in the talent level.

THE ROOKIES: In an effort to upgrade the secondary, the Bills moved quickly, using three of their first four choices on DBs,

BILLS VETERAN ROSTER

HEAD COACH—Marv Levy. Assistant Coaches—Tom Bresnahan, Walt Corey, Bruce DeHaven, Chuck Dickerson, Rusty Jones, Don Lawrence, Chuck Lester, Ted Marchibroda, Nick Nicolau, Elijah Pitts, Dick Roach.

No.	Name	Pos.	Ht.	Wt.	NFL Exp.	College
54	Bailey, Carlton	LB	6-2	237	4	North Carolina
92	Baldinger, Gary	NT	6-3	270	5	Wake Forest
75	Ballard, Howard	T	6-6	315	4	Alabama A&M
52	Bavaro, David	LB	6-0	235	2	Syracuse
82	Beebe, Don	WR	5-11	177	3	Chadron State
97	Bennett, Cornelius	LB	6-2	238	5	Alabama
50	Bentley, Ray	LB	6-2	235	6	Central Michigan
81	Burton, Leonard	C	6-3	277	5	South Carolina
58	Conlan, Shane	LB	6-3	235	5	Penn State
65	Davis, John	T	6-4	310	5	Georgia Tech
23	Davis, Kenneth	RB	5-10	209	6	Texas Christian
45	Drane, Dwight	SS	6-2	205	6	Oklahoma
85	Edwards, Al	WR	5-8	188	2	NW Louisiana State
59	Frerotte, Mitch	G	6-3	280	3	Penn State
33	Fuller, Eddie	RB	5-9	199	1	Louisiana State
35	Gardner, Carwell	FB	6-2	235	2	Louisville
99	Garner, Hal	LB	6-4	235	5	Utah State
7	Gilbert, Gale	QB	6-3	210	4	California-Berkeley
81	Glover, Deval	WR	5-11	184	1	Syracuse
93	Haggins, Odell	NT	6-2	275	1	Florida State
26	Hale, Chris	CB	5-7	161	3	USC
27	Hicks, Clifford	CB	5-10	188	5	Oregon
67	Hull, Kent	C	6-4	275	6	Mississippi State
47	Jackson, Kirby	CB	5-10	180	5	Mississippi State
12	Kelly, Jim	QB	6-3	218	6	Miami (Fla.)
38	Kelso, Mark	FS	5-11	185	6	William & Mary
63	Lingner, Adam	C	6-4	268	9	Illinois
73	Lodish, Mike	NT	6-3	260	2	UCLA
80	Lofton, James	WR	6-3	190	14	Stanford
42	Manuel, Lionel	WR	5-11	180	8	Pacific
84	McKeller, Keith	TE	6-4	245	4	Jacksonville State
88	Melzelaars, Pete	TE	6-7	250	10	Wabash
57	Monger, Matt	LB	6-1	235	6	Oklahoma State
41	Mueller, Jamie	FB	6-1	230	5	Benedictine
11	Norwood, Scott	K	6-0	207	7	James Madison
37	Odomes, Nate	CB	5-10	188	5	Wisconsin
74	Parker, Glenn	G	6-5	301	2	Arizona
26	Paterra, Greg	FB	5-11	220	3	Slippery Rock
53	Patton, Marvcus	LB	6-2	216	2	UCLA
94	Pike, Mark	DE	6-4	272	5	Georgia Tech
29	Pool, David	CB	5-9	188	2	Carson-Newman
83	Reed, Andre	WR	6-2	190	7	Kutztown State
14	Reich, Frank	QB	6-4	210	7	Maryland
51	Ritcher, Jim	G	6-3	273	12	North Carolina State
77	Rogers, Reggie	DE	6-6	280	2	Washington
87	Rolle, Butch	TE	6-4	245	6	Michigan State
96	Seals, Leon	DE	6-5	267	5	Jackson State
25	Smiley, Tim	SS	6-0	190	1	Arkansas State
78	Smith, Bruce	DE	6-4	275	7	Virginia Tech
46	Smith, Leonard	SS	5-11	202	9	McNeese State
79	Staysniak, Joe	T	6-5	295	1	Ohio State
56	Talley, Darryl	LB	6-4	235	9	West Virginia
89	Tasker, Steve	WR	5-9	185	7	Northwestern
21	Taylor, Brian	CB	5-10	195	3	Oregon State
34	Thomas, Thurman	RB	5-10	198	4	Oklahoma State
24	Tucker, Brett	SS	5-11	195	2	Northern Illinois
86	Turner, Vernon	WR	5-8	185	2	Carson-Newman
10	Tuten, Rick	P	6-2	218	3	Florida State
31	Williams, James	CB	5-10	172	2	Fresno State
69	Wolford, Will	T	6-5	290	6	Vanderbilt
91	Wright, Jeff	NT	6-2	270	4	Central Missouri State
30	Young, Brett	FS	5-10	195	1	Oregon

TOP DRAFT CHOICES

Rd.	Name	Sel. No.	Pos.	Ht.	Wt.	College
1	Jones, Henry	26	CB	6-0	187	Illinois
2	Hansen, Phil	54	DE	6-5	258	North Dakota State
3	Wren, Darryl	82	DB	6-0	186	Pittsburgh State
5	Wilbourn, Shawn	138	DB	6-3	205	Cal State-Long Beach
6	Hamilton, Millard	166	WR	5-10	180	Clark

headed by Jones and Pittsburgh State's Darryl Wren. DE Phil Hanson, a second-rounder from North Dakota State, is a dominating pass-rusher.

OUTLOOK: They've learned how to avoid beating themselves and they showed their toughness in the Super Bowl. Between those attributes and the physical talent, Marv Levy's team is odds-on choice to repeat as AFC champion.

BILL PROFILES

JIM KELLY 31 6-3 218 Quarterback

He was the highest-rated quarterback in the league (101.2) and he got the Bills to the Super Bowl, but no ring . . . Missed the last two regular-season games with a knee injury and came back to soar in the playoffs against the Dolphins and the Raiders . . . Threw 24 touchdown passes and only nine interceptions in the regular season . . . Added five touchdown passes and two interceptions in the playoffs . . . A product of the University of Miami, he was the third quarterback chosen on the first round in 1983 (after John Elway and Todd Blackledge) . . . Played two years with the Houston Gamblers in the USFL before joining the Bills . . . Second to Jack Kemp among Bills' quarterbacks in career completions and yards . . . Born Feb. 14, 1960, in Pittsburgh . . . Was paid $3.3 million in 1990 for the first year in a six-year pact that guarantees him $1.4 million in base salary each year.

THURMAN THOMAS 25 5-10 198 Running Back

You could make a legitimate case for his being the NFL's MVP last year . . . He led the league in total yards for the second straight season, with 1,829 yards . . . Gained 1,297 yards on 272 rushes, a 4.8 average . . . Caught 49 passes for 532 yards, nearly an 11-yard average . . . He's been voted to the Pro Bowl the last two years and was a starter last year . . Rushed for over 100 yards five times last year, including 154 yards on 30 carries against the Dolphins with Kelly out and the Bills needing a victory to clinch the AFC East . . . The most valuable Bill in the Super Bowl . . . A second-round pick out of Oklahoma State in 1988 . . . Born April 16, 1966, in Houston . . . 1990 salary: $600,000.

ANDRE REED 27 6-2 190 **Wide Receiver**

The Bills' all-time leading receiver with 348 catches, he's been voted to three straight Pro Bowls . . . Led the Bills in receptions for the fifth straight year with 71 catches for 945 yards, including eight touchdowns . . . A fourth-round selection in 1985, he earned $425,000 last year, the first year of a new contract that will average $1.16 million, including a $500,000 signing bonus . . . He's had 10 multi-touchdown games in his career and now has 39 TDs, passing Elbert "Golden Wheels" Dubenion as the Bills' highest-scoring wide receiver . . . Born Jan. 29, 1964, in Allentown, Pa.

KENT HULL 30 6-4 275 **Center**

The mainstay of the Bills' offensive line . . . He was signed as a free agent out of the USFL in 1986 and has started 76 consecutive games since joining the NFL . . . Been voted to the Pro Bowl for four straight years . . . Blocked for Herschel Walker with the New Jersey Generals, who selected him on the seventh round of the 1983 USFL draft . . . His father, Charles, is the Director of Agriculture for the state of Mississippi . . . They raise brood cows on a 350-acre farm in Greenwood, Miss. . . . Born Jan. 13, 1961, in Ponotoc, Miss., and played at Mississippi State, 80 miles from his home . . . 1990 salary: $400,000.

JAMES LOFTON 35 6-3 190 **Wide Receiver**

He provided the perfect complement to Andre Reed on the outside and averaged 20.3 yards on his 35 catches . . . He has 642 catches in his 13 NFL seasons, putting him second to Art Monk among active receivers and sixth on the all-time list . . . His 11,889 yards put him in third place among the NFL's all-time list in that category . . . Now in his third decade as a receiver, he entered the league as the Packers' first-round pick in 1978. Was with the Packers through 1986 before being traded to the Raiders . . . Joined the Bills in 1989 as a free agent . . . Played for Bill Walsh at Stanford, where he was also a three-time All-American in track . . . Born July 5, 1956, in Fort Ord, Cal. . . . 1990 salary: $525,000.

CORNELIUS BENNETT 25 6-2 238 Linebacker

Obtained in 1987 in the Mother of All NFL Trades. The deal sent Eric Dickerson to the Colts, a hatful of draft choices to the Rams and Bennett to the Bills . . . He was the Colts' first pick (second player overall) in the 1987 draft after being a three-time All-SEC linebacker at Alabama and a two-time All-American . . . Twice named to the Pro Bowl . . . Became the first player in NFL history to be voted Player of The Week on consecutive weeks (against the Raiders and Broncos) . . . Started all 16 regular-season games and was the Bills' fourth-leading tackler with 96 . . . Added four sacks and 18 pressures . . . A great pass-rusher from his left outside linebacker position, he's at his best chasing down plays from the backside . . . Born Aug. 25, 1966, in Birmingham, Ala. . . . 1990 salary: $575,000.

DARRYL TALLEY 31 6-4 235 Outside Linebacker

Even though he played in only his first Pro Bowl, the eight-year veteran has been considered one of the most underrated players in the AFC . . . At this year's Super Bowl, Bills' defensive coordinator Walt Corey said that Talley is the team's most complete linebacker . . . He doesn't have the sack totals of Cornelius Bennett but he covers better and plays the run more effectively . . . A second-round draft pick out of West Virginia in 1983 . . . Led the Bills with 123 tackles in 1990 and added four sacks and five pressures. . . . Scored the first touchdown of his NFL career last year when he returned an interception against the Browns. One of the Cleveland players chasing him on the play was his brother John, a Browns' tight end . . . Despite undergoing surgery on both elbows and a knee in the offseason, he started every game in 1990 . . . A second-round draft pick out of West Virginia in 1983 . . . Born July 10, 1960, in Cleveland . . . 1990 salary: $475,000.

BRUCE SMITH 28 6-4 275 Defensive End

The first player taken in the 1985 draft, he's been selected to the Pro Bowl the last four seasons . . . The consensus choice as the AFC's best defensive lineman and at a level with Philadelphia's Reggie White among all defensive ends in the NFL . . . He earned $1.3 million in 1990, when he finished second in the NFL in sacks with 19 . . . He had four of those sacks against Jeff George of the Colts and had at least one sack in 10 of the first 13 games of the season . . . Finished the season with 99 tackles, 82 of them unassisted . . . Tremendous quickness off the ball . . . Consensus All-American and Outland Trophy winner at Virginia Tech . . . Born on June 18, 1963, in Norfolk, Va.

SHANE CONLAN 27 6-3 235 Inside Linebacker

He was the AFC's Rookie of the Year in 1987 and has been to the Pro Bowl the last three years . . . A first-round draft pick from Penn State in 1987, he earned $302,500 in 1990 . . . At the beginning of his rookie year, he struggled as the Bills moved him to outside linebacker. But when they traded for Cornelius Bennett, Conlan was shifted to the more natural inside linebacker spot. Since then, he's been a force against the run . . . He had 114 tackles in his rookie year and 93 last season, 72 unassisted . . . A consensus All-American at Penn State, he played on the national championship Nittany Lions team in 1986 . . . Penn State coach Joe Paterno said Conlan was the best linebacker he'd coached at Linebacker U. . . . Born April 3, 1964, in Frewsburg, N.Y., and played his high school ball at Frewsburg High, which is only 70 miles from Rich Stadium.

NATE ODOMES 26 5-10 188 Cornerback

Another of the underrated Bills, he came to the Bills in 1987 as part of the same trade that brought Shane Conlan . . . The Bills had the third pick in that draft and traded it to Houston (which took Alonzo Highsmith). In exchange, the Bills got the Oilers' first- and second-round picks and used them to take Conlan and Odomes . . . A second-round pick from Wisconsin . . . He had 16 pass deflections to go along with his one interception, and many teammates felt he should have been voted to the Pro Bowl . . . He received a game ball against the Eagles when he "pitched a shutout," allowing none of his men to catch a pass throughout the game . . . Born Aug. 25, 1965, in Columbus, Ga. . . . 1990 salary: $265,000.

COACH MARV LEVY: Came within a field goal of a Super Bowl ring to go with his Phi Beta Kappa key . . . The NFL's professor of coaches (he also has a master's degree in English history from Harvard) has established Buffalo as a power, winning the AFC East the last three years, capped by the SB XXV cliff-hanger loss to the Giants . . . Enters fifth full season with the Bills with a 43-27 regular-season mark . . . Organized and unflappable, he has kept the Bills together despite internal bickering late in the 1989 season . . . A running back at Coe College, he was head coach at New Mexico, California and William & Mary . . . Coached the Montreal Alouettes in the Canadian Football League before taking over the Kansas City Chiefs (1977-82) . . . Led Chicago Blitz in the USFL (1984) and was director of football operations for the Alouettes when the Bills hired him to replace Hank Bullough in November 1986 . . . Was NFL Coach of the Year in 1988 . . . Overall NFL regular-season record is 74-69 . . . Born Aug. 3, 1928, in Chicago.

GREATEST PUNTER

Before he became a TV analyst for NFL games, Paul Maguire played in them—as a punter with the Bills, he provided Buffalo with the best punting in its history.

A free-agent linebacker/punter from The Citadel, Maguire averaged 42.1 yards on 552 punts between his rookie year, 1964, through 1970. He also holds the Bills' records for longest punt (64 yards) and highest average in a game (46.8 yards against San Diego in 1964) and shares the record for most punts in a game (8) with Darryl Lamonica.

Marv Bateman is a close second to Maguire, averaging 41.7 yards on the 262 punts he made between 1974 and 1977.

INDIVIDUAL BILL RECORDS

Rushing

Most Yards Game:	273	O. J. Simpson, vs Detroit, 1976
Season:	2,003	O. J. Simpson, 1973
Career:	10,183	O. J. Simpson, 1969-77

Passing

Most TD Passes Game:	5	2 times, most recently Jim Kelly, vs Houston, 1989
Season:	26	Joe Ferguson, 1983
Career:	181	Joe Ferguson, 1973-84

Receiving

Most TD Passes Game:	4	Jerry Butler, vs N.Y. Jets, 1979
Season:	10	Elbert Dubenion, 1964
Career:	39	Andre Reed, 1985-90

Scoring

Most Points Game:	30	Cookie Gilchrist, vs N.Y. Jets, 1963
Season:	138	O. J. Simpson, 1975
Career:	560	Scott Norwood, 1985-90
Most TDs Game:	5	Cookie Gilchrist, vs N.Y. Jets, 1963
Season:	23	O. J. Simpson, 1975
Career:	70	O. J. Simpson, 1969-77

CINCINNATI BENGALS

TEAM DIRECTORY: Chairman: Austin E. Knowlton; Pres.: John Sawyer; VP/GM: Paul Brown; Asst. GM: Michael Brown; Dir. Player Personnel: Pete Brown; Dir. Pub. Rel.: Allan Heim; Bus. Mgr.: Bill Connelly; Head Coach: Sam Wyche. Home field: Riverfront Stadium (59,754). Colors: Orange, black and white.

James Brooks averaged 5.1 for 1,004 yards rushing.

SCOUTING REPORT

OFFENSE: Through adversity, the 9-7 Bengals might have improved as a team. Their offense survived many aches to win nine games and advance into the second round of the playoffs. Boomer Esiason's left wrist ached and his accuracy suffered. Throughout October, injuries prevented receivers Tim McGee and Eddie Brown from being on the field together.

The talented left side of the offensive line—tackle Anthony Munoz and guard Bruce Reimers—were sidelined, but somehow the Bengals gave the Raiders a battle in the playoffs. They lost, but gained momentum for this season.

Few teams are as blessed with the weapons of the Bengals. Healthy or hurt, Esiason is dangerous. Brown and McGee are 50-catch receivers whose numbers decreased because Esiason simply didn't throw enough to them. Coach Sam Wyche is trying to develop two young receivers—Mike Barber and Reggie Rembert—to complement their skills.

Competition for featured back will be intense. James Brooks had another 1,000-yard season, Ickey Woods is healthy and Harold Green, who had 353 yards as a rookie, is promising.

DEFENSE: The Bengals have some hitters. David Fulcher is a strong safety in a linebacker's body. James Francis is a linebacker trapped inside a defensive end's body. What the Bengals don't have is stoppers. Opponents averaged 4.7 yards a carry and 350.3 yards a game.

The secondary should be healthier. Unless he tries to drive to the hoop again, cornerback Eric Thomas, who blew out his knee in an offseason basketball game, could provide Pro-Bowl pass coverage. During his absence, the Bengals acquired depth for their secondary in Rod Jones from Tampa Bay. Teamed with Lewis Billips, the Bengals are three-deep with cover guys.

Their coverage, however, will suffer unless the Bengals can toughen their defensive line. David Grant, young, inconsistent but good, found a home at defensive right end. Tim Krumrie can chase down people from the nose-tackle position and accumulate more tackles than most nose tackles. Still, nobody intimidates blockers up front.

SPECIAL TEAMS: Punter Lee Johnson and Jim Breech are a good team. Johnson's powerful left leg gives the Bengals the long punt. Breech, the 35-year-old placekicker, rarely misses short field

BENGALS VETERAN ROSTER

HEAD COACH—Sam Wyche. Assistant Coaches—Jim Anderson, Dana Bible, Marv Braden, Dick LeBeau, Jim McNally, Dick Selcer, Dave Shula, Mike Stock, Chuck Studley, Kim Wood.

No.	Name	Pos.	Ht.	Wt.	NFL Exp.	College
42	Ball, Eric	RB	6-2	214	3	UCLA
86	Barber, Mike	WR	5-11	172	3	Marshall
53	Barker, Leo	LB	6-2	230	8	New Mexico State
24	Billups, Lewis	CB	5-11	182	6	North Alabama
74	Blados, Brian	G	6-5	296	8	North Carolina
55	Brady, Ed	LB	6-2	236	8	Illinois
3	Breech, Jim	K	5-6	161	13	California
60	Brennan, Mike	T	6-5	274	2	Notre Dame
21	Brooks, James	RB	5-10	182	11	Auburn
81	Brown, Eddie	WR	6-0	185	7	Miami (Fla.)
99	Buck, Jason	DE	6-5	264	5	Brigham Young
27	Bussey, Barney	S	6-0	210	6	South Carolina
45	Carter, Carl	CB	5-11	180	6	Texas Tech
57	Clark, Bernard	LB	6-2	248	2	Miami (Fla.)
62	Crigler, Eric	T	6-5	295	1	Murray State
29	Dixon, Rickey	CB	5-11	191	4	Oklahoma
7	Esiason, Boomer	QB	6-5	220	8	Maryland
50	Francis, James	LB	6-5	252	2	Baylor
33	Fulcher, David	S	6-3	238	6	Arizona State
58	Gordon, Alex	LB	6-5	245	5	Cincinnati
98	Grant, David	NT	6-5	278	4	West Virginia
28	Green, Harold	RB	6-2	222	2	South Carolina
82	Holman, Rodney	TE	6-3	238	10	Tulane
80	James, Lynn	WR	6-0	191	2	Arizona State
36	Jennings, Stanford	RB	6-1	212	8	Furman
68	Jetton, Paul	G	6-4	288	3	Texas
11	Johnson, Lee	P	6-2	200	7	Brigham Young
25	Jones, Rod	CB	6-0	185	6	Southern Methodist
84	Kattus, Eric	TE	6-5	251	5	Michigan
64	Kozerski, Bruce	G	6-4	287	8	Holy Cross
69	Krumrie, Tim	NT	6-2	274	9	Wisconsin
72	McClendon, Skip	DE	6-7	287	5	Arizona State
85	McGee, Tim	WR	5-10	183	6	Tennessee
73	Moyer, Ken	T	6-7	297	4	Toledo
78	Munoz, Anthony	T	6-6	284	12	Southern California
52	Ogletree, Craig	LB	6-2	236	2	Auburn
32	Price, Mitchell	CB	5-9	181	2	Tulane
75	Reimers, Bruce	T	6-7	298	8	Iowa State
88	Rembert, Reggie	WR	6-5	245	5	West Virginia
87	Riggs, Jim	TE	6-5	245	5	Clemson
76	Scrafford, Kirk	T	6-6	255	2	Montana
83	Smith, Kendal	WR	5-10	189	4	Utah State
97	Stewart, Andrew	DE	6-5	265	2	Cincinnati
20	Taylor, Craig	RB	5-11	228	4	West Virginia
22	Thomas, Eric	CB	5-11	181	5	Tulane
96	Tuatagaloa, Natu	DE	6-4	274	3	California
59	Walker, Kevin	LB	6-3	244	4	Maryland
63	Walter, Joe	T	6-7	292	7	Texas Tech
51	White, Leon	LB	6-3	242	6	Brigham Young
12	Wilhelm, Erik	QB	6-3	217	4	Oregon State
30	Woods, Ickey	RB	6-2	232	4	Nevada-Las Vegas
91	Zander, Carl	LB	6-2	235	6	Tennessee

TOP DRAFT CHOICES

Rd.	Name	Sel. No.	Pos.	Ht.	Wt.	College
1	Williams, Alfred	18	LB	6-6	237	Colorado
2	Rogers, Lamar	52	DT	6-3	265	Auburn
3	Dahl, Bob	72	DT	6-5	267	Notre Dame
4	Hollas, Donald	99	QB	6-3	215	Rice
4	Carpenter, Rob	109	WR	6-2	183	Syracuse

goals. He made 17 of his 21 attempts. Cornerback Mitchell Price returned a 66-yard punt for a touchdown against the Seahawks, but averaged only 6.6 yards on his other tries. Running back Eric Ball is a steady kick-returner with a 22.9-yard average. In Bengal tradition, the coverage teams ranked among the league's worst.

THE ROOKIES: Not surprisingly, the Bengals loaded up on defense with three of their top four choices. The mystery is how they will be used. Colorado linebacker Alfred Williams, the first-round choice, is a lot like Francis, last year's top pick. Francis might be moved to inside linebacker. Defensive linemen Lamar Rogers of Auburn and Bob Dahl of Notre Dame have great potential as pass-rushers, but they have had attitude problems in college.

OUTLOOK: Coach Sam Wyche might wage war against Commissioner Paul Tagliabue, battle on locker-room access issues and help the homeless, but he matured as a coach last year. His star players are getting older now, so he needs to keep attention on the field and return to the Super Bowl. He's blessed with an offense that could win 12 games and a defense that could lose 10.

BENGAL PROFILES

BOOMER ESIASON 30 6-5 220 — Quarterback

Bothered by a sore left wrist that affected his accuracy during different parts of the season . . . His total of 22 interceptions doubled his 1989 total . . . Still one of the game's premier quarterbacks and has no peers for being able to run a no-huddle offense . . . Has thrown 24 touchdown passes in five of past six seasons . . . Completed 224 of 402 passes for 3,031 yards, his sixth consecutive 3,000-yard season . . . Has 77.0 quarterback rating (92.1 in 1989) . . . Color analyst for World League games for USA Network during offseason . . . His uncanny left-handed release allows him to be more accurate than most quarterbacks . . . Called Boomer by his parents because he kicked his mother during pregnancy . . . A second-round draft choice in 1984 after breaking Maryland's passing records . . . Born April 17, 1961, in East Islip, N.Y. . . . 1991 salary: $1.2 million.

EDDIE BROWN 28 6-0 185 — Wide Receiver

Defenses floated more defenders toward Brown's side, limiting him to 44 receptions, the second-lowest total during his six-year career . . . Coach Sam Wyche admits that not enough attempts went to his side . . . Bothered by knee injury following Oct. 1 game against the Seahawks and took a month to regain full speed . . . Has 304 career receptions for 5,307 yards . . . Runs precise routes and can break tackles after making reception . . . Extremely dangerous near the goal line . . . Has averaged six touchdowns a season . . . Won All-American honors at the University of Miami after attending Navarro Junior College in Corsicana, Tex. . . . First-round draft choice in 1985 . . . Named NFL Offensive Rookie of the Year in 1985 after 53-catch season . . . Strengthens his hands by squeezing "Play Doh" . . . Averaged 24 yards a reception in 1988 . . . Born Dec. 17, 1962, in Miami . . . 1991 salary: $925,000.

JAMES BROOKS 32 5-10 182 — Halfback

Has the body of a back in his twenties . . . Works hard during offseason to stay in condition . . . Crossed the 1,000-yard rushing plateau for the second consecutive year . . . Gained 1,004 yards on only 195 carries . . . His 5.1-yard average marked the third consecutive year he averaged more than five yards an attempt . . . Caught 26 passes to bring his career total to 334 . . . Shows no sign of wearing down . . . Willing to play hurt . . . A compound fracture of the left thumb limited him during the playoffs . . . Upset that he wasn't among top three for Pro Bowl, but he went as an alternate . . . Has been to four Pro Bowls . . . Acquired in 1984 from Chargers for fullback Pete Johnson . . . Averaged 5.7 yards an attempt during brilliant career at Auburn . . . Born Dec. 28, 1958, in Warner Robins, Ga. . . . 1991 salary: $1.15 million.

ANTHONY MUNOZ 33 6-6 284 **Tackle**

Injuries are starting to finally catch up to the blocker of the 1980s . . . Had severe shoulder problems that forced him to miss the Bengals' playoff game against the Raiders, the first missed start during his career . . . Sets the standard for tackles in the NFL . . . Has been to the Pro Bowl 10 times . . . Shoulder problems have prevented him from playing in two of the past three Pro Bowls . . . Will occasionally sneak off the line to catch touchdown passes, something he's done four times during his career . . . One of the best offensive linemen ever to come out of Southern Cal . . . Can be beaten by the quick pass-rushing linebackers or ends, but is rarely overpowered . . . Went to the Sports Medicine Institute in Fargo, N.D., to improve his speed . . . Acted in two movies, *Borderline* and *The Right Stuff* . . . Born Aug. 19, 1958, in Ontario, Cal. . . . 1991 salary: $900,000.

RODNEY HOLMAN 31 6-3 238 **Tight End**

Considered by many the league's top tight end . . . A 40-catch season sent him to his third Pro Bowl . . . One of Boomer Esiason's favorite plays last year was a naked bootleg in which he fired a completion to Holman . . . A dangerous deep threat who caught a 53-yarder last season . . . One of the best blockers for sweeps because of his low, powerful hits on linebackers . . . Has 261 career receptions and 21 touchdowns . . . Cousin of former Steeler halfback Preston Pearson . . . Caught only two passes during first two seasons . . . A two-time All-American at Tulane . . . Third-round draft choice in 1982 . . . Born April 20, 1960, in Ypsilanti, Mich. . . . 1991 salary: $558,300.

JAMES FRANCIS 23 6-5 252 **Linebacker**

One of the best rookie defenders last season . . . Led team with 78 tackles and eight sacks . . . Participated in 92 percent of the team's defensive plays . . . Received double-team blocking on most passing downs after recording seven sacks during first seven games . . . Key 17-yard interception return for touchdown in season-finale against Cleveland helped to put Bengals in playoffs . . . Added 15 pounds of muscle before senior year at Baylor and earned first-team All-American honors . . . To inspire better practices at Baylor, he instructed safety Robert Blackmon (now a Seahawk) to knock out undergraduates on the scout teams once a week . . . Was sixth man on Baylor basketball team that went to 1987 NCAA tournament . . . Born Aug. 4, 1968, in Houston . . . 1991 salary: $350,000.

DAVID FULCHER 26 6-3 238 Strong Safety

Earned third consecutive trip to the Pro Bowl . . . Diagnosed after the season as having an arthritic condition in a knee . . . Was asked by management to weigh under 230 pounds to prolong his great career . . . Second on the team with 75 tackles, but led with five interceptions . . . Former NFL great Bill Dudley dubbed him a future Hall of Famer . . . Loves to deck running backs and force fumbles . . . "I love to force the run," he said . . . Nicknamed "The Rock." . . . Started at Arizona State as a freshman and had 105 tackles . . . A grade screwup forced him to make late application for 1986 draft, in which he was a third-round selection . . . Was a consensus All-American at Arizona State . . . Born Sept. 28, 1964, in Los Angeles . . . 1991 salary: $775,000.

ERIC THOMAS 26 5-11 181 Cornerback

Proved value during final weeks of season by shutting down receivers . . . Was expected to miss season after tearing up his knee in an off-season basketball game . . . Had surgery on right knee in May but completely rehabilitated the injury in seven months . . . Considered one of the best coverage cornerbacks in the game . . . Took over as a starter during rookie year in 1987 and gained instant stardom . . . A second-round draft choice from Tulane who was also a track star . . . Loves to play man-to-man coverage . . . Had seven interceptions in 1988 . . . Attended Pasadena City College . . . Born Sept. 11, 1964, in Sacramento . . . 1990 salary: $210,000.

DAVID GRANT 25 6-5 278 — Defensive End

Finally found a home at right defensive end . . . Moved up and down the line from nose guard to end during his first three seasons . . . Recorded 44 tackles and two sacks . . . Might have replaced talented Tim Krumrie as the toughest Bengals' defensive lineman to block . . . Was a fourth-round choice from West Virginia in 1988 who was known for his pass-rushing skills . . . In 1989, he led the team in injuries with four—knee tendinitis, sprained wrist, torn pectoral muscle and torn bicep . . . Changing positions also slowed him down during his first two years . . . Moved into a starting job late in his rookie season . . . Replaced Krumrie as the nose tackle during Super Bowl XXIII . . . Born Sept. 17, 1965, in Belleville, N.J. . . . 1990 salary: $140,000.

BRUCE REIMERS 30 6-7 298 — Guard

Broke his foot during the preseason and missed first four games . . . Suffered a severely sprained ankle that forced him to miss the Raiders' playoff game . . . Without Anthony Munoz and Reimers, the Bengals' left side of the line collapsed . . . Has developed into one of the game's best run-blockers . . . Overpowers defenders with the style that his position coach, Jim McNally, describes as being that of a lumberjack . . . An eighth-round choice who waited his turn to start . . . Was an All-Big Eight blocker at Iowa State . . . His long arms help to make him an excellent pass-blocker . . . Can also play tackle if needed . . . If he returns healthy, Bengals will rank among the league's best rushing teams . . . Has a business degree . . . Born Sept. 18, 1960, in Humboldt, Iowa . . . 1991 salary: $275,000.

COACH SAM WYCHE: Might have had his best coaching year . . . Took a team battered by injuries and surrounded by controversy into the second round of the playoffs . . . Fined approximately $28,000—one game check—for banning a *USA Today* female reporter from entering the team's locker room after a loss to the Seahawks . . . Turned the event into a national platform to speak out about inappropriate media access . . . Received more than $40,000 of donations from fans around the country . . . A brilliant offensive mind who created the no-huddle offense . . . Tends to become too emotional and put his squad on an emotional roller-coaster . . . A former journeyman quarterback who started in semipro ball and finished his career in 1976 with the Bills . . . After being as assistant with the 49ers and a head coach at Indiana, he became Paul Brown's fifth head coach . . . Compiled 58-53 record since 1983 . . . The loss of offensive coordinator Bruce Coslet to the Jets as head coach might have created a transition problem for the offense . . . Ran sporting goods store for three years after retiring as a player . . . Spends time helping the homeless . . . Born Jan. 5, 1945, in Atlanta.

GREATEST PUNTER

Starting with David Lewis, the Bengals have had a rich tradition in punting excellence. From 1970 to 1973, Lewis averaged 43.8 yards a kick. David Green followed with a 40-yard average the next two seasons.

Pat McInally imported the Ivy League approach. A Harvard grad, McInally became a folk hero. From 1976 through 1985, McInally, part-time receiver and full-time punter, became the unofficial team spokesman. His statements were as eloquent as his punts, which maintained a 42-yard average through the years.

The latest in the line of quality punters might become the best. Lee Johnson bounced around the AFC Central in Cleveland and Houston before finding a home in Cincinnati. Coach Sam Wyche loves Johnson's powerful left leg. He uses Johnson on kickoffs and in punt formation. Last year, Johnson averaged 42.3 yards per kick, and, as always, boomed a few 60-plus-yard punts.

Years of experimenting taught Johnson to wear a shoe when

he punted. With a shoe, Johnson gained consistency. He also gained job security.

INDIVIDUAL BENGAL RECORDS

Rushing

Most Yards Game:	201	James Brooks, vs Houston, 1990
Season:	1,087	James Brooks, 1986
Career:	5,876	James Brooks, 1984-90

Passing

Most TD Passes Game:	5	2 times, most recently Boomer Esiason, vs Tampa Bay, 1989
Season:	29	Ken Anderson, 1981
Career:	196	Ken Anderson, 1971-85

Receiving

Most TD Passes Game:	3	3 times, most recently Isaac Curtis, vs Baltimore, 1979
Season:	10	Isaac Curtis, 1974
Career:	53	Isaac Curtis, 1973-83

Scoring

Most Points Game:	24	Larry Kinnebrew, vs Houston, 1984
Season:	115	Jim Breech, 1981
Career:	875	Jim Breech, 1981-89
Most TDs Game:	4	Larry Kinnebrew, vs Houston, 1984
Season:	16	Pete Johnson, 1981
Career:	70	Pete Johnson, 1977-83

CLEVELAND BROWNS

TEAM DIRECTORY: Owner/Pres.: Art Modell; Exec. VP-Legal Administration: Jim Bailey; Exec. VP-Football Operations: Ernie Accorsi; VP-Pub. Rel.: Kevin Byrne; Head Coach: Bill Belichick. Home field: Cleveland Stadium (80,098). Colors: Seal brown, orange and white.

Michael Dean Perry pounds the QBs en route to Pro Bowl.

SCOUTING REPORT

OFFENSE: Quarterback Bernie Kosar considered the problems mental. Outsiders believe it's physical. Whatever, the Browns have one sick offense. They were last on the ground (76.3 yards a game), next to last in scoring (14.25 points) and fourth-worst in total offense (272.9 yards).

So after years of turbulence, the Browns take a Tranquill approach. Gary Tranquill, with no NFL coaching experience, will be the latest to coordinate the Browns' offense. Good luck. Kosar hasn't been the same since damaging ligaments in his right elbow in 1988. His game-breaking halfback (Eric Metcalf) simply can't run inside. There really isn't a receiving threat to take pressure off Webster Slaughter, one of the game's toughest receivers. And the offensive line? Resumes are being accepted.

The situation is passable in the middle of the line. Paul Farren will move from tackle to guard. With center Mike Babb, guard-center Gregg Rakoczy, Plan B acquisition John Reinstra and a healthier Dan Fike, the Browns have plenty of interior options. They are vulnerable at tackle.

Kevin Mack's inspired running should improve the ground attack. Getting Metcalf into the open field to catch more passes should create a few more big plays. The Browns have to replace retired tight end Ozzie Newsome. The rest is up to Kosar.

DEFENSE: For seven years, Bill Belichick was considered the behind-the-scenes technician who directed Bill Parcells' Giant defense. Now, he's emerged from the meeting room to see how good he really is. But the 39-year-old Belichick can't be expected to produce miracles.

Except for Pro Bowl defensive tackle Michael Dean Perry (26), Belichick must rebuild an aging unit that lacks speed. Linebacker Clay Matthews (35) is entering the role-playing stage of his career. Cornerback Frank Minnifield (31) wanted to be traded last season. Raymond Clayborn (36) can't be expected to hold down the other cornerback job for an entire season. One bright spot is inside linebacker Mike Johnson (28), who made his second Pro Bowl.

The Browns were the sixth-worst team against the run, allowing 131.6 yards a game. Continued development of young defensive ends Rob Burnett and Anthony Pleasant could help, but the Browns lack another proven tackle. Switching to a 3-4 could be appealing if they had the four linebackers. Van Waiters hasn't progressed as quickly as management would like. David Grayson has speed but is still raw.

BROWNS VETERAN ROSTER

HEAD COACH—Bill Belichick. Assistant Coaches—Ernie Adams, Jim Bates, Don Blackmon, Steve Crosby, Hal Hunter, Richard Mann, John Mitchell, Scott O'Brien, Nick Saban, Phil Savage, Jerry Simmons, Gary Tranquill.

No.	Name	Pos.	Ht.	Wt.	NFL Exp.	College
48	Arbuckle, Charles	TE	6-2	240	1	UCLA
61	Baab, Mike	C	6-4	275	10	Texas
37	Barnett, Harlon	S	5-11	200	2	Michigan State
24	Blaylock, Tony	CB	5-11	190	4	Winston-Salem
36	Braggs, Stephen	DB	5-9	180	5	Texas
58	Brandon, David	LB	6-4	230	4	Memphis State
86	Brennan, Brian	WR	5-10	185	8	Boston College
52	Brown, Richard	LB	6-3	240	4	San Diego State
90	Burnett, Rob	DL	6-4	270	2	Syracuse
26	Clayborn, Raymond	CB	6-1	190	15	Texas
79	Cunningham, Ed	T	6-7	295	1	Texas
74	Farren, Paul	T-G	6-6	270	9	Boston University
69	Fike, Dan	G	6-7	285	7	Florida
25	Florence, Anthony	CB	6-0	185	1	Bethune-Cookman
13	Francis, Jeff	QB	6-4	225	2	Tennessee
27	Gainer, Derrick	RB	5-11	235	2	Florida A&M
81	Galbraith, Scott	TE	6-3	260	2	Southern California
30	Gash, Thane	S	6-0	195	4	East Tennessee State
71	Gibson, Tom	DL	6-8	275	3	Northern Arizona
56	Grayson, David	LB	6-3	230	5	Fresno State
11	Hansen, Brian	P	6-4	220	7	Sioux Falls
23	Harper, Mark	CB	5-9	185	6	Alcorn State
64	Hawthorne, George	T	6-6	275	1	Iowa
39	Hilliard, Randy	CB	5-11	160	2	Northwestern State
93	Hines, John	DE	6-4	260	1	Alabama State
33	Hoard, Leroy	RB	5-11	230	2	Michigan
62	Jefferson, Ben	T	6-9	330	2	Maryland
51	Johnson, Eddie	LB	6-1	235	11	Louisville
16	Johnson, Flip	WR	5-9	181	3	McNeese State
59	Johnson, Mike	LB	6-1	230	6	Virginia Tech
80	Joines, Vernon	WR	6-2	210	2	Maryland
55	Jones, Jock	LB	6-2	230	2	Virginia Tech
66	Jones, Tony	T	6-5	290	4	Western Carolina
19	Kosar, Bernie	QB	6-5	215	7	Miami
40	Kramer, Kyle	S	6-3	190	2	Bowling Green
88	Langhorne, Reggie	WR	6-2	205	7	Elizabeth City State
49	Lyons, Robert	S	6-2	200	2	Akron
34	Mack, Kevin	FB	6-0	230	7	Clemson
57	Matthews, Clay	LB	6-2	245	14	Southern California
21	Metcalf, Eric	RB	5-10	190	3	Texas
31	Minnifield, Frank	CB	5-9	180	8	Louisville
20	Morris, Joe	RB	5-7	195	9	Syracuse
67	Morris, Mike	C	6-5	285	4	NE Missouri State
22	Newsome, Vince	S	6-1	185	9	Washington
89	Oliphant, Mike	WR-KR	5-9	171	2	Puget Sound
92	Perry, Michael Dean	DT	6-1	285	4	Clemson
17	Philcox, Todd	QB	6-4	225	2	Syracuse
98	Pleasant, Anthony	DE	6-5	258	2	Tennessee State
73	Rakoczy, Gregg	G-C	6-5	295	5	Miami
77	Reeves, Ken	OL	6-5	277	7	Texas A&M
70	Rienstra, John	G	6-5	275	6	Temple
72	Robbins, Kevin	OL	6-6	295	2	Michigan State
44	Rouson, Lee	RB	6-1	222	7	Colorado
83	Rowell, Eugene	WR	6-1	180	2	Southern Mississippi
95	Sanders, Terrence	DL	6-7	319	1	Grambling
28	Shavers, Tyrone	WR	6-3	210	1	Lamar
97	Sims, Darryl	DE	6-3	275	5	Wisconsin
84	Slaughter, Webster	WR	6-1	170	6	San Diego State
4	Smith, Billy	P	5-11	190	1	Tenn.-Chattanooga
3	Stover, Matt	K	5-11	178	1	Louisiana Tech
87	Talley, John	TE	6-5	245	2	West Virginia
65	Tamm, Ralph	G-C	6-4	280	2	West Chester
85	Tillman, Lawyer	WR	6-5	230	2	Auburn
50	Waiters, Van	LB	6-4	250	4	Indiana
91	Weston, Rhondy	DL	6-5	280	2	Florida
99	Williams, Marlin	DE	6-3	255	1	Western Illinois
78	Woods, Rob	T	6-5	295	1	Arizona

TOP DRAFT CHOICES

Rd.	Name	Sel. No.	Pos.	Ht.	Wt.	College
1	Turner, Eric	2	S	6-0	206	UCLA
2	King, Ed	29	G	6-4	297	Auburn
3	Jones, James	57	NT	6-2	299	Northern Iowa
4	Sagapolutele, Pio	85	DT	6-3	262	San Diego State
6	Jackson, Michael	141	WR	6-4	195	Southern Mississippi

Plan B swept away safety Felix Wright, leaving a big hole at safety. Expect hard-hitting Thane Gash to move to strong safety for starters. Former Ram castoff Vince Newsome could offer some assistance and rookie Eric Turner should earn a starting job at safety.

SPECIAL TEAMS: The kicking game was so bad last year that punter Bryan Wagner and placekicker Jerry Kauric were released in April. Unproven former Giant kicker Matt Stover was recruited through Plan B. Brian Hansen, who had a 41.7 average for the Patriots, will be given a chance at the punting job. No problem with the return teams. The Browns still have Metcalf and speedy but too-often injured Mike Oliphant.

THE ROOKIES: UCLA's Turner might have been a reach as the second choice in the draft, but scouts agree that his range and hitting ability make him a better prospect than Bears' free safety Mark Carrier, the NFC Defensive Rookie of the Year. The rest of the draft looked like a cattle drive—guards Ed King of Auburn (297 pounds) and Todd Jones of Henderson State (320-plus) and defensive tackles James Jones of Northern Iowa (299), Tio Sagapolutele of San Diego State (285) and Frank Conover of Syracuse (320).

OUTLOOK: The Browns are much better than their 3-13 record, but no one can say how much better. Through all the turmoil and the transition, Belichick would do well to add three or four wins. For what it's worth, impatient owner Art Modell gave him a five-year contract. Of course, that might not mean as much as it used to in Cleveland.

BROWN PROFILES

MICHAEL DEAN PERRY 26 6-1 285 Defensive Tackle

Continues as one of the more dominating tackles in pro football . . . Amazing quickness and first step . . . Went to the Pro Bowl as a starter, his second trip in three years . . . Led Browns with 11½ sacks and 27 quarterback pressures . . . Outpaced his older, bigger brother, Bears' William "The Refrigerator" as a football star, if not a media figure . . . Weight has not been a problem during his pro career . . . Broke his brother's career sack record at Clemson with 28, three more than "The Refrigerator" . . . One of 12 children . . . Drafted in the second round in 1988 . . . Faced a contract negotiation that could rank him among the highest-paid defensive linemen . . . Said he was embarrassed by some of the team's efforts during games . . . Born Aug. 27, 1965, in Aiken, S.C. . . . 1990 base salary: $231,000.

BERNIE KOSAR 27 6-5 215 **Quarterback**

Had another difficult season . . . Bothered by chronic elbow problems and a sore thumb, he had the lowest percentage of completions (54.4) since rookie year . . . His 15 interceptions were most in six-year career . . . Threw only 10 touchdown passes, eight less than in 1989 . . . Career has been held back by numerous head-coaching and offensive-coordinator changes . . . Disagreed with former head coach Bud Carson's ball-control approach because he felt personnel was suited for more passing . . . Played only two seasons at the University of Miami, graduated and entered the pros through a supplemental draft . . Plays for the team he followed growing up . . . Said Browns needed a lot of "soul-searching" during the season . . . Born Nov. 25, 1963, in Boardman, Ohio . . . 1991 base salary: $1.75 million.

FRANK MINNIFIELD 31 5-9 180 **Cornerback**

Negotiated away last season . . . Reported late and played only nine games . . . Infuriated management to a point where they tried to trade him . . . Almost swapped him to the Atlanta Falcons for guard Bill Fralic . . . Before last year, was a Pro-Bowl caliber cornerback . . . Still has the ability but does he have the desire to display it in Cleveland? . . . Uses a laptop computer to prepare for games and enters in every play formation, down and distance . . . Missed the Pro Bowl for the first time in four years . . . Signed with the Chicago Blitz of the USFL before 1983 draft, killing his chances of being a high NFL draft choice . . . Signed as a free agent with the Browns in 1984 . . . Established "The Dogs" with former teammate Hanford Dixon when they barked at receivers . . . Walk-on at Louiville but ended up the leader of the school's nationally-ranked secondary in 1982 . . . Born Jan. 1, 1960, in Lexington, Ky. . . . 1991 base salary: $800,000.

WEBSTER SLAUGHTER 26 6-1 170 Wide Receiver

One of the toughest and most exciting receivers in football . . . Also one of the most hated because of tendency to talk, taunt and hit defensive backs . . . Led Browns with 59 receptions for 847 yards . . . Has averaged 48 catches a season during his first five years . . . Flows downfield similar to Paul Warfield and catches cornerbacks off-guard with his deceptive speed . . . During senior year at San Diego State, he finished fourth in the nation with 82 catches . . . A superb basketball player capable of 50-point nights in charity games . . . Plays the saxaphone . . . Missed seven games in 1988 because of a broken arm . . . Born Oct. 19, 1964, in Stockton, Cal. . . . 1991 base salary: $500,000.

ERIC METCALF 23 5-10 190 Halfback

Best described as being a running back and a third receiver all at once . . . One of the most exciting open-field runners in the game . . . Improved as receiver, catching 57 passes for 452 yards . . . Rushed for only 248 yards, a disappointing 3.1-yard average . . . Simply can't run inside the tackles . . . Said Bengal halfback James Brooks, "If you see the things I do on the field, his running and my running are two different things. When I run, I push the pile. When he runs, he takes a lick and falls." . . . Was the 13th choice in the 1989 draft, out of Texas . . . Father Terry starred for the St. Louis Cardinals and the Redskins . . . Set Southwest Conference record for career all-purpose yards with 5,705 . . . Two-time NCAA long-jump champion . . . Born Jan. 23, 1968, in Seattle . . . 1991 base salary: $350,000.

CLAY MATTHEWS 35 6-2 245 **Linebacker**

Might be entering the role-player phase of his career but there aren't many better linebackers on the roster to replace him . . . Has bounced all over the field in recent years, playing weak-side and strong-side . . . Played for the Browns in three different decades . . . Made five trips to the Pro Bowl . . . Played every down of the 1989 season at left outside linebacker . . . Finished fourth on the team last year with 102 tackles, 72 of which were solo . . . Ranked with some of the great linebackers of the 1980s . . . Was an All-American linebacker at Southern Cal . . . Drafted by the Browns in the first round of 1978 . . . Brother, Bruce, plays for the Oilers . . . Born March 15, 1956, in Palo Alto, Cal. . . . 1991 base salary: $825,000.

MIKE JOHNSON 28 6-1 230 **Linebacker**

Has become the team's steadiest linebacker . . . Went to the Pro Bowl for the second consecutive time as a middle linebacker . . . Shows some of those Mike Singletary qualities for awareness . . . Doesn't dominate but makes plays . . . Led the team with 161 tackles . . . Like so many Browns, he came through a supplemental draft from the USFL . . Played 35 games for the Philadelphia-Baltimore Stars of the USFL . . . Earned academic and All-American honors at Virginia Tech . . . Held out for 42 days during training camp . . . Born Nov. 26, 1962, in Southport, N.C. . . . 1990 base salary: $550,000.

KEVIN MACK 29 6-0 230 **Fullback**

The inspirational leader of the offense . . . Played every play as though it were the Super Bowl . . . Came back from personal problems to lead the Browns with 702 yards and a 4.4-yard average, his best season since 1987 . . . Had a 30-day jail sentence in 1989 for illegal-substance abuse . . . Missed two games last year with a broken finger . . . Went to the Pro Bowl two times . . Was Clemson's leading rusher in 1983 and then signed with the Los Angeles Express of the USFL . . . Came to the Browns as a supplemental draft choice in 1984 . . . Has gone to two Pro Bowls for the Browns . . . Born Aug. 9, 1962, in Kings Mountain, N.C. . . . 1990 base salary: $600,000.

THANE GASH 26 6-0 195 **Safety**

Outside of Cleveland, few recognized his skills . . . At times last year, some wondered whether Browns' coaches recognized his skills . . . Played at free safety, where he roamed the field and finished second on the Browns with 134 tackles . . . Might be better suited to play strong safety even though he lacks coverage skills . . . A seventh-round draft choice in 1988 who sneaked up on people . . . Beat out Brian Washington for the strong safety job in 1989 . . . Known as a kamikaze-type hitter . . . Played for four defensive coordinators in four years at East Tennessee State . . Started his career as a special-teams player . . . Born Sept. 1, 1965, in Henderson, N.C. . . . 1991 base salary: $305,000.

LAWYER TILLMAN 25 6-5 230 **Wide Receiver**

Missed last season with a foot injury . . . Caught only six passes as a rookie . . . Is he the biggest draft bust since Mike Junkin, or a potential star? . . . The Browns have this season to learn the outcome of the most unsettling question mark on their offense . . . At an offseason minicamp, he was tried at the tight end position . . . Coming out of the run-dominated Auburn program, he didn't have many chances to catch passes . . . Played four seasons at Auburn and caught only 93 passes, third-best in school history . . . The Browns traded three draft choices, including a first-runder, to select him in 1989 . . . Born May 20, 1966, in Mobile, Ala. . . . 1991 base salary: $240,000.

COACH BILL BELICHICK: A product of the film room and a coaching family . . . Started career breaking down film for the Baltimore Colts in 1975 and bounced around the NFL as an assistant . . . Hired as a special-teams coach for Bill Parcells' Giants in 1983 and was the defensive coordinator of the team that yielded the fewest points in the NFL last season on the way to its Super Bowl triumph . . . Earned his first Super Bowl ring in SB XXI . . . Signed five-year contract worth $2.5 million . . . His dad, Steve, was a fullback with the Detroit Lions in 1941 and an assistant coach at the U.S. Naval Academy for 35 years . . . Bill was a 170-pound center, defensive end, tight end and occasional linebacker at Wesleyan University, where he majored in economics . . . Has hired a staff filled with college coaches who have limited pro experience . . . Said he will have a balanced offense instead of relying on the ball-control approach stressed by Parcells, his former boss . . . Not considered a self-promoter . . . Born April 16, 1952, in Nashville, Tenn.

GREATEST PUNTER

Ahead of his time, Paul Brown always came equipped. The coach who revolutionized the profession with his innovations wasn't about to move from the All-America Football Conference to the NFL without the best of everything. Not only did he have great players, but he had great specialists.

Which brings us to Horace Gillom. Brown's punter set a standard of kicking in the early 1950s that young, strong legs have yet to match in the 42-year history of the franchise. In 1951 and 1952, Gillom led the league with 45.5- and 45.7-yard averages. No Brown has come within seven yards of his 80-yard punt in 1954.

The Gillom-Brown relationship dated back to Massillon High in the 1940s. Brown rarely let great talents slip away, so when he needed a punter and a wide receiver, he called upon Gillom, who averaged 43.8 yards a kick from 1950 through 1956.

After Gillom marched several multi-talented punting stars—Gary Collins, Don Cockroft, Sam Baker and Steve Cox. But it was Gillom who set the standard.

INDIVIDUAL BROWN RECORDS

Rushing

Most Yards Game:	237	2 times, most recently Jim Brown, vs Philadelphia, 1961
Season:	1,863	Jim Brown, 1963
Career:	12,312	Jim Brown, 1957-65

Passing

Most TD Passes Game:	5	3 times, most recently Brian Sipe, vs Pittsburgh, 1979
Season:	30	Brian Sipe, 1980
Career:	154	Brian Sipe, 1974-83

Receiving

Most TD Passes Game:	3	7 times, most recently Calvin Hill, vs Baltimore, 1978
Season:	13	Gary Collins, 1963
Career:	70	Gary Collins, 1962-71

Scoring

Most Points Game:	36	Dub Jones, vs Chicago Bears, 1951
Season:	126	Jim Brown, 1965
Career:	1,349	Lou Groza, 1950-59, 1961-67
Most TDs Game:	6	Dub Jones, vs Chicago Bears, 1951
Season:	21	Jim Brown, 1965
Career:	126	Jim Brown, 1957-65

DENVER BRONCOS

TEAM DIRECTORY: Owner: Pat Bowlen; Treas. and CFO: Bob Hurley; Dir. Football Oper.: Lide Huggins; Dir. Player Pers.: Reed Johnson; Dir. Media Rel.: Jim Saccomano; VP/Head Coach: Dan Reeves. Home field: Mile High Stadium (76,273). Colors: Orange, blue and white.

A whole Bobby Humphrey is a bull of a Bronco.

SCOUTING REPORT

OFFENSE: Dan Reeves has always depended upon his offense. That unit has all the money players. John Elway is the passer. Bobby Humphrey is the runner. Mark Jackson and Vance Johnson make the big catches. The system still works. The Broncos outscored teams, 207-145, in the first halves of games.

Then things went crazy. Humphrey severely sprained an ankle in a Sept. 30 game against the Bills and he wasn't the same for the remainder of the season. Without a healthy Humphrey, the Broncos couldn't hold onto their leads. In the third quarter alone, they were outscored, 95-46. Elway would be forced to rally in the fourth quarter and the mistakes mounted.

Each of the four offensive headliners return, but the supporting cast is in transition. Sammy Winder retired, leaving the Broncos without a dependable backup halfback. Shannon Sharpe, a tall receiver, is being groomed for the H-back job. Clarence Kay, after regaining Reeves' confidence with a 29-catch season, jeopardized his career with another arrest for driving under the influence.

Big changes are evident on the offensive line. The trade of left tackle Gerald Perry to the Rams leaves a void. Newcomers Sean Farrell and Crawford Ker will battle for one of the starting jobs at guard.

DEFENSE: Blame it on injuries, but the Broncos' defense was horrible. There were reasons. Knee injuries sidelined their best defensive lineman against the run (Alphonso Carreker) and their best coverage cornerback (Tyrone Braxton). Defensive end Ron Holmes held out 50 days but didn't earn his raise. Chronic knee problems are threatening to shorten the career of linebacker Karl Mecklenburg.

If Holmes, Carreker and Braxton come close to their 1989 performances, the Broncos could shoot back to the top of the division. If they don't, they are in deep trouble. Reeves hopes he has found the linebacker in Mike Croel of Nebraska to fit in with Mecklenburg, Simon Fletcher and Michael Brooks.

An interesting move was made in the secondary. Charles Dimry, beaten for 13 touchdowns with the Falcons, was signed through Plan B. The safety corps of hard-hitters Steve Atwater and Dennis Smith still prevents many crossing patterns. Of course, as vulnerable as the Broncos were on the corners, why go inside anyway?

BRONCOS VETERAN ROSTER

HEAD COACH—Dan Reeves. Assistant Coaches—Marvin Bass, Barney Chavous, Joe DeCamillis, Mo Forte, George Henshaw, Pete Mangurian, Al Miller, Mike Nolan, Wade Phillips, Harold Richardson, Mike Shanahan, Ernie Stautner, Charlie Waters.

No.	Name	Pos.	Ht.	Wt.	NFL Exp.	College
27	Atwater, Steve	S	6-3	213	3	Arkansas
64	Beavers, Scott	OL	6-4	277	2	Georgia Tech
32	Bratton, Melvin	RB	6-1	225	3	Miami (Fla.)
34	Braxton, Tyrone	CB	5-11	185	5	North Dakota State
56	Brooks, Michael	LB	6-1	235	5	Louisiana State
92	Carreker, Alphonso	DE	6-6	272	8	Florida State
20	Clark, Kevin	OB	5-10	185	4	San Jose State
25	Corrington, Kip	S	6-0	175	3	Texas A&M
58	Curtis, Scott	LB	6-1	230	4	New Hampshire
62	Davidson, Jeff	G	6-5	309	2	Ohio State
55	Dennison, Rick	LB	6-3	220	10	Colorado State
—	Dimry, Charles	CB	6-0	175	5	Nevada-Las Vegas
7	Elway, John	QB	6-3	215	9	Stanford
35	Ezor, Blake	RB	5-9	183	2	Michigan State
63	Farrell, Sean	OG	6-3	260	10	Penn State
73	Fletcher, Simon	LB	6-5	240	7	Houston
99	Galloway, David	DE	6-3	265	10	Florida
—	Green, Gaston	RB	5-11	192	5	UCLA
87	Green, Paul	TE	6-3	230	3	Southern California
93	Haliburton, Ronnie	LB	6-4	230	2	Louisiana State
69	Hamilton, Darrell	T	6-5	298	3	North Carolina
24	Henderson, Wymon	CB	5-9	186	5	Nevada-Las Vegas
90	Holmes, Ron	DE	6-4	265	7	Washington
2	Horan, Mike	P	5-11	190	8	Long Beach State
26	Humphrey, Bobby	RB	6-1	201	3	Alabama
80	Jackson, Mark	WR	5-9	180	6	Purdue
82	Johnson, Vance	WR	5-11	185	7	Arizona
66	Juriga, Jim	G-T	6-6	275	4	Illinois
72	Kartz, Keith	C	6-4	270	5	California
88	Kay, Clarence	TE	6-2	237	8	Georgia
—	Ker, Crawford	G	6-3	285	8	Florida
71	Kragen, Greg	NT	6-3	265	7	Utah State
8	Kubiak, Gary	QB	6-0	192	9	Texas A&M
21	Lang, Le-Lo	DB	5-11	185	2	Washington
76	Lanier, Ken	T	6-3	290	11	Florida State
59	Lucas, Tim	LB	6-3	230	5	California
77	Mecklenburg, Karl	LB	6-3	240	9	Minnesota
52	Mills, Jeff	LB	6-3	238	2	Nebraska
22	Montgomery, Alton	OB	6-0	195	2	Houston
84	Nattiel, Ricky	WR	5-9	180	5	Florida
75	Parkinson, Brent	OL	6-5	267	2	Southern California
—	Perryman, Robert	RB	6-2	233	6	Michigan
91	Powers, Warren	DE	6-6	287	3	Maryland
48	Robbins, Randy	S	6-2	189	8	Arizona
30	Sewell, Steve	RB	6-3	210	7	Oklahoma
81	Sharpe, Shannon	WR	6-2	225	2	Savannah State
49	Smith, Dennis	S	6-3	200	11	Southern California
65	Smith, Monte	G	6-4	270	3	North Dakota
85	Stallworth, Tim	WR	5-10	185	2	Washington State
94	Szymanski, Jim	DE	6-5	268	2	Michigan State
53	Thompson, Anthony	LB	6-1	227	2	East Carolina
61	Townsend, Andre	DE-NT	6-3	265	8	Mississippi
9	Treadwell, David	K	6-1	175	3	Clemson
86	Verhulst, Chris	TE	6-2	249	4	Cal State-Chico
79	Widell, Dave	T	6-6	292	4	Boston College
67	Widell, Doug	G	6-4	287	3	Boston College
83	Young, Mike	WR	6-1	183	7	UCLA

TOP DRAFT CHOICES

Rd.	Name	Sel. No.	Pos.	Ht.	Wt.	College
1	Croel, Mike	4	LB	6-3	232	Nebraska
2	Johnson, Reggie	30	TE	6-2	256	Florida State
3	Traylor, Keith	61	LB	6-2	260	Central State
4	Russell, Derek	89	WR	6-0	179	Arkansas
5	Lewis, Greg	115	RB	5-10	214	Washington

SPECIAL TEAMS: Kevin Clark, a Canadian Football League import, led the Broncos with a 25.3 kickoff-return average and a 7.6 punt-return mark. Rich Horan rejected a three-year, $1.32 million offer from the Redskins to keep punting in the mile-high air. Placekicker David Treadwell, after an inconsistent year, found few takers on the Plan B market.

THE ROOKIES: The Broncos had a great draft. Croel, who has 4.5 speed, may be the outside linebacker they've been seeking for a decade. Third-round choice Keith Traylor of Central State (Okla.) can learn from the aging Mecklenburg at inside linebacker. Tight end Reggie Johnson of Florida State, considered the best blocker in the draft, can allow the Broncos to faze out Kay.

OUTLOOK: The AFC West is no longer an easy division, and the 5-11 Broncos might find it difficult to return to the 10- and 11-victory plateau. Those 7-1 division records are over, for now. Unless the Broncos add more talent to their defense and fix holes in their offense line, they might have trouble reaching the .500 mark.

BRONCO PROFILES

JOHN ELWAY 31 6-3 215 **Quarterback**

Proved that his powerful right arm can't compensate for team's inadequacies . . . Had highest completion percentage (58.6) in his career, but the Broncos won only five games . . . Completed between 70 and 80 percent of his attempts in three games . . . Passed for 3,526 yards . . . Played some of the best games of his career at the end of the season, showing his desire to win . . . Second-leading rusher with 258 yards and needs 67 yards to cross career plateau of 2,000 . . . Holds NFL record for six consecutive 3,000-yard passing and 200-yard rushing seasons . . . Threw only 15 touchdown passes, fewest since his rookie season in 1983 . . . Has brought the Broncos from behind in fourth quarters to win 17 games during career . . . Stanford All-American was first player picked in '83 draft, by Baltimore Colts, but didn't want to play in Baltimore and was traded to Broncos . . . Born

June 28, 1960, in Port Angeles, Wash. . . 1991 salary: $1.525 million.

BOBBY HUMPHREY 24 6-1 201 **Halfback**

Hobbled for three months with a severely sprained ankle suffered during a 177-yard game against the Bills on Sept. 30 . . . Finished third in American Conference with 1,202 rushing yards . . . Rushed for 132, 129 and 177 yards in consecutive games in September . . . Had eight 80-yard-plus rushing games . . . In two seasons, he has rushed for 2,353 yards and has gone to two Pro Bowls . . . Ranks fifth on team's all-time rushing list . . . Has developed his receiving skills and caught 24 passes as he becomes more versatile . . . A brilliant career at Alabama was shortened when he broke the a metatarsal bone in his left foot twice in one year . . . Skipped his senior season and went to the Broncos in the first round of a 1989 supplemental draft . . . Had five 100-yard games as a rookie . . . Gained 3,733 yards in three seasons at Alabama . . . Born Oct. 11, 1966, in Birmingham, Ala. . . . 1991 salary: $315,000.

STEVE ATWATER 24 6-3 213 **Free Safety**

Nicknamed the "Smiling Assassin" . . . NFL Films put a microphone on him for a Monday night game against the Chiefs and gave audience a classic display of violent hits . . . Perhaps the only player in league to knock Chiefs' fullback Christian Okoye completely off his feet . . . After that hit, he shouted to Okoye, "Yeah, you tried, baby." . . . Second to linebacker Michael Brooks on the Broncos with 173 combined tackles . . . In just two seasons, has 10 of the Broncos' top 25 games single-game tackle totals, highlighted by his 18-tackle game against the Steelers on Oct. 14 . . . Was a high-school basketball star who failed to attend the McDonald's All-Star Classic because of chicken pox . . . Made the All-Southwest Conference team three times and All-American twice at Arkansas . . . Was a first-round draft choice in 1989 . . . Cousin of Giants' wide receiver Mark Ingram . . . Born Oct. 28, 1966, in Chicago . . . 1991 salary: $300,000.

SIMON FLETCHER 29 6-5 240 **Linebacker**

Established himself as the team's most efficient pass-rusher with 11 sacks last season . . . Ranks seventh in team history with 42½ sacks, including 32 during the past three seasons . . . Tied team record with four-sack performance against the Vikings on Nov. 4 . . . Remains the Broncos' fastest linebacker with 4.7 speed in the 40 . . . Broncos weren't sure whether he was a defensive end or a linebacker when they drafted him in the second round of the 1985 draft . . . Gave him a chance to start in 1987 at linebacker after two seasons as a defensive end . . . Recorded 209 tackles during three seasons as a starting defensive lineman at the University of Houston . . . Switched from defensive tackle to defensive end in college . . . Born Feb. 18, 1962, in Bay City, Tex. . . . 1991 salary: $535,000.

MARK JACKSON 28 5-9 180 **Wide Receiver**

Ended Vance Johnson's three-year reign as the Broncos' leading receiver with 57 catches for 926 yards . . . Ranked eighth in the American Conference . . . Has 195 career catches for 3,398 yards . . . Had six of the team's top 11 yardage days . . . Has been inconsistent during his first five seasons, having his best years on even years (1986, 1988 and 1990) and following them with bad seasons . . . A big-play threat who has a 17.43 career reception average . . . Had 98 receptions during his final two seasons at Purdue on passes thrown by Jim Everett . . . A big-play receiver in the playoffs . . . Was an honorable mention All-Big Ten receiver . . . His 1989 season was marred by a broken collarbone, but he finished the year strong . . . Born July 23, 1963, in Chicago . . . 1991 salary: $475,000.

KARL MECKLENBURG 31 6-3 240 **Linebacker**

Chronic knee problems could make this his final season . . . Started 1990 as an outside linebacker for his pass-rushing ability, but coach Wade Phillips decided to move him inside . . . Though his range has declined, he is still one of the game's more dominating players . . . Returned a fumble for a touchdown against Seattle in September and recorded his first career safety in the season-finale against the Packers . . . Some believe that he hasn't played as well since he was leg-whipped by 49ers' guard Guy McIntyre during Super Bowl XXIV and suffered a knee injury that required surgery . . . Is the franchise's fourth-leading all-time quarterback sacker with 51½ . . . A former 12th-round draft choice who has played each of the positions on the defensive line and at linebacker . . . Is an accomplished guitar player . . . Holds a biology degree from University of Minnesota . . . Born Sept. 1, 1960, in Edina, Minn. . . . 1991 salary: $900,000.

VANCE JOHNSON 28 5-11 185 **Wide Receiver**

Hard to believe that the oft-injured Vance has played 50 consecutive games . . . He always complains about injuries, but he continues to stay on the field . . . His numbers dropped from 76 passes a year ago to 54 because of coach Dan Reeves' desire to pass less . . . Has 322 career catches and needs 31 to pass Steve Watson for third place on the team's all-time reception list . . . Had a nine-reception game against the Seahawks, but claimed he was permanently scarred because of a eye-gouge from cornerback Melvin Jenkins in a September game . . . A four-year tailback at Arizona who was the 1982 NCAA long-jump champion (26-11) . . . Joined Simon Fletcher as a second-round 1985 draft choice . . . Considered one of the most marketable artists in Colorado . . . Born March 13, 1963, in Trenton, N.J. . . . 1991 salary: $400,000 plus a $250,000 roster bonus.

KEN LANIER 32 6-3 290 **Tackle**

Several teams in the AFC West, including the Seahawks, gave him Pro Bowl votes . . . Is a senior member of an offensive line in transition . . . Has played in 141 games, including 133 in succession . . . Has 99 straight starts . . . At the end of 1990, he had started more games than the rest of the offensive line combined (136 to 128) . . . At Florida State, he was known as "Ironman" because he played 46 consecutive games . . . Was a fifth-round choice in 1981 and moved into the starting right-tackle spot the next season . . . Seahawks' defensive end Jacob Green ranks him as the best right tackle in AFC . . . Holds Florida State shot-put record of 60 feet, two inches . . . Born July 8, 1959, in Columbus, Ohio . . . 1991 salary: $750,000.

TYRONE BRAXTON 26 5-11 185 Cornerback

Considered the Broncos' best coverage cornerback until he blew out a knee against the Seahawks on Sept. 30 . . . After the injuries, he feared about his financial future because he had no contract after the season . . . Without him, the Broncos had difficulty covering receivers . . . His replacement, Elliott Smith, eventually had to be treated for a chemical dependency and was cut . . . Reeves believes the knee was ahead of schedule during its recovery . . . A 12th-round choice from North Dakota State in 1987 who entered the pros as a safety . . . Never played cornerback until asked by the Broncos . . . Ran on the 400-meter relay team at North Dakota State . . . Born Dec. 12, 1964, in Madison, Wisc. . . . 1990 salary: $184,000.

DOUG WIDELL 24 6-4 287 Guard

A powerful run-blocker who has yet to perfect his pass-blocking skills . . . At times, he ranks among the best run-blockers in the league . . . Brother, Dave, joined him with the Broncos after a trade and finished the season as the starting left guard . . . His performance slipped slightly after being named to the 1989 all-rookie team . . . Being a starter, he was removed from special-teams coverage units, where he excelled as a rookie . . . Came to the Broncos as a second-round choice from Boston College in 1989 . . . Had to play right tackle during his senior year in college, but he felt that he was out of position . . . Nonetheless, he made honorable mention All-American . . . Born Sept. 23, 1966, in Hartford, Conn. . . . 1991 salary: $210,000.

COACH DAN REEVES: Recovered from a training-camp heart problem and was back on the field coaching before the start of the regular season . . . Received a high-tech operation that cleaned out three of the arteries leading to his heart . . . Went on limited diet that dropped his weight into the 190s, less than his college playing weight . . . Perhaps had his most emotional season, displaying his frustration several times with tears . . . Has the fourth-best record among active coaches (90-61-1 during the regular season) . . . Has five first-place and three second-place finishes in 10 seasons . . . Has coached or played in eight Super Bowls . . . Spent two seasons as a Cowboys' player-coach in 1970-71 at the end of an eight-year career as a running back . . . Rushed for 1,990 yards and scored 25 touchdowns . . . Inducted into the South Carolina Hall of Fame after a fine career as a quarterback at South Carolina . . . Went into private business in 1973 before rejoining the Cowboys' coaching staff the next season . . . Was the NFL's youngest coach when he took over as head coach in 1981 . . . Bugged by rap that his teams make the Super Bowl but never win one . . . Born Jan. 19, 1944, in Americus, Ga.

GREATEST PUNTER

In Denver, it's supposed to be the thin mile-high air that makes punters great. Two punters—Al Fraser and Robert Scarpitto—had career averages of more than 44 yards a punt during the 1960s, and they only punted part-time.

Punting in Denver is a matter of brains and foot. Mike Horan combines those two elements. He has the leg to average 44 yards per kick during a season. He did that in 1988 and last year. But he has the brains to use the air for accuracy. During the past three seasons, he has averaged 19 punt placements inside the 20.

Horan is the king of the Denver air. He has a degree in mechanical engineering and has worked for Hughes Aircraft. On those offseason jobs, he designed radar and sonar equipment.

During the season, he punts those "smart bombs," those seemingly laser-guided punts that land inside opponents' 10-yard lines.

INDIVIDUAL BRONCO RECORDS

Rushing

Most Yards Game:	183	Otis Armstrong, vs Houston, 1974
Season:	1,407	Otis Armstrong, 1974
Career:	6,323	Floyd Little, 1967-75

Passing

Most TD Passes Game:	5	2 times, most recently John Elway, vs Minnesota, 1984
Season:	24	Frank Tripucka, 1960
Career:	135	John Elway, 1983-90

Receiving

Most TD Passes Game:	3	4 times, most recently Steve Watson, vs Baltimore, 1981
Season:	13	Steve Watson, 1981
Career:	44	Lionel Taylor, 1960-66
	44	Haven Moses, 1972-81

Scoring

Most Points Game:	21	Gene Mingo, vs Los Angeles, 1960
Season:	137	Gene Mingo, 1962
Career:	736	Jim Turner, 1971-79
Most TDs Game:	3	11 times, most recently Gerald Willhite, vs Kansas City, 1986
Season:	13	3 times, most recently Steve Watson, 1981
Career:	54	Floyd Little, 1967-75

HOUSTON OILERS

TEAM DIRECTORY: Pres./Owner: K.S. (Bud) Adams; Exec. VP/GM: Mike Holovak; Exec. VP/Adm.: Mike McClure; VP/Marketing and Broadcasting: Don MacLachlan; Dir. College Scouting: Dick Corrick; Dir. Business Oper.: Lewis Mangum; Dir. Media Services: Chip Namias; Head Coach: Jack Pardee. Home field: Astrodome (60,502). Colors: Scarlet, Columbia blue and white.

It should be thumbs-up again for the Moon man.

SCOUTING REPORT

OFFENSE: Coaches and GMs start worrying about players once they reach the age of 35, so naturally they're concerned about quarterback Warren Moon and wide receiver Drew Hill. Hill turns 35 in October and Moon does the same in November. As much as the Oilers' Run-n'-Shoot scheme is hyped, those two players are the main reason it works.

Moon, despite passing for 4,689 yards in 15 games, finished the season with a compound fracture of the thumb. Hill was benched during the 41-14 playoff loss to the Bengals in favor of Bernard Ford. Hill still doesn't know why that happened. All he knows is that he caught 74 passes for 1,019 yards.

Unless both players go over the hill, the Oilers will shoot for the Moon this year. With the Fab Four receivers, Moon could crack the 5,000-yard passing plateau. Had Curtis Duncan caught four more passes, the Oilers would have had four receivers at the 70-catch mark, a remarkable achievement. Duncan, Ernest Givins and Haywood Jeffires are all 27 or younger and are entering their prime.

After cutting their running back corps in half with the departures of Alonzo Highsmith and Mike Rozier, the Oilers don't have a back that is a natural fit in the Run-n'-Shoot. Lorenzo White filled the spot with a 702-yard season, but the Oilers will be on the lookout for a more adaptable back. Despite tackle Dean Steinkuhler's chronic elbow problems and the demotion of center Jay Pennison, the Oilers maintain an overpowering offensive line, featuring Pro Bowlers Bruce Matthews and Mike Munchak.

DEFENSE: Coach Jack Pardee doesn't offer a flashy defense; it's a basic 4-3. It might lack the excitement of his offense, but this defense is effective. Last year, the Oilers allowed only 30 defensive touchdowns—18 less than in 1989—and trimmed 36 yards (325.7 to 289.7) from their defensive statistics.

Pardee keeps opening opportunities for younger players by releasing some of the older Jerry Glanville mainstays. Before the draft, he rid the Oilers of cornerbacks Patrick Allen and Steve Brown and middle linebacker John Grimsley. Richard Johnson, formerly a backup in Glanville's doghouse, resurrected his career and worked in the "Air Patrol" secondary that ranked sixth in the league with 22 interceptions. Johnson led the squad with eight.

The Oilers' defense, led by Pro Bowl defensive tackle Ray Childress, has a mixture of power and brains. Linebacker Johnny Meads is a poor man's right outside linebacker who lacks the

OILERS VETERAN ROSTER

HEAD COACH—Jack Pardee. Assistant Coaches—Jim Eddy, Kevin Gilbride, Frank Novak, Chris Palmer, Richard Smith, Jim Stanley, Pat Thomas, Steve Watterson, Bob Young.

No.	Name	Pos.	Ht.	Wt.	NFL Exp.	College
76	Aim, Jeff	DT	6-6	269	1	Notre Dame
97	Banks, Robert	DE-DT	6-5	260	4	Notre Dame
37	Bergeson, Eric	S	5-11	192	2	Brigham Young
14	Carlson, Cody	QB	6-3	202	5	Baylor
79	Childress, Ray	DT-DE	6-6	272	7	Texas A&M
66	Dawson, Doug	G-C	6-3	288	4	Texas
28	Dishman, Cris	CB	6-0	178	4	Purdue
80	Duncan, Curtis	WR	5-11	184	5	Northwestern
51	Fairs, Eric	LB	6-3	244	6	Memphis State
88	Ford, Bernard	WR	5-10	171	3	Central Florida
95	Fuller, William	DE	6-3	265	6	North Carolina
8	Garcia, Teddy	PK	5-9	172	4	NE Louisiana
81	Givins, Ernest	WR	5-9	172	6	Louisville
93	Graf, Rick	LB	6-5	250	5	Wisconsin
22	Hagy, John	S	6-0	190	4	Texas
83	Harris, Leonard	WR	5-8	162	6	Texas Tech
85	Hill, Drew	WR	5-9	172	12	Georgia Tech
84	Jeffires, Haywood	WR	6-2	201	4	North Carolina State
90	Johnson, Ezra	DE	6-4	257	15	Morris Brown
23	Johnson, Richard	CB	6-1	195	7	Wisonsin
87	Johnson, Richard L.	WR	5-6	185	3	Colorado
86	Jones, Cedric	WR	6-1	184	10	Duke
96	Jones, Sean	DE	6-7	264	3	Northeastern
82	Jones, Tony	WR	5-7	139	2	Texas
32	Jordan, Tony	RB	6-2	220	3	Kansas State
27	Kinard, Terry	S	6-1	198	9	Clemson
21	Knight, Leander	DB	6-1	192	3	Montclair State
56	Kozak, Scott	LB	6-3	222	3	Oregon
57	Lathon, Lamar	LB	6-3	244	2	Houston
78	Maggs, Don	T-G	6-5	290	5	Tulane
74	Matthews, Bruce	G-C	6-5	291	9	Southern California
25	McDowell, Bubba	S	6-1	198	3	Miami (Fla.)
89	McNeil, Gerald	WR-KR	5-8	142	6	Baylor
91	Meads, Johnny	LB	6-2	226	8	Nicholls State
94	Montgomery, Glenn	DT	6-0	268	3	Houston
9	Montgomery, Greg	P	6-4	215	4	Michigan State
1	Moon, Warren	QB	6-3	212	8	Washington
63	Munchak, Mike	G	6-3	284	10	Penn State
64	Norgard, Erik	C-G	6-1	278	2	Colorado
26	Orlando, Bo	S	5-10	180	2	West Virginia
72	Peguese, Willis	DE	6-4	267	2	Miami (Fla.)
20	Pinkett, Allen	RB	5-9	196	6	Notre Dame
31	Porter, Kerry	RB	6-2	220	4	Washington State
53	Seale, Eugene	LB	5-10	253	5	Lamar
10	Slack, Reggie	QB	6-1	221	1	Auburn
54	Smith, Al	LB	6-1	244	5	Utah State
99	Smith, Doug	DT	6-6	314	7	Auburn
70	Steinkuhler, Dean	T	6-3	287	8	Nebraska
68	Stewart, Alex	DE	6-4	260	1	Cal-Fullerton
36	Thomas, Dee	CB	5-10	176	2	Nicholls State
44	White, Lorenzo	RB	5-11	222	4	Michigan State
73	Williams, David	T	6-5	292	3	Florida

TOP DRAFT CHOICES

Rd.	Name	Sel. No.	Pos.	Ht.	Wt.	College
2	Dumas, Mike	28	S	5-11	173	Indiana
2	Lewis, Darryl	38	DB	5-8	193	Arizona
2	Flannery, John	44	C	6-3	304	Syracuse
3	Jackson, Steve	71	DB	5-8	182	Purdue
3	Donnalley, Kevin	79	OT	6-5	290	North Carolina

recognition he deserves. For power, the Oilers offer strong safety Bubba McDowell and last-year's top choice Lamar Lathon, a 244-pound assault machine with 4.5 speed. Up front, ends Sean Jones and William Fuller combined for 20½ sacks.

SPECIAL TEAMS: Greg Montgomery might be the least-used punter in pro football, but he is one of the most appreciated. His 45-yard average would have earned him a trip to the Pro Bowl, but the successful Run-n'-Shoot offense doesn't give him a chance. Kicker Teddy Garcia has one of the strongest unrefined legs in the sport. He made 14-of-20 field goals, including 12 of his last 16, in nine games, but he was lent to the World League for additional experience. Gerald "Ice Cube" McNeil didn't provide the expected excitement as the return-specialist.

THE ROOKIES: The Oilers saved money by trading out of the first round. With seven choices between the 28th and 102nd, they filled needs adequately. They grabbed a short but promising safety (Mike Dumas of Indiana), a tough nickel cornerback (Darryl Lewis of Arizona), two speedy cover guys (Steve Jackson of Purdue and Marcus Robertson of Iowa State), a 300-pound center (John Flannery of Syracuse), a powerful tackle (Kevin Donnalley of North Carolina) and a defensive tackle (David Rocker of Auburn).

OUTLOOK: Gradually, teams might learn to defense the Run-n'-Shoot, but it will take years. If his receivers hold onto more passes, Moon could not only pass the 5,000-yard plateau, but he could increase his touchdown tosses from 33 into the forties. The 9-7 Oilers struggled to a 2-3 start learning Pardee's ways, but a fast launch this year could mean a trip to the playoffs.

OILER PROFILES

WARREN MOON 34 6-3 212 **Quarterback**

Could have shattered NFL single-season records had he not suffered an open-thumb dislocation in the final two minutes of a Dec. 23 loss to the Bengals . . . The injury forced him to miss the Oilers' season-finale but he returned for the Pro Bowl . . . Needed 17 completions, 40 passing attempts and 396 yards to break Dan Marino's single-season records . . . Finished with 362 completions, 584 attempts and 4,689 yards . . . Has only missed nine games during his seven-year NFL career . . . Tied NFL single-season record with 18 fumbles . . . Became only the third quarterback in NFL history to pass for more than 4,000 yards, joining Marino and Dan Fouts, and almost become the second 5,000-yard thrower . . . Unwanted by the NFL, Moon played six seasons for the Edmonton Eskimos in the Canadian Football League before joining the Oilers in 1984 . . . Scheduled to make $4 million in final year of his contract in 1993 . . . Was the MVP of 1978 Rose Bowl in University of Washington's victory over Michigan . . . Born Nov. 18, 1956, in Los Angeles . . . 1991 salary: $1.5 million.

RAY CHILDRESS 28 6-6 272 Defensive Lineman

Successfully made the switch from end to tackle in Jack Pardee's 4-3 defense . . . Though he isn't the pass-rusher Bruce Smith is, Childress is one of the game's most dominating defenders . . . Made the Pro Bowl at end and at tackle . . . One of toughest defenders against the run in the league . . . Had eight quarterback sacks . . . Led Oiler linemen for sixth consecutive year in tackles with 65 . . . Was the third player selected in the 1985 draft . . . A shrewd businessman who owns a construction business in Dallas and is a partner in apartment syndicates and cattle ranches . . . Earned starting defensive-line job during his freshman season at Texas A&M . . . Born Oct. 20, 1962, in Memphis, Tenn. . . . 1991 salary: $700,000 plus $120,000 roster bonus.

BRUCE MATTHEWS 30 6-5 291 Guard-Center

Perhaps the most versatile and most valuable offensive lineman in the league . . . Could earn Pro Bowl honors at virtually every position on the line . . . Recruited to play center in the final weeks of the season because of poor play by Jan Pennison, and he stuffed nose tackles from Pittsburgh and Cincinnati . . . Might stay at center this season . . . Has gone to the past three Pro Bowls . . . Was the ninth player chosen in the 1983 draft after a brilliant career at Southern Cal . . . Dominating run-blocker as well as a great pass-blocker . . . Brother, Clay, plays linebacker for the rival Browns and father played linebacker for the 49ers during the 1950s . . . Faced difficult offseason contract negotiation . . . Deep-snaps on punts and kicks . . . Born Aug. 8, 1961, in Raleigh, N.C. . . . 1990 salary: $425,000.

ERNEST GIVINS 26 5-9 172 **Wide Receiver**

Youthful leader of the Fab Four receivers who became the first quartet in NFL history to catch 65 passes each . . . Made 72 receptions for 979 yards and a team-high nine touchdowns . . . Not the fastest receiver on the team, but he is extremely dangerous with the hitch passes . . . The ideal slot receiver for a Run-n'-Shoot offense . . . Not a disciplined route-runner and does drop too many passes . . . Concerned about mounting number of concussions suffered during career . . . Caught 301 passes during his first five seasons . . . Came to the Oilers in the second round of the 1986 draft . . . Caught 67 passes during two-year starting career at Louisville . . . Has 4.36 speed in the 40 . . . Born Sept. 3, 1964, in St. Petersburg, Fla. . . . 1991 salary: $700,000.

BUBBA McDOWELL 24 6-1 198 **Strong Safety**

Plays much bigger than his size . . . Like a linebacker in a safety's body . . . Finished third on the team with 81 tackles . . . Loves to play the run . . . Blocked three punts during his first two NFL seasons . . . Blocked nine punts during career at the University of Miami . . . Despite being a third-round choice in 1989, McDowell has played like a first-rounder . . . One of only nine rookies to start every game of the 1989 season . . . Made instant impact at Miami by blocking five punts during sophomore season . . . Made 181 career tackles in college . . . Born Nov. 4, 1966, in Missouri City, Tex. . . . 1991 salary: $185,000.

DREW HILL 34 5-9 172 **Wide Receiver**

Ageless receiver retains his ability to get behind defenders . . . Tied with teammate Haywood Jeffires for first in the American Conference with 74 receptions . . . Has 1,000-yard receiving years in four of his six seasons with the Oilers . . . Acquired from the Rams for fourth- and seventh-round draft choices in 1985 . . . Was upset late in the season when coach Jack Pardee started inserting other receivers for him for matchup purposes . . . Has had amazing career since being drafted by the Rams in the 12th round in 1979 . . . Caught 450 passes during his career . . . Was one of the nation's top return specialists at Georgia Tech . . . Has five seasons with at least 60 catches . . . Caught more passes in all but one Oiler season than he did during a five-year Rams' career in which he caught 60 passes . . . Born Oct. 5, 1956, in Newman, Ga. . . . 1991 salary: $700,000 plus $200,000 roster bonus.

MIKE MUNCHAK 31 6-3 284 **Guard**

Went to the Pro Bowl for the sixth time . . . The prototype NFL guard who can pull to the outside and overpower defenders at the line of scrimmage . . . He is the most honored Oiler since Earl Campbell . . . Isn't as versatile as Bruce Matthews and wouldn't do as well at tackle . . . Had no lingering effects from off-season elbow surgery . . . Many scouts considered him to be the best athlete available in 1982 draft but lasted until the eighth choice . . . Had brilliant career at Penn State, blocking for Curt Warner and other top backs . . . Knee injury in 1986 jeopardized his future but he recovered to go to the Pro Bowl the next season . . . Has been a Pro Bowl starter four times . . . Born March 5, 1960, in Scranton, Pa. . . . 1991 salary: $800,000.

JOHNNY MEADS 30 6-2 226 **Linebacker**

He's called the poor man's outside linebacker . . . Quiet and unassuming, Meads gets his job done quietly and without his own fanfare, a trademark that works better in Jack Pardee's system than it did when Jerry Glanville was coach . . . Does an excellent job dropping into zone and rarely has passes thrown in his area . . . Finished second to linebacker Al Smith (101) with 95 tackles . . . His nickname is "Sandman" because he puts quarterbacks to sleep . . . Came to the Oilers in 1984 as a third-round draft choice . . . Walk-on at Nicholls State and ended up starting three seasons, mostly as a defensive lineman . . . His second pro season was marred by knee surgery . . . Is an effective blitzer . . . Born June 25, 1961, in New Orleans . . . 1990 salary: $350,000.

HAYWOOD JEFFIRES 26 6-2 201 Wide Receiver

Is the only tall receiver among the Oilers, whom some call Haywood and the Seven Dwarfs . . . Listed at 6-2, he might be 6-4 and still growing . . . Made the biggest improvement among the Oiler receivers . . . Has great downfield speed . . . Had 47 receptions in 1989 and 74 for 1,048 yards last year . . . Coaches also liked the way that he blocked downfield . . . On a receiving corps that dropped numerous passes, he made corrections to enable him to become a more sure-handed receiver . . . Started only one game and caught only nine passes during first two seasons . . . Has competed in the NFL's "Fastest Man" contest . . . Accomplished receiver at North Carolina State who was drafted by Oilers in the first round of 1987 draft . . . Born Dec. 12, 1964, in Shreveport, La. . . . 1990 salary: $250,000.

RICHARD JOHNSON 29 5-6 185 Wide Receiver

Joins Oilers from the Lions via Plan B . . . Small, daring receiver was ideal for Detroit's Silver Stretch offense . . . Led Lions in receptions for the second year in a row . . . Caught 64 passes for 727 yards and six TDs . . . Started all 16 games . . . Caught seven passes in three different games . . . USFL refugee bounced around several NFL camps before landing in Detroit in 1989 . . . Caught 70 passes for 1,091 yards and eight TDs in 1989 . . . Led USFL in receiving as quarterback Jim Kelly's favorite target with Houston Gamblers in 1984 and 1985 . . . Caught 115 passes in 1984 and 103 in 1985 . . . Played running back at Colorado . . . Born Oct. 19, 1961, in San Pedro, Cal. . . . 1991 salary: $300,000 plus $25,000 signing bonus.

LORENZO WHITE 25 5-11 222 Halfback

Had an up-and-down season but emerged as the Oilers' lone setback . . . Led team with 702 yards and a 4.2-yard average and rushed for eight touchdowns . . . Might not be considered ideal for the Run-n'-Shoot, but filled the job adequately . . . The Oilers traded Alonzo Highsmith to Dallas and cut Mike Rozier, opening White's chance to start . . . Needs to correct a fumbling problem after putting ball on the ground seven times last year . . . Set Big Ten records for 991 carries during four-year career at Michigan State . . . Was 22nd choice in 1988 draft . . . Rushed for 3,500 yards and scored 34 touchdowns in high school . . . Had tough contract negotiation scheduled during offseason . . . Born April 12, 1966, in Hollywood, Fla. . . . 1990 salary: $250,000.

COACH JACK PARDEE: Overhauled offense and defense last year . . . By putting in the 4-3 defense, the Oilers became one of the most difficult teams to move the ball against, allowing only 290 yards a game . . . The Run-n'-Shoot approach to the offense came close to breaking numerous NFL records . . . Has won everywhere he has coached . . . Coached in four leagues (the NFL, WFL, USFL and the Southwest Conference) . . . Was the head coach of the Redskins and the Bears before taking job as the defensive coordinator of the Chargers in 1981 . . . Brought the Run-n'-Shoot to the Houston Gamblers of the USFL in 1984 and 1985 . . . The University of Houston hired him from 1987 through 1989 . . . His NFL career record is 53-53 . . . Was All-American linebacker for Bear Bryant at Alabama and had two Pro-Bowl seasons during a 15-year NFL career . . . Survived a bout with cancer . . . He is the 14th coach in the 31-year history of the Oilers . . . Was the Coach of the Year in 1979 for the Redskins . . . Born April 19, 1936, in Exira, Iowa.

GREATEST PUNTER

Greg Montgomery is the Maytag repairman without the endorsements. Maytag won a warm spot in the hearts of appliance-lovers by advertising washing machines that never needed repair. As the ads went, the loneliest job in town was that of the Maytag repairman.

In Houston, loneliness is being a punter in a Run-n'-Shoot offense. Warren Moon moved the offense so effectively that Montgomery only punted 34 times in 16 games, only 18 times in the final 11. "Greg's happy for the success of the offense," GM Mike Holovak said, "but he would like to kick some more."

Montgomery's inactivity cost him a trip to the Pro Bowl. The good news was that he averaged 45 yards a punt, best in the NFL. The bad news was that he failed to meet the 40-punt requirement for his statistics to count.

Only in Houston is Montgomery appreciated. Around the NFL, few know that he has done everything to justify his selection in the third round of the 1988 draft. His average jumped from 38.8 to 43.3 in 1989, convincing management they had selected the best punter in franchise history. Now, if they can figure out a way to use him . . .

INDIVIDUAL OILER RECORDS

Rushing

Most Yards Game:	216	Billy Cannon, vs N.Y. Jets, 1961
Season:	1,934	Earl Campbell, 1980
Career:	8,574	Earl Campbell, 1978-84

Passing

Most TD Passes Game:	7	George Blanda, vs N.Y. Titans, 1961
Season:	36	George Blanda, 1961
Career:	165	George Blanda, 1960-66

Receiving

Most TD Passes Game:	3	8 times, most recently Drew Hill, vs Washington, 1988
Season:	17	Bill Groman, 1961
Career:	51	Charlie Hennigan, 1960-66

Scoring

Most Points Game:	30	Billy Cannon, vs N.Y. Titans, 1961
Season:	115	2 times, most recently Tony Zendejas, 1989
Career:	596	George Blanda, 1960-66
Most TDs Game:	5	Billy Cannon, vs N.Y. Titans, 1961
Season:	19	Earl Campbell, 1979
Career:	73	Earl Campbell, 1978-84

INDIANAPOLIS COLTS

TEAM DIRECTORY: Pres./Tres.: Robert Irsay; VP/GM: Jim Irsay; VP/Gen. Counsel: Michael Chernoff; Dir. Player Personnel: Jack Bushofsky; Dir. Pub. Rel.: Craig Kelley; Head Coach: Ron Meyer. Home field: Hoosier Dome (60,127). Colors: Royal blue and white.

SCOUTING REPORT

OFFENSE: The metamorphosis began last year, thanks to the rapid development of rookie quarterback Jeff George. Instead of being a run-run-run team that was totally reliant on Eric Dickerson,

By George, Jeff proved a comer in rookie campaign.

the Colts found there are yards to be gained via the pass as well. Part of that was by necessity. Dickerson missed the early part of the 1990 season because of his injury/contract problems.

The Colts had to go to the air and they found that George was as good as they hoped when they traded Andre Rison, Chris Hinton and a first-round pick for him. He threw the ball well, hung in under pressure and was actually something of a team leader.

Not having Rison deprived George of the deep blazer, but the Colts compensated with veterans Stanley Morgan, Clarence Verdin and Bill Brooks. That combination sparked a late surge that saw the Colts go 5-3 (7-9 overall) over the second half despite a ragged running game.

The Colts rushed the ball only 335 times, a non-strike-year franchise low. The 1,282 rushing yards were also a franchise low. Dickerson rushed for only 677 yards, ending his NFL-record string of seven straight 1,000-yard seasons. Look for a resurgence this year.

The offensive line is a weak point. It really struggled last year and George, despite his Marino-esque release, was sacked 37 times in the 13 games he played.

DEFENSE: Like all Ron Meyer teams, the Colts' defense doesn't give up any easy yards. Their secondary may have problems and their front seven may not be All-Pro material, but they play well together and they make you pay for the territory you gain.

The linebackers are the strength, particularly Jeff Herrod and Duane Bickett, a former Pro Bowler who has to re-establish that level again. Fredd Young has been a major disappointment while Chip Banks, another veteran acquired in a trade, was capable.

Up front, Jon Hand and Harvey Armstrong are dependable veterans but age and contract hassles held Donnell Thompson to 39 tackles last year.

None of the cornerbacks is able to handle people man-to-man, so they're very vulnerable when the Colts gamble with the blitz.

SPECIAL TEAMS: The Colts have two of the best kickers in the division and perhaps the league. Rohn Stark is a Pro Bowl punter and Dean Biasucci has proven to be a big-game, crunch-time placekicker.

Verdin set up several victories with his punt returns.

THE ROOKIES: The Colts, without a first-round pick, chose Shane Curry, Miami defensive lineman, as their No. 1 and then went for a couple of Colorado Buffaloes in defensive back Dave

COLTS VETERAN ROSTER

HEAD COACH—Ron Meyer. Assistant Coaches—Leon Burtnett, George Catavolos, Sylvester Croom, Steve Furness, Milt Jackson, Bill Muir, Brad Seely, Rick Venturi, Tom Zupancic.

No.	Name	Pos.	Ht.	Wt.	NFL Exp.	College
79	Armstrong, Harvey	NT	6-3	282	9	Southern Methodist
62	Baldinger, Brian	OG	6-4	278	9	Duke
31	Ball, Michael	DB	6-0	220	4	Southern University
51	Banks, Chip	LB	6-4	245	9	Southern California
94	Bates, Stephen	NT	6-4	253	1	James Madison
36	Baylor, John	DB	6-0	203	3	Southern Mississippi
81	Beach, Pat	TE	6-4	249	9	Washington State
20	Bentley, Albert	RB	5-11	217	7	Miami
4	Biasucci, Dean	K	6-0	190	7	Western Carolina
50	Bickett, Duane	LB	6-5	251	7	Southern California
80	Brooks, Bill	WR	6-0	189	6	Boston University
71	Call, Kevin	OT	6-7	305	8	Colorado State
76	Clancy, Sam	DE	6-7	300	8	Pittsburgh
66	Cline, Michael	LB	6-4	279	1	Arkansas State
66	Conlin, Chris	OL	6-4	290	3	Penn State
72	Cunningham, Pat	OT	6-6	312	1	Texas A&M
38	Daniel, Eugene	DB	5-11	188	8	Louisiana State
95	Davis, Travis	NT	6-2	283	2	Michigan State
35	Davis, Willie	DB	5-11	202	1	Southern Illinois
29	Dickerson, Eric	RB	6-3	224	9	Southern Methodist
69	Dixon, Randy	OG	6-3	302	5	Pittsburgh
53	Donaldson, Ray	C	6-3	300	12	Georgia
58	Ficaro, Cedric	LB	6-3	258	4	Notre Dame
75	Gabalczyk, Mark	DL	6-6	281	3	Western Michigan
11	George, Jeff	QB	6-4	221	2	Illinois
37	Goode, Chris	DB	6-0	196	5	Alabama
26	Grant, Alan	DB	5-10	187	2	Stanford
2	Green, Jarrod	WR	6-1	200	1	Oklahoma State
78	Hand, Jon	DE	6-7	301	6	Alabama
9	Herrmann, Mark	QB	6-4	220	10	Purdue
54	Herrod, Jeff	LB	6-0	246	4	Mississippi
84	Hester, Jessie	WR	5-11	172	6	Florida State
12	Hilger, Rusty	QB	6-4	209	6	Oklahoma State
25	Holloway, Cornell	DB	5-11	182	2	Pittsburgh
44	Howard, William	RB	6-1	250	3	Tennessee
1	Huffman, Darvell	WR	5-8	158	1	Boston University
59	Jaworski, Matthew	LB	6-1	227	1	Colgate
23	Johnson, Anthony	FB	6-0	222	2	Notre Dame
57	Johnson, Walter	LB	6-0	240	4	Louisiana Tech
33	Lattimore, Brian	RB	6-1	202	1	SE Missouri State
90	McCullough, Richard	DE	6-5	284	3	Clemson
96	McDonald, Quintus	LB	6-3	263	3	Penn State
87	Mobley, Orson	TE	6-5	259	6	Salem College
86	Morgan, Stanley	WR	5-11	185	15	Tennessee
73	Moss, Zepross	OT	6-6	338	3	Alabama State
61	Pozderac, Phil	OT	6-9	292	7	Notre Dame
39	Prior, Mike	DB	6-0	210	6	Illinois State
97	Radecic, Scott	LB	6-3	236	8	Penn State
34	Robinson, Ron	DB	6-0	185	1	Kentucky
74	Schultz, William	OT	6-5	305	2	Southern California
85	Simmons, Stacey	WR	5-9	183	2	Florida
98	Siracusa, Tony	NT	6-3	303	2	Pittsburgh
3	Stark, Rohn	P	6-3	203	10	Florida State
30	Streeter, George	DB	6-2	215	3	Notre Dame
27	Taylor, Keith	DB	5-11	206	4	Illinois
99	Thompson, Donnell	DE	6-4	280	11	North Carolina
40	Thornton, Reggie	WR	5-10	170	1	Bowling Green
68	Tomberlin, Pat	OT	6-2	310	2	Florida State
10	Trudeau, Jack	QB	6-3	219	6	Illinois
83	Verdin, Clarence	WR	5-8	162	6	SW Louisiana
92	Walker, Tony	LB	6-3	235	2	SE Missouri State
93	Weir, Robert	DL	6-3	287	1	Southern Methodist

TOP DRAFT CHOICES

Rd.	Name	Sel. No.	Pos.	Ht.	Wt.	College
2	Curry, Shane	40	DE	6-4	259	Miami
3	McCloughan, Dave	69	DB	6-0	180	Colorado
4	Vander Poel, Mark	96	OT	6-7	303	Colorado
5	Cash, Kerry	125	TE	6-4	247	Texas
6	Agee, Mel	152	DT	6-5	282	Illinois

McCloughan and tackle Mark Vander Poel. McCloughan, a track man, has the speed and Vander Poel the bulk at 303 pounds.

OUTLOOK: If they can come up with a cornerback or two to cover people deep and can get Dickerson back in a football mode, this team could surprise some people and might even contend for a playoff spot.

COLT PROFILES

JEFF GEORGE 23 6-4 221 **Quarterback**

It cost the Colts Andre Rison, Chris Hinton and a first-round pick to get George, but after one year it looks like they got a bargain . . . The rookie showed leadership, poise and a strong arm . . . Although he was 5-7 in starts, the team was 5-3 under his direction in the second half on the season . . . Only the eighth QB in NFL history to throw more touchdowns (16) than interceptions (13) as a rookie . . . Completed 181 of 334 passes for 2,152 yards . . . Completed 50 percent of his passes in nine of his 13 games . . . Over the second half of the season, he completed 120 of 220 passes (54.5 percent) for 1,553 yards and 14 touchdowns, with seven interceptions . . . The first player taken in the 1990 draft, he earned $900,000 in base pay as well as a $2,750,000 signing bonus . . . Left the University of Illinois after his junior year to enter the NFL draft . . . National high school Player of the Year from Warren Central High School in Indianapolis . . . Born Dec. 8, 1967, in Indianapolis.

BILL BROOKS 27 6-0 189 **Wide Receiver**

Finished second on the team in receptions with 62 for 823 yards and five touchdowns, trailing only Albert Bentley (71 catches) . . . Led the team in receiving yardage for the third straight year . . . Needs only 229 yards to pass Roger Carr into fifth place among Colts' all-time receivers . . . Had at least four receptions in nine games last year . . . A fourth-round draft pick from Boston University in 1986, he earned $550,000 last year . . . Born April 6, 1964, in Boston.

ERIC DICKERSON 30 6-3 224 **Running Back**

Missed the first five games of the season after being suspended for "conduct detrimental to the team" for failure to report . . . As a result, his NFL-record string of seven straight 1,000-yard seasons was ended . . . Finished the season with 677 yards and four touchdowns on 166 carries . . . Over his career, Dickerson has gained 11,903 yards on 2,616 attempts and rushed for 86 touchdowns, fifth on the NFL's all-time list . . . A six-time Pro Bowler, he was the second player taken in the 1983 draft . . . Played at SMU under current head coach Ron Meyer . . . Has four rushing titles in his career, putting him in second place in NFL history in that category . . . Despite his off-field problems last year, he wound up accounting for 41 of the team's 81 rushing first downs . . . Born Sept. 2, 1960, in Sealy, Tex. . . . 1990 salary: $1,450,000.

ALBERT BENTLEY 31 5-11 217 **Running Back**

The Colts' most productive offensive player in 1990 . . . Led the team in receptions with 71 for 664 yards, both career highs . . . Second to Eric Dickerson in rushing yardage with 556 yards and four touchdowns on 137 carries . . Started in 15 games . . . He's played six seasons with the Colts after two years in the USFL . . . The Colts' second-round pick, out of University of Miami, in the supplemental draft of 1984 . . . His 137 rushing attempts were second-most of his Colts' career . . . One of only five Colts to have more than 70 receptions in one season . . . One of the most complete backs in the league, he is also an excellent blocker . . . Born Aug. 15, 1960, in Immokalee, Fla. . . . 1990 salary: $425,000.

DUANE BICKETT 28 6-5 251 **Linebacker**

Second to Jeff Herrod in tackles, he had 117 hits, 84 of them unassisted . . . Recorded 10 or more tackles in six games and has had 27 games of double-digit tackles . . . Missed an October game against Kansas City because of a hamstring injury, snapping a run of 80 consecutive starts . . . A first-round draft pick from USC in 1985 . . . Prototypical outside linebacker, he's big enough to take on the run and fast enough to either rush the passer or drop back in coverage . . . A Pro Bowl starter following the 1987 season . . . Born Dec. 1, 1962, in Los Angeles . . . 1990 salary: $850,000.

JON HAND 27 6-7 301 **Defensive End**

Missed the first week of the season because of a contract dispute and then sat out three games late in the year because of a knee injury . . . Finished the season with only 3½ sacks but was the leading tackler among the defensive linemen with 63 tackles, 44 of them unassisted . . . The fourth player taken in the 1986 draft, Hand played at Alabama . . . He earned $690,000 in base pay as well as a $650,000 signing bonus last year . . . Had his best year in 1989, recording 10 sacks, nine pressures and 85 tackles . . . Born Nov. 13, 1963, in Sylacauga, Ala.

JEFF HERROD 25 6-0 246 **Linebacker**

One of the unsung heroes of the Colts, he was the leading tackler in 11 of the 13 games he played and finished the season with a team-high 155 tackles, 95 unassisted . . . Also had 4½ sacks . . . He had double-figure tackle totals in 11 of the 13 games he played and had 16 tackles in each of three games . . . Missed the first game of the season because of a contract dispute and another two because of injury . . . A ninth-round draft pick from Mississippi in 1988, he earned $400,000 in base salary as well as another $100,000 as a reporting bonus as part of a new contract . . . First cousin of the actor Mr. T . . . Born July 29, 1966, in Birmingham, Ala.

CHIP BANKS 31 6-4 245 **Linebacker**

The only Colts' linebacker to start all 16 games last year, he finished the season with 69 tackles, sixth on the team . . . A former first-round pick (third player taken) by the Browns in 1982, he went to the Colts in 1988 in a trade with San Diego and earned $375,000 last year . . . Missed all of 1988 and first half of 1989 following drug involvement but the Colts took a chance and traded a third-round pick to acquire Banks from San

Diego . . . Went to the Chargers from Cleveland in a draft-day trade in 1987 and was voted first alternate for the AFC Pro Bowl team . . . Born Sept. 18, 1959, in Fort Lawton, Okla.

ROHN STARK 32 6-3 203 **Punter**

A second-round pick in the 1982 draft, Stark has twice been the AFC's punter in the Pro Bowl . . . Last year, he had a 43.4-yard average (longest punt a 61-yarder) and led the NFL for much of the year before finishing third to Mike Horan of the Broncos and Sean Landeta of the Giants . . . Has won three NFL punting championships . . . Earned $415,000 as well as a $100,000 signing bonus last year . . . A four-year letterman at Florida State, he played in 1980 and 1981 Orange Bowls and Japan and Olympia Gold Bowls . . . Has a pilot's license . . . Born April 4, 1959, in Minneapolis.

MIKE PRIOR 28 6-0 210 **Free Safety**

Led the secondary in tackles (third on the team) with 113 last year and 81 of them were unassisted . . . Also had three interceptions and 15 deflections as the center fielder in the Colts' defense . . . With 18 career interceptions, he's three away from ninth place on the Colts' all-time list . . . A free-agent acquisition in 1986, he earned $325,000 last year . . . Has a degree in business administration from Illinois State . . . Born Nov. 14, 1963, in Chicago Heights, Ill.

COACH RON MEYER: A specialist in reclamation projects, he went to Indianapolis late in 1986 after turning around programs at Nevada-Las Vegas and SMU and with the New England Patriots . . . The Pats had fired him in 1984 even though team was 5-3 . . . Colts were 0-13 when he took over and they went from a finesse, passing team to a physical, grind-it-out club . . . Won all three remaining games that season and in 1987 they won the AFC East with a 9-6 mark . . . Colts went 9-7 and

8-8 the next two years and wound up at 7-9 last season by winning five of their last eight games . . . NFL record with Pats and Colts is 44-45 . . . Born Feb. 17, 1941, in Westerville, Ohio . . . Was a walk-on defensive back at Purdue, where he won school's Nobel Kizer Award for athletic and academic achievement in 1963.

GREATEST PUNTER

The Colts' surprising decision to use a second-round draft pick, the 34th choice overall, in the 1982 draft to select Rohn Stark, a punter from Florida State, turned out to be a wise choice. Stark's career average is at the 44-yard level. That puts him in fourth place on the NFL's all-time punting list behind Sammy Baugh (45.1), Tommy Davis (44.78) and Yale Lary (44.3).

Stark has been selected to the Pro Bowl three times and has led the league in punting three times. In 1990 he ranked third among punters with a 43.4 average (third-lowest of his career), trailing Mike Horan of Denver (44.8) and Sean Landeta of the Giants (43.8). If Stark had finished first, it would have been his fourth NFL punting title and would have tied him with Jerrel Wilson and Baugh for the most punting championships in league history. With three titles, Stark is tied with Ray Guy, Lary and Jim Fraser.

INDIVIDUAL COLT RECORDS

Rushing

Most Yards Game:	198	Norm Bulaich, vs N.Y. Jets, 1971
Season:	1,659	Eric Dickerson, 1988
Career:	5,487	Lydell Mitchell, 1972-77

Passing

Most TD Passes Game:	5	2 times, most recently Gary Hogeboom, vs Buffalo, 1987
Season:	32	John Unitas, 1959
Career:	287	John Unitas, 1956-72

Receiving

Most TD Passes Game:	3	6 times, most recently Roger Carr, vs Cincinnati, 1976
Season:	14	Raymond Berry, 1959
Career:	68	Raymond Berry, 1955-67

Scoring

Most Points Game:	24	5 times, most recently Eric Dickerson, vs Denver, 1988
Season:	120	Lenny Moore, 1964
Career:	678	Lenny Moore, 1956-67
Most TDs Game:	4	5 times, most recently Eric Dickerson, vs Denver, 1988
Season:	20	Lenny Moore, 1964
Career:	113	Lenny Moore, 1956-67

Eric Dickerson looks to return to a 1,000-yard season.

KANSAS CITY CHIEFS

TEAM DIRECTORY: Owner: Lamar Hunt; Pres./COO/GM: Carl Peterson; Exec. VP-Adm.: Tim Connolly; Player Personnel Dir.: Whitey Dovell; Dir. Pub. Rel.: Robert Moore; Head Coach: Marty Schottenheimer. Home field: Arrowhead Stadium (78,097). Colors: Red and gold.

SCOUTING REPORT

OFFENSE: Steve DeBerg has never been put in this position. Thoughout his 15-year career, he was always the quarterback destined for replacement. Now, he's the 37-year-old quarterback upon whom the Chiefs are depending for a trip to the Super Bowl.

Can DeBerg stage an encore to his amazing 1990 season? He ranked third in the league with a 96.3 rating, and his four interceptions in 444 attempts was the second-best ratio in league history. And few can still believe he threw for seven passes of 60 yards or more in an offense that lacks a deep threat. This might be DeBerg's last chance at the brass ring, but the Chiefs, 11-5 last year, will give him every chance to grab it.

With that in mind, they added tight end Pete Holohan, who caught 49 passes for the Rams, and scatback Troy Stradford from Miami via Plan B. Certainly DeBerg has two overpowering running backs—Barry Word and Christian Okoye—to take the pressure off him. And the Chiefs added young blood—and insurance—in the form of rookie running back Harvey Williams of Louisiana State.

What DeBerg lacks is deep speed. J.J. Birden and unproven Freddie Jones might become those targets. Dependable Stephone Paige catches defenders asleep with his deceptive speed. But the Chiefs' success falls on DeBerg's right arm.

DEFENSE: What can you give a defense that has everything? With the addition of inside linebacker Percy Snow, the Chiefs have six of their front seven defenders capable of making the Pro Bowl. Their front three of Bill Maas, Dan Saleaumua and Neil Smith are awesome. Their linebacking corps of Derrick Thomas, Snow, Dino Hackett and Chris Martin is fearsome.

Cornerbacks Albert Lewis and Kevin Ross are the game's best coverage tandem. With Kevin Porter developing into a great run-stopper at strong safety, the only question mark in the defense is at free safety, where former Pro Bowler Deron Cherry battles knee

Speedy cornerback Albert Lewis is a menace to receivers.

problems and age. With six Pro Bowls behind him and the knee healed, Cherry is ready for a fling at a title.

Team president Carl Peterson and coach Marty Schottenheimer acquired defensive end Ron Stallworth from the Jets in a trade. Linebackers Ricky Shaw (Eagles) and Marc Mumford (Broncos) offer backup support.

SPECIAL TEAMS: The Plan B departure of Naz Worthen left the Chiefs without their most active return specialist. Of course, with Worthen, the Chiefs had substandard return units (6.9 per punt and 17 yards a kickoff). Kicking is secure, with Nick Lowery making 34-of-37 attempts. Bryan Barker replaced Kelly Goodburn as the punter.

CHIEFS VETERAN ROSTER

HEAD COACH—Marty Schottenheimer. Assistant Coaches—Bruce Arians, Bill Cowher, Tony Dungy, Jim Erkenbeck, Howard Mudd, Joe Pendry, Tom Pratt, Dave Redding, Al Saunders, Kurt Schottenheimer, Darvin Wallis.

No.	Name	Pos.	Ht.	Wt.	NFL Exp.	College
76	Alt, John	T	6-7	300	8	Iowa
77	Baldinger, Rich	T	6-4	291	10	Wake Forest
4	Barker, Bryan	P	6-1	187	2	Santa Clara
40	Bell, Billy	CB	5-10	170	2	Lamar
99	Bell, Mike	DE	6-4	266	11	Colorado State
26	Bell, Richard	RB	6-0	200	2	Nebraska
88	Birden, J.J.	WR-KR	5-9	160	3	Oregon
25	Boysaw, Greg	S-CB	6-1	207	1	Illinois
34	Burruss, Lloyd	S	6-0	211	11	Maryland
55	Charlton, Clifford	LB	6-3	245	3	Florida
20	Cherry, Deron	S	5-11	205	11	Rutgers
84	Davis, Willie	WR	6-0	159	1	Central Arkansas
17	DeBerg, Steve	QB	6-3	214	15	San Jose State
19	Dixon, Titus	WR	5-6	152	2	Troy State
94	Dunn, Chris	LB	6-3	235	1	Cal Poly-SLO
10	Elkins, Mike	QB	6-3	225	3	Wake Forest
91	Fears, Willie	DE-NT	6-4	287	3	Northwestern State
22	Gamble, Kenny	RB-KR	5-10	206	4	Colgate
74	Graham, Derrick	T	6-4	306	2	Appalachian State
98	Griffin, Leonard	DE	6-4	275	6	Grambling
61	Grunhard, Tim	C	6-2	302	2	Notre Dame
56	Hackett, Dino	ILB	6-3	230	6	Appalachian State
86	Harry, Emile	WR	5-11	188	5	Stanford
85	Hayes, Jonathan	TE	6-5	254	7	Iowa
89	Holohan, Pete	TE	6-4	235	11	Notre Dame
41	Hoskins, Eric	CB-S	5-11	175	1	Missouri Western
43	Jones, Bill	RB	5-11	228	3	SW Texas State
80	Jones, Fred	WR-KR	5-9	175	2	Grambling
29	Lewis, Albert	CB	6-2	198	9	Grambling
8	Lowery, Nick	K	6-4	205	12	Dartmouth
72	Lutz, David	G	6-6	305	9	Georgia Tech
63	Maas, Bill	DE	6-5	270	8	Pittsburgh
57	Martin, Chris	OLB	6-2	245	9	Auburn
51	Marts, Lonnie	OLB	6-1	235	2	Tulane
48	McNair, Todd	RB-KR	6-1	197	3	Temple
30	Mitchell, Stump	RB	5-9	194	10	The Citadel
50	Munford, Marc	LB	6-2	231	5	Nebraska
35	Okoye, Christian	RB	6-1	260	5	Azusa Pacific
83	Paige, Stephone	WR	6-2	188	9	Fresno State
24	Pearson, Jayice	CB	5-11	180	6	Washington
11	Pelluer, Steve	QB	6-4	212	8	Washington
45	Petry, Stan	CB	5-11	180	3	Texas Christian
27	Porter, Kevin	S	5-10	214	4	Auburn
52	Rogers, Tracy	ILB	6-2	241	2	Fresno State
31	Ross, Kevin	CB	5-9	182	8	Temple
87	Sadowski, Troy	TE	6-5	265	2	Georgia
97	Saleaumua, Dan	NT	6-0	285	5	Arizona State
21	Saxon, James	RB	5-11	225	4	San Jose State
93	Shaw, Ricky	LB	6-4	240	4	Oklahoma State
54	Simien, Tracy	LB	6-1	245	1	Texas Christian
95	Sims, Tom	NT	6-2	285	2	Pittsburgh
90	Smith, Neil	DE	6-4	275	4	Nebraska
59	Snow, Percy	ILB	6-2	248	2	Michigan State
96	Stallworth, Ron	DE	6-5	260	3	Auburn
25	Stradford, Troy	RB	5-9	192	5	Boston College
79	Szott, David	G	6-4	278	2	Penn State
58	Thomas, Derrick	OLB	6-3	234	3	Alabama
81	Thomas, Robb	WR	5-11	174	3	Oregon State
32	Thompson, Ernest	RB	6-2	236	1	Georgia Southern
13	Vlasic, Mark	QB	6-3	206	4	Iowa
46	Washington, Charles	CB	6-1	210	3	Cameron
82	Whitaker, Danta	TE	6-4	248	3	Miss. Valley State
70	Williams, Larry	G	6-5	290	4	Notre Dame
65	Winters, Frank	G-C	6-3	285	5	Western Illinois
23	Word, Barry	RB	6-2	230	3	Virginia

TOP DRAFT CHOICES

Rd.	Name	Sel. No.	Pos.	Ht.	Wt.	College
1	Williams, Harvey	21	RB	6-2	215	LSU
2	Valerio, Joe	50	OT	6-5	293	Penn
3	Barnett, Tim	77	WR	6-1	201	Jackson State
5	Mincy, Charles	133	DB	5-11	187	Washington
6	Malone, Darrell	162	DB	5-10	182	Jacksonville State

THE ROOKIES: Schottenheimer loves to stockpile running backs. Williams, plagued by knee troubles in college, could be a 1,000-yard producer in the Chiefs' offense. Penn's Joe Valerio is the type of sleeper tackle that Schottenheimer usually grooms into greatness. Tim Barnett of Jackson State is raw, but has great jumping ability and could become the next Paige.

OUTLOOK: The Chiefs will battle the Raiders again for the division and the chance to go to the Super Bowl. Their defense is younger and has more impact players than the Raiders, but the Raiders offer more striking power. The 17-week chase will be among the most interesting in the NFL this year.

CHIEF PROFILES

ALBERT LEWIS 30 6-2 198 **Cornerback**

A remarkable athlete who's actually improved his speed as he's aged . . . Instead of running the 4.45 40s he sprinted in college, he fires off consistent 4.36s . . . During a 51-day holdout last summer, he stared at tapes of receivers running pass routes . . . Has a tape library on 400 receivers . . . Played in 129 games and has 28 career interceptions . . . Went the entire season without surrendering a touchdown but was beaten by Mark Clayton for a fourth-quarter touchdown in a playoff loss to the Dolphins . . . Went to his fourth Pro Bowl . . . Blocked four punts to increase his career total to nine . . . Drafted in the third round of the 1983 draft and won a starting job in the final week of the season . . . Intercepted 11 passes during his final two seasons at Grambling . . . Born Oct. 6, 1960, in Mansfield, La. . . . 1991 base salary: $700,000.

KEVIN ROSS 29 5-9 182 **Cornerback**

Gets more action on his side than Albert Lewis but enjoys it more because of his love for contact . . . Intercepted five passes to increase his career total to 26 and went to his second Pro Bowl . . . Deflected a team-high 16 passes . . . Has averaged 5½ tackles a game since becoming a starter in 1984 . . . Former Steeler receiver John Stallworth embarrassed Ross by beating him often in the 1984 season-opener, but Ross quickly rebounded to become Chiefs' best rookie . . . Came to the Chiefs as an unknown seventh-round choice from Temple . . . Held out 43 days last year . . . Intercepted 13 passes and made 249 tackles at Temple . . . Nickname is "Rock" . . . Born Jan. 16, 1962, in Camden, N.J.

DERRICK THOMAS 25 6-3 234 Linebacker

In his second year, started establishing Lawrence Taylor-type sack numbers (20) . . . Has 30 sacks in 31 NFL games . . . His seven-sack performance against Seahawk quarterback Dave Krieg was unforgettable, but Krieg broke from his arms to throw the game-winning touchdown pass with no time left on the clock . . . Has started in the past two Pro Bowls . . . Led Chiefs with six forced fumbles . . . His father, Air Force Capt. Robert Thomas, was shot down during a mission in Vietnam when Derrick was five years old . . . Considered the nation's top pass-rusher during his final two years at Alabama, when he recorded 52 sacks . . . Has 4.52 speed in the 40 . . . Named Defensive Rookie of the Year in 1989 . . . Born March 29, 1966, in Miami . . . 1991 base salary: $500,000.

STEVE DeBERG 37 6-3 214 Quarterback

Stunned the pro football world by making his 14th season his best . . . Was the league's third-rated passer (96.3) . . . Threw only four interceptions in 444 attempts, second-best in NFL history to Joe Ferguson . . . Failed to throw an interception in 14 of 16 games, a remarkable total for a veteran who averaged 1.2 interceptions per game during his first 13 seasons . . . Ranks 17th on career passing-yardage list (28,490) . . . Considered one of the best play-action passers in football because of his ability to fake handoffs . . . Passed for 3,444 yards and 23 touchdowns . . . Brought the big play to the Chiefs' offense by completing seven passes for 60 or more yards . . . Is 16-6 since he took over as starter in 1989 . . . Has been with five NFL teams since the Cowboys made him a 10th-round choice out of San Jose State in 1977 . . . Played with Joe Montana, John Elway and Vinny Testaverde and eventually lost his job . . . Born Jan. 19, 1954, in Oakland . . . 1990 base salary: $675,000.

BARRY WORD 27 6-2 230 Fullback

A remarkable comeback story of a player who virtually went from prison to the Pro Bowl . . . Convinced Chiefs' management that his mistakes—a six-month prison term for drug distribution—were behind him . . . After starting the season as a backup, rushed for 1,105 yards and became the sixth Chief to rush for 1,000 yards . . . Had team-record 200 yards rushing against Detroit and three 100-yard games . . . A former NCAA 110-meter hurdler when he was at Virginia. Word offers more moves than Christian Okoye . . . Entered the NFL as a third-round choice of the Saints but played in only two games during the 1988 and 1989 seasons . . . Gained only 133 yards and had only 36 NFL carries before last season . . . Gained 1,224 yards during his senior year at Virginia . . . Born July 17, 1964, in Long Island, Va. . . . 1990 base salary: $114,000.

CHRISTIAN OKOYE 30 6-1 260 Fullback

Never achieved the same success that enabled him to lead the NFL in rushing in 1989 . . . Took a physical beating early in the season and had a modest 3.3-yard-per-carry average . . . Finished the season with 805 yards . . . Had only one 100-yard game—seven less than a year ago—and only three games in which he rushed for at least 85 yards . . . In four seasons, he has 3,418 rushing yards . . . Began NFL career with 4.46 speed in the 40-yard dash . . . Didn't have the moves to slip past gang-tackling defenders . . . A former Nigerian track-and-field star who was coaxed into trying out for the Azusa Pacific football team . . . Born Aug. 16, 1961, in Enugu, Nigeria . . . 1991 base salary: $625,000.

NEIL SMITH 25 6-4 275 Defensive End

Should have collected more Pro Bowl votes than he did . . . Selected as the second pick in the 1988 draft, Smith has become one of the league's most dominating defensive ends . . . Attacks blockers on every play . . . Known at Nebraska as a supreme run-stopper, he learned pass-rushing skills, recorded 9½ sacks and led the Chiefs with 44 quarterback pressures . . .

Came to Nebraska as a 208-pound freshman with 5.09 speed in the 40 . . . Now runs sub-4.6 40s . . . Former GM Jim Schaaf received public criticism for giving the Lions a second-round choice to move up to take Smith, but Schaaf looks like a genius . . . Born April 10, 1966, in New Orleans . . . 1991 base salary: $500,000.

JOHN ALT 29 6-7 300 **Tackle**

One of the least recognized pass-blockers . . . Because of his quick feet and long arms, he shuts out charging defenders . . . Allowed only one sack last season . . . Worked on his run-blocking last summer and now is becoming dominant in that category . . . Plays on an overpowering offensive line that averages 6-5, 294 pounds per man . . . Started his college career at Iowa as a tight end but moved over to tackle after two seasons . . . Increased weight from 230 to 279 pounds to make the transition . . . The Chiefs made him the 21st player selected in the 1984 draft . . . Played tight end, punter and kicker in high school. . . . Best tackle not be selected to a Pro Bowl . . . Born May 30, 1962, in Stuttgart, Germany . . . 1991 base salary: $425,000.

STEPHONE PAIGE 29 6-2 188 **Wide Receiver**

Finished second in the AFC with 1,021 yards and led the Chiefs with 65 catches . . . Became the third Chief to cross the 1,000-yard barrier, joining Carlos Carson and Otis Taylor . . . Has caught passes in 80 consecutive games . . . Though he is considered a possession receiver, he has averaged more than 17.2 yards a catch . . . Has deceptive speed, similar to Jerry Rice . . . Overshadowed at Fresno State by Henry Ellard, he joined the Chiefs in 1983 as a free agent and became a starter midway through his third season . . . Had touchdowns of 83 and 96 yards last season . . . Caught only 44 passes in 1989 because of the Chiefs' run-oriented offense . . . Played two years at Saddleback (Cal.) Junior College . . . Born Oct. 15, 1961, in Slidell, La. . . . 1991 base salary: $675,000.

NICK LOWERY 35 6-4 189 Kicker

Went to his second Pro Bowl after leading the NFL with 139 points and a 91.9 field-goal accuracy percentage, fourth-highest in NFL history . . . Made 34-of-37 field-goal attempts . . . His 79-percent career average (259 of 328) is the best in history . . . Made 21 consecutive field goals during one stretch last year . . . Missed his only attempt outside of the 50-yardline last season, but holds NFL record with 18 field goals longer than 50 . . . Was unsuccessful in tryouts with eight teams until he joined the Chiefs as a free agent in 1980 . . . Graduated from Dartmouth with a government degree . . . Worked as an intern for U.S. Senator John Chafee . . . Born May 27, 1956, in Munich, Germany . . . 1991 base salary: $425,000.

PETE HOLOHAN 32 6-4 235 Tight End

Plan B signee from the Rams, where he was key to team's potent passing game . . . Lined up as "H-back" in one-back formation and served as one of quarterback Jim Everett's favorite receivers . . . Third on Rams in catches in 1990 with 49 . . . Twenty of his receptions came on third-down conversions and resulted in first downs . . . Had caught 151 passes in three seasons with the Rams . . . Best season was 1988 with 59 catches . . . Spent seven seasons with San Diego . . . Rams acquired him in exchange for fourth-round draft pick in 1988 . . . Chargers' seventh-round pick out of Notre Dame in 1981 . . . Born Aug. 25, 1959, in Albany, N.Y. . . . 1990 base salary: $325,000.

COACH MARTY SCHOTTENHEIMER: He's Mr. Playoffs, going to the playoffs in five of his six full seasons as head coach . . . Has coached the Chiefs to two of their four winning seasons since 1974 . . . Builds his team around a powerful running attack and aggressive man-to-man cornerbacks . . . A positive thinker who tries to make his team believe that it will go to the Super Bowl . . . His reg-

ular-season record is 63-39-1 . . . Playoff record is 2-5 . . . During the past 21 games with the Chiefs, his record is 15-6, fourth-best in the NFL . . . After being an All-American linebacker at the University of Pittsburgh in the 1960s, he bounced around the NFL as a special-teams player and defensive backup . . . Coaching career began in 1974 with the Portland Storm of the World Football League after starting the season as a player . . . Was Lawrence Taylor's first position coach when he was with the Giants . . . Left the Browns in 1988 after a spat with owner Art Modell over the makeup of his coaching staff . . . Had taken the Browns to two consecutive trips to the AFC title game . . . Born Sept. 23, 1943, in Canonsburg, Pa.

GREATEST PUNTER

Hank Stram snickered at the thought. The former Chiefs' coach was asked why Jerrel Wilson never gently placed his punts. Finesse, outsiders said, might make the American Football League all-time punter that much better. Why, folks wondered, didn't Stram ever tame the punter known as "Thunderfoot?"

"Would you try to make a boxer out of Rocky Marciano?" Stram replied.

Wilson was to punting what Marciano was to boxing, a knockout artist. He stood 6-4 and weighed 225 pounds. Some called him "Duck," a reference either to his swagger or his reputation as a hunter. Others yelled it when he boomed low line drives. Once, he drove a punt off the rear end of a teammate. The ball richocheted to the back of the end zone for a safety.

His powerful body survived from 1963 to 1977. During that span, he averaged a remarkable 43.6 yards a punt. Talk about going the distance? His 1,014 punts traveled 44,185 yards. If needed, he'd play fullback or linebacker. Finesse? No way.

INDIVIDUAL CHIEF RECORDS

Rushing

Most Yards Game:	200	Barry Word. vs Detroit. 1990
Season:	1.480	Christian Okoye. 1989
Career:	4.451	Ed Podolak. 1969-77

Passing

Most TD Passes Game:	6	Len Dawson, vs Denver, 1964
Season:	30	Len Dawson, 1964
Career:	237	Len Dawson, 1962-75

Receiving

Most TD Passes Game:	4	Frank Jackson, vs San Diego, 1964
Season:	12	Chris Burford, 1962
Career:	57	Otis Taylor, 1965-75

Scoring

Most Points Game:	30	Abner Haynes, vs Oakland, 1961
Season:	139	Nick Lowery, 1990
Career:	1,231	Jan Stenerud, 1967-79
Most TDs Game:	5	Abner Haynes, vs Oakland, 1961
Season:	19	Abner Haynes, 1962
Career:	60	Otis Taylor, 1965-75

LOS ANGELES RAIDERS

TEAM DIRECTORY: President: Al Davis; Exec. Asst.: Al LoCasale; Sr. Exec.: John Herrera; Sr. Administrator: Morris Bradshaw; Business Mgr.: John Novak; Publications: Mike Taylor; Head Coach: Art Shell. Home field: Los Angeles Memorial Coliseum (92,487). Colors: Silver and black.

SCOUTING REPORT

OFFENSE: Raiders' boss Al Davis doesn't sit still. When he's not plotting a course to move the franchise to another city, he fiddles with the roster. Fearless, Davis isn't afraid to gamble. After all, didn't he risk a seventh-round draft choice on Bo Jackson, steal Max Montoya from the Cincinnati Bengals, etc., etc.?

Roger Craig is the latest attempt to keep the offense moving. After hearing that the 49ers questioned whether Craig could still be a Pro Bowl back, Davis jumped in and gave him a two-year contract. If Craig can regain any of his 1989 skills, his addition will minimize the loss of Jackson, whose hip dislocation put his football career in jeopardy. Jackson led the Raiders with 698 rushing yards, but Davis will have Craig, Marcus Allen and Greg Bell at halfback for a complete season.

Under the guidance of quarterback coach Mike White, Jay Schroeder minimized mistakes and had a great season, throwing 19 touchdown passes and only nine interceptions. Outsiders doubt whether Schroeder is right for the job, but Davis stays with him. He put Steve Beuerlein on the sidelines with a clipboard all season to keep Schroeder free of controversy. With Schroeder, the bomb returned to the Raiders' offense.

Montoya's addition placed the Raiders among the best blocking teams in the league. Center Don Mosebar and guard Steve Wisniewski went to the Pro Bowl and Montoya played well enough to join them.

DEFENSE: Still smarting from a 51-3 loss to the Bills in the AFC championship game, Davis brought in future Hall-of-Fame safety Ronnie Lott. A disenchanted 49er, like Craig, Lott won't be asked to play 16 games. He'll share the strong-safety job with veteran Mike Harden and also work with Eddie "The Hitman" Anderson, a Jack Tatum-like free safety.

The Raiders keep teams guessing about their linebacking corps. Jerry Robinson will be 35 in December and needs a partner to

Jay Schroeder comes off best year since '86 as a Redskin.

share the position. Aaron Wallace, a second-round choice last year, is being groomed for that job. Thomas Benson and Riki Ellison are destined for replacement at the other starting job. O'Brien Alston, a Plan B signee with a history of knee problems, could challenge Benson for the job at left outside. Ellison played the middle well despite a bad knee.

RAIDERS VETERAN ROSTER

HEAD COACH—Art Shell. Assistant Coaches—Dave Adolph, Fred Biletnikoff, Gunther Cunningham, Kim Helton, Earl Leggert, Steve Ortmayer, Terry Robiskie, Joe Scanella, Jack Stanton, Tom Walsh, Mike White, Doug Wilkerson.

No.	Name	Pos.	Ht.	Wt.	NFL Exp.	College
44	Adams, Stefon	WR	5-10	185	6	East Carolina
80	Alexander, Mike	WR	6-3	185	2	Penn State
32	Allen, Marcus	RB	6-2	210	10	Southern California
59	Alston, O'Brien	LB	6-6	245	3	Maryland
33	Anderson, Eddie	S	6-1	205	6	Fort Valley State
28	Bell, Greg	RB	5-10	210	8	Notre Dame
54	Benson, Tom	LB	6-2	240	8	Oklahoma
7	Beuerlein, Steve	QB	6-2	210	3	Notre Dame
24	Brown, Ron	CB	5-11	185	8	Arizona State
81	Brown, Tim	WR	6-0	195	3	Notre Dame
97	Burton, Ron	LB	6-1	245	5	North Carolina
95	Charles, Mike	DT	6-4	315	9	Syracuse
55	Cofield, Tim	LB	6-2	240	5	Elizabeth City State
22	Craig, Roger	RB	6-0	224	9	Nebraska
23	Crudup, Derrick	S	6-2	215	2	Oklahoma
70	Davis, Scott	DE	6-7	275	4	Illinois
46	Dorn, Torin	CB	6-0	190	2	North Carolina
84	Dyal, Mike	TE	6-2	240	3	Texas A&I
50	Ellison, Riki	LB	6-2	230	8	Southern California
86	Fernandez, Mervyn	WR	6-3	200	5	San Jose State
73	FitzPatrick, James	T	6-7	320	6	Southern California
83	Gault, Willie	WR	6-1	180	9	Tennessee
26	Glenn, Vencie	S	6-0	190	6	Indiana State
79	Golic, Bob	DT	6-2	275	12	Notre Dame
6	Gossett, Jeff	P	6-2	195	10	Eastern Illinois
85	Graddy, Sam	WR	5-10	180	4	Tennessee
60	Graves, Rory	T	6-6	295	4	Ohio State
45	Harden, Mike	S	6-1	200	12	Michigan
62	Harrell, Newt	G	6-5	285	1	West Texas State
82	Holland, Jamie	WR	6-1	195	5	Ohio State
88	Horton, Ethan	TE	6-4	240	5	North Carolina
34	Jackson, Bo	RB	6-1	230	5	Auburn
18	Jaeger, Jeff	K	5-11	195	4	Washington
58	Jimerson, A.J.	LB	6-3	235	2	Norfolk State
92	King, Emanuel	DE	6-4	270	6	Alabama
53	Klostermann, Bruce	LB	6-4	235	4	South Dakota State
25	Land, Dan	S	6-0	195	3	Albany State
21	Lewis, Garry	CB	5-11	185	2	Alcorn State
37	Lloyd, Doug	RB	6-1	220	1	North Dakota State
75	Long, Howie	DE	6-5	270	11	Villanova
42	Lott, Ronnie	S	6-0	200	11	Southern California
91	Mark, Greg	DE	6-3	260	2	Miami
41	McCallum, Napoleon	RB	6-2	225	3	Naval Academy
36	McDaniel, Terry	CB	5-10	180	3	Tennessee
77	McElroy, Reggie	T	6-6	285	9	West Texas State
65	Montoya, Max	G	6-5	290	13	UCLA
72	Mosebar, Don	C	6-6	280	9	Southern California
99	Moss, Winston	LB	6-3	245	5	Miami
31	Mueller, Vance	RB	6-0	220	6	Occidental
71	Patten, Joel	T	6-7	305	7	Duke
43	Patterson, Elvis	CB	5-11	195	8	Kansas
66	Peat, Todd	G	6-2	315	4	Northern Illinois
57	Robinson, Jerry	LB	6-2	230	13	UCLA
78	Rother, Tim	DT	6-7	280	3	Nebraska
13	Schroeder, Jay	QB	6-4	215	8	UCLA
94	Smith, Anthony	DE	6-3	265	1	Arizona
35	Smith, Steve	RB	6-1	240	5	Penn State
93	Townsend, Greg	DE	6-3	270	9	Texas Christian
67	Turk, Dan	C	6-4	275	8	Wisconsin
89	Tyler, Rob	TE	6-5	255	2	South Carolina State
51	Wallace, Aaron	LB	6-3	235	2	Texas A&M
48	Washington, Lionel	CB	6-0	185	9	Tulane
68	Wilkerson, Bruce	T	6-5	295	5	Tennessee
40	Wilson, Marcus	S	6-1	200	1	Virginia
90	Wise, Mike	DE	6-7	270	5	Cal-Davis
76	Wisniewski, Steve	G	6-4	280	3	Penn State
66	Wright, Steve	T	6-6	280	9	Northern Iowa

TOP DRAFT CHOICES

Rd.	Name	Sel. No.	Pos.	Ht.	Wt.	College
1	Marinovich, Todd	24	QB	6-4	210	USC
2	Bell, Nick	43	RB	6-2	252	Iowa
4	Ismail, Raghib	100	WR	5-10	175	Notre Dame
6	Harrison, Nolan	146	DT	6-5	290	Indiana
8	Jones, Brian	213	LB	6-1	242	Texas

Anthony Smith, the surprising first-round choice a year ago, has recovered from a knee injury and will try to fit into the defensive line. Earl Leggett returns to the line as coach, so Smith will be taught the Raider way. With Howie Long, Bob Golic and Greg Townsend growing older, potential replacements should be developing.

SPECIAL TEAMS: No change between the kicking teams. Jeff Jaeger made 15 of his 20 field goals. Jeff Gossett, despite having two kicks blocked, has the quickest release time among league punters. The Raiders improved their speed on the coverage teams, but their speedier returners didn't break many big plays.

THE ROOKIES: It was a typical Davis draft. Quarterback Todd Marinovich of USC has Raider blood in his veins because his father, Marv, played for the Raiders. Give him a couple years and another Ken Stabler could emerge. The 252-pound Nick Bell of Iowa is a tough inside runner. If Raghib "Rocket" Ismail tires of the Canadian Football League, he could become a Raider next year.

OUTLOOK: The Raiders, 12-4 last year, are close. Had they not stumbled in the AFC championship game, Davis would have been spouting "Just Win, Baby" at the Super Bowl. The one problem they have is age. By midseason, their defense could be starting eight players in their 30s. That's why the Lott acquisition is important. The Raiders are also close to another rebuilding program.

RAIDER PROFILES

JAY SCHROEDER 30 6-4 215 Quarterback

Talked Raiders' boss Al Davis into giving him a $100,000 paycut and a chance to win back the starting job . . . Davis hired former Illinois coach Mike White to rebuild him as a thrower . . . White restructured his drop and timed his retreat with the routes of receivers . . . Completed 54.5 percent of his attempts, the first time in four years he's completed more than half of his passes . . . Averaged only 21 attempts per game, limiting his chances of making mistakes . . . Threw 19 touchdown passes and only nine interceptions . . . A former UCLA quarterback who played four seasons of minor-league baseball before switching back to football and becoming the Redskins' third-round choice in 1984 . . . Came to the Raiders in a trade involving tackle Jim Lachey in 1988 . . . Debuted with the Redskins after Joe Theismann suffered a career-ending injury . . . Passed for 4,109 yards in 1986, but was benched several times by coach Joe Gibbs in next couple of seasons . . . Born June 28, 1961, in Milwaukee . . . 1990 salary: $900,000.

HOWIE LONG 31 6-5 270 **Defensive End**

Became a dominating defender again after two injury-plagued seasons . . . Remains a blocking problem for any line . . . Still receives double-team blocking . . . Recorded six sacks to increase his career total to 71½ . . . Should have gone to the Pro Bowl a seventh time . . . NFL Defensive Player of the Year in 1984 and 1986 . . . Played college ball at Villanova, where he also established himself as a boxing champion . . . Despite back problems, came to the Raiders in the second round of the 1981 draft . . . His best season was 1983, when he had 13 sacks . . . Calf problems plagued him in 1988 . . . Born Jan. 6, 1960, in Somerville, Mass. . . . 1991 salary: $1.25 million.

ROGER CRAIG 31 6-0 224 **Halfback**

He went from the cover of the 49ers' press guide to the unprotected list, from the Pro Bowl to Plan B . . . Signed during the very last hours of Plan B upon a recommendation of former 49ers' teammate Ronnie Lott . . . The 49ers thought his Pro Bowl days were over after a 439-yard season in which he averaged 3.1-yards per carry . . . For the past two years, he dropped weight to improve speed and he might have lost his strength . . . Weighed 215 pounds in 1988, 205 in 1989 and 190 last year . . . First player in 49ers' history to rush for three consecutive 1,000-yard seasons . . . Will share the halfback position with Marcus Allen and Greg Bell . . . Rushed for 7,064 yards during eight-year career with the 49ers . . . His reception total dropped from 62 in 1989 to 25 last year . . . Was Nebraska's fourth-leading rusher (2,446 yards) at tailback and fullback . . . Taken in second round of 1983 draft . . . Born July 10, 1960, in Preston, Miss. . . . 1991 salary: $750,000.

MARCUS ALLEN 31 6-2 210 **Halfback**

This dependable back was present when the Raiders needed him, rushing for 140 yards during a playoff victory over the Bengals . . . Scored 13 touchdowns, including 12 on the ground, his best offensive production since 1985 . . . Had scored 22 touchdowns during the previous four seasons . . . Rushed for 682 yards on 179 carries, sharing the halfback job with Bo Jackson and Greg Bell . . . Had 15 receptions, his lowest total in NFL career . . . Hasn't been to the Pro Bowl since 1987, when Jackson became a Raider . . . In nine seasons, he's rushed for 7,957 yards . . . Was the 10th player chosen in the 1982 draft, out of Southern Cal, where he won the 1981 Heisman Trophy . . . Has annual contract problems and had to hold out seven days during 1990 training camp . . . Born March 26, 1960, in San Diego . . . 1990 salary: $1.1 million.

GREG TOWNSEND 29 6-3 270 **Defensive End**

Gambled during a contract holdout in 1990 that he could have a Pro-Bowl year and won . . . Missed 30 days of training camp but still had one of his best seasons . . . After leading the team with 12½ sacks, he expects a big raise . . . Shaved his head to establish himself as one of the true Raider characters . . . Admitted that he let the excesses of success—too much partying—get the best of him during his early Raider days . . . Holds talks for people wanting to recover from chemical dependency . . . Has 84 sacks during his first eight seasons, but always seems to make the right play when one-on-one against a ball-carrier . . . Was a fourth-round choice in 1983 from Texas Christian . . . Irritated opponents by standing close to huddles before plays . . . Spent some of his career at linebacker, but fits in better as a defensive end in the 4-3 scheme . . . Born Nov. 3, 1961, in Los Angeles . . . 1991 salary: $1.1 million.

MERVYN FERNANDEZ 31 6-3 200 Wide Receiver

Demands passes in critical moments of games . . . A tough, lanky receiver with speed who is willing to go into the middle of a defense for catches and can break free of tackles . . . Led Raiders with 52 receptions and five touchdown passes . . . Has 109 receptions during the past two seasons . . . His numbers dropped slightly because Jay Schroeder only threw 21 and completed 11 passes a game . . . Came to Raiders from the B.C. Lions of the Canadian Football League, where he caught 374 passes in five seasons . . . Was CFL MVP in 1985 . . . Nicknamed "Swervin' Mervyn" . . . In 1988, he led NFL with 26-yard average . . . Was a 10th-round draft choice from San Jose State in 1983 . . . Born Dec. 29, 1959, in Merced, Cal. . . . 1990 salary: $500,000.

STEVE WISNIEWSKI 24 6-4 280 Guard

Went to the Pro Bowl in his second season . . . The guidance of veteran linemen Don Mosebar and Max Montoya helped to bring out the best in this former Penn State All-American . . . Raiders made a draft-day trade with Dallas Cowboys in 1989 to make him their second-round choice . . . Al Davis considered him the best pure blocker in that draft . . . Started 15 games as a rookie . . . Older brother Leo played nose tackle for the Baltimore Colts . . . Started three seasons in college . . . Only third offensive linemen in Penn State history to be named first-team All-American . . . Made all-rookie team in 1989 . . . Was youngest player on Raider roster at the age of 22 . . . Born April 7, 1967, in Rutland, Vt. . . . 1991 salary: $250,000.

DON MOSEBAR 29 6-6 280 Center

Changed the thinking about NFL center . . . Considered too tall for the position when he entered the league in 1983, Mosebar has watched taller, massive centers become the norm . . . Played 13 games at tackle in 1988 because of team needs but returned to his natural position . . . Was the 26th player selected in the 1983 draft, out of Southern Cal . . . Only the third regular center in Raider history, joining Jim Otto and Dave Dalby . . . Not an overpowering blocker, he is recognized for his flawless technique . . . Bothered by back problems early in his career . . . Selected to Pro Bowl last year and in 1989 . . . Was a shot-putter and discus-thrower in college . . . Born Sept. 11, 1961, in Yakima, Wash. . . . 1990 salary: $585,000.

MAX MONTOYA 35 6-5 290 **Guard**

One of the great Plan B steals in 1990 after an 11-year career with the Bengals . . . Heard from the Raiders while staying at a Hawaiian condo before the 1990 Pro Bowl . . . Was a seventh-round choice of the Bengals in 1979 . . . Has been to three Pro Bowls for the Bengals . . . Despite his age, he is still one of the better pass-blockers in the league . . . Provided leadership for young linemen such as Steve Wisniewski and Rory Graves . . . Started at guard in Bengals' two Super Bowl games during the 1980s . . . Once honored as being NFL's best pass-blocking guard . . . Owns a Mexican restaurant in Cincinnati . . . Born May 12, 1956, in Montebello, Cal. . . . 1991 salary: $700,000.

RONNIE LOTT 32 6-0 200 **Strong Safety**

Left the 49ers after a contract tiff with owner Eddie DeBartolo . . . Was willing to take a $200,000 pay cut to stay with the 49ers, but became upset when they wanted him to retire after this season . . . Signed a two-year contract with the Raiders . . . Still one of the game's most punishing hitters . . . Will switch from free safety to strong safety to help the Raider defense . . . Al Davis hopes that Lott will work with free safety Eddie "The Hitman" Anderson, whom he considers a Jack Tatum-type safety . . . Went to the Pro Bowl for the eighth time . . . Has lost most of his speed, but plays the safety position like an extra mobile linebacker . . . Has missed 10 games during past two seasons . . . A two-time All-American at Southern Cal . . . Born May 8, 1959, in Albuquerque, N.M. . . . 1991 salary: $100,000 signing bonus and $825,000 salary.

COACH ART SHELL: Quickly established himself as one of the league's best motivators . . . He's a man of few words who knows how to bring out the best from players . . . Has a 21-9 record since replacing Mike Shanahan as the Raiders' coach in 1989 . . . Erased petty rules Shanahan imposed, such as prohibiting players from sitting on their helmets . . . A former Hall-of-Fame tackle with the Raiders who went to the Pro Bowl eight times . . . Was a Raider assistant since 1983 . . . Missed only five games during 15-year career . . . During his playing days, Raiders were 150-56-7 and went to the playoffs 11 times . . . Though he was quiet, teammates respected him and stayed away from him if he was angry . . . Has a 13-1 record in the Los Angeles Coliseum as a head coach . . . Prepares the team's running-game plan while friend and former teammate Terry Robiskie works the passing offense. . . . Two-time All-American at Maryland State . . . Came to the Raiders as a third-round choice in 1968 . . . Born Nov. 26, 1946, in Charleston, S.C.

GREATEST PUNTER

Tom Flores, then an assistant Raiders' coach, noticed something funny during their 1973 training camp. Ray Guy, their first-round draft choice, wore a defensive jersey and worked a few reps with the secondary. Wasn't Guy a punter?

"Ray was a great, great athlete," Flores said. "He could throw a football 75 yards. In college [Southern Mississippi], he played defensive back."

As a punter, he was The Guy. A Hall of Fame candidate this year, Guy set the standards for modern-day punters. In 14 seasons, he averaged 42.4 yards per punt and went to seven Pro Bowls. But the Raiders wanted more than just long kicks. They asked for placement, so Guy never achieved the 45.3-yard average he had during his rookie year.

"He had tremendous explosion, and when he punted, he put on a show," Flores said. "I remember one time, punting from his 20, he tried to put a ball out of bounds inside the opponents' 20. He was amazing."

Once, he came to the sidelines with a bloodied face. Coaches thought someone attacked him. Guy explained that his foot extended so far that he hit himself in the face. What a Guy.

INDIVIDUAL RAIDER RECORDS

Rushing

Most Yards Game:	221	Bo Jackson, vs Seattle, 1987
Season:	1,759	Marcus Allen, 1985
Career:	7,957	Marcus Allen, 1982-90

Passing

Most TD Passes Game:	6	2 times, most recently Daryle Lamonica, vs Buffalo 1969
Season:	34	Daryle Lamonica, 1969
Career:	150	Ken Stabler, 1970-79

Receiving

Most TD Passes Game:	4	Art Powell, vs Houston, 1963
Season:	16	Art Powell, 1963
Career:	76	Fred Biletnikoff, 1965-78

Scoring

Most Points Game:	24	2 times, most recently Marcus Allen, vs San Diego, 1984
Season:	117	George Blanda, 1968
Career:	863	George Blanda, 1967-75
Most TDs Game:	4	2 times, most recently Marcus Allen, vs San Diego, 1984
Season:	18	Marcus Allen, 1984
Career:	93	Marcus Allen, 1982-90

MIAMI DOLPHINS

TEAM DIRECTORY: Pres.: Timothy J. Robbie; Dir. Player Personnel: Charley Winner; Dir. Media Relations: Harvey Greene; Head Coach: Don Shula. Home field: Joe Robbie Stadium (73,000). Colors: Aqua and orange.

Dan Marino enters 1991 with 59.3 career passing pct.

SCOUTING REPORT

OFFENSE: In terms of touchdowns, Dan Marino had his least productive season, throwing 21 scoring passes (against only 11 interceptions). However, the development of Sammie Smith as a running back took much of the pressure off Marino. As a result, the Dolphins won 12 regular-season games and returned to the playoffs.

Smith had a great first game (159 yards against New England) and a solid finale (108 yards vs. Indianapolis). But, in-between he had trouble with fumbles and was inconsistent. Those were the only two games in which he rushed for more than 100 yards all year. Tony Paige showed that he can catch the ball and pick up the tough short yardage.

The Marks Brothers still have the ability to beat you deep, although there are concerns that Mark Duper is no longer the big-play receiver he's been. Mark Clayton, however, is clearly the most dangerous receiver the Dolphins have. Ferrell Edmunds was inconsistent, but still was voted to the Pro Bowl. And the Dolphins made wide receiver Randal Hill of the U. of Miami their top draft pick.

The offensive line was dominating (only 16 sacks allowed), thanks to the play of rookies Richmond Webb, a Pro Bowler, and Keith Sims, a wide-body guard who supplanted the departed (Plan B) Roy Foster in the starting lineup beside Webb. Jeff Uhlenhake started all 16 games and provided stability to the center of the line.

DEFENSE: No Name II gave the Dolphins an unexpectedly productive season and, until the playoff loss to the Bills, they had shown remarkable improvement. The defense allowed 15 points per game, compared to 24 the previous year, and 284 total yards per outing, compared to 356 in 1989. Midway through the season, they went 13 quarters without allowing a touchdown and 25 quarters without surrendering a rushing touchdown.

Jeff Cross was voted to the Pro Bowl on the strength of a quick start even though his performance tailed off. T.J. Turner started 12 games at the left end, while Shawn Lee took over for Alfred Oglesby in the final 10 games.

John Offerdahl was again the dominant linebacker, starting every game. A key to the defensive excellence was the fact that all four linebackers—Offerdahl, Hugh Green, Cliff Odom and David Griggs—started all 16 games. Ditto in the secondary, where

DOLPHINS VETERAN ROSTER

HEAD COACH—Don Shula. Assistant Coaches—George Hill, Tony Nathan, Tom Olivadotti, Mel Phillips, John Sandusky, Larry Seiple, Dan Sekanovich, Mike Shula, Gary Stevens, Carl Taseff, Junior Wade, Mike Westoff.

No.	Name	Pos.	Ht.	Wt.	NFL Exp.	College
86	Banks, Fred	WR	5-10	185	6	Liberty
84	Baty, Greg	TE	6-5	240	5	Stanford
53	Bolcar, Ned	LB	6-1	235	2	Notre Dame
82	Brown, Andre	WR	6-3	210	2	Miami (Fla.)
37	Brown, J.B.	CB	6-0	192	3	Maryland
83	Clayton, Mark	WR	5-9	185	9	Louisville
50	Cooper, Louis	LB	6-2	238	7	Western Carolina
91	Cross, Jeff	DE	6-4	272	4	Missouri
65	Dellenbach, Jeff	T-C	6-6	285	7	Wisconsin
74	Dennis, Mark	T	6-6	295	5	Illinois
85	Duper, Mark	WR	5-9	192	10	NW Louisiana
80	Edmunds, Ferrell	TE	6-6	254	4	Maryland
22	Fullwood, Brent	RB	5-11	210	5	Auburn
62	Galbreath, Harry	G	6-1	275	4	Tennessee
35	Glenn, Kerry	CB	5-9	178	5	Minnesota
41	Grant, African	S	6-0	200	1	Illinois
55	Green, Hugh	LB	6-2	230	11	Pittsburgh
92	Griggs, David	LB	6-3	248	3	Virginia
59	Grimsley, John	LB	6-2	238	8	Kentucky
45	Harden, Bobby	S	6-0	192	1	Miami (Fla.)
87	Henry, Charles	TE	6-4	230	1	Miami (Fla.)
21	Higgs, Mark	RB	5-7	195	4	Kentucky
29	Hobley, Liffort	S	6-0	202	6	Louisiana State
38	Holt, Leroy	FB	5-10	224	1	Southern California
24	Jackson, Vestee	CB	6-0	186	6	Washington
11	Jensen, Jim	WR-RB	6-4	224	11	Boston University
54	Junior, E.J.	LB	6-3	242	11	Alabama
99	Klingbeil, Chuck	NT	6-1	260	1	Northern Michigan
58	Krauss, Barry	LB	6-3	250	12	Alabama
44	Lankford, Paul	CB	6-1	191	10	Penn State
98	Lee, Shawn	NT	6-2	285	4	North Alabama
32	Limbrick, Garrett	FB	6-2	240	2	Oklahoma State
72	Linn, Jack	T	6-5	278	1	West Virginia
20	Logan, Marc	FB	5-11	222	5	Kentucky
13	Marino, Dan	QB	6-4	224	9	Pittsburgh
89	Martin, Tony	WR	6-0	180	2	Mesa
28	McGruder, Michael	CB	5-11	190	2	Kent State
19	Mitchell, Scott	QB	6-6	236	1	Utah
27	Moore, Stevon	S	5-11	204	2	Mississippi
93	Odom, Cliff	LB	6-2	243	11	Texas-Arlington
56	Offerdahl, John	LB	6-2	238	6	Western Michigan
96	Oglesby, Alfred	NT	6-3	278	2	Houston
25	Oliver, Louis	S	6-2	226	3	Florida
49	Paige, Tony	FB	5-10	235	8	Virginia Tech
90	Price, Terry	DE	6-4	272	2	Texas A&M
23	Ray, Pat	CB	5-10	180	1	Missouri
52	Reichenbach, Mike	LB	6-2	240	8	East Stroudsburg
4	Roby, Reggie	P	6-2	246	9	Iowa
68	Rose, Blaine	G	6-5	271	1	Maryland
9	Secules, Scott	QB	6-3	220	4	Virginia
88	Sievers, Eric	TE	6-4	238	11	Maryland
69	Sims, Keith	G	6-2	305	2	Iowa State
30	Smith, Don	RB	5-11	200	5	Mississippi State
33	Smith, Sammie	RB	6-2	230	3	Florida State
70	Sochia, Brian	NT-DE	6-3	278	9	NW Oklahoma State
10	Stoyanovich, Pete	K	5-10	185	3	Indiana
95	Turner, T.J.	DE	6-4	280	6	Houston
63	Uhlenhake, Jeff	C	6-3	284	3	Ohio State
78	Webb, Richmond	T	6-6	295	2	Texas A&M
60	Weidner, Bert	G-C	6-3	284	2	Kent State
26	Williams, Jarvis	S	5-11	200	4	Florida

TOP DRAFT CHOICES

Rd.	Name	Sel. No.	Pos.	Ht.	Wt.	College
1	Hill, Randal	23	WR	5-11	177	Miami
3	Craver, Aaron	60	RB	6-0	214	Fresno State
5	Cox, Bryan	113	LB	6-3	235	Western Illinois
5	Williams, Gene	121	G	6-3	208	Iowa State
7	Green, Chris	191	DB	5-10	188	Illinois

Tim McKyer, J.B. Brown, Louis Oliver and Jarvis Williams started every game. McKyer, however, was traded to the Falcons.

SPECIAL TEAMS: Don Shula's kickers are among the best in the league. Reggie Roby had his lowest average (42.0) since joining the team in 1983 and still finished fourth in the AFC in punting. Pete Stoyanovich, a two-year man, ranked near the top of the AFC kicking charts as he made 21-of-26 field-goal attempts, including six of eight from 40 yards or more and two of three from 50 yards or longer. Marc Logan is a dangerous kickoff man and Scott Schwedes averaged nearly 10 yards on punt returns.

THE ROOKIES: The receiving corps needs new blood and the Dolphins found it in Hill, who was clocked in 4.3 by the scouts. Getting Fresno State running back Aaron Craver on the third round was a steal; he'll provide depth behind Smith. And they feel they have a good one in Western Illinois linebacker Brian Cox, a third-rounder.

OUTLOOK: Marino will be Marino and Shula is Shula, so two main ingredients for success are there. But can the defense rebound from the disaster in the playoffs and repeat its regular-season success? That's the key question for the Fish in 1991.

DOLPHIN PROFILES

DAN MARINO 29 6-4 224 **Quarterback**

Although he's played only eight seasons, Marino has left his mark: he is 14th among all-time NFL quarterbacks in pass attempts with 4,181 . . . Ranks 10th in career passing yardage (31,416) and seventh in touchdown passes (241) . . . The Pitt product was the sixth quarterback chosen in the 1983 draft, behind John Elway, Todd Blackledge, Jim Kelly, Tony Eason and Ken O'Brien . . . In 119 regular-season games, he's been held to less than 50 percent completions only 14 times, even though he rarely has a running game to take the pressure off him . . . For his career, he has completed 2,480 passes in 4,181 attempts for

31,417 yards and 241 touchdowns, with 136 interceptions . . . He reached the 30,000-yard mark in 114 games, faster than any other quarterback in NFL history . . . He and Johnny Unitas are the only NFL quarterbacks to throw at least 20 touchdown passes in eight straight years and Marino is the only quarterback to pass for 30 TDs over three straight years . . . Born Sept. 15, 1961, in Pittsburgh . . . 1990 salary: $1.5 million.

MARK DUPER 32 5-9 192 **Wide Receiver**

Led the Dolphins in both receptions (52) and yardage gained via the pass (810) . . . Injuries slowed him in 1987 and 1988 but he rebounded with 49 catches in 1989 and 52 last year . . . A second-round draft pick from Northwestern (La.) State in 1982 . . . After scoring just two touchdowns in 1988 and 1989, he had five scoring catches last year . . . When he grabbed a 69-yard touchdown pass against the Jets on Oct. 7, it was his first TD in 16 games . . . Has 397 career receptions for 7,022 yards (17.7-yard average) and 47 touchdowns . . . With Mark Clayton out of the lineup for five consecutive games, Duper responded with 19 catches for 306 yards and two touchdowns . . . Third on the Dolphins' all-time receiver list, behind Nat Moore (510) and Clayton (437) . . . His 7,022 yards put him second to Moore (7,547) in that category . . . Born Jan. 25, 1959, in Pineville, La. . . . 1990 salary: $1.5 million.

MARK CLAYTON 30 5-9 185 **Wide Receiver**

Ligament damage to his right knee caused him to miss a career-high six games and resulted in his making only 32 catches for 406 yards . . . That was the least since his rookie year (six catches) and half his 1989 total of 64 grabs . . . An eighth-round pick from Louisville in 1983 . . . Spent five games on the injured-reserve list last year—the first time he had been on IR in his career . . . Prior to that, he had missed only three games since becoming a starter in 1984 . . . His 437 catches put him second to Nat Moore (510) among Dolphin receivers . . . Has at least one catch in the last 63 games he's played . . . If he has another 1,000-yard season in 1991, he would become the seventh player in NFL history to break that mark five times . . . Born April 8, 1961, in Indianapolis . . . 1990 salary: $1 million.

SAMMIE SMITH 24 6-2 230 **Running Back**

He opened the 1990 season with his best effort—159 yards on 23 carries against the Patriots for the fourth-best single-game rushing performance in Dolphin history . . . Finished the season in seventh place among AFC rushers with 831 yards . . . As a rookie in 1989, he had 659 yards . . . A first-round pick from Florida State in 1989 . . . His 226 rushing attempts last year was the second-most in Dolphin history, trailing only the 272 Delvin Williams had in 1978 . . . Fumbling was a problem. His eight (four of them lost) was one shy of the Dolphin team record . . . A powerful straight-ahead runner, his numbers over two years are better than any other Dolphin in history in yards (1,490), attempts (426) and touchdowns (14) . . . Born May 16, 1967, in Orlando, Fla . . . 1990 salary: $390,000.

RICHMOND WEBB 24 6-6 295 **Tackle**

The first rookie offensive tackle to be selected to the Pro Bowl since Chris Hinton went in 1984 . . . A first-round pick in 1990 (ninth overall) from Texas A&M . . . Started all 16 games and is considered the new Anthony Munoz among offensive linemen in the league . . . First Dolphin offensive lineman in the Pro Bowl since Dwight Stephenson in 1987 . . . Joins Marino and John Offerdahl as the only Dolphins to be selected to the Pro Bowl as rookies . . . He handled Bruce Smith in all three games against the Bills' All-Pro pass-rusher . . . Born Jan. 11, 1967, in Dallas . . . 1990 salary: $325,000 plus $1.35-million signing bonus.

JEFF CROSS 25 6-4 272 **Defensive End**

He was one of four Dolphins selected to the 1990 Pro Bowl after recording 11½ sacks, eighth in the AFC . . . A ninth-round draft pick from Missouri in 1988 . . . First Dolphin DE to make the Pro Bowl since Doug Betters went in 1983 . . . His 11½-sack performance was the fourth-best single-season effort in Dolphin history . . . As a ninth-round selection, he's the lowest-round draftee in Dolphin history to make the Pro Bowl . . . Slumped at the end of the season, with only 1½ sacks in his last six games. In the previous six, however, he had eight sacks . . . Finished sixth on the team with 60 tackles, 51 solo . . . Born March 25, 1966, in Riverside, Cal. . . . 1990 salary: $350,000.

JOHN OFFERDAHL 27 6-3 238 Linebacker

Started in the Pro Bowl in 1990 and has been selected to the game five times in his five-year career . . . A second-round draft pick in 1986 from Western Michigan . . . In 1989, he sat out the first five games in a contract dispute and still was voted to the Pro Bowl . . . He led the Dolphins in tackles last year with 116, including 98 solo . . . Has registered more than 100 tackles in three of his five seasons . . . Led the team or tied in tackles in seven games and was second three other times . . . Very strong against the run . . . Has a degree in bio-medicine . . . Dolphins' nominee for NFL Man of the Year in 1989 and 1990 . . . Born Aug. 17, 1964, in Wisconsin Rapids, Wisc. . . . 1990 salary: $850,000.

PETE STOYANOVICH 24 5-10 185 Placekicker

The second-year kicker made his first 13 field-goal attempts in 1990 before missing a 53-yard attempt against the Jets in Week 9 . . . Included in his conversions were boots of 51 and 53 yards . . . Finished the season with the best percentage in Dolphin history (.840) after making 21 of his 25 field-goal attempts. It was the fourth-best percentage in the AFC last year . . . An eighth-round pick out of Indiana in 1989 . . . Over his two-year career, Stoyanovich has made 40-of-51 field-goal attempts for a .784 average . . . Has converted 27-of-31 attempts of under 50 yards . . . His 59-yard boot against the Jets in 1989 was the third-longest field goal in NFL history, behind Tom Dempsey's 63-yarder for New Orleans in 1970 and Steve Cox's 60-yarder for the Browns in 1984 . . . Born April 28, 1967, in Dearborn, Mich. . . . 1990 salary: $80,000.

COACH DON SHULA: How good a coach is he? . . . Let the

record speak for itself: starting 29th year as a head coach in the NFL, 22nd with the Dolphins, and Miami has won or shared the division championship an astounding 13 times and achieved back-to-back Super Bowl crowns in 1972 and 1973 . . . Has appeared in more Super Bowls (six) than any other coach . . . Took over the Dolphins in 1970 after outstanding career with the Colts that began in 1963 when, at age 33, he became the youngest head coach in NFL history . . . Played running back at John Carroll University and was a defensive back in the NFL with Browns, Colts and Redskins before he joined the Lions' coaching staff in 1960 . . . NFL regular-season record is 218-123-6 and his victories are second to George "Papa Bear" Halas' 325 among all-time NFL coaches . . . But it took Halas 40 years . . . Born Jan. 4, 1930, in Grand River, Ohio.

GREATEST PUNTER

Reginald Henry Roby is not only the best punter in Dolphins' history but his 43.2-yard average over his eight-year career puts him in ninth place on the NFL's all-time list. He's only had two punts blocked.

A sixth-round draft pick from Iowa in 1983, Roby has been selected to two Pro Bowls (1984 and 1989). He ranks second to Larry Seiple in punts attempted (466 to Seiple's 633), but none of the other Miami punters can match his production. Roby has the five-best season averages and four of the five best single-game records, including the incredible 58.5-yard average on four punts against the 49ers in 1986. He also has had individual punts of 77 and 73 (twice) yards, which ranks him 1-2-3 in the Dolphin book.

INDIVIDUAL DOLPHIN RECORDS

Rushing

Most Yards Game:	197	Mercury Morris, vs New England, 1973
Season:	1,258	Delvin Williams, 1978
Career:	6,737	Larry Csonka, 1968-74, 1979

Passing

Most TD Passes Game:	6	2 times, most recently Dan Marino, vs N.Y. Jets, 1986
Season:	48	Dan Marino, 1984
Career:	241	Dan Marino, 1983-90

Receiving

Most TD Passes Game:	4	Paul Warfield, vs Detroit, 1973
Season:	18	Mark Clayton, 1984
Career:	74	Nat Moore, 1974-86

Scoring

Most Points Game:	24	Paul Warfield, vs Detroit, 1973
Season:	117	Garo Yepremian, 1971
Career:	830	Garo Yepremian, 1970-78
Most TDs Game:	4	Paul Warfield, vs Detroit, 1973
Season:	18	Mark Clayton, 1984
Career:	75	Nat Moore, 1974-86

NEW ENGLAND PATRIOTS

TEAM DIRECTORY: Chairman: Victor K. Kiam II; Vice Chairman: Francis W. Murray; Pres.: William Sullivan Jr.; CEO: Sam Jankovich; VP-Adm.: Patrick Forte; VP: Bucko Kilroy; VP-Player Oper.: Joe Mendes; VP-Pub. Rel.: Tom Bass; Dir. Pub. Rel.: Pat Hanlon; Head Coach: Dick MacPherson. Home field: Foxboro Stadium (60,794). Colors: Red, white and blue.

SCOUTING REPORT

OFFENSE: A major rebuilding chore here for first-year coach Dick MacPherson and his staff.

In 1990, the 1-15 Patriots ranked 26th in the league in total

Bruce Armstrong won his first berth in the Pro Bowl.

offense, 28th in scoring. Their 181 points was the lowest by an NFL team since the merger of the two leagues. In the final eight games, they were held to one touchdown or less seven times.

The development of a quality starting quarterback—Tommy Hodson and Hugh Millen will compete—is the top priority. Neither Hodson, Steve Grogan nor Marc Wilson was able to generate any sustained offense.

Running back John Stephens played well at times, but injuries and inconsistency were factors in his up-and-down season. Marvin Allen is a better runner than Stephens but has been plagued by injuries. So the Patriots hope for help from their second first-round draft pick, Arizona State's Leonard Russell.

The offensive line was atrocious and the Patriots responded by making USC tackle Pat Harlow their first pick. Only Bruce Armstrong, a Pro Bowl starter, performed well up front.

There is a decent group of receivers, headed by Irving Fryar and Hart Lee Dykes. Second-year man Michael Timpson has the speed to make an impact. Marv Cook is an underrated but effective tight end.

DEFENSE: The foundation is there. The defensive line has better depth than the Pats have enjoyed in a decade. Ray Agnew was a solid rookie and Tim Goad and Brent Williams have been staples. Youngsters Sean Smith and Marion Hobby showed promise. If Garin Veris can remain healthy, it will be a big plus.

The linebacking corps, led by Andre Tippett and Johnny Rembert, is solid. Add Cowboy LB Eugene Lockhart, who came with cornerback Ron Francis in the deal for first pick in the draft (remember Notre Dame's Raghib "Rocket" Ismail?). Safeties Roland James and Fred Marion are veterans coming off injuries. Cornerback Maurice Hurst is the Pats' best coverage man, but Ronnie Lippett has to rebound from a subpar season.

SPECIAL TEAMS: Jason Staurovsky, a dependable field-goal kicker, had a 16-for-22 season, including a 53-yarder. The punting position is up for grabs since Brian Hansen signed with the Browns in Plan B.

Sammy Martin was injured last year but he's a quality kick-returner. Fryar has handled the punt-return chores for the last seven years but he'll hand that role over to somebody new.

THE ROOKIES: MacPherson got his wish in the draft. He wanted big and he got BIG. The Pats used three of their first four

PATRIOTS VETERAN ROSTER

HEAD COACH—Dick MacPherson. Assistant Coaches—Joe Collier, Joel Collier, Dick Coury, Ivan Fears, Norm Gerber, Bobby Grier, Rod Humenuik, Stan Jones, Myrel Moore, Dante Scarnecchia, Dave Uyrus, Charlie West.

No.	Name	Pos.	Ht.	Wt.	NFL Exp.	College
33	Adams, George	RB	6-1	225	6	Kentucky
92	Agnew, Ray	DE	6-3	280	2	North Carolina State
39	Allen, Marvin	RB	5-10	208	4	Tulane
78	Armstrong, Bruce	T	6-4	284	5	Louisville
59	Brown, Vincent	LB	6-2	245	4	Miss. Valley State
76	Clayton, Stan	T-G	6-3	265	4	Penn State
63	Chilton, Gene	C	6-3	286	5	Texas
22	Coleman, Eric	CB	6-0	190	3	Wyoming
85	Cook, Marv	TE	6-4	234	3	Iowa
65	Crawford, Elbert	C/G	6-3	280	2	Arkansas
71	DeRiggi, Fred	NT	6-2	268	2	Syracuse
88	Dykes, Hart Lee	WR	6-4	218	3	Oklahoma State
28	Francis, Ron	CB	5-9	186	5	Baylor
80	Fryar, Irving	WR-PR	6-0	200	8	Nebraska
74	Gambol, Chris	G-T	6-6	303	4	Iowa
91	Gannon, Chris	DE	6-6	260	3	SW Louisiana
43	Gibson, Ernest	CB	5-10	185	7	Furman
72	Goad, Tim	NT	6-3	280	4	North Carolina
28	Gordon, Tim	FS	6-0	188	5	Tulsa
58	Harvey, Richard	LB	6-1	227	2	Tulane
60	Hobby, Marion	DE	6-4	277	2	Tennessee
13	Hodson, Tom	QB	6-2	195	2	Louisiana State
99	Howard, David	LB	6-1	230	7	Long Beach State
45	Hunter, Ivy Joe	RB	6-1	248	3	Kentucky
37	Hurst, Maurice	CB	5-10	185	3	Southern
38	James, Roland	SS	6-2	191	12	Tennessee
50	Jarostchuk, Ilia	LB	6-3	245	5	New Hampshire
30	Jones, Victor	RB	5-8	212	2	Louisiana State
35	Landry, Anthony	RB	5-9	200	1	Stephen F. Austin
42	Lippett, Ronnie	CB	5-11	180	8	Miami (Fla.)
54	Lockhart, Eugene	LB	6-2	230	8	Houston
31	Marion, Fred	FS	6-2	191	10	Miami (Fla.)
82	Martin, Sammy	WR	5-11	175	4	Louisiana State
86	McMurtry, Greg	WR	6-2	207	2	Michigan
64	Melander, Jon	T	6-7	280	1	Minnesota
7	Millen, Hugh	QB	6-5	216	5	Washington
81	Mowatt, Zeke	TE	6-3	240	8	Florida State
52	Rembert, Johnny	LB	6-3	234	9	Clemson
95	Reynolds, Ed	LB	6-5	242	9	Virginia
27	Robinson, Junior	CB	5-9	181	2	East Carolina
55	Singleton, Chris	LB	6-2	247	2	Arizona
97	Smith, Sean	DE	6-7	280	2	Georgia Tech
4	Staurovsky, Jason	K	5-9	170	5	Tulsa
44	Stephens, John	RB	6-1	215	4	NW Louisiana State
34	Strachan, Steve	RB	6-1	225	6	Boston College
53	Tardits, Richard	LB	6-2	235	1	Georgia
83	Timpson, Michael	WR	5-10	175	3	Penn State
56	Tippett, Andre	LB	6-3	241	9	Iowa
90	Veris, Garin	DE	6-4	255	6	Stanford
70	Viaene, David	T	6-5	300	3	Minnesota-Duluth
75	Villa, Danny	C-T	6-5	305	5	Arizona State
47	Warner, Kirk	TE	6-4	225	1	Georgia
21	Washington, Mickey	CB	5-9	187	2	Texas A&M
96	Williams, Brent	DE	6-4	275	6	Toledo
25	Zackery, Tony	FS	6-2	195	2	Washington

TOP DRAFT CHOICES

Rd.	Name	Sel. No.	Pos.	Ht.	Wt.	College
1	Harlow, Pat	11	OT	6-6	288	Southern California
1	Russell, Leonard	14	RB	6-2	237	Arizona State
2	Henderson, Jerome	41	CB	5-11	189	Clemson
3	Stephens, Calvin	56	G	6-4	262	South Carolina
4	Zolak, Scott	84	QB	6-5	222	Maryland

picks on offensive players. They took Harlow, a 290-pounder; Russell, 235, and Calvin Stephens, a 285-pound South Carolina guard, with the first pick in the third round.

OUTLOOK: The Patriots will be better if only because they can't be worse. But they're a couple of years away from contending for the division.

PATRIOT PROFILES

BRUCE ARMSTRONG 25 6-4 284 — Offensive Tackle

The only Patriots' representative in the Pro Bowl last year . . . Has started 60 consecutive games since coming to the Patriots as a first-round draft pick out of Louisville in 1987 . . . First rookie to start on the Pats' offensive line since John Hannah in 1973 . . . Considered to be one of the top tackles ever to play for the Patriots . . . Began his college career as a tight end but switched to tackle as a sophomore at Louisville . . . Equally adept at pass-blocking and power-blocking on the run . . . Born Sept. 7, 1965, in Miami . . . 1990 salary: $650,000.

HART LEE DYKES 24 6-4 218 — Wide Receiver

One of the best high-school athletes ever to come out of Texas, he's been slow to develop as an NFL wide receiver . . . Third on the team with 34 receptions for 549 yards last year even though he missed a half-dozen games after being involved in an early-morning brawl outside a Providence nightclub . . . Suffered an eye injury in the fight and for a time there was fear that he wouldn't be able to play football again . . . As a rookie, he had only 10 catches in his first nine games but exploded down the stretch, making 39 grabs for 654 yards in the final seven games . . . A first-round draft pick from Oklahoma State in 1989, he earned $250,000 last year . . . Set Big Eight conference record for receptions with 203, good for 3,171 yards and 29 touchdowns . . . Excellent hands combined with size make him a prime target . . . Born Sept. 2, 1966, in Bay City, Tex.

IRVING FRYAR 28 6-0 200 — Wide Receiver

First player taken in the 1984 draft has been in the headlines for off-field problems rather than on-field exploits . . . Had his best year in 1990, leading the team in receptions (54) and yardage (856) . . . Both figures were career highs . . . Also a dangerous punt-returner who is the Pats' all-time leader in return yardage . . . A consensus All-American at Nebraska, he earned $750,000 last year . . . Not a happy camper, he has repeatedly asked to be traded, claiming that he needs to go to a team with a proven quarterback . . . Makes the sensational catches and is also one of the best-blocking wide receivers in the league . . . Born Sept. 28, 1962, in Mt. Holly, N.J. . . . 1990 salary: $750,000.

JOHN STEPHENS 25 6-1 215 — Running Back

Has led the Patriots in rushing all three years with the club . . . Selected to the Pro Bowl as a rookie in 1988 after gaining 1,168 yards . . . A severe ankle injury held him to 833 yards in 244 carries in 1989 . . . Last year, he was inconsistent but still gained team-high 808 yards on 212 carries . . . Strong straight-ahead runner, he is also a capable receiver and blocker . . . A first-round pick in the 1988 draft (17th player overall) . . He was the second Patriot player to make the Pro Bowl as a rookie, following cornerback Mike Haynes (1976) . . . Broke into the starting lineup in third game of his rookie year and carried the Pats to within one game of the playoffs . . . Born Feb. 23, 1966, in Shreveport, La., and attended Northwestern (La.) State . . . 1990 salary: $450,000.

TOMMY HODSON 24 6-2 195 — Quarterback

After Steve Grogan was injured and Marc Wilson was ineffective, Hodson stepped into the lineup for the final six games of the disastrous 1990 season and performed well . . . Completed 85 of 156 passes for 968 yards and four touchdowns, with five interceptions . . . Showed leadership ability and poise and put himself in position to battle for the starting job in 1991 . . . A third-round draft pick, he earned $160,000 in base pay last year as well as a $160,000 signing bonus . . Chosen All-SEC for four straight years at LSU, where he set conference passing records . . . Passed for 9,115 yards in his career; no other SEC quarterback has passed for more than 8,000 . . . Started every game but one in his college days . . . Born Jan. 28, 1967, in Matthews, La.

JOHNNY REMBERT 30 6-3 234 — Inside Linebacker

A Pro Bowl selection following the 1988 and 1989 seasons, he missed most of last year with a knee injury . . . Still, he finished with 43 tackles, one sack and three deflections . . . Strong against the run, he ranks high among linebackers in defending against passes . . . Had two interceptions and three deflections last year before being injured . . . A fourth-round draft pick from Clemson in 1983, he earned $300,000 last year . . . Born Jan. 19, 1961, in Hollandale, Miss., one of a brood of 11 children.

ANDRE TIPPETT 31 6-3 241 — Outside Linebacker

Rebounded well last year after missing all of 1989 because of shoulder surgery that ended a string of five straight Pro Bowl appearances . . . Was not used as a pass-rusher because the coaches wanted to utilize him more in pass-coverage than they had in the past . . . Remained a force against the run . . . Had 3½ sacks . . . Holder of black belts in karate and runs a string of karate schools in the New England area . . . A second-round draft pick from Iowa in 1982, Tippett earned $750,000 last year . . . Extremely quick off the ball, he averaged 12 sacks a season between 1983 and 1988 . . . Had 83 tackles last year, second among Patriots' linebackers even though most people ran away from him . . . Born Dec. 27, 1959, in Birmingham, Ala.

BRENT WILLIAMS 26 6-4 275 — Defensive End

Has led the Patriots in sacks the last four years . . . Had six to lead the team in 1990 . . . Originally a seventh-round draft pick from Toledo in 1986, he's been a starter for the last four years and has been one of the few dependable players on the injury-riddled Pats' defense . . . Started every game over the last three years . . . Grew up with Carl Banks, Eugene Marve and Lonnie Young in Flint, Mich . . . Played college ball at Toledo and earned $250,000 last year . . . Born Oct. 23, 1964, in Flint, Mich.

TIM GOAD 25 6-3 280 **Defensive Tackle**

Hasn't missed a game in three years as a Patriot and has been a starter since the third game of his rookie year (1988) . . . Finished third on the team and first among defensive linemen in tackles last year with 87 . . . Also had 2½ sacks . . . Co-winner of team's best-lineman award in 1989 . . . Not a pass-rusher, he's at his best clogging up the middle on running plays, allowing linebackers to make the tackles . . . Frequently double-teamed . . . A fourth-round draft pick from the University of North Carolina in 1988, he earned $127,000 last year . . . Played every position on his high-school team (Patrick County H.S. in Stuart, Va.) . . . First player from his high school to play at a Division I college . . . Born Feb. 28, 1966, in Claudville, Va.

RAY AGNEW 23 6-3 280 **Defensive End**

Started 1990 at left tackle and played 12 games, nine as a starter . . . Missed two games with a calf injury and two more with a knee injury . . . Finished ninth on the team with 52 tackles, 38 solo . . . Also had 2½ sacks and forced a fumble . . . Had a season-high seven tackles against Washington in Week 14 . . . A first-round pick (10th player chosen) from North Carolina State in 1990, he earned a base salary of $335,000 as well as a signing bonus of $1 million . . . Not flashy, but a relentless defender who is the kind of player around whom the Patriots will build their future . . . Born Dec. 9, 1967, in Winston-Salem, N.C.

EUGENE LOCKHART 30 6-2 230 **Linebacker**

Became a Patriot in the deal that gave the Cowboys the No. 1 pick in the 1991 draft . . . Led Cowboys in tackles (139) for the fourth time in his seven seasons . . . It was his fifth 100-tackle season . . . Second-team All-NFC by UPI . . . Has started a team-high 48 consecutive games . . . Best season was 1989, with astounding 222 tackles . . . Had at least 10 tackles in every game that season . . . Has been credited with 897 tackles in his career . . . Intense, emotional player . . . Cowboys' sixth-round pick out of Houston in 1984 . . . Nicknamed "The Hitting Machine" . . . Born March 8, 1961, in Crockett, Tex. . . . 1990 base salary: $360,000.

COACH DICK MacPHERSON: When the 60-year-old

MacPherson was hired to replace Rod Rust as the Patriots' head coach in January, it marked a homecoming . . . His first head-coaching job was at the University of Massachusetts, where the Patriots held their training camp . . . Prior to arriving at UMass, where he led the Minutemen to a 45-27-1 record in seven seasons, MacPherson was linebacker coach with the Broncos . . . He left UMass to re-enter pro ball as linebacker coach with the Browns in 1978 under head coach Sam Rutigliano . . . Three years later, MacPherson moved up to Syracuse, where he directed the rebuilding stage of that program . . . In his 10 years there prior to taking over the Patriots, the Orangemen were 66-46-4 and qualified for bowl appearances in five of his last six seasons . . . Born Dec. 4, 1930, in Old Towne, Maine . . . He is a graduate of Springfield College, where he centered the unbeaten 1956 football team, and he has a master's degree from Illinois.

GREATEST PUNTER

Rich Camarillo didn't last through training camp in his first NFL tryout, back in 1981. A free agent from the University of Washington, he was waived by the Patriots prior to the regular season even though he was clearly the best punter in camp. However, at the time, the Pats were experimenting with the concept of having one kicker handle both the punting and placekicking, so they gave the job to Mike Hubach.

Midway through the season, however, Hubach was struggling with both responsibilities so the team abandoned the two-for-one approach, and re-signed Camarillo. Hubach was released at the end of that season but Camarillo remained with the Pats through 1987, when he was waived. He later played for the Rams and Cardinals, going to the Pro Bowl while with Phoenix in 1989.

As a Patriot, Camarillo averaged 42.6 yards a punt, highest in franchise history. His 468 punts was nearly 100 more than runnerup Tom Yewcic, who averaged 39.2 yards a punt from 1961 through 1966.

INDIVIDUAL PATRIOT RECORDS

Rushing

Most Yards Game:	212	Tony Collins, vs N.Y. Jets, 1983
Season:	1,458	Jim Nance, 1966
Career:	5,453	Sam Cunningham, 1973-79, 1981-82

Passing

Most TD Passes Game:	5	3 times, most recently Steve Grogan, vs N.Y. Jets, 1979
Season:	31	Babe Parilli, 1964
Career:	182	Steve Grogan, 1975-90

Receiving

Most TD Passes Game:	3	6 times, most recently Stanley Morgan, vs Seattle, 1986
Season:	12	Stanley Morgan, 1979
Career:	67	Stanley Morgan, 1977-89

Scoring

Most Points Game:	28	Gino Cappelletti, vs Houston, 1965
Season:	155	Gino Cappelletti, 1964
Career:	1,130	Gino Cappelletti, 1960-70
Most TDs Game:	3	14 times, most recently Stanley Morgan, vs Seattle, 1986
Season:	13	2 times, most recently Stanley Morgan, 1979
Career:	67	Stanley Morgan, 1977-89

NEW YORK JETS

TEAM DIRECTORY: Chairman: Leon Hess; Pres.: Steve Gutman; VP/GM: Dick Steinberg; Dir. Pro Personnel: Jim Royer; Dir. Pub. Rel.: Frank Ramos; Head Coach: Bruce Coslet. Home field: Giants Stadium (77,311). Colors: Kelly green and white.

Blair Thomas' rookie performance heralds bright future.

SCOUTING REPORT

OFFENSE: The critical need here is a dependable, healthy Ken O'Brien at quarterback. With second-year men Blair Thomas and Brad Baxter sharing the bulk of the running load, the Jets should be able to do some damage via the run and cause teams to send their safeties on run support.

O'Brien had some big games last year, but he had some bombs as well. If he gets time to throw and reaches deep threats Al Toon and Rob Moore, the Jets should be able to put some big numbers on the board again. Toon, Moore and Terance Mathis, who showed big-play ability as a rookie, will have secondaries backing up. Thomas has the kind of Freeman McNeil moves that can turn a two-yard hole into a 12-yard gain.

Last year, the 6-10 Jets had to field a patchwork offensive line most of the time. Even when they were healthy, the blockers up front weren't that effective on the run. The new schemes brought by first-year coach Bruce Coslet resulted in only 40 sacks, the team's lowest total since the strike-shortened 1982 season.

DEFENSE: With Marty Lyons retired and Ron Stallworth traded, the Jets have to upgrade their defensive line to make a run for the division.

Dennis Byrd is the new leader of the line although Jeff Lageman, drafted as a linebacker in the first round two years ago, has made a decent adjustment into a down lineman. Darrel Davis could be a surprisingly effective pass-rusher if given a regular opportunity.

Kyle Clifton anchors a linebacking corps that could use some added depth but the secondary is in pretty good shape. Tony Stargell, a second-year cornerback, should learn from his rookie mistakes; he showed talent at times. Safety Erik McMillan is an an excellent centerfielder who had five more interceptions last year and has 19 in his three-year career.

SPECIAL TEAMS: Pat Leahy, the oldest player in the NFL at 39, looks like the next George Blanda. Last year, his 16th in the NFL, he was voted the Jets' MVP following a Pro Bowl season in which he made 23-of-26 field-goal attempts and all 32 of his PAT tries. Unless he loses it suddenly, the placekicking should be a strength once again.

Veteran Joe Prokop is the punter but was merely average last year, with a 40-yard gross average and a 34-yard net. Mathis is a potential game-breaker as a return man on punt and kickoffs.

JETS VETERAN ROSTER

HEAD COACH—Bruce Coslet. Assistant Coaches—Larry Beightol, Kippy Brown, Pete Carroll, Joe Daniels, Ed Donatell, Foge Fazio, Greg Mackrides, Chip Myers, Al Roberts, Greg Robinson, Bob Wylie.

No.	Name	Pos.	Ht.	Wt.	NFL Exp.	College
30	Baxter, Brad	RB	6-1	231	2	Alabama State
18	Bell, Grantis	WR-KR	5-9	156	1	West Virginia
99	Bosa, John	DE	6-4	275	4	Boston College
80	Boyer, Mark	TE	6-4	242	7	Southern California
43	Brim, Mike	CB	6-0	192	4	Virginia Union
29	Brown, A.B.	RB	5-9	215	2	West Virginia
87	Burkett, Chris	WR	6-4	200	7	Jackson State
90	Byrd, Dennis	DT	6-5	270	3	Tulsa
66	Cadigan, Dave	G-T	6-4	285	4	Southern California
59	Clitton, Kyle	LB	6-4	236	8	Texas Christian
69	Criswell, Jeff	T	6-7	291	5	Graceland
49	Curtis, Travis	S	5-10	180	5	West Virginia
98	Davis, Darrell	DE	6-2	264	2	Texas Christian
89	Dawkins, Dale	WR	6-1	190	2	Miami
84	Dressel, Chris	TE	6-4	239	8	Stanford
62	Duffy, Roger	C	6-3	285	2	Penn State
11	Eason, Tony	QB	6-4	212	9	Illinois
75	Eatman, Irv	T	6-7	298	6	UCLA
44	Egu, Patrick	RB	5-11	206	2	Nevada-Reno
91	Frase, Paul	DT	6-5	270	3	Syracuse
52	Galvin, John	LB	6-3	230	4	Boston College
76	Goetz, Chris	G	6-2	272	1	Pittsburgh
79	Haight, Mike	G	6-4	291	6	Iowa
40	Hasty, James	CB	6-0	201	4	Washington State
34	Hector, Johnny	RB	5-11	214	9	Texas A&M
54	Holmes, Bruce	LB	6-2	241	1	Minnesota
55	Houston, Bobby	LB	6-2	235	1	North Carolina State
26	Johnson, Kenneth	S	6-2	216	2	Florida A&M
95	Johnson, Troy	LB	6-2	236	4	Oklahoma
58	Kelly, Joe	LB	6-2	235	6	Washington
82	Kelly, Pat	TE	6-6	252	3	Syracuse
25	Kors, R.J.	S	6-0	195	1	Long Beach State
56	Lageman, Jeff	DE	6-5	265	3	Virginia
5	Leahy, Pat	K	6-0	200	18	St. Louis
47	Levells, John	LB	6-2	236	1	C.W. Post
81	Mathis, Terance	WR-KR	5-10	170	2	New Mexico
64	Matich, Trevor	C-G-T	6-4	297	7	Brigham Young
70	Mattes, Ron	T	6-6	302	5	Virginia
23	Mayes, Mike	CB	5-10	179	2	Louisiana State
22	McMillan, Erik	S	6-2	200	4	Missouri
92	McNeil, Emanuel	DT	6-3	277	1	Tennessee-Martin
24	McNeil, Freeman	RB	5-11	208	11	UCLA
94	Mersereau, Scott	DT	6-3	277	5	Southern Connecticut
72	Miller, Brett	T	6-7	286	9	Iowa
85	Moore, Rob	WR	6-3	205	2	Syracuse
51	Mott, Joe	LB	6-4	234	3	Iowa
77	Nichols, Gerald	DT-DE	6-2	260	5	Florida State
7	O'Brien, Ken	QB	6-4	212	9	Cal-Davis
21	Odegard, Don	CB	6-0	180	2	Nevada-Las Vegas
71	Pickel, Bill	DT	6-5	265	9	Rutgers
20	Price, Dennis	CB	6-1	175	3	UCLA
6	Prokop, Joe	P	6-2	225	6	Cal Poly-Pomona
15	Schonert, Turk	QB	6-1	200	9	Stanford
45	Stargell, Tony	CB	5-11	180	2	Tennessee State
57	Stephens, Mac	LB	6-3	220	2	Minnesota
53	Sweeney, Jim	C-G	6-4	277	8	Pittsburgh
14	Taylor, Troy	QB	6-4	200	2	California
32	Thomas, Blair	RB	5-10	195	2	Penn State
88	Toon, Al	WR	6-4	205	7	Wisconsin
83	Townsell, JoJo	WR-KR	5-9	182	7	UCLA
48	Washington, Brian	S	6-1	212	3	Nebraska
97	Washington, Marvin	DE-DT	6-6	276	3	Idaho
86	Wellsandt, Doug	TE	6-3	248	2	Washington State
67	White, Dwayne	G	6-2	312	2	Alcorn State
63	Zawatson, Dave	G-T	6-5	287	3	California

TOP DRAFT CHOICES

Rd.	Name	Sel. No.	Pos.	Ht.	Wt.	College
2	Nagle, Browning	34	QB	6-2	220	Louisville
3	Lewis, Morris	63	LB	6-4	240	Georgia
4	Gunn, Mark	94	DT	6-6	283	Pittsburgh
6	Bryant, Blaise	148	RB	5-11	198	Iowa State
6	Riley, Mike	160	DB	5-11	175	Tulane

THE ROOKIES: The Jets, without a first-round pick, made Louisville QB Browning Nagle, a rifle-firing pocket passer, the 34th choice. Their next pick, third-rounder Morris Lewis of Georgia, is highly regarded as a pass-rusher.

OUTLOOK: Give this team a couple of years, a couple of offensive linemen and an outside linebacker or two, and it could make waves. The problem is that by the time the supporting cast is ready to do its job, O'Brien may be too beaten up to do his.

JET PROFILES

KEN O'BRIEN 30 6-4 212 — Quarterback

The second-most productive passer in Jets' history, trailing only Joe Namath. O'Brien has passed for 20,444 yards; Namath threw for 27,055 . . . Started all 16 games in 1990 and finished eighth in the AFC in passing with a 77.3 rating . . . Completed 226 of 411 attempts for 2,855 yards and 13 touchdowns, with 10 interceptions . . . Had his best game against the Patriots in Week 15, completing 11 of 12 attempts for 210 yards and two touchdowns . . . Passed the 20,000-yard mark in passing and had his 15th 300-yard game during the season . . . Although he didn't play a game in his rookie year, he was named the Jets' starting quarterback prior to the 1984 season and has held the job ever since . . . A 1983 first-rounder from Cal-Davis (fifth quarterback taken) . . . Born Nov. 27, 1960, in Brooklyn, N.Y. . . . 1990 salary: $1.3 million.

FREEMAN McNEIL 32 5-11 208 — Running Back

The Jets' all-time leading rusher with 7,604 yards (and 36 touchdowns) . . . Still has the speed to turn the corner and has retained the ability to make tacklers miss . . . Third-leading rusher in 1990 with 458 yards and six touchdowns (tying his career high) . . . Teammates voted him winner of the Ed Block Award for courage and determination . . . Jets' first-round pick from UCLA (third player taken) in the 1981 draft . . . He holds team record with 29 100-plus-yard games, including three in playoffs . . . He's averaged more than four yards a carry in each of his 10 seasons . . . Born April 27, 1959, in Jackson, Miss. . . . 1990 salary: $900,000.

BLAIR THOMAS 23 5-10 195 **Running Back**

Heir apparent to Freeman McNeil as the Jets' prime-time running back . . . He was the second player taken in the 1990 draft (McNeil was the third in 1981) and has a similar, darting type of running style . . . Called by Penn State's Joe Paterno "probably the best all-around back I've ever coached," Thomas struggled through his rookie year because of nagging ankle and hamstring injuries that followed a contract holdout . . . Still, he played in 15 games and started 13 . . . Picked after Jeff George, Thomas earned $525,000 in base salary last year and also received a $3-million signing bonus . . . Led NFL rookies in average gain (5.0) and topped the AFC rookies with 620 yards on 123 carries . . . Born Oct. 7, 1967, in Philadelphia.

AL TOON 28 6-4 205 **Wide Receiver**

The Jets' leading receiver, with 57 grabs for 757 yards and six touchdowns . . . Has a reception in 77 straight games, second-highest among all-time Jets' receivers and fourth behind Art Monk (114), Anthony Carter and Stephone Paige (80) among active receivers . . . A first-round pick from Wisconsin in 1985, he earned $1,150,000 last year . . . He ranks fourth among Jets' all-time receivers in catches (412) and is third in yardage (5,331) in only six years with the club . . . Reached the 400-catch plateau in only 81 games, third-quickest in NFL history behind Kellen Winslow (72) and Lionel Taylor (74) . . . Had more catches in his first five years (355) than any receiver in NFL history . . . Born April 30, 1963, in Newport News, Va.

ROB MOORE 22 6-3 205 **Wide Receiver**

Selected on the first round of the 1990 supplemental draft after skipping senior year at Syracuse . . . Finished second on the team in receptions with 44, good for 692 yards and six touchdowns . . . Second to Cards' Ricky Proehl among NFL rookie receivers in catches and third in yards gained . . . Highlight of season was his nine-catch, 175-yard, one-touchdown effort against New England in Week 4. That included a 69-yard TD, the longest Jets' TD pass since 1986 . . . Earned base salary of $400,000 as well as a signing bonus of $1.5 million . . . The Orangemen's all-time leader in yardage (2,122) and touchdowns (22) and second in catches (106) and average (20.0) . . . He had nine 100-yard games in college . . . Born Sept. 27, 1968, in Hempstead, N.Y., and grew up just three miles from the Jets' training complex.

ERIK McMILLAN 26 6-2 200 — Defensive Back

Mr. Opportunism, he has 19 career interceptions in just 45 NFL games and has returned three of them for touchdowns . . . Also returned two fumble recoveries for scores . . . A third-round draft pick from Missouri in 1988, he went to the Pro Bowl after each of his first two seasons . . . Excellent anticipation and hands, he led the AFC in interceptions with eight as rookie . . . Last year, he finished second on the team in tackles with 92 and added five more interceptions . . . His gambling style resulted in his getting burned for big plays more often last year than in first two seasons . . . Needs only two interceptions to take over fourth place on Jets' all-time list . . . He and his father Ernie (defensive lineman, Cardinals) are only father-son combination in NFL history to play in the Pro Bowl . . . Born May 3, 1965, in St. Louis . . . 1990 salary: $525,000.

KYLE CLIFTON 29 6-4 236 — Linebacker

The Jets' leading tackler in five of his seven years at inside linebacker . . . Last year, he led the team with 195 tackles, 103 more than the runnerup . . . Also led the AFC in interceptions by a linebacker with three, tying career high . . . A third-round draft pick from TCU in 1984, he earned $375,000 last year . . . Recruited by TCU as a quarterback but shifted to outside linebacker for his sophomore and junior years before settling in as inside linebacker as a senior . . . Had 22 tackles in a game against San Diego last season . . . Had two of his interceptions in Game 4 against the Pats. One set up a field goal and the other stopped a Pats' drive in the end zone . . . Born Aug. 23, 1962, in Onley, Tex.

JIM SWEENEY 29 6-4 275 **Center-Guard**

The Jets have had documented problems in their offensive line in recent years, but Sweeney has been solid . . . Started all 16 games the last three years . . . In 1990, he started 14 games at center and two more at left guard, filling in for an injured Mike Haight . . . Missed all of training camp because of a contract dispute but was in the starting lineup for Opening Day . . . Second-round pick from Pittsburgh in 1984, he earned $635,000 last season . . . Has played every position on the offensive line . . . Became a starter in rookie year . . . Born Aug. 8, 1962, in Pittsburgh.

DENNIS BYRD 24 6-5 270 **Defensive Tackle**

Led team in sacks with 13, the most by a Jet since Mark Gastineau's 13½ in 1985 . . . Fourth in the AFC in sacks last year, when he started 16 games as the team's "Eagle" tackle, a role filled by Keith Millard for Pete Carroll when the Jets' defensive coordinator was with the Vikings . . . The only NFL linemen with more sacks last year were Bruce Smith (19) and Reggie White (15) . . . Had 5½ of his sacks in the last three games . . . A second-round draft pick from Tulsa in 1989, he earned $200,000 last year . . . Born Oct. 5, 1966, in Oklahoma City.

BRAD BAXTER 24 6-1 231 **Running Back**

Blair Thomas and Rob Moore were first-round draft picks, but the most productive Jet rookie last year was Baxter . . . He spent the 1989 season on the developmental squad but last year developed into a big-time power runner . . . Was second on team in rushing with 539 yards and scored six touchdowns, the most ever by a Jets' rookie runner . . . He provides the straight-ahead power to Thomas' and McNeil's slashing big-play ability . . . Also a tremendous blocker who has surprised even the Jets' coaches. "He's made the most improvement of all the guys on the team since I first saw him. I thought . . . this guy doesn't have a chance,'' said Bruce Coslet . . . Started 10 games . . . The free agent from Alabama State was born April 5, 1967, in Dothan, Ala.

COACH BRUCE COSLET: Beginning his second year as a head coach, following a successful career as Sam Wyche's top assistant in Cincinnati . . . Considering the fact that the staff was new, the management team was new and the team was both inexperienced and injured, Coslet did a solid job in directing the Jets to six wins . . . Born Aug. 5, 1946, in Oakdale, Cal., he played tight end at College of the Pacific and for the Bengals from 1969 through 1976 . . . Began his coaching career with the 49ers in 1980 and moved to Cincinnati as special teams/ tight end coach . . . Promoted to offensive coordinator in 1986 and held that position until taking over the Jets last year . . . ''He's a strong, solid coach,'' former 49ers' coach Bill Walsh said. ''He's very creative and has a solid knowledge of offensive football. He is extremely bright. His intellect is not common in athletics.''

GREATEST PUNTER

Curly Johnson shares the longevity award among Jets' punters with Chuck Ramsey. Both held that job for eight years—Ramsey, 1977–1984, and Johnson, 1961–1968. In terms of productivity, however, no Jets' punter is in Johnson's league. Johnson averaged 42.8 yards and had 40-plus yard averages in seven of his eight years. His low was 39.9, in 1962. His 45.3 average in 1965 (72 kicks for 3,260 yards) is the highest single-season punting performance in Jets' history.

Ramsey is in third place among Jets' punters with a career 40.1 average, trailing Johnson and Steve O'Neal, who was with the Jets from 1969 through 1972 and averaged 40.4 yards. Those were busy times for Jet punters. O'Neal's 11 punts against the Colts in 1971 and 10 against New England in the same year are team highs.

INDIVIDUAL JET RECORDS

Rushing

Most Yards Game:	192	Freeman McNeil, vs Buffalo, 1985
Season:	1,331	Freeman McNeil, 1985
Career:	7,604	Freeman McNeil, 1981-90

Passing

Most TD Passes Game:	6	Joe Namath, vs Baltimore, 1972
Season:	26	2 times, most recently Joe Namath, 1967
Career:	170	Joe Namath, 1965-76

Receiving

Most TD Passes Game:	4	Wesley Walker, vs Miami, 1986
Season:	14	2 times, most recently Don Maynard, 1965
Career:	88	Don Maynard, 1960-72

Scoring

Most Points Game:	19	2 times, most recently Pat Leahy, vs Cincinnati, 1984
Season:	145	Jim Turner, 1968
Career:	1,362	Pat Leahy, 1974-90
Most TDs Game:	4	Wesley Walker, vs Miami, 1986
Season:	14	3 times, most recently Emerson Boozer, 1972
Career:	88	Don Maynard, 1960-72

PITTSBURGH STEELERS

TEAM DIRECTORY: Pres.: Daniel Rooney; VP: John McGinley; VP: Art Rooney Jr.; Dir. Player Personnel: Dick Haley; Dir. Communications: Joe Gordon; Dir. Pub. Rel.: Dan Edwards; Head Coach: Chuck Noll. Home field: Three Rivers Stadium (59,492). Colors: Black and gold.

Return specialist Rod Woodson earned ticket to Pro Bowl.

SCOUTING REPORT

OFFENSE: A disc jockey fasted during a Steelers' touchdown drought. Radio stations competed with each other for variations of "Joe Must Go" songs. Nasty signs started sprinkling through the Three Rivers Stadium crowds. In one year, former Jets' coach Joe Walton made an impact on the offense.

Walton runs a complex offense. General Norman Schwarzkopf communicated to his troups in the Middle East in less time than it took a Walton play to go from sidelines to huddle. That's why quarterback Bubby Brister complained and coach Chuck Noll demanded some simplicity. But being a former head coach, Walton stubbornly stuck by a plan that believes the system is more important than the players who execute it.

In the end, the 9-7 Steelers finished with a feeble offensive unit that ranked 22nd in the NFL and scored only 31 touchdowns. During their 1-3 start, they went without an offensive touchdown. The Steelers do have weapons. Despite fighting Walton's changes, Brister completed 57.6 percent of his passes and ranked sixth in the conference with an 81.6 rating. Fullback Merril Hoge (1,116 combined yards), wide receiver Louis Lipps (50 catches) and rookie sensation Eric Green (34 catches and seven touchdowns) played well.

Through Plan B, the Steelers weeded out high draft choices such as guard John Reinstra and wide receiver Derek Hill. Unless halfback Tim Worley (418 yards and a 3.8-yard average) produces, he might be the next to go. Youngster Wayne Williams and Barry Foster offer more production for less money.

DEFENSE: It's not the Steel Curtain, but the Steeler secondary offers the best air defense this side of the Patriot missile. Led by Pro Bowl cornerback Rod Woodson, the secondary allowed only nine touchdown passes in 16 games, the fewest in more than a decade. The Steelers intercepted virtually every bomb thrown their way.

Overall, they might be a defensive tackle and a healthy Aaron Jones away from being a dominating defense. At the moment, they are frustrating to an offense. Opponents completed only 51.3 percent of their attempts and ran for a scant 3.6 yards a carry. The Steelers also caused 42 turnovers.

Woodson and young David Johnson are a fine cornerback combo. Carnell Lake and Thomas Everett provide quick striking capabilities from the safety positions. Inside linebacker David Little was finally recognized for his Pro Bowl-caliber play. Greg

STEELERS VETERAN ROSTER

HEAD COACH—Chuck Noll. Assistant Coaches—Ron Blackledge, Dave Brazil, John Fox, Joe Greene, Jack Henry, Dick Hoak, Jon Kolb, Dwain Painter, Rod Rust, George Stewart, Bob Valesente, Joe Walton.

No.	Name	Pos.	Ht.	Wt.	NFL Exp	College
1	Anderson, Gary	PK	5-11	184	10	Syracuse
60	Blankenship, Brian	G	6-1	280	5	Nebraska
6	Brister, Bubby	QB	6-3	208	6	NE Louisiana
88	Calloway, Chris	WR	5-10	185	2	Michigan
64	Davidson, Kenny	DE	6-5	272	2	Louisiana State
89	Davis, Lorenzo	WR	5-11	185	2	Youngstown State
63	Dawson, Dermontti	C	6-2	279	4	Kentucky
96	Dunbar, Karl	DL	6-4	275	1	Louisiana State
66	Evans, Donald	DE	6-2	265	3	Winston-Salem
27	Everett, Thomas	FS	5-9	182	5	Baylor
80	Fair, Ron	WR	5-11	190	1	Arizona State
29	Foster, Barry	RB	5-10	223	2	Arkansas
68	Freeman, Lorenzo	DL	6-5	319	5	Pittsburgh
86	Green, Eric	TE	6-5	274	2	Liberty
22	Griffin, Larry	S	6-0	202	6	North Carolina
35	Hall, Delton	CB	6-1	208	5	Clemson
77	Haselrig, Carlton	G	6-1	291	2	Pitt-Johnstown
21	Herds, Tyreese	DB	5-11	205	1	Kansas State
53	Hinkle, Bryan	LB	6-2	220	10	Oregon
33	Hoge, Merril	RB	6-2	229	5	Idaho State
62	Ilkin, Tunch	OT	6-3	274	12	Indiana State
65	Jackson, John	OT	6-6	290	4	Eastern Kentucky
99	Jenkins, A.J.	DE	6-2	237	3	Cal-Fullerton
44	Johnson, David	CB	6-0	185	3	Kentucky
97	Jones, Aaron	DE	6-5	269	4	Eastern Kentucky
25	Jones, Gary	S	6-1	203	2	Texas A&M
37	Lake, Carnell	SS	6-1	207	3	UCLA
51	Lanza, Chuck	C	6-2	265	3	Notre Dame
83	Lipps, Louis	WR	5-10	186	8	Southern Mississippi
50	Little, David	LB	6-1	236	11	Florida
95	Lloyd, Greg	LB	6-2	225	4	Fort Valley State
74	Long, Terry	G	5-11	278	8	East Carolina
56	McGovern, Rob	LB	6-2	234	3	Holy Cross
84	Mularkey, Mike	TE	6-4	238	9	Florida
54	Nickerson, Hardy	LB	6-2	225	5	California
14	O'Donnell, Neil	QB	6-3	221	2	Maryland
55	Olsavsky, Jerry	LB	6-1	218	3	Pittsburgh
85	O'Shea, Terry	TE	6-4	238	3	California (Pa.)
71	Ricketts, Tom	OT-G	6-5	293	3	Pittsburgh
20	Stone, Dwight	WR-RB	6-0	190	5	Middle Tenn. State
11	Strom, Rick	QB	6-2	201	3	Georgia Tech
4	Stryzinski, Dan	P	6-1	193	2	Indiana
73	Strzelczyk, Justin	OT	6-5	291	2	Maine
91	Veasey, Craig	DL	6-2	280	2	Houston
36	Walsh, Dan	RB	6-0	215	[illegible]	Montclair State
98	Williams, Gerald	NT	6-3	291	6	Auburn
57	Williams, Jerrol	LB	6-5	244	3	Purdue
42	Williams, Warren	RB	6-0	201	4	Miami (Fla.)
93	Willis, Keith	DE	6-1	263	9	Northeastern
49	Woodruff, Dwayne	CB	6-0	196	12	Louisville
26	Woodson, Rod	CB-KR	6-0	197	5	Purdue
38	Worley, Tim	RB	6-2	223	3	Georgia
76	Wyatt, Willie	NT	6-0	275	2	Alabama

TOP DRAFT CHOICES

Rd.	Name	Sel. No.	Pos.	Ht.	Wt.	College
1	Richardson, Huey	15	DE	6-4	233	Florida
2	Graham, Jeff	46	WR	6-1	193	Ohio State
3	Mills, Ernie	73	WR	5-11	175	Florida
4	Walker, Sammy	88	DB	5-10	192	Texas Tech
4	Cooper, Adrian	103	TE	6-4	253	Oklahoma

Lloyd, a hard-hitting outside linebacker, has emerged as one of their best hitters.

Consideration, however, might be given to switching to a 4-3. Aaron Jones has proven to be too brittle as a 3-4 end and could benefit by charging more from the outside. Though he's an adequate nose tackle, Gerald Williams plays better at end. In a 4-3, the Steelers could fill the middle with less talented tackles and still be effective.

SPECIAL TEAMS: They don't come better returning kicks than Woodson, who averaged 10.5 yards a punt return and 21.8 yards on kickoffs. Kickoff-coverage teams did poorly, allowing 22.2 yards. Gary Anderson remains one of pro football's most accurate kickers. Dan Stryzinski doesn't kick long (37.8 yards) but his 34.1-yard net is passable.

THE ROOKIES: It wouldn't be a draft without the Steelers taking a defensive lineman. Florida defensive end-linebacker Huey Richardson becomes this year's Aaron Jones. They've taken defensive linemen in the first two rounds of seven of the past 11 drafts. For wide-receiving help, they grabbed Jeff Graham of Ohio State and Ernie Mills of Florida.

OUTLOOK: If Brister adjusts to Walton's game and Worley lives up to his salary, the Steelers could graduate to the 10-win plateau. Ten victories is usually enough to win this balanced division.

STEELER PROFILES

ROD WOODSON 26 6-0 197 **Cornerback**

Went to the Pro Bowl as a starter . . . Was an unsigned restricted free agent after the season and had several teams, particularly the Falcons, seriously interested in him . . . One of the quickest players in the league, he finished second in the 1988 NFL Fastest Man competitition . . . Elected the Steelers' MVP last year and was co-MVP in 1988 . . . Led Steelers with five interceptions and deflected 16 passes . . . One of the league's most dangerous return specialists (10.6 yards per punt and 21.8 per kickoff) . . . Led AFC with 398 punt-return yards, including a 52-yard return for a touchdown . . . Qualified for Olympic trials in 100-meter high hurdles . . . Wants to play wide receiver and cornerback . . . Broke 13 Purdue records during a career that enabled him to be a first-round draft choice . . . Born March 10, 1965, in Fort Wayne, Ind. . . . 1990 salary: $350,000.

MERRIL HOGE 26 6-2 229 **Fullback**

Might be the most valuable man on the offense . . . Led Steelers with 772 rushing yards, increasing his career total to 2,106 . . . Scored 10 touchdowns, including seven rushing . . . Caught 40 passes for 342 yards and has averaged 33 receptions during his first four years . . . If Tim Worley continues to struggle and Barry Foster continues to develop, he might be tried at halfback . . . Performs best in big games, illustrated by consecutive 100-yard games in 1989 playoffs . . . Set 11 offensive records at Idaho State, primarily as a workhorse running back . . . Scored 44 touchdowns in college . . . Came to the Steelers as a 10th-round draft choice in 1987 . . . Born Jan. 26, 1965, in Pocatello, Idaho . . . 1991 salary: $199,000.

BUBBY BRISTER 29 6-3 208 **Quarterback**

Had trouble learning Joe Walton's complicated offense and often voiced his disapproval . . . Was so upset after Dallas exhibition game about the Walton offense, he slammed a forearm into a locker-room door . . . Eventually, Chuck Noll stepped in and made communication with the sidelines easier . . . Completed 57.62 percent of his passes (223 of 387), the second-best percentage in Steeler history . . . Had arthroscopic surgery on right shoulder in March to relieve bursitis problem . . . Struggled early in the season on an offense that failed to score a touchdown during its first four games . . . His 20 touchdown passes were the most for the Steelers since Terry Bradshaw in 1981 . . . Juggled a football and baseball career in college and came to the Steelers as a third-round draft choice from Northeast Louisiana . . . When he weighed 70 pounds, youth football league officials in Louisiana promoted him to 150-pound division because of his skills . . . Born Aug. 15, 1962, in Alexandria, La. . . . 1991 salary: $900,000.

DAVID LITTLE 32 6-1 236 **Linebacker**

Honored by going to the Pro Bowl for the first time . . . Though he's quiet, he let it be known around the locker room that he is one of the league's top inside linebackers . . . Led team in tackles (80) for the fourth consecutive year and for the fifth time in the past six seasons . . . A heady player who has a knack for making the right defensive call at the right time . . . Younger brother of former Miami Dolphin Hall of Famer Larry Little, who was considered too short to be a great inside linebacker . . . "He's the most unsung player I've been around," Steelers' defensive coordinator David Brazil said . . . Replaced Jack Lambert in 1984 . . . Made a school-record 287 unassisted tackles in 33 career games at Florida . . . A seventh-round draft choice in 1981 . . . Born Jan. 3, 1959, in Miami . . . 1991 salary: $340,000.

ERIC GREEN 24 6-5 274 **Tight End**

Who said Chuck Noll would never throw to a tight end? . . . He broke a single-season record for touchdown receptions by a Steeler tight end (seven) . . . His 34 receptions was the most by a Steeler tight end since 1983 . . . He did this despite missing training camp and not playing a down until the second week of the regular season . . . Held out 54 days and had to play himself into shape. Only played in 13 games and started six . . . Had seven catches for 105 yards in season-ending game against the Oilers . . . Had 99 career receptions and 16 touchdowns for Sam Rutigliano at Liberty College and earned first-round draft choice honors . . . Steelers want him to play at 260 pounds . . . Runs a 4.79 40 . . . Had 99 catches in college career for 1,442 yards . . . Born June 22, 1967, in Savannah, Ga. . . . 1991 salary: $300,000.

CARNELL LAKE 24 6-1 207 **Strong Safety**

Could be the next Steelers' defensive back to earn Pro Bowl honors . . . At UCLA he was considered to be too small to be a linebacker and too big to be a defensive back . . . Progressed from all-rookie season into second-year stardom . . . Can easily cover tight ends and is a devastating hitter . . . *Sports Illustrated* selected him on its All-Pro team . . . Tied for third on the Steelers with 67 tackles . . . He's not as big as David Fulcher of the Bengals but he certainly plays like him . . . A three-year starter at outside linebacker at UCLA who had 24½ sacks and 275 tackles . . . Steelers made him a second-round draft choice in 1989 . . . Averaged 151 yards and 2.4 touchdowns a game as a high-school running back before suffering injury five games into his senior year . . . Born July 15, 1967, in Salt Lake City . . . 1991 salary: $220,000.

GERALD WILLIAMS 27 6-3 291 **Nose Tackle**

Has steadily improved under the guidance of former Hall of Fame defensive tackle Joe Greene . . . Came into the league as a 290-pound nose tackle but might eventually be better at end . . . Plays his best weighing around 275 pounds . . . Has great range for a big defensive lineman . . . Led Steelers with six sacks, including five in final five games . . . Has started 47 of past 48 games . . . Came to the Steelers as a second-round draft choice in 1986 out of Auburn . . . Took over starting job in 1988 when Gary Dunn was waived . . . Solid run-stopper in short-yardage situations . . . Started for three seasons at defensive end at Auburn . . . Born Sept. 8, 1963, in Waycross, Ga. . . . 1991 salary: $300,000.

LOUIS LIPPS 29 5-10 186 **Wide Receiver**

Remains a dangerous receiver who survives despite double coverage . . . Caught 50 passes for 682 yards but scored only three touchdowns . . . His per-catch average dropped from 19 yards to 13.6, which could be because of Joe Walton's short-passing offense . . . Has 303 career receptions for 5,347 yards . . . Has been team MVP twice . . . Lacks the deep speed he once possessed . . . Continues as a solid downfield run-blocker . . . A first-round draft choice out of Southern Mississippi in 1984 . . . Struggled with hamstring problems in 1987, when his reception total dropped to 11 . . . Had five 100-yard receiving games as a college senior . . . Was a talented punt-returner in his early years . . . Caught 200 passes during his first five seasons . . . Born Aug. 9, 1962, in New Orleans . . . 1991 salary: $750,000.

DERMONTTI DAWSON 26 6-2 279 Center

The Steelers finally believe they have found a replacement for Hall-of-Famer Mike Webster . . . Played guard as a rookie but has settled into the center position the past two years . . . Is a finesse blocker who is excellent in pass protection . . . Suffered a knee injury in 1988 when defensive end Art Still, an uncle by marriage, fell on his leg and kept him out two months . . . Played guard at Kentucky and was second-team All-Southeastern Conference . . . Steelers saw his potential as a center . . . An avid weightlifter who finished first in Southeastern Conference with 1,507-pound total lift . . . Feared initial challenge of playing center because doubted whether he could switch from guard . . . Born June 17, 1965, in Lexington, Ky. . . . 1991 salary: $220,000.

GARY ANDERSON 32 5-11 184 Kicker

Was eight points short of his fifth 100-point season . . . His next extra point will tie Roy Gerela's team record of 293 . . . Hit on 20-of-25 field goals . . . Increased his consecutive field-goal streak inside the 35-yard-line to 50 . . . Ranks third in NFL history in field-goal accuracy . . . Came to the Steelers after being cut by the Bills in 1982 . . . Never saw a football before arriving in the United States from South Africa as a youth . . . Father was a professional soccer player in England . . . Was a placekicker for Syracuse and had an NCAA record 87.4 percent field-goal rating . . . Played rugby in college . . . Born July 16, 1959, in Parys, Orange Free State, South Africa . . . 1991 salary: $350,000, plus $50,000 roster bonus.

COACH CHUCK NOLL: The fifth-winningest coach in NFL history with 202-147-1 record . . . Has won nine AFC Central titles . . . His 16-8 postseason record is the best among all-time coaches . . . Will be 60 years old at the end of the season . . . Delegated the offense to former Jets coach Joe Walton, marking the first time he surrendered control of that unit . . . Likes to work with the Steelers' young blockers . . . Considered resigning in 1988 over flap with owners about his coaching staff . . . Has a pilot's license . . . Was a messenger guard and linebacker on Paul Brown's Cleveland Browns' teams during the 1950s . . . Took over a perennial loser as head coach of the Steelers in 1969 and led them to four Super Bowl titles . . . A quiet man who refuses to make speaking engagements or accept commercial endorsements . . . Embarks on 23rd season as Steeler coach this year . . . Was team captain at Dayton . . . Was assistant under Sid Gillman with Chargers and Don Shula with Colts . . . Born Jan. 5, 1932, in Cleveland.

GREATEST PUNTER

In Pittsburgh, Pat Brady remains a legend. Steelers fans were asked in 1982 to vote for their all-time team in celebration of the 50th anniversary of the franchise. This list was loaded with heroes from the Super Bowl years, but the punter was Pat Brady, who had retired in 1954.

Steelers' president Dan Rooney remembers the time a suburban Pittsburgh punter talked his way into a tryout. The lad was persistent, spending the better part of an afternoon sending punts throughout Forbes Field, where the Steelers were working out. In the locker room sat Brady.

"Somebody asked him when he was going to go out and show the kid how to punt," Rooney said. "Brady said to let the kid go out there and tire himself out."

Finally, Brady emerged. He strolled to the 50-yard line with ball in hand. With one swift left-footed motion, Brady boomed the ball out of the stadium. Then he walked to the locker room. The kid rode back to the suburbs.

From 1952 to 1954, Brady averaged 44.5 yards a kick. His best season was 1953, when he maintained a 46.9-yard average. His career ended when he tore an Achilles tendon trying to jump to catch a high snap on a punt.

INDIVIDUAL STEELER RECORDS

Rushing

Most Yards Game:	218	John Fuqua, vs Philadelphia, 1970
Season:	1,246	Franco Harris, 1975
Career:	11,950	Franco Harris, 1972-83

Passing

Most TD Passes Game:	5	2 times, most recently Mark Malone, vs Indianapolis, 1985
Season:	28	Terry Bradshaw, 1978
Career:	210	Terry Bradshaw, 1970-82

Receiving

Most TD Passes Game:	4	Roy Jefferson, vs Atlanta, 1968
Season:	12	2 times, most recently Louis Lipps, 1985
Career:	63	John Stallworth, 1974-87

Scoring

Most Points Game:	24	2 times, most recently Roy Jefferson, vs Atlanta, 1968
Season:	139	Gary Anderson, 1985
Career:	910	Gary Anderson, 1982-90
Most TDs Game:	4	2 times, most recently Roy Jefferson, vs Atlanta, 1968
Season:	14	Franco Harris, 1976
Career:	100	Franco Harris, 1972-83

SAN DIEGO CHARGERS

TEAM DIRECTORY: Chairman/Pres.: Alex G. Spanos; Vice Chairman: Dean Spanos; GM: Bobby Beathard; Dir. Pub. Rel.: Bill Johnston; Head Coach: Dan Henning. Home field: San Diego Jack Murphy Stadium (60,750). Colors: Navy, white and gold.

Marion Butts emerged as third-leading rusher in NFL.

SCOUTING REPORT

OFFENSE: Welcome to the NFL series, "Who's in Charge?" The coach, Dan Henning, wants to start quarterback Billy Joe Tolliver, but the general manager, Bobby Beathard, is double-teaming with John Friesz and Plan B acquisition Bob Gagliano. Beathard let 11 players, including tackle Joel Patten and receivers Quinn Early and Wayne Walker, slip away. Henning kind of liked Patten.

After three 6-10 seasons, Henning is rebuilding the offense again. The quarterback controversy will linger, but a debate on the running attack won't. Fullback Marion Butts makes everything too simple. He rushed for 1,225 yards, and despite gang-tackling on defense, he still gained 4.6 yards a carry. Beathard and the press had to convince Henning the value of halfback Ronnie Harmon, but their opinions were correct. Harmon caught 46 passes out of the backfield. Rod Bernstine contributed 589 yards rushing.

Henning and Beathard agree on several things. Among them are the lack of a receiving threat to pair up with Pro Bowler Anthony Miller and any sign of having a left tackle. Any help Beathard supplies in those two areas will be greatly appreciated by Henning. His job might depend on it.

DEFENSE: Holes in the defense were apparent when Beathard released his Plan B list. He voided himself of all but one of the team's safeties, releasing Vencie Glenn and Lester Lyles. Letting 300-pound tackle Les Miller go to the Saints opened another hole.

The task this year will be filling around the edges of five Pro Bowl-caliber defenders and former Pro Bowl linebacker Billy Ray Smith, whose skills are declining because of age and injuries. The Chargers have three top pass-rushers—ends Lee Williams and Burt Grossman and linebacker Leslie O'Neal. Linebacker Junior Seau, a Pro-Bowl alternate at inside linebacker, will be incorporated in a rush that registered 45 sacks last season.

The voids at safety will probably force the Chargers to move cornerback Gill Byrd, the best cornerback not in the Pro Bowl, to free safety. Martin Bayless, the only safety survivor, could retain his starting job. Or will he? With the Chargers' defense, there are no guaranties.

Will defensive tackle Joe Phillips recover from head injuries suffered in an assault outside of a bar? Will Smith rebound from his many injuries? Is Henry Rolling the right replacement for Smith? Can the Chargers survive in this division with two starting

CHARGERS VETERAN ROSTER

HEAD COACH—Dan Henning. Assistant Coaches—Chuck Clausen, Alex Gibbs, Mike Haluchak, Bobby Jackson, Charlie Joiner, Ron Lynn, LeCharls McDaniel, Jim Mora, Larry Pasquale, Jack Reilly, Ted Tollner, Ed White.

No.	Name	Pos.	Ht.	Wt.	NFL Exp.	College
44	Bayless, Martin	SS	6-2	212	8	Bowling Green
95	Benson, Mitchell	DT	6-4	300	3	Texas Christian
82	Bernstine, Rod	TE	6-3	238	5	Texas A&M
71	Brown, Dean	T	6-3	311	1	Notre Dame
35	Butts, Marion	RB	6-1	248	3	Florida State
22	Byrd, Gill	CB-S	5-11	198	9	San Jose State
46	Caravello, Joe	HB	6-3	262	5	Tulane
3	Carney, John	K	5-11	170	3	Notre Dame
29	Carrington, Darren	CB-S	6-2	200	3	Northern Arizona
63	Cornish, Frank	C-G	6-4	295	2	UCLA
88	Cox, Arthur	TE	6-2	277	9	Texas Southern
28	Elder, Donnie	CB	5-9	178	6	Memphis State
61	Floyd, Eric	G-T	6-5	300	2	Auburn
27	Frank, Donald	CB	6-0	200	2	Winston-Salem State
17	Friesz, John	QB	6-4	209	1	Idaho
16	Gagliano, Bob	QB	6-3	205	5	Utah
67	Goeas, Leo	G-T	6-4	285	2	Hawaii
92	Grossman, Burt	DE	6-4	255	3	Pittsburgh
53	Hall, Courtney	C-G	6-1	269	3	Rice
33	Harmon, Ronnie	RB	5-11	200	6	Iowa
86	Heard, Ron	WR	5-10	180	1	Bowling Green
34	Hendrickson, Steve	LB	6-0	250	3	California
97	Hinkle, George	DE	6-5	269	4	Arizona
48	Humphery, Bobby	CB-S	5-11	180	9	New Mexico State
21	Kelson, Derrick	DB	6-0	187	1	Purdue
10	Kidd, John	P	6-3	208	8	Northwestern
80	Kyles, Troy	WR	6-1	188	2	Howard
81	Lewis, Nate	WR	5-11	189	2	Oregon Tech
73	May, Mark	G-T	6-6	290	10	Pittsburgh
41	McDonald, Keith	WR	5-9	170	3	San Jose State
31	McEwen, Craig	HB	6-1	220	5	Utah
83	Miller, Anthony	WR	5-11	185	4	Tennessee
91	O Neal, Leslie	OLB	6-4	259	5	Oklahoma State
37	Orr, Terry	HB	6-2	235	6	Texas
75	Phillips, Joe	NT	6-5	315	6	Southern Methodist
50	Plummer, Gary	ILB	6-2	240	6	California
25	Radachowsky, George	S	6-0	195	7	Boston College
65	Richards, David	G-T	6-4	310	4	UCLA
64	Rodenhauser, Mark	C	6-5	263	4	Illinois State
57	Rolling, Henry	OLB	6-2	225	4	Nevada-Reno
79	Savage, Tony	NT	6-3	300	1	Washington State
30	Seale, Sam	CB	5-9	185	3	Western State
55	Seau, Junior	LB	6-3	250	2	Southern California
23	Shelton, Anthony	CB	6-1	195	2	Tennessee State
68	Simmonds, Mike	G	6-4	295	2	Indiana State
54	Smith, Billy Ray	OLB	6-3	236	9	Arkansas
43	Spencer, Tim	RB	6-1	223	7	Ohio State
72	Swayne, Harry	T	6-5	290	5	Rutgers
85	Taylor, Kitrick	WR	5-11	191	4	Washington State
56	Thaxton, Galand	ILB	6-1	240	2	Wyoming
76	Thompson, Broderick	G-T	6-4	295	7	Kansas
11	Tolliver, Billy Joe	QB	6-1	218	3	Texas Tech
39	Walker, Derrick	TE	6-0	244	2	Michigan
99	Williams, Lee	DE	6-5	271	8	Bethune-Cookman
84	Wilson, Walter	WR	5-10	185	2	East Carolina
70	Zandofsky, Mike	G	6-2	285	3	Washington

TOP DRAFT CHOICES

Rd.	Name	Sel. No.	Pos.	Ht.	Wt.	College
1	Richard, Stanley	9	CB	6-1	198	Texas
2	Thornton, George	36	DT	6-3	301	Alabama
2	Bieniemy, Eric	39	RB	5-7	204	Colorado
2	Moten, Eric	47	G	6-3	307	Michigan State
4	Thigpen, Yancey	90	WR	6-0	207	Winston-Salem

cornerbacks—Sammy Seale and Anthony Shelton—acquired from the waiver wire?

SPECIAL TEAMS: Here is where Beathard solved problems with an open checkbook and a quick hook. He found the right kicking combination with punter John Kidd and John Carney, who made 19-of-21 field goals after replacing inept Fuad Reviez. Nate Lewis and Donnie Elder—Beathard acquisitions—spiced up the return game. Henning added Larry Pasquale as his special-teams coach and watched the units rank collectively as the best in the league.

THE ROOKIES: Free safety Stanley "The Sheriff" Richard of Texas not only fills the void in the secondary but his coverage ability opens plenty of options. Defensive tackle George Thornton of Alabama might have been a reach in the second round, but the Chargers were desperate for a 300-pounder on the line. Halfback Eric Bieniemy of Colorado was a steal in the second round, but Michigan State's Eric Moten wasn't. Beathard traded next year's first-rounder to move into position to take him.

OUTLOOK: When they were 6-7, the Chargers were close to breaking into the upper end of the AFC West. How the constant turnover of personnel and the quarterback questions are resolved will determine whether the Chargers can reach that .500 mark.

CHARGER PROFILES

BILLY JOE TOLLIVER 25 6-1 218 Quarterback

His progress is the single most important story on this team . . . Coach Dan Henning has faith he will develop into a top pro but GM Bobby Beathard, who drafted John Friesz and gave Bob Gagliano $630,000 a year to replace him, doesn't . . . Has a strong arm and is a fiery leader but tends to overthrow receivers and make critical mistakes late in games . . . Threw 16 interceptions, but went through a six-week stretch in which he threw 140 passes without being intercepted . . . Started 14 games and had a 6-8 record . . . Completed 216 of 410 attempts (52.7

percent) for 2,574 yards and 16 touchdowns . . . Acquired in the third round of the 1989 draft following draft-day trade in which the Chargers surrendered three choices . . . A four-year starter at Texas Tech . . . Threw 14 no-hitters in high school with a 92-mile-an-hour fastball . . . Holds Texas Tech record for attempts (1,007), completions (493), yards (6,756) and touchdowns (38) . . . Missed six weeks of 1989 season with broken collarbone . . . Born Feb. 7, 1966, in Dallas . . . 1991 salary: $300,000.

MARION BUTTS 25 6-1 248 Fullback

Carried only 64 times at Florida State, where he was a blocking back for Sammie Smith, whom the Miami Dolphins drafted in the first round . . . Might be the Chargers' best seventh-round choice in team history . . . Finished third in the NFL with 1,225 yards on 265 carries, earning a spot in the Pro Bowl . . . Virtually impossible to strip the ball from his hands; he fumbled only two times in 435 carries . . . A foot injury forced him to miss final two games and the Pro Bowl . . . Slowly developing his receiving skills, improving his reception total from seven to 16 . . . Impressed Florida State coaches with his unflinching style on special teams . . . Loves to punish defenders either running or blocking . . . Career almost ended during junior year in college when he broke his leg . . . Played two seasons at Northeast Oklahoma A&M Junior College . . . Born Aug. 1, 1966, in Worth County, Ga. . . . 1990 salary: $85,000.

LESLIE O'NEAL 27 6-4 259 Linebacker

Went to the Pro Bowl for his second consecutive year . . . Led Chargers with 13½ sacks, improving his career total to 42½ in 54 games . . . Plays right outside linebacker on rushing downs but rushes from a three-point stance in passing situations . . . His ego tends to cause friction on the team when he mouths off about not receiving enough publicity or local promotions . . . His 1988 season marked his first full campaign after missing 23 months due to near career-ending knee injury . . . Came to the Chargers as the eighth player selected in the 1986 draft . . . Finished third on the team with 81 tackles . . . Missed 23 days of training camp because of contract holdout . . . Played defensive end until switch to outside linebacker after 1988 season . . . Named NFL Defensive Rookie of the Year in 1986 . . . Born May 7, 1964, in Little Rock, Ark. . . . 1991 salary: $850,000.

ANTHONY MILLER 26 5-11 185 — Wide Receiver

One of the most feared receivers because of his speed and ability to get open . . . Selected to the Pro Bowl for the second time, his first as a starter . . . Despite double coverage and having no receiving threat on the other side of the field, he caught 63 passes for 933 yards and seven touchdowns . . . Had a nine-reception game in the second week against the Bengals . . . Played only one year of high-school football before accepting a track scholarship at San Diego State . . . Bench-presses twice his weight . . . Eventually ended up at Tennessee, where he played football and ran track . . . Finished second to Redskins' cornerback Darrell Green in 1989 NFL's Fastest Man Competition . . . Has 10.3 speed at 100 meters . . . Named team MVP in 1989 . . . Born April 15, 1965, in Pasadena, Cal. . . . 1991 salary: $300,000.

JUNIOR SEAU 22 6-3 250 — Linebacker

Immediately established himself as an impact player at inside linebacker and was selected a second alternate to the Pro Bowl . . . Coaches want to give him more work rushing the passer after a one-sack season . . . Missed all but two practices during training camp negotiating a contract, but still finished second on team with 85 tackles . . . Born in Samoa and didn't learn to speak English until he was seven . . . After being ruled a Prop 48 student at Southern Cal, he became an honor student . . . Was the fifth player chosen in 1990 draft after deciding to skip his senior season . . . Motivated himself in training before draft by reports that Alabama linebacker Keith McCants could become top choice . . . Runs 4.61 40 . . . Bench-presses 440 pounds . . . Born Jan. 19, 1969, in American Samoa . . . 1991 salary: $375,000.

LEE WILLIAMS 28 6-5 271 **Defensive End**

Wasn't happy that coaches moved him to tackle in pass-rush situations to accommodate pass-rushers Burt Grossman and Leslie O'Neal . . . Sack total dropped from 14 to 7½, ending his two-year string of going to the Pro Bowl . . . Walked out during training camp because of a contract dispute . . . Received enough votes to be a Pro Bowl alternate . . . Remains one of the game's best pass-rushers and has 65½ career sacks . . . A durable player who participated in 99 consecutive non-strike games since 1984 . . . Started career with the Los Angeles Express of the USFL and came to the Chargers in a supplemental draft . . . Played college ball at Bethune-Cookman . . . Lives by motto, "Attack, seek out and destroy." . . . Born Oct. 15, 1962, in Ft. Lauderdale, Fla. . . . 1991 salary: $500,000.

ROD BERNSTINE 26 6-3 238 **Running Back**

Had been in the doghouse until final two games of the season, when he rushed for 190 yards . . . Might have stopped the numerous trade rumors that have haunted him the past few years . . . Needs to stay healthy for 16 weeks because he has missed a minimum of two games in each of his first four seasons . . . Ranked second on the team with 589 yards on 124 carries despite missing four games with hamstring problems . . . Has been used as a tight end and an H-back . . . The Chargers made him the 24th choice in 1987 draft after a controversial trade with the Browns to acquire linebacker Chip Banks . . . Played fullback and tight end at Texas A&M . . . Played tight end in 1988 and caught 14 passes . . . Had anterior cruciate knee tear in 1988 . . . Born Feb. 8, 1965, in Fairfield, Cal. . . . 1990 salary: $270,000.

GILL BYRD 30 5-11 198 **Cornerback**

Had his third consecutive seven-interception season, but can't crack the talent-rich AFC Pro Bowl squad . . . Because of changes in the secondary he might be moved to free safety after Bobby Beathard released all but two of the team's safeties after last season . . . Despite lacking great speed, he takes advantage of the team's great pass rush and knows how to read quarterbacks and receivers . . . Has 32 career interceptions in eight seasons after coming to the Chargers as a 1983 first-round draft choice . . . A walk-on at San Jose State who ended up starting four years at cornerback . . . "I'm not a thoroughbred; I'm just a plow-horse," Byrd said of his skills . . . Won starting left-cornerback position as a rookie in 1983 minicamp . . . Uncle, Mac Byrd, played for Rams and Vikings . . . Opened a hair boutique in San Diego called "Hair Studio 22." . . . Born Feb. 20, 1961, in San Francisco . . . 1991 salary: $675,000.

BURT GROSSMAN 24 6-4 255 Defensive End

A pure pass-rush specialist who has 18 sacks in 23 career games . . . Improved a little against the run but might not ever gain a reputation as a great run-stopper . . . Started every game . . . Fractured a rib and missed most of the season-finale against the Raiders . . . Was a pass-rush demon at the University of Pittsburgh, where he recorded 26½ sacks in three years . . . Lost 25 pounds as a college freshman because of mono . . . The Chargers made him the eighth player selected in the 1989 draft . . . Has former Wade Boggs girlfriend Margo Adams as a half-sister and former Steeler tight end Randy Grossman as a cousin . . . Admitted taking steroids before a pre-draft workout . . . Was named to all-rookie team in 1989 . . . Born April 10, 1967, in Philadelphia . . . 1991 salary: $375,000.

COURTNEY HALL 23 6-1 269 Guard-Center

Moved to guard last season to fill team's needs but will probably switch back to center . . . Entered the league as its youngest player and is recognized as being one of its best young linemen . . . Started every game since coming to the Chargers in the second round of the 1989 draft . . . A brilliant student who earned economic and business degrees at Rice and plans to earn a masters' in business . . . Started 44 games on the offensive line at Rice . . . Entered kindergarten at the age of four and was 16 when he started college . . . One of two rookies to start every game in 1989 . . . Bench-presses 430 pounds and squats 650 pounds . . . Born Aug. 26, 1968, in Los Angeles . . . 1991 salary: $262,000.

COACH DAN HENNING: Pressure is on him after three consecutive 6-10 seasons . . . Has revamped the offensive line twice and is rebuilding the receiving corps around wide receiver Anthony Miller . . . Known as a quarterback teacher, Henning must bring rapid maturity to Billy Joe Tolliver, who will be pressured by John Friesz and Bob Gagliano for a starting job . . . Preaches the one-back passing attack that is known for ball control . . . So far, ball control has meant low-scoring because the Chargers have scored 20 or more points in only 16 of Henning's 48 games . . . Former head coach of the Falcons who has a 34-61-1 career record . . . Was a Chargers' backup quarterback in 1967 . . . Has coached in the NFL since 1972, when he started with the Oilers . . . After being fired by the Falcons in 1986, he spent a year as quarterback coach of the Redskins . . . Was the nation's 14th-ranked quarterback during his senior year at William & Mary . . . Close friend of former Giants' coach Bill Parcells and they have a pact to hire the other if one needs a job . . . Born June 21, 1942, in Bronx, N.Y.

GREATEST PUNTER

One season does not a punter make. But in San Diego, where the punt is missing in the Punt, Pass and Kick Contest, John Kidd might have made history in his first season (1990) wearing the lightning helmet. He was consistent, averaging 40 yards a kick and placing 23 percent of those kicks inside the 20.

You simply don't return punts on The Kidd. Only 28 of 61 punts were returned for a modest 4.7-yard average. For that kind of consistency, GM Bobby Beathard was willing to invest a $150,000 signing bonus to lure Kidd away from the Buffalo Bills last year.

Kidd is appreciated. Some of his predecessors weren't. Ralf Mojsiejenko set club records in his four seasons in San Diego. He averaged 42.9 every time he punted the ball, but management thought he was vulnerable to long returns, so they traded him to the Chargers in 1988. The rest of Charger history is filled with journeymen punters such as Maury Buford and Dennis Partee.

A good season this fall could make Kidd a man among Charger punters.

INDIVIDUAL CHARGER RECORDS

Rushing

Most Yards Game:	206	Keith Lincoln, vs Boston, 1964
Season:	1,225	Marion Butts, 1990
Career:	4,963	Paul Lowe, 1960-67

Passing

Most TD Passes Game:	6	Dan Fouts, vs Oakland, 1981
Season:	33	Dan Fouts, 1981
Career:	254	Dan Fouts, 1973-87

Receiving

Most TD Passes Game:	5	Kellen Winslow, vs Oakland, 1981
Season:	14	Lance Alworth, 1965
Career:	81	Lance Alworth, 1962-70

Scoring

Most Points Game:	30	Kellen Winslow, vs Oakland, 1981
Season:	118	Rolf Benirschke, 1980
Career:	766	Rolf Benirschke, 1977-86
Most TDs Game:	5	Kellen Winslow, vs Oakland, 1981
Season:	19	Chuck Muncie, 1981
Career:	83	Lance Alworth, 1962-70

SEATTLE SEAHAWKS

TEAM DIRECTORY: Pres./GM: Tom Flores; VP/Asst. GM: Chuck Allen; Dir. Player Personnel: Mike Allman; VP/Dir. Pub. Rel.: Gary Wright; Head Coach: Chuck Knox. Home field: Kingdome (64,757). Colors: Blue, green and silver.

John L. Williams does it all from his fullback slot

SCOUTING REPORT

OFFENSE: Ground Chuck is back, but for how long? Coming off his finest coaching season, Chuck Knox returned the power to the running offense, but his owner, Ken Behring, dragged out contract-extension talks and finally gave him a two-year extension through 1993. Written into the deal is a provision where either side could cancel the contract after each season.

Under Knox, the offense will never be that imaginative. He tried the Run-n'-Shoot, but pretty much cancelled the project halfway into a season-opening loss to the Bears. Instead, he resumed the "Hard Knox" approach to the game. With four 225-pound bound backs, the Seahawks rushed for 109.3 yards a game, a 22-yard improvement over 1989.

Fullback John Williams made the Pro Bowl with his blocks, runs and catches. Derrick Fenner, a once-troubled 230-pound halfback, put his past behind and moved ahead for 859 yards. Backed up by veteran fullback James Jones and young halfback Chris Warren, the Seahawks can maintain their no-nonsense approach to offense.

Aging quarterback Dave Krieg made big plays, but his mistakes don't go away. Without a deep receiving threat, the Seahawks (9-7 in 1990) might not be able to compensate for his 16 fumbles and 20 interceptions. The offensive line, featuring veteran guard Bryan Millard and young left tackle Andy Heck, is steady. The receiving team of Brian Blades and Tommy Kane combined for 101 receptions.

DEFENSE: Defensive coordinator Tom Catlin did miracles as every linebacker except backup Joe Cain spent time on the injured-reserve list. Catlin started the season with two rookie starters and had to teach first-round tackle Cortez Kennedy the defense after his training-camp holdout.

With schemes and mirrors, the Seahawks moved from the bottom of the defensive statistics into the Top 10. They ranked ninth in the NFL, 10th against the run. A year ago, the Seahawks ranked 23rd against the run with their pint-sized 3-4. Catlin tried the 4-3 and alternated the 293-pound Kennedy and 297-pound Eric Hayes into the line.

Linebacker Terry Wooden, coming off anterior-cruciate surgery, was an instant starter on the left outside. Knee tendinitis hindered safety Robert Blackmon, but the coaching staff will find a way to get his aggressiveness onto the field.

SEAHAWKS VETERAN ROSTER

HEAD COACH—Chuck Knox. Assistant Coaches—John Becker, Tom Catlin, George Dyer, Chick Harris, Ken Meyer, Paul Moyer, Rod Perry, Russ Purnell, Frank Raines, Kent Stephenson, Rusty Tillman, Joe Vitt.

No.	Name	Pos.	Ht.	Wt.	NFL Exp.	College
50	Ahrens, Dave	LB	6-4	247	11	Wisconsin
52	Andrews, Ricky	LB	6-2	236	2	Washington
65	Bailey, Edwin	G	6-4	279	11	South Carolina State
25	Blackmon, Robert	S	6-0	198	2	Baylor
89	Blades, Brian	WR	5-11	191	4	Miami
64	Brilz, Darrick	G	6-3	281	5	Oregon State
77	Bryant, Jeff	DT	6-5	281	10	Clemson
93	Buczkowski, Bob	DE	6-5	261	3	Pittsburgh
59	Cain, Joe	LB	6-1	233	3	Oregon Tech
88	Chadwick, Jeff	WR	6-3	189	9	Grand Valley State
84	Clark, Louis	WR	6-0	198	5	Mississippi State
53	Comeaux, Darren	LB	6-1	239	10	Arizona State
51	Cotton, Marcus	LB	6-3	237	4	Southern California
34	Davis, Brian	CB	6-2	190	5	Nebraska
3	Donnelly, Rick	P	6-0	203	6	Wyoming
75	Dyko, Chris	T	6-6	295	2	Washington State
68	Eisenhooth, Stan	C	6-5	291	3	Towson State
54	Feasel, Grant	C	6-7	279	7	Abilene Christian
44	Fenner, Derrick	RB	6-3	228	3	North Carolina
7	Ford, John	WR	6-2	204	2	Virginia
22	Glasgow, Nesby	S	5-10	187	13	Washington
79	Green, Jacob	DE	6-3	256	12	Texas A&M
29	Harper, Dwayne	CB	5-11	174	4	South Carolina State
78	Hayes, Eric	DT	6-3	297	2	Florida State
66	Heck, Andy	T	6-6	286	3	Notre Dame
85	Heller, Ron	TE	6-3	242	5	Oregon State
76	Hitchcock, Bill	T	6-6	308	1	Purdue
27	Hunter, Patrick	CB	5-11	186	6	Nevada-Reno
26	Jefferson, James	CB	6-1	199	3	Texas A&I
9	Johnson, Norm	K	6-2	203	10	UCLA
30	Jones, James	FB	6-2	232	9	Florida
83	Junkin, Trey	TE	6-2	240	9	Louisiana Tech
81	Kane, Tommy	WR	5-11	181	4	Syracuse
15	Kemp, Jeff	QB	6-0	201	11	Dartmouth
96	Kennedy, Cortez	DT	6-3	293	2	Miami
17	Krieg, Dave	QB	6-1	192	12	Milton
63	Lee, Ronnie	T	6-3	295	13	Baylor
20	Loville, Derek	RB	5-9	196	2	Oregon
31	McElroy, Vann	S	6-2	190	10	Baylor
40	McLemore, Chris	FB	6-1	230	3	Arizona
86	McNeal, Travis	TE	6-3	244	3	Tennessee-Chattanooga
71	Millard, Bryan	G	6-5	277	8	Texas
99	Miller, Donald	LB	6-2	223	2	Idaho State
95	Morris, Robert	DE	6-6	279	1	Valdosta State
72	Nash, Joe	DT	6-3	278	10	Boston College
58	Newbill, Richard	LB	6-1	240	2	Miami
97	Porter, Rufus	LB	6-1	226	4	Southern
41	Robinson, Eugene	S	6-0	190	7	Colgate
73	Singer, Curt	T	6-5	292	4	Tennessee
82	Skansi, Paul	WR	5-11	187	9	Washington
94	Stephens, Rod	LB	6-1	237	3	Georgia Tech
11	Stouffer, Kelly	QB	6-3	207	3	Colorado State
23	Thompson, Kevin	S	5-10	190	1	Oklahoma
87	Tice, Mike	TE	6-7	247	11	Maryland
56	Tofflemire, Joe	C	6-2	273	3	Arizona
42	Warren, Chris	RB	6-2	225	2	Ferrum
74	Wheat, Warren	G	6-6	274	2	Brigham Young
32	Williams, John L.	FB	5-11	231	6	Florida
90	Wooden, Terry	LB	6-3	232	2	Syracuse
57	Woods, Tony	DE	6-4	269	5	Pittsburgh
92	Wyman, David	LB	6-2	250	5	Stanford

TOP DRAFT CHOICES

Rd.	Name	Sel. No.	Pos.	Ht.	Wt.	College
1	McGwire, Dan	16	QB	6-8	243	San Diego State
2	Thomas, Doug	51	WR	5-9	176	Clemson
3	Daniels, David	74	WR	6-1	192	Penn State
4	Kasay, John	98	K	5-10	186	Georgia
5	Davis, Harlan	128	DB	6-0	191	Tennessee

Age is still a factor. Three-fourths of the defensive line—Jacob Green, Joe Nash and Jeff Bryant—are in their thirties. Defensive end Tony Woods is coming off major knee surgery. The leader of a secondary that lacks consistent cornerback play is 34-year-old strong safety Nesby Glasgow.

SPECIAL TEAMS: Despite surrendering two punt returns for touchdowns early in the season, the coverage teams finished strong. Special-teams coach Rusty Tillman, who interviewed for the Cleveland head-coaching job, was pleased. Rick Donnelly, a 1990 Plan B signee, ended years of inconsistent Seahawk punting, but kicker Norm Johnson cost the team a couple of games by missing clutch field-goal attempts. Warren, despite weighing 225 pounds, earned the return job and almost broke several for touchdowns.

THE ROOKIES: The Seahawks drafted little that could help Knox this year. The 6-8 quarterback, Dan McGwire of San Diego State, will need a year or two of spectating before he can take over for Krieg. Elsewhere, they gained speed and little else. Receivers Doug Thomas of Clemson and David Daniels of Penn State run 4.4 40s, but are projects. So is bump-and-run cornerback Harlan Davis of Tennesee. Kicker John Kasay, the fourth-round choice from Georgia, could beat out the inconsistent Johnson.

OUTLOOK: The Seahawks and the Broncos match up with less talent than their other three division opponents. Despite the addition of some promising young talent over the last two years, Seattle still isn't ready to dominate.

SEAHAWK PROFILES

JOHN L. WILLIAMS 26 5-11 231 Fullback

Finally made a well-deserved trip to the Pro Bowl, as a replacement for injured Bo Jackson . . . Considered football's best fullback because of his all-around contributions . . . After Curt Warner's departure following 1989 season, he took a more vocal role in the huddle, encouraging better play from his teammates . . . Rushed for 714 yards and caught 73 passes for

699 yards . . . Only Bills' halfback Thurman Thomas (1,413 yards) gained more combined yards . . . Blocking ability opened holes so that unproven Derrick Fenner could lead the team with 859 rushing yards . . . Has become Dave Krieg's emergency target in passing situations . . . Was Seahawks' first-round choice in 1986 after rushing for 2,409 yards at Florida . . . Reunited with James Jones, the former Florida fullback who taught him how to block . . . Started since his rookie season . . . Born Nov. 23, 1964, in Palatka, Fla. . . . 1991 salary: $900,000.

DAVE KRIEG 32 6-1 192 Quarterback

Amazingly durable, he joined Phoenix's Timm Rosenbach to be the only NFL quarterback to take every snap last season . . . Has brought the Seahawks from behind to win games 16 times in fourth quarters during his career . . . Fits in well under offensive coordinator John Becker's short-passing offense . . . Has 102 career fumbles, needing four to tie Dan Fouts' all-time NFL record . . . Had 16 fumbles, including four that were returned for touchdowns, in 1990 . . . Completed 265 of 448 passes for 3,194 yards . . . Threw only 15 touchdown passes, lowest total since becoming a starter in 1982 . . . A free agent who came recommended by his Milton College coach, Rudy Gaddini . . . Teammates nicknamed him "Mudbone" . . . Signed a new five-year contract before last season . . . Born Oct. 20, 1958, in Schofield, Wisc. . . . 1991 salary: $1.4 million.

CORTEZ KENNEDY 23 6-3 293 Defensive Tackle

Missed 1990 training camp because of contract problems and his play suffered . . . Alternated behind Jeff Bryant at right tackle . . . Joined Eagles' defensive tackle Jerome Brown working out with a conditioning trainer in Orlando during offseason . . . Became highest-paid defensive rookie in NFL history after signing a five-year, $6.75-million contract . . . Seahawks swapped four draft choices with the Patriots to move up five spots in the 1990 draft to select him third overall . . . Played well toward the end of the season and had a 10-tackle game against the Dolphins

. . . Played at Northwest Mississippi Junior College before transferring to Miami in 1988 . . . Went on to All-American selection in 1989 as the Hurricanes became No. 1 . . . Born Aug. 23, 1968, in Osceola, Fla. . . . 1991 salary: $600,000 plus $100,000 roster bonus.

BRIAN BLADES 26 5-11 191 **Wide Receiver**

Retirement of Steve Largent pushed double coverage to him and production suffered . . . Reception numbers dropped from 77 to 49, which cost him a second trip to the Pro Bowl . . . Brother Bennie is starting safety for the Lions . . . Brought his family to watch season-ending game against the Lions in which he caught seven passes and received a cheap shot from his brother . . . Because he played defensive back in high school, he doesn't mind blocking downfield on running plays . . . Walked out of training camp because of a contract problems . . . Doesn't have the great breakaway speed to be considered a deep threat . . . Was a backup at the University of Miami as a senior but drew the Seahawks' call in the second round of 1988 draft . . . Born July 24, 1965, in Ft. Lauderdale, Ky. . . . 1991 salary: $235,000.

DERRICK FENNER 24 6-3 228 **Halfback**

One of many great comeback stories of 1990 . . . Showed power and elusiveness, rushing for 859 yards and a 4.0-yard average . . . Battled back from a murder charge (he was cleared) and from being shot in the chest outside of a Washington, D.C., bar . . . Could have been a first-round choice had his off-the-field problems not forced him out of North Carolina . . . Well worth the 10th-round choice invested in him . . . Didn't play football in 1987 and 1988 after leading the ACC in rushing at North Carolina in 1986 . . . Ran for a career-high 144 yards and three touchdowns against the Broncos in September . . . Played despite knee and ankle spur problems late in the season . . . Tried at fullback during rookie season but learned halfback is his natural position . . . Born April 6, 1967, in Washington, D.C. . . . 1990 salary: $85,000.

ANDY HECK 24 6-6 286 **Tackle**

One of the best young pass-blocking tackles in the NFL . . . Started 25 games in first two seasons . . . Quarterback Dave Krieg believes his blindside is protected with Heck at left tackle . . . Corrected rookie problem of allowing defenders to beat him on inside rushes . . . After playing most of his Notre Dame career at tight end, he switched to tackle as a senior . . . Ate six meals a day to put on the required weight for the transformation . . . Improved so much that he ended up being the 15th player selected in the 1989 NFL draft . . . Missed blocks by Heck allowed two safeties in 1989 . . . Didn't miss a down while recovering from torn rib ligaments last year . . . Caught 16 passes during college career . . . A first-team all-rookie selection in 1989 . . . Born Jan. 1, 1967, in Fargo, N.D. . . . 1991 salary: $325,000.

BRYAN MILLARD 30 6-5 277 **Guard**

Did not miss an offensive play for the second consecutive season . . . After an off year in 1989, re-established himself as one of the AFC's top blocking guards . . . Twice during his career has been selected as a Pro Bowl alternate but has never played in the game . . . Has started 83 of 105 games since joining the Seahawks in 1984 . . . After starting two seasons on the Texas offensive line, he developed his pro skills as a starter for the New Jersey Generals of the USFL, blocking for Herschel Walker . . . Came to the Seahawks during a 1984 supplemental draft . . . An avid weightlifter who trains year-round . . . He is a fisherman who holds annual celebrity tournament . . . Born Dec. 2, 1960, in Sioux City, Iowa . . . 1991 salary: $550,000.

DAVE WYMAN 27 6-2 250 **Linebacker**

The leader of the Seahawks' defense at middle linebacker . . . Missed the first eight games last season because of a knee tendon problem but finished the season with 48 tackles and two interceptions in eight games . . . Suffered serious knee injury while playing linebacker at Stanford in 1984 and was in a cast for four months . . . After major reconstruction, he returned the next season . . . The knee figured in his being a second-rounder in the 1987 draft . . . Bulked up to 250 pounds after the coaching staff decided to switch to a 4-3 last season . . . Traded to the 49ers during rookie season, but trade was nullified because of shoulder injury . . . Had 458 career tackles at Stanford . . . Born March 31, 1964, in San Diego . . . 1991 salary: $450,000.

JACOB GREEN 34 6-3 256 — Defensive End

Rebounded after two disappointing seasons, thanks to switch to a 4-3 alignment . . . Playing left end with an additional lineman, Green received less double-team blocking and watched his sack total jump from three to 12½ . . . Because of his $1-million salary, he was left unprotected . . . Rejected $1.05-million offer from the Oilers during final days of Plan B . . . Involved in Seattle community during season and stages a charity golf tournament . . . Seahawks' defensive captain . . . Has a strange contract that defers all earnings for at least three years, but he lives off $350,000 paid from past deferred contracts . . . Was a first-round draft choice from Texas A&M in 1980 . . . Undersized, injured and double-teamed in the Seahawks' old 3-4 scheme, he recorded only 12 sacks during 1988 and 1989 seasons . . . Born Jan. 21, 1957, in Pasadena, Tex. . . . 1991 salary: $1 million.

TONY WOODS 25 6-4 269 — Defensive End

Added 20 pounds and successfully made the switch from linebacker to defensive end . . . Surprised people with his ability to stop the run . . . Despite being a pass-rusher in college, he had to relearn his pass-rushing techniques and recorded three sacks during the final month of the season . . . Suffered an anterior cruciate tear to his right knee during the season-finale against the Lions . . . Was a first-round draft choice in 1987 as an outside linebacker out of the University of Pittsburgh, where he was an All-American . . . Received a contract extension at the end of 1990 season . . . Born Sept. 11, 1965, in Newark, N.J. . . . 1990 salary: $375,000.

COACH CHUCK KNOX: Moved ahead of Bud Grant into seventh place among all-time NFL coaches with a 164-105-1 career record . . . Eleven of his 18 teams have made the playoffs . . . Should have picked up his fifth Coach-of-the-Year honor after coaching the team to a 9-4 finish despite losing his entire linebacker corps to injuries . . . Signed two-year contract extension through 1993 . . . Proponent of a strong run attack, he fooled with the Run-n'-Shoot offense last season without success . . . Needs three victories to pass Paul Brown on the all-time victory list . . . Lost 63 pounds before last season to win a diet challenge against five other NFL coaches . . . Wrote a book *Hard Knox*, in which he told of his rise from a tough neighborhood outside of Pittsburgh and how he endured physical abuse from his father . . . Majored in history at Juniata College, where he played tackle . . . Coached the Rams and Bills before joining the Seahawks in 1983 . . . Was an NFL assistant for 10 seasons . . . Started as a high-school football coach . . . So determined to win, he came to work at 5 AM every day last season . . . Born April 27, 1932, in Sewickley, Pa.

GREATEST PUNTER

Seattle was a franchise that ached for a good punter. Last year, they signed a good punter who ached. Rick Donnelly established a consistency in the position that had been missing since the inception of the franchise.

But, oh, that aching back. "It's something I'm always going to have," said Donnelly, who has a history of great punting and back pain. "Stiffness. I get up in the morning, and I can straighten out in five or 10 minutes. After two back surgeries, I'm going to have to really expect to live with it."

Donnelly can certainly punt despite the back. His 40.8-yard average was exactly what special teams coach Rusty Tillman wanted. "Rick is consistent and very professional," Tillman said.

Signed through Plan B, Donnelly left a Falcon team that turned its back on him when his pain forced him to miss the 1989 season. Management feared that those near-Pro Bowl years might be gone. In Seattle, Donnelly found some pats on the back.

INDIVIDUAL SEAHAWK RECORDS

Rushing

Most Yards Game:	207	Curt Warner, vs Kansas City, 1983
Season:	1,481	Curt Warner, 1986
Career:	6,705	Curt Warner, 1983-89

Passing

Most TD Passes Game:	5	3 times, most recently Dave Krieg, vs L.A. Raiders, 1988
Season:	32	Dave Krieg, 1984
Career:	184	Dave Krieg, 1980-90

Receiving

Most TD Passes Game:	4	Daryl Turner, vs San Diego, 1985
Season:	13	Daryl Turner, 1985
Career:	100	Steve Largent, 1976-89

Scoring

Most Points Game:	24	2 times, most recently Curt Warner, vs Denver, 1988
Season:	110	Norm Johnson, 1984
Career:	810	Norm Johnson, 1982-90
Most TDs Game:	4	2 times, most recently Curt Warner, vs Denver, 1988
Season:	15	3 times, most recently Derrick Fenner, 1990
Career:	101	Steve Largent, 1976-89

San Diego State QB Dan McGwire was Seattle's first pick.

OFFICIAL 1990 NFL STATISTICS

(Compiled by Elias Sports Bureau)

RUSHING

TOP TEN RUSHERS

	Att	Yards	Avg	Long	TD
Sanders, Barry, Det.	255	1304	5.1	t45	13
Thomas, Thurman, Buff.	271	1297	4.8	t80	11
Butts, Marion, S.D.	265	1225	4.6	52	8
Byner, Earnest, Wash.	297	1219	4.1	22	6
Humphrey, Bobby, Den.	288	1202	4.2	t37	7
Anderson, Neal, Chi.	260	1078	4.1	52	10
Word, Barry, K.C.	204	1015	5.0	t53	4
Brooks, James, Cin.	195	1004	5.1	t56	5
Cunningham, Randall, Phil.	118	942	8.0	t52	5
Smith, Emmitt, Dall.	241	937	3.9	t48	11

AFC - INDIVIDUAL RUSHERS

	Att	Yards	Avg	Long	TD
Thomas, Thurman, Buff	271	1297	4.8	t80	11
Butts, Marion, S.D.	265	1225	4.6	52	8
Humphrey, Bobby, Den.	288	1202	4.2	t37	7
Word, Barry, K.C.	204	1015	5.0	t53	4
Brooks, James, Cin.	195	1004	5.1	t56	5
Fenner, Derrick, Sea.	215	859	4.0	36	14
Smith, Sammie, Mia.	226	831	3.7	33	8
Stephens, John, N.E.	212	808	3.8	26	2
Okoye, Christian, K.C.	245	805	3.3	32	7
Hoge, Merril, Pitt.	203	772	3.8	t41	7
Williams, John L., Sea.	187	714	3.8	25	3
Mack, Kevin, Clev.	158	702	4.4	26	5
White, Lorenzo, Hou.	168	702	4.2	22	8
Jackson, Bo, Raiders	125	698	5.6	88	5
Allen, Marcus, Raiders	179	682	3.8	28	12
Dickerson, Eric, Ind.	166	677	4.1	43	4
Thomas, Blair, Jets	123	620	5.0	41	1

t = Touchdown
Leader based on yards gained

	Att	Yards	Avg	Long	TD
Bernstine, Rod, S.D.	124	589	4.8	t40	4
Bentley, Albert, Ind.	137	556	4.1	t26	4
Baxter, Brad, Jets	124	539	4.3	t28	6
McNeil, Freeman, Jets	99	458	4.6	29	6
Worley, Tim, Pitt.	109	418	3.8	38	0
Williams, Warren, Pitt.	68	389	5.7	t70	3
Hector, Johnny, Jets	91	377	4.1	22	2
Harmon, Ronnie, S.D.	66	363	5.5	41	0
Green, Harold, Cin.	83	353	4.3	39	1
Smith, Steve, Raiders	81	327	4.0	17	2
Logan, Marc, Mia.	79	317	4.0	17	2
Davis, Kenneth, Buff.	64	302	4.7	47	4
Pinkett, Allen, Hou.	66	268	4.1	19	0
Woods, Ickey, Cin.	64	268	4.2	32	6
Elway, John, Den.	50	258	5.2	21	3
Metcalf, Eric, Clev.	80	248	3.1	17	1
Allen, Marvin, N.E.	63	237	3.8	29	1
Taylor, Craig, Cin.	51	216	4.2	24	2
Moon, Warren, Hou.	55	215	3.9	17	2
Mueller, Jamie, Buff.	59	207	3.5	20	2
Foster, Barry, Pitt.	36	203	5.6	38	1
Bell, Greg, Raiders	47	164	3.5	21	1
Esiason, Boomer, Cin.	49	157	3.2	21	0
Hoard, Leroy, Clev.	58	149	2.6	42	3
Stradford, Troy, Mia.	37	138	3.7	15	1
Winder, Sammy, Den.	42	120	2.9	19	2
Krieg, Dave, Sea.	32	115	3.6	25	0
Adams, George, N.E.	28	111	4.0	13	0
Perryman, Bob, N.E.	32	97	3.0	13	1
Paige, Tony, Mia.	32	95	3.0	11	2
Bratton, Mel, Den.	27	82	3.0	10	3
Smith, Don, Buff.	20	82	4.1	13	2
Ezor, Blake, Den.	23	81	3.5	15	0
Gainer, Derrick, Clev.	30	81	2.7	9	1
Schroeder, Jay, Raiders	37	81	2.2	17	0
Hodson, Tom, N.E.	12	79	6.6	23	0
Jones, Victor, Hou.	14	75	5.4	14	0
Ball, Eric, Cin.	22	72	3.3	15	1
O'Brien, Ken, Jets	21	72	3.4	15	0
Higgs, Mark, Mia.	10	67	6.7	27	0
Givins, Ernest, Hou.	3	65	21.7	31	0
Brister, Bubby, Pitt.	25	64	2.6	11	0
Kelly, Jim, Buff.	22	63	2.9	15	0
McNair, Todd, K.C.	14	61	4.4	13	0
Tatupu, Mosi, N.E.	16	56	3.5	15	0
Carlson, Cody, Hou.	11	52	4.7	16	0
Kubiak, Gary, Den.	9	52	5.8	18	0
Jones, Bill, K.C.	10	47	4.7	14	0
Jennings, Stanford, Cin.	12	46	3.8	13	1
Sewell, Steve, Den.	17	46	2.7	8	3
Mueller, Vance, Raiders	13	43	3.3	12	0
Gardner, Carwell, Buff.	15	41	2.7	14	0
Secules, Scott, Mia.	8	34	4.3	17	0

	Att	Yards	Avg	Long	TD
Eason, Tony, Jets	7	29	4.1	24	0
Marino, Dan, Mia.	16	29	1.8	15	0
Slaughter, Webster, Clev.	5	29	5.8	17	0
Jackson, Mark, Den.	5	28	5.6	t16	1
Trudeau, Jack, Ind.	10	28	2.8	9	0
Lewis, Nate, S.D.	4	25	6.3	t10	1
McCallum, Napoleon, Raiders	10	25	2.5	6	0
Reich, Frank, Buff.	15	24	1.6	9	0
Beebe, Don, Buff.	1	23	23.0	23	0
Reed, Andre, Buff.	3	23	7.7	26	0
Tolliver, Billy Joe, S.D.	14	22	1.6	14	0
Jones, James, Sea.	5	20	4.0	5	0
Taylor, Troy, Jets	2	20	10.0	15	1
Blades, Brian, Sea.	3	19	6.3	12	0
Bell, Richard, Pitt.	5	18	3.6	12	0
Kinnebrew, Larry, Buff.	9	18	2.0	4	1
Stryzinski, Dan, Pitt.	3	17	5.7	9	0
Saxon, James, K.C.	3	15	5.0	8	0
Limbrick, Garrett, Mia.	5	14	2.8	5	0
Nelson, Darrin, S.D.	3	14	4.7	5	0
Kosar, Bernie, Clev.	10	13	1.3	5	0
Miller, Anthony, S.D.	3	13	4.3	10	0
Loville, Derek, Sea.	7	12	1.7	4	0
James, Lynn, Cin.	1	11	11.0	11	0
Warren, Chris, Sea.	6	11	1.8	4	1
Clark, Ken, Ind.	7	10	1.4	11	0
Fernandez, Mervyn, Raiders	3	10	3.3	9	0
Strom, Rick, Pitt.	4	10	2.5	10	0
Hester, Jessie, Ind.	4	9	2.3	10	0
Mathis, Terance, Jets	2	9	4.5	10	0
Brown, A.B., Jets	1	8	8.0	8	0
Martin, Tony, Mia.	1	8	8.0	8	0
Overton, Don, N.E.	5	8	1.6	6	0
Wilson, Marc, N.E.	5	7	1.4	6	0
Jensen, Jim, Mia.	4	6	1.5	2	0
Pelluer, Steve, K.C.	5	6	1.2	5	0
Wilhelm, Erik, Cin.	6	6	1.0	4	0
Morris, Jamie, N.E.	2	4	2.0	3	0
Goodburn, Kelly, K.C.	1	5	5.0	5	0
Banks, Fred, Mia.	1	3	3.0	3	0
Friesz, John, S.D.	1	3	3.0	3	0
Plummer, Gary, S.D.	2	3	1.5	2	1
Porter, Kerry, Den.	1	3	3.0	3	0
George, Jeff, Ind.	11	2	0.2	6	1
McNeal, Travis, Sea.	1	2	2.0	2	0
Prokop, Joe, Jets	3	2	0.7	8	0
Gannon, Chris, N.E.	1	0	0.0	0	0
Hansen, Brian, N.E.	1	0	0.0	0	0
Vlasic, Mark, S.D.	1	0	0.0	0	0
Wilson, Walter, S.D.	1	0	0.0	0	0
Jones, Fred, K.C.	1	-1	-1.0	-1	0
Pagel, Mike, Clev.	3	-1	-0.3	0	0
Redden, Barry, Clev.	1	-1	-1.0	-1	0

	Att	Yards	Avg	Long	TD
Evans, Vince, Raiders	1	-2	-2.0	-2	0
Jones, Tony, Hou.	1	-2	-2.0	-2	0
Chadwick, Jeff, Sea.	1	-3	-3.0	-3	0
Wellsandt, Doug, Jets	1	-3	-3.0	-3	0
Fryar, Irving N.E.	2	-4	-2.0	-1	0
Moore, Rob, Jets	2	-4	-2.0	4	0
DeBerg, Steve, K.C.	21	-5	-0.2	6	0
Grogan, Steve, N.E.	4	-5	-1.3	0	0
Lipps, Louis, Pitt.	1	-5	-5.0	-5	0
Stone, Dwight, Pitt.	2	-6	-3.0	10	0
Edmunds, Ferrell, Mia.	1	-7	-7.0	-7	0
Barber, Mike, Cin.	1	-13	-13.0	-13	0

NFC - INDIVIDUAL RUSHERS

Sanders, Barry, Det.	255	1304	5.1	t45	13
Byner, Earnest, Wash.	297	1219	4.1	22	6
Anderson, Neal, Chi.	260	1078	4.1	52	10
Cunningham, Randall, Phil.	118	942	8.0	t52	5
Smith, Emmitt, Dall.	241	937	3.9	t48	11
Johnson, Johnny, Phoe.	234	926	4.0	41	5
Gary, Cleveland, Rams	204	808	4.0	48	14
Anderson, Ottis, Giants	225	784	3.5	28	11
Walker, Herschel, Minn.	184	770	4.2	t58	5
Rozier, Mike, Hou.-Atl.	163	717	4.4	67	3
Sherman, Heath, Phil.	164	685	4.2	36	1
Muster, Brad, Chi.	141	664	4.7	28	6
Anderson, Gary, T.B.	166	646	3.9	22	3
Heyward, Craig, N.O.	129	599	4.6	t47	4
Mayes, Rueben, N.O.	138	510	3.7	18	7
Cobb, Reggie, T.B.	151	480	3.2	17	2
Riggs, Gerald, Wash.	123	475	3.9	20	6
Rosenbach, Timm, Phoe.	86	470	5.5	25	3
Carter, Dexter, S.F.	114	460	4.0	t74	1
Hampton, Rodney, Giants	109	455	4.2	41	2
Broussard, Steve, Atl.	126	454	3.6	t50	4
Toney, Anthony, Phil.	132	452	3.4	20	1
Craig, Roger S.F.	141	439	3.1	26	1
Thompson, Anthony, Phoe.	106	390	3.7	40	4
Fenney, Rick Minn.	87	376	4.3	27	2
Peete, Rodney, Det.	47	363	7.7	37	6
Fenerty, Gill, N.O.	73	355	4.9	t30	2
Harbaugh, Jim, Chi.	51	321	6.3	17	4
Rathman, Tom, S.F.	101	318	3.1	22	7
Haddix, Michael, G.B.	98	311	3.2	13	0
Hilliard, Dalton, N.O.	90	284	3.2	17	0
Testaverde, Vinny, T.B.	38	280	7.4	t48	1
Gannon, Rich, Minn.	52	268	5.2	27	1
Thompson, Darrell, G.B.	76	264	3.5	37	1
Green, Gaston, Rams	68	261	3.8	31	0

	Att	Yards	Avg	Long	TD
McGee, Buford, Rams	44	234	5.3	19	1
Tillman, Lewis, Giants	84	231	2.8	17	1
Agee, Tommie, Dall.	53	213	4.0	28	0
Sanders, Thomas, Phil.	56	208	3.7	39	1
Anderson, Alfred, Minn.	59	207	3.5	14	2
Hostetler, Jeff, Giants	39	190	4.9	30	2
Majkowski, Don, G.B.	29	186	6.4	24	1
Jones, Keith, Atl.	49	185	3.8	22	0
Woodside, Keith, G.B.	46	182	4.0	21	1
Aikman, Troy, Dall.	40	172	4.3	20	1
Sydney, Harry, S.F.	35	166	4.7	19	2
Meggett, Dave, Giants	22	164	7.5	51	0
Montana, Joe, S.F.	40	162	4.1	20	1
Young, Steve, S.F.	15	159	10.6	31	0
Gagliano, Bob, Det.	46	145	3.2	22	0
Carthon, Maurice, Giants	36	143	4.0	12	0
Byars, Keith, Phil.	37	141	3.8	23	0
Warner, Curt, Rams	49	139	2.8	9	1
Green, Mark, Chi.	27	126	4.7	14	0
Fullwood, Brent, G.B.	44	124	2.8	16	1
Dilweg, Anthony, G.B.	21	114	5.4	22	0
Harvey, John, T.B.	27	113	4.2	14	0
Humphries, Stan, Wash.	23	106	4.6	17	2
Johnson, Tracy, Atl.	30	106	3.5	12	3
Miller, Chris, Atl.	26	99	3.8	18	1
Bailey, Johnny, Chi.	26	86	3.3	9	0
Dupard, Reggie, Wash.	19	85	4.5	11	0
Flagler, Terrence, Phoe.	13	85	6.5	t29	1
Mitchell, Brian, Wash.	15	81	5.4	21	1
Wilson, Wade, Minn.	12	79	6.6	24	0
Fourcade, John, N.O.	15	77	5.1	12	1
Fontenot, Herman, G.B.	17	76	4.5	18	0
Rice, Allen, Minn.	22	74	3.4	13	0
Dupree, Marcus, Rams	19	72	3.8	13	0
Chandler, Chris, T.B.	13	71	5.5	18	1
Ware, Andre, Det.	7	64	9.1	30	0
Simms, Phil, Giants	21	61	2.9	20	1
Monk, Art, Wash.	7	59	8.4	26	0
Vick, Roger, Phil.	16	58	3.6	17	1
Rouse, James, Chi.	16	56	3.5	10	0
Delpino, Robert, Rams	13	52	4.0	13	0
Wilder, James, Det.	11	51	4.6	13	0
Workman, Vince, G.B.	8	51	6.4	31	0
Clark, Jessie, Minn.	16	49	3.1	11	0
Highsmith, Alonzo, Dall.	19	48	2.5	7	0
Dixon, James, Dall.	11	43	3.9	18	0
Gentry, Dennis, Chi.	11	43	3.9	11	0
Tomczak, Mike, Chi.	12	41	3.4	14	2
Query, Jeff, G.B.	3	39	13.0	18	0
Campbell, Scott, Atl.	9	38	4.2	20	0
Perkins, Bruce, T.B.	13	36	2.8	9	0
Johnston, Daryl, Dall.	10	35	3.5	8	1
Drummond, Robert, Phil.	8	33	4.1	9	1

	Att	Yards	Avg	Long	TD
Jones, Ernie, Phoe.	4	33	8.3	15	0
Everett, Jim, Rams	20	31	1.6	15	1
Morris, Ron, Chi.	2	26	13.0	16	0
Wright, Alexander, Dall.	3	26	8.7	14	0
Walsh, Steve, Dall.-N.O.	20	25	1.3	18	0
Bryant, Kelvin, Wash.	6	24	4.0	12	0
Lang, Gene, Atl.	9	24	2.7	9	0
Ellard, Henry, Rams	2	21	10.5	13	0
Saxon, Mike, Dall.	1	20	20.0	20	0
Williams, Calvin, Phil.	2	20	10.0	18	0
Smith, Cedric, Minn.	9	19	2.1	7	0
Sanders, Ricky, Wash.	4	17	4.3	12	0
Carter, Anthony, Minn.	3	16	5.3	11	0
Settle, John, Atl.	9	16	1.8	4	0
Henderson, Keith, S.F.	6	14	2.3	9	0
Rouson, Lee, Giants	3	14	4.7	6	0
Sharpe, Sterling, G.B.	2	14	7.0	10	0
Anderson, Willie, Rams	1	13	13.0	13	0
Barnett, Fred, Phil.	2	13	6.5	12	0
Dozier, D.J., Minn.	6	12	2.0	4	0
Rutledge, Jeff, Wash.	4	12	3.0	t12	1
Kiel, Blair, G.B.	5	9	1.8	4	1
Pringle, Mike, Atl.	2	9	4.5	9	0
Sikahema, Vai, Phoe.	3	8	2.7	4	0
Carter, Cris, Minn.	2	6	3.0	8	0
Laufenberg, Babe, Dall.	2	6	3.0	5	0
Smith, Timmy, Dall.	6	6	1.0	3	0
Tate, Lars, Chi.	3	5	1.7	4	0
Bates, Bill, Dall.	1	4	4.0	4	0
Ingram, Mark, Giants	1	4	4.0	4	0
Proehl, Ricky, Phoe.	1	4	4.0	4	0
Rypien, Mark, Wash.	15	4	0.3	8	0
Smith, J.T., Phoe.	1	4	4.0	4	0
Baker, Stephen, Giants	1	3	3.0	3	0
Feagles, Jeff, Phil.	2	3	1.5	3	0
Wolfley, Ron, Phoe.	2	3	1.5	2	0
Clark, Gary, Wash.	1	1	1.0	1	0
McMahon, Jim, Phil.	3	1	0.3	3	0
Carlson, Jeff, T.B.	1	0	0.0	0	0
Hill, Bruce, T.B.	1	0	0.0	0	0
Mojsiejenko, Ralf, Wash.	1	0	0.0	0	0
Rice, Jerry, S.F.	2	0	0.0	2	0
Tupa, Tom, Phoe.	1	0	0.0	0	0
Kemp, Perry, G.B.	1	-1	-1.0	-1	0
Perry, William, Chi.	1	-1	-1.0	-1	0
Martin, Kelvin, Dall.	4	-2	-0.5	3	0
Newsome, Harry, Minn.	2	-2	-1.0	0	0
Jones, Hassan, Minn.	1	-7	-7.0	-7	0
McKinnon, Dennis, Dall.	1	-8	-8.0	-8	0
Buford, Maury, Chi.	1	-9	-9.0	-9	0
Camarillo, Rich, Phoe.	1	-11	-11.0	-11	0
Millen, Hugh, Atl.	7	-12	-1.7	2	0
English, Keith, Rams	2	-19	-9.5	-8	0

49ers' Joe Montana led NFC in completion percentage.

49ers' Jerry Rice caught career-high 100 passes.

PASSING

TOP TEN PASSERS

	Att	Comp	Pct Comp	Yds	Avg Gain
Kelly, Jim, Buff.	346	219	63.3	2829	8.18
Moon, Warren, Hou.	584	362	62.0	4689	8.03
DeBerg, Steve, K.C.	444	258	58.1	3444	7.76
Simms, Phil, Giants	311	184	59.2	2284	7.34
Cunningham, Randall, Phil.	465	271	58.3	3466	7.45
Schroeder, Jay, Raiders	334	182	54.5	2849	8.53
Montana, Joe, S.F.	520	321	61.7	3944	7.58
Marino, Dan, Mia.	531	306	57.6	3563	6.71
Harbaugh, Jim, Chi.	312	180	57.7	2178	6.98
Brister, Bubby, Pitt.	387	223	57.6	2725	7.04

AFC - INDIVIDUAL PASSERS

Kelly, Jim, Buff.	346	219	63.3	2829	8.18
Moon, Warren, Hou.	584	362	62.0	4689	8.03
DeBerg, Steve, K.C.	444	258	58.1	3444	7.76
Schroeder, Jay, Raiders	334	182	54.5	2849	8.53
Marino, Dan, Mia.	531	306	57.6	3563	6.71
Brister, Bubby, Pitt.	387	223	57.6	2725	7.04
Elway, John, Den.	502	294	58.6	3526	7.02
O'Brien, Ken, Jets	411	226	55.0	2855	6.95
Esiason, Boomer, Cin.	402	224	55.7	3031	7.54
George, Jeff, Ind.	334	181	54.2	2152	6.44
Krieg, Dave, Sea.	448	265	59.2	3194	7.13
Tolliver, Billy Joe, S.D.	410	216	52.7	2574	6.28
Kosar, Bernie, Clev.	423	230	54.4	2562	6.06
Wilson, Marc, N.E.	265	139	52.5	1625	6.13

(Nonqualifiers)

Taylor, Troy, Jets	10	7	70.0	49	4.90
Carlson, Cody, Hou.	55	37	67.3	383	6.96
Reich, Frank, Buff.	63	36	57.1	469	7.44
Wilhelm, Erik, Cin.	19	12	63.2	117	6.16
Trudeau, Jack, Ind.	144	84	58.3	1078	7.49

t = Touchdown
Leader based on rating points, minimum 224 attempts

TD	Pct TD	Long	Int	Pct Int	Sack	Yds Lost	Rating Points
24	6.9	71	9	2.6	20	158	101.2
33	5.7	t87	13	2.2	36	252	96.8
23	5.2	t90	4	0.9	22	191	96.3
15	4.3	t80	4	1.3	20	104	92.7
30	6.5	t95	13	2.8	49	431	91.6
19	5.7	t68	9	2.7	29	197	90.8
26	5.0	t78	16	3.1	29	153	89.0
21	4.0	t69	11	2.1	15	90	82.6
10	3.2	t80	6	1.9	31	206	81.9
20	5.2	90	14	3.6	28	213	81.6

24	6.9	71	9	2.6	20	158	101.2
33	5.7	t87	13	2.2	36	252	96.8
23	5.2	t90	4	0.9	22	191	96.3
19	5.7	t68	9	2.7	29	197	90.8
21	4.0	t69	11	2.1	15	90	82.6
20	5.2	90	14	3.6	28	213	81.6
15	3.0	66	14	2.8	43	311	78.5
13	3.2	t69	10	2.4	34	262	77.3
24	6.0	53	22	5.5	31	198	77.0
16	4.8	75	13	3.9	37	320	73.8
15	3.3	t63	20	4.5	40	360	73.6
16	3.9	t45	16	3.9	19	150	68.9
10	2.4	50	15	3.5	37	220	65.7
6	2.3	t36	11	4.2	29	228	61.6

1	10.0	15	0	0.0	2	3	114.2
4	7.3	t53	2	3.6	3	15	96.3
2	3.2	43	0	0.0	6	41	91.3
0	0.0	19	0	0.0	1	2	80.4
6	4.2	73	6	4.2	14	104	78.4

	Att	Comp	Pct Comp	Yds	Avg Gain
Grogan, Steve, N.E.	92	50	54.3	615	6.68
Gilbert, Gale, Buff.	15	8	53.3	106	7.07
Strom, Rick, Pitt.	21	14	66.7	162	7.71
Hodson, Tom, N.E.	156	85	54.5	968	6.21
Friesz, John, S.D.	22	11	50.0	98	4.45
Eason, Tony, Jets	28	13	46.4	155	5.54
Pagel, Mike, Clev.	148	69	46.6	819	5.53
Vlasic, Mark, S.D.	40	19	47.5	168	4.20
Kubiak, Gary, Den.	22	11	50.0	145	6.59
(Fewer than 10 attempts)					
Allen, Marcus, Raiders	1	0	0.0	0	0.00
Evans, Vince, Raiders	1	1	100.0	36	36.00
Ferguson, Joe, Ind.	8	2	25.0	21	2.63
Francis, Jeff, Clev.	2	2	100.0	26	13.00
Herrmann, Mark, Ind.	1	1	100.0	6	6.00
Humphrey, Bobby, Den.	2	0	0.0	0	0.00
James, Lynn, Cin.	1	0	0.0	0	0.00
Jensen, Jim, Mia.	1	1	100.0	31	31.00
Johnson, Lee, Cin.	1	1	100.0	4	4.00
Pelluer, Steve, K.C.	5	2	40.0	14	2.80
Philcox, Todd, Cin.	2	0	0.0	0	0.00
Secules, Scott, Mia.	7	3	42.9	17	2.43
Sewell, Steve, Den.	1	0	0.0	0	0.00
Smith, Don, Buff.	1	0	0.0	0	0.00
Stark, Rohn, Ind.	1	1	100.0	40	40.00
Stephens, John, N.E.	1	0	0.0	0	0.00
Toon, Al, Jets	2	0	0.0	0	0.00

NFC - INDIVIDUAL PASSERS

Simms, Phil, Giants	311	184	59.2	2284	7.34
Cunningham, Randall, Phil.	465	271	58.3	3466	7.45
Montana, Joe, S.F.	520	321	61.7	3944	7.58
Harbaugh, Jim, Chi.	312	180	57.7	2178	6.98
Peete, Rodney, Det.	271	142	52.4	1974	7.28
Everett, Jim, Rams	554	307	55.4	3989	7.20
Miller, Chris, Atl.	388	222	57.2	2735	7.05
Rypien, Mark, Wash.	304	166	54.6	2070	6.81
Testaverde, Vinny, T.B.	365	203	55.6	2818	7.72
Majkowski, Don, G.B.	264	150	56.8	1925	7.29
Rosenbach, Timm, Phoe.	437	237	54.2	3098	7.09
Gannon, Rich, Minn.	349	182	52.1	2278	6.53
Walsh, Steve, Dall.-N.O.	336	179	53.3	2010	5.98
Aikman, Troy, Dall.	399	226	56.6	2579	6.46

TD	Pct TD	Long	Int	Pct Int	Sack	Yds Lost	Rating Points
4	4.3	48	3	3.3	9	68	76.1
2	13.3	23	2	13.3	1	9	76.0
0	0.0	22	1	4.8	5	29	69.9
4	2.6	56	5	3.2	20	147	68.5
1	4.5	17	1	4.5	1	7	58.5
0	0.0	31	1	3.6	4	35	49.0
3	2.0	32	8	5.4	5	40	48.2
1	2.5	27	2	5.0	0	0	46.7
0	0.0	36	4	18.2	3	19	31.6

0	0.0	0	1	100.0	0	0	0.0
0	0.0	36	0	0.0	0	0	118.8
0	0.0	13	2	25.0	0	0	0.0
0	0.0	17	0	0.0	0	0	118.8
0	0.0	6	0	0.0	0	0	91.7
0	0.0	0	0	0.0	0	0	39.6
0	0.0	0	0	0.0	0	0	39.6
0	0.0	31	0	0.0	0	0	118.8
1	100.0	t4	0	0.0	0	0	122.9
0	0.0	11	1	20.0	0	0	8.3
0	0.0	0	1	50.0	2	9	0.0
0	0.0	8	1	14.3	1	9	10.7
0	0.0	0	0	0.0	0	0	39.6
0	0.0	0	0	0.0	0	0	39.6
0	0.0	40	0	0.0	0	0	118.8
0	0.0	0	1	100.0	0	0	0.0
0	0.0	0	0	0.0	0	0	39.6

15	4.8	t80	4	1.3	20	104	92.7
30	6.5	t95	13	2.8	49	431	91.6
26	5.0	t78	16	3.1	29	153	89.0
10	3.2	t80	6	1.9	31	206	81.9
13	4.8	t68	8	3.0	27	173	79.8
23	4.2	t55	17	3.1	30	198	79.3
17	4.4	t75	14	3.6	26	167	78.7
16	5.3	t53	11	3.6	6	33	78.4
17	4.7	t89	18	4.9	38	330	75.6
10	3.8	t76	12	4.5	32	178	73.5
16	3.7	t68	17	3.9	43	285	72.8
16	4.6	t78	16	4.6	34	188	68.9
12	3.6	58	13	3.9	10	76	67.2
11	2.8	t61	18	4.5	39	288	66.6

	Att	Comp	Pct Comp	Yds	Avg Gain
(Nonqualifiers)					
Young, Steve, S.F.	62	38	61.3	427	6.89
Willis, Peter Tom, Chi.	13	9	69.2	106	8.15
Hostetler, Jeff, Giants	87	47	54.0	614	7.06
Rutledge, Jeff, Wash.	68	40	58.8	455	6.69
Millen, Hugh, Atl.	63	34	54.0	427	6.78
Wilson, Wade, Minn.	146	82	56.2	1155	7.91
Kiel, Blair, G.B.	85	51	60.0	504	5.93
Gagliano, Bob, Det.	159	87	54.7	1190	7.48
Dilweg, Anthony, G.B.	192	101	52.6	1267	6.60
Campbell, Scott, Atl.	76	36	47.4	527	6.93
Humphries, Stan, Wash.	156	91	58.3	1015	6.51
Fourcade, John, N.O.	116	50	43.1	785	6.77
Ware, Andre, Det.	30	13	43.3	164	5.47
Tomczak, Mike, Chi.	104	39	37.5	521	5.01
Chandler, Chris, T.B.	83	42	50.6	464	5.59
Laufenberg, Babe, Dall.	67	24	35.8	279	4.16
(Fewer than 10 attempts)					
Bailey, Johnny, Chi.	1	1	100.0	22	22.00
Byars, Keith, Phil.	4	4	100.0	53	13.25
Byner, Earnest, Wash.	2	1	50.0	31	15.50
Feagles, Jeff, Phil.	1	0	0.0	0	0.00
Green, Roy, Phoe.	1	1	100.0	20	20.00
Helton, Barry, S.F.	1	1	100.0	0	0.00
Heyward, Craig, N.O.	1	0	0.0	0	0.00
Johnson, Johnny, Phoe.	1	0	0.0	0	0.00
Jones, Keith, Atl.	1	1	100.0	37	37.00
Kramer, Tommy, N.O.	3	1	33.3	2	0.67
Long, Chuck, Rams	5	1	20.0	4	0.80
McGee, Buford, Rams	2	2	100.0	23	11.50
McMahon, Jim, Phil.	9	6	66.7	63	7.00
Mitchell, Brian, Wash.	6	3	50.0	40	6.67
Walker, Herschel, Minn.	2	1	50.0	12	6.00

TD	Pct TD	Long	Int	Pct Int	Sack	Yds Lost	Rating Points
2	3.2	t34	0	0.0	8	41	92.6
1	7.7	18	1	7.7	1	7	87.3
3	3.4	t44	1	1.1	9	38	83.2
2	2.9	40	1	1.5	6	34	82.7
1	1.6	53	0	0.0	11	43	80.6
9	6.2	t75	8	5.5	15	90	79.6
2	2.4	22	2	2.4	8	62	74.8
10	6.3	t47	10	6.3	13	83	73.6
8	4.2	59	7	3.6	22	150	72.1
3	3.9	70	4	5.3	9	55	61.7
3	1.9	44	10	6.4	9	62	57.5
3	2.6	t68	8	6.9	8	44	46.1
1	3.3	33	2	6.7	4	22	44.3
3	2.9	48	5	4.8	11	70	43.8
1	1.2	t68	6	7.2	15	103	41.4
1	1.5	t27	6	9.0	4	29	16.9
0	0.0	22	0	0.0	0	0	118.8
4	100.0	t18	0	0.0	0	0	158.3
1	50.0	t31	0	0.0	0	0	135.4
0	0.0	0	0	0.0	0	0	39.6
0	0.0	20	0	0.0	0	0	118.8
0	0.0	0	0	0.0	0	0	79.2
0	0.0	0	1	100.0	0	0	0.0
0	0.0	0	1	100.0	0	0	0.0
0	0.0	37	0	0.0	0	0	118.8
0	0.0	2	1	33.3	2	11	2.8
0	0.0	4	0	0.0	0	0	39.6
1	50.0	t22	0	0.0	0	0	154.2
0	0.0	21	0	0.0	1	7	86.8
0	0.0	18	0	0.0	1	3	71.5
0	0.0	12	0	0.0	0	0	68.8

TOP TEN PASS RECEIVERS

	No	Yards	Avg	Long	TD
Rice, Jerry, S.F.	100	1502	15.0	t64	13
Rison, Andre, Atl.	82	1208	14.7	t75	10
Byars, Keith, Phil.	81	819	10.1	54	3
Ellard, Henry, Rams	76	1294	17.0	t50	4
Clark, Gary, Wash	75	1112	14.8	t53	8
Jeffires, Haywood, Hou.	74	1048	14.2	t87	8
Hill, Drew, Hou.	74	1019	13.8	57	5
Williams, John L., Sea.	73	699	9.6	60	0
Givins, Ernest, Hou	72	979	13.6	t80	9
Reed, Andre, Buff.	71	945	13.3	t56	8
Bentley, Albert, Ind	71	664	9.4	73	2

TOP TEN RECEIVERS BY YARDS

	Yards	No	Avg	Long	TD
Rice, Jerry, S.F.	1502	100	15.0	t64	13
Ellard, Henry, Rams	1294	76	17.0	t50	4
Rison, Andre, Atl.	1208	82	14.7	t75	10
Clark, Gary, Wash.	1112	75	14.8	t53	8
Sharpe, Sterling, G.B.	1105	67	16.5	t76	6
Anderson, Willie, Rams	1097	51	21.5	t55	4
Jeffires, Haywood, Hou.	1048	74	14.2	t87	8
Paige, Stephone, K.C.	1021	65	15.7	t86	5
Hill, Drew, Hou.	1019	74	13.8	57	5
Carter, Anthony, Minn.	1008	70	14.4	t56	8

TOP TEN INTERCEPTORS

	No	Yards	Avg	Long	TD
Carrier, Mark, Chi.	10	39	3.9	14	0
Johnson, Richard, Hou.	8	100	12.5	35	1
Haddix, Wayne, T.B.	7	231	33.0	t65	3
Browner, Joey, Minn	7	103	14.7	31	1
Waymer, Dave, S.F.	7	64	9.1	24	0
Byrd, Gill, S.D.	7	63	9.0	24	0
Mayhew, Martin, Wash.	7	20	2.9	15	0
Walls, Everson, Giants.	6	80	13.3	40	1
Stinson, Lemuel, Chi.	6	66	11.0	30	0
White, William, Det.	5	120	24.0	48	1
Ross, Kevin, K.C.	5	97	19.4	40	0
McMillan, Erik, Jets	5	92	18.4	25	0
Oliver, Louis, Mia.	5	87	17.4	35	0
Williams, Jarvis, Mia.	5	82	16.4	t42	1
Woodson, Rod, Pitt.	5	67	13.4	34	0
Hopkins, Wes, Phil.	5	45	9.0	21	0
Hamilton, Harry, T.B.	5	39	7.8	27	0
Jackson, Greg, Giants	5	8	1.6	5	0

TOP TEN KICKOFF RETURNERS

	No	Yards	Avg	Long	TD
Clark, Kevin, Den.	20	505	25.3	75	0
Elder, Donnie, S.D.	24	571	23.8	90	0
Meggett, David, Giants	21	492	23.4	58	0
Gray, Mel, Det.	41	939	22.9	65	0
Wilson, Charles, G.B.	35	798	22.8	36	0
Green, Gaston, Rams	25	560	22.4	t99	1
Walker, Herschel, Minn.	44	966	22.0	64	0
Woodson, Rod, Pitt.	35	764	21.8	49	0
Sanders, Deion, Atl.	39	851	21.8	50	0
Warren, Chris, Sea.	23	478	20.8	71	0

TOP TEN PUNT RETURNERS

	No	FC	Yards	Avg	Long	TD
Verdin, Clarence, Ind	31	3	396	12.8	36	0
Bailey, Johnny, Chi	36	13	399	11.1	t95	1
Meggett, David, Giants	43	12	467	10.9	t68	1
Gray, Mel, Det	34	7	361	10.6	39	0
Woodson, Rod, Pitt	38	8	398	10.5	t52	1
Query, Jeff, G.B	32	7	308	9.6	25	0
Warren, Chris, Sea	28	16	269	9.6	39	0
Brown, Tim, Raiders	34	8	295	8.7	39	0
Price, Mitchell, Cin	29	14	251	8.7	t66	1
Sanders, Deion, Atl	29	13	250	8.6	t79	1

TOP TEN LEADERS - SACKS

Thomas, Derrick, K.C.	20.0
Smith, Bruce, Buff.	19.0
Haley, Charles, S.F.	16.0
White, Reggie, Phil	14.0
O'Neal, Leslie, S.D.	13.5
Byrd, Dennis, Jets	13.0
Greene, Kevin, Rams	13.0
Green, Jacob, Sea	12.5
Jones, Sean, Hou.	12.5
Townsend, Greg, Raiders	12.5

TOP TEN PUNTERS

	No	Yards	Long	Avg
Horan, Mike, Den	58	2575	67	44.4
Landeta, Sean, Giants	75	3306	67	44.1
Stark, Rohn, Ind	71	3084	61	43.4
Saxon, Mike, Dall	79	3413	62	43.2
Camarillo, Rich, Phoe	67	2865	63	42.8
Barnhardt, Tommy, N.O	70	2990	65	42.7
Newsome, Harry, Minn	78	3299	61	42.3
Johnson, Lee, Cin	64	2705	70	42.3
Feagles, Jeff, Phil	72	3026	60	42.0
Roby, Reggie, Mia	72	3022	62	42.0

TOP TEN SCORERS - KICKERS

	XP	XPA	FG	FGA	PTS
Lowery, Nick, K C.	37	38	34	37	139
Lohmiller, Chip, Wash.	41	41	30	40	131
Butler, Kevin, Chi.	36	37	26	37	114
Cofer, Mike, S.F	39	39	24	36	111
Norwood, Scott, Buff.	50	52	20	29	110
Treadwell, David, Den.	34	36	25	34	109
Ruzek, Roger, Phil.	45	48	21	29	108
Davis, Greg, Atl.	40	40	22	33	106
Johnson, Norm Sea.	33	34	23	32	102
Leahy, Pat, Jets	32	32	23	26	101

Total Punts	TB	Blk	Opp Ret	Ret Yds	In 20	Net Avg
59	6	1	22	159	14	33.9
75	11	0	41	291	24	37.3
72	3	1	42	334	24	37.4
79	8	0	43	438	20	35.6
67	5	0	41	258	16	37.4
71	6	1	43	302	20	36.2
79	8	1	44	513	19	33.2
64	8	0	36	352	12	34.3
74	3	2	37	338	20	35.5
72	3	0	40	397	20	35.6

TOP TEN SCORERS - NONKICKERS

	TD	TDR	TDP	TDM	PTS
Sanders, Barry, Det.	16	13	3	0	96
Fenner, Derrick, Sea.	15	14	1	0	90
Gary, Cleveland, Rams	15	14	1	0	90
Allen, Marcus, Raiders	13	12	1	0	78
Anderson, Neal, Chi.	13	10	3	0	78
Rice, Jerry, S.F.	13	0	13	0	78
Thomas, Thurman, Buff.	13	11	2	0	78
White, Lorenzo, Hou.	12	8	4	0	72
Anderson, Ottis, Giants	11	11	0	0	66
Smith, Emmitt, Dall.	11	11	0	0	66

NFL STANDINGS 1921–1990

1921

	W	L	T	Pct.
Chicago Staleys	10	1	1	.909
Buffalo All-Americans	9	1	2	.900
Akron, Ohio, Pros	7	2	1	.778
Green Bay Packers	6	2	2	.750
Canton, Ohio, Bulldogs	4	3	3	.571
Dayton Triangles	4	3	1	.571
Rock Island Independents	5	4	1	.556
Chicago Cardinals	2	3	2	.400
Cleveland Indians	2	6	0	.250
Rochester Jeffersons	2	6	0	.250
Detroit Heralds	1	7	1	.125
Columbus Panhandles	0	6	0	.000
Cincinnati Celts	0	8	0	.000

1922

	W	L	T	Pct.
Canton, Ohio, Bulldogs	10	0	2	1.000
Chicago Bears	9	3	0	.750
Chicago Cardinals	8	3	0	.727
Toledo Maroons	5	2	2	.714
Rock Island Independents	4	2	1	.667
Dayton Triangles	4	3	1	.571
Green Bay Packers	4	3	3	.571
Racine, Wis., Legion	5	4	1	.556
Akron, Ohio, Pros	3	4	2	.429
Buffalo All-Americans	3	4	1	.429
Milwaukee Badgers	2	4	3	.333
Marion, O., Oorang Indians	2	6	0	.250
Minneapolis Marines	1	3	0	.250
Evansville Crimson Giants	0	2	0	.000
Louisville Brecks	0	3	0	.000
Rochester Jeffersons	0	3	1	.000
Hammond, Ind., Pros	0	4	1	.000
Columbus Panhandles	0	7	0	.000

1923

	W	L	T	Pct.
Canton, Ohio, Bulldogs	11	0	1	1.000
Chicago Bears	9	2	1	.818
Green Bay Packers	7	2	1	.778
Milwaukee Badgers	7	2	3	.778
Cleveland Indians	3	1	3	.750
Chicago Cardinals	8	4	0	.667
Duluth Kelleys	4	3	0	.571
Buffalo All-Americans	5	4	3	.556
Columbus Tigers	5	4	1	.556
Racine, Wis., Legion	4	4	2	.500
Toledo Maroons	2	3	2	.400
Rock Island Independents	2	3	3	.400
Minneapolis Marines	2	5	2	.286
St. Louis All-Stars	1	4	2	.200
Hammond, Ind., Pros	1	5	1	.167
Dayton Triangles	1	6	1	.143
Akron, Ohio, Indians	1	6	0	.143
Marion, O., Oorang Indians	1	10	0	.091
Rochester Jeffersons	0	2	0	.000
Louisville Brecks	0	3	0	.000

1924

	W	L	T	Pct.
Cleveland Bulldogs	7	1	1	.875
Chicago Bears	6	1	4	.857
Frankford Yellowjackets	11	2	1	.846
Duluth Kelleys	5	1	0	.833
Rock Island Independents	6	2	2	.750
Green Bay Packers	8	4	0	.667
Buffalo Bisons	6	4	0	.600
Racine, Wis., Legion	4	3	3	.571
Chicago Cardinals	5	4	1	.556
Columbus Tigers	4	4	0	.500
Hammond, Ind., Pros	2	2	1	.500
Milwaukee Badgers	5	8	0	.385
Dayton Triangles	2	7	0	.222
Kansas City Cowboys	2	7	0	.222
Akron, Ohio, Indians	1	6	0	.143
Kenosha, Wis., Maroons	0	5	1	.000
Minneapolis Marines	0	6	0	.000
Rochester Jeffersons	0	7	0	.000

1925

	W	L	T	Pct.
Chicago Cardinals	11	2	1	.846
Pottsville, Pa., Maroons	10	2	0	.833
Detroit Panthers	8	2	2	.800
New York Giants	8	4	0	.667
Akron, Ohio, Indians	4	2	2	.667
Frankford Yellowjackets	13	7	0	.650
Chicago Bears	9	5	3	.643
Rock Island Independents	5	3	3	.625
Green Bay Packers	8	5	0	.615
Providence Steamroller	6	5	1	.545
Canton, Ohio, Bulldogs	4	4	0	.500
Cleveland Bulldogs	5	8	1	.385
Kansas City Cowboys	2	5	1	.286
Hammond, Ind., Pros	1	3	0	.250
Buffalo Bisons	1	6	2	.143
Duluth Kelleys	0	3	0	.000
Rochester Jeffersons	0	6	1	.000
Milwaukee Badgers	0	6	0	.000
Dayton Triangles	0	7	1	.000
Columbus Tigers	0	9	0	.000

1926

	W	L	T	Pct.
Frankford Yellowjackets	14	1	1	.933
Chicago Bears	12	1	3	.923
Pottsville, Pa., Maroons	10	2	1	.833
Kansas City Cowboys	8	3	1	.727
Green Bay Packers	7	3	3	.700
Los Angeles Buccaneers	6	3	1	.667
New York Giants	8	4	1	.667
Duluth Eskimos	6	5	2	.545
Buffalo Rangers	4	4	2	.500
Chicago Cardinals	5	6	1	.455
Providence Steamroller	5	7	0	.417
Detroit Panthers	4	6	2	.400
Hartford Blues	3	7	0	.300
Brooklyn Lions	3	8	0	.273
Milwaukee Badgers	2	7	0	.222
Akron, Ohio, Indians	1	4	3	.200
Dayton Triangles	1	4	1	.200
Racine, Wis., Legion	1	4	0	.200
Columbus Tigers	1	6	0	.143
Canton, Ohio, Bulldogs	1	9	3	.100
Hammond, Ind., Pros	0	4	0	.000
Louisville Colonels	0	4	0	.000

1927

	W	L	T	Pct.
New York Giants	11	1	1	.917
Green Bay Packers	7	2	1	.778
Chicago Bears	9	3	2	.750
Cleveland Bulldogs	8	4	1	.667
Providence Steamroller	8	5	1	.615
New York Yankees	7	8	1	.467
Frankford Yellowjackets	6	9	3	.400
Pottsville, Pa., Maroons	5	8	0	.385
Chicago Cardinals	3	7	1	.300
Dayton Triangles	1	6	1	.143
Duluth Eskimos	1	8	0	.111
Buffalo Bisons	0	5	0	.000

1928

	W	L	T	Pct.
Providence Steamroller	8	1	2	.889
Frankford Yellowjackets	11	3	2	.786
Detroit Wolverines	7	2	1	.778
Green Bay Packers	6	4	3	.600
Chicago Bears	7	5	1	.583
New York Giants	4	7	2	.364
New York Yankees	4	8	1	.333
Pottsville, Pa., Maroons	2	8	0	.200
Chicago Cardinals	1	5	0	.167
Dayton Triangles	0	7	0	.000

1929

	W	L	T	Pct.
Green Bay Packers	12	0	1	1.000
New York Giants	13	1	1	.929
Frankford Yellowjackets	9	4	5	.692
Chicago Cardinals	6	6	1	.500
Boston Bulldogs	4	4	0	.500
Orange, N.J., Tornadoes	3	4	4	.429
Stapleton Stapes	3	4	3	.429
Providence Steamroller	4	6	2	.400
Chicago Bears	4	9	2	.308
Buffalo Bisons	1	7	1	.125
Minneapolis Red Jackets	1	9	0	.100
Dayton Triangles	0	6	0	.000

1930

	W	L	T	Pct.
Green Bay Packers	10	3	1	.769
New York Giants	13	4	0	.765
Chicago Bears	9	4	1	.692
Brooklyn Dodgers	7	4	1	.636
Providence Steamroller	6	4	1	.600
Stapleton Stapes	5	5	2	.500
Chicago Cardinals	5	6	2	.455
Portsmouth, O., Spartans	5	6	3	.455
Frankford Yellowjackets	4	14	1	.222
Minneapolis Red Jackets	1	7	1	.125
Newark Tornadoes	1	10	1	.091

1931

	W	L	T	Pct.
Green Bay Packers	12	2	0	.857
Portsmouth, O., Spartans	11	3	0	.786
Chicago Bears	8	5	0	.615
Chicago Cardinals	5	4	0	.556
New York Giants	7	6	1	.538
Providence Steamroller	4	4	3	.500
Stapleton Stapes	4	6	1	.400
Cleveland Indians	2	8	0	.200
Brooklyn Dodgers	2	12	0	.143
Frankford Yellowjackets	1	6	1	.143

1932

	W	L	T	Pct.
Chicago Bears	7	1	6	.875
Green Bay Packers	10	3	1	.769
Portsmouth, O., Spartans	6	2	4	.750
Boston Braves	4	4	2	.500
New York Giants	4	6	2	.400
Brooklyn Dodgers	3	9	0	.250
Chicago Cardinals	2	6	2	.250
Stapleton Stapes	2	7	3	.222

1933

EASTERN DIVISION

	W	L	T	Pct.	Pts.	OP
N.Y. Giants	11	3	0	.786	244	101
Brooklyn	5	4	1	.556	93	54
Boston	5	5	2	.500	103	97
Philadelphia	3	5	1	.375	77	158
Pittsburgh	3	6	2	.333	67	208

WESTERN DIVISION

	W	L	T	Pct.	Pts.	OP
Chi. Bears	10	2	1	833	133	82
Portsmouth	6	5	0	545	128	87
Green Bay	5	7	1	417	170	107
Cincinnati	3	6	1	333	38	110
Chi. Cardinals	1	9	1	100	52	101

NFL Championship: Chicago Bears 23, N.Y. Giants 21

1934

EASTERN DIVISION

	W	L	T	Pct.	Pts.	OP
N.Y. Giants	8	5	0	.615	147	107
Boston	6	6	0	.500	107	94
Brooklyn	4	7	0	.364	61	153
Philadelphia	4	7	0	.364	127	85
Pittsburgh	2	10	0	.167	51	206

WESTERN DIVISION

	W	L	T	Pct.	Pts.	OP
Chi. Bears	13	0	0	1.000	286	86
Detroit	10	3	0	.769	238	59
Green Bay	7	6	0	.538	156	112
Chi. Cardinals	5	6	0	.455	80	84
St. Louis	1	2	0	.333	27	61
Cincinnati	0	8	0	.000	10	243

NFL Championship: N.Y. Giants 30, Chicago Bears 13

1935

EASTERN DIVISION

	W	L	T	Pct.	Pts.	OP
N.Y. Giants	9	3	0	.750	180	96
Brooklyn	5	6	1	.455	90	141
Pittsburgh	4	8	0	.333	100	209
Boston	2	8	1	.200	65	123
Philadelphia	2	9	0	.182	60	179

WESTERN DIVISION

	W	L	T	Pct.	Pts.	OP
Detroit	7	3	2	.700	191	111
Green Bay	8	4	0	.667	181	96
Chi. Bears	6	4	2	.600	192	106
Chi. Cardinals	6	4	2	.600	99	97

NFL Championship: Detroit 26, N.Y. Giants 7

One game between Boston and Philadelphia was canceled.

1936

EASTERN DIVISION

	W	L	T	Pct.	Pts.	OP
Boston	7	5	0	.583	149	110
Pittsburgh	6	6	0	.500	98	187
N.Y. Giants	5	6	1	.455	115	163
Brooklyn	3	8	1	.273	92	161
Philadelphia	1	11	0	.083	51	206

WESTERN DIVISION

	W	L	T	Pct.	Pts.	OP
Green Bay	10	1	1	.909	248	118
Chi. Bears	9	3	0	.750	222	94
Detroit	8	4	0	.667	235	102
Chi. Cardinals	3	8	1	.273	74	143

NFL Championship: Green Bay 21, Boston 6

1937

EASTERN DIVISION

	W	L	T	Pct.	Pts.	OP
Washington	8	3	0	.727	195	120
N.Y. Giants	6	3	2	.667	128	109
Pittsburgh	4	7	0	.364	122	145
Brooklyn	3	7	1	.300	82	174
Philadelphia	2	8	1	.200	86	177

WESTERN DIVISION

	W	L	T	Pct.	Pts.	OP
Chi. Bears	9	1	1	.900	201	100
Green Bay	7	4	0	.636	220	122
Detroit	7	4	0	.636	180	105
Chi. Cardinals	5	5	1	.500	135	165
Cleveland	1	10	0	.091	75	207

NFL Championship: Washington 28, Chicago Bears 21

1938

EASTERN DIVISION

	W	L	T	Pct.	Pts.	OP
N.Y Giants	8	2	1	.800	194	79
Washington	6	3	2	.667	148	154
Brooklyn	4	4	3	.500	131	161
Philadelphia	5	6	0	.455	154	164
Pittsburgh	2	9	0	.182	79	169

WESTERN DIVISION

	W	L	T	Pct.	Pts.	OP
Green Bay	8	3	0	.727	223	118
Detroit	7	4	0	.636	119	108
Chi. Bears	6	5	0	.545	194	148
Cleveland	4	7	0	.364	131	215
Chi. Cardinals	2	9	0	.182	111	168

NFL Championship: N.Y. Giants 23, Green Bay 17

1939

EASTERN DIVISION

	W	L	T	Pct.	Pts.	OP
N.Y. Giants	9	1	1	.900	168	85
Washington	8	2	1	.800	242	94
Brooklyn	4	6	1	.400	108	219
Philadelphia	1	9	1	.100	105	200
Pittsburgh	1	9	1	.100	114	216

WESTERN DIVISION

	W	L	T	Pct.	Pts.	OP
Green Bay	9	2	0	.818	233	153
Chi. Bears	8	3	0	.727	298	157
Detroit	6	5	0	.545	145	150
Cleveland	5	5	1	.500	195	164
Chi. Cardinals	1	10	0	.091	84	254

NFL Championship: Green Bay 27, N.Y. Giants 0

1940

EASTERN DIVISION

	W	L	T	Pct.	Pts.	OP
Washington	9	2	0	.818	245	142
Brooklyn	8	3	0	.727	186	120
N.Y. Giants	6	4	1	.600	131	133
Pittsburgh	2	7	2	.222	60	178
Philadelphia	1	10	0	.091	111	211

WESTERN DIVISION

	W	L	T	Pct.	Pts.	OP
Chi. Bears	8	3	0	.727	238	152
Green Bay	6	4	1	.600	238	155
Detroit	5	5	1	.500	138	153
Cleveland	4	6	1	.400	171	191
Chi. Cardinals	2	7	2	.222	139	222

NFL Championship: Chicago Bears 73, Washington 0

1941

EASTERN DIVISION

	W	L	T	Pct.	Pts.	OP
N.Y. Giants	8	3	0	.727	238	114
Brooklyn	7	4	0	.636	158	127
Washington	6	5	0	.545	176	174
Philadelphia	2	8	1	.200	119	218
Pittsburgh	1	9	1	.100	103	276

WESTERN DIVISION

	W	L	T	Pct.	Pts.	OP
Chi. Bears	10	1	0	.909	396	147
Green Bay	10	1	0	.909	258	120
Detroit	4	6	1	.400	121	195
Chi. Cardinals	3	7	1	.300	127	197
Cleveland	2	9	0	.182	116	244

Western Division playoff: Chicago Bears 33, Green Bay 14

NFL Championship: Chicago Bears 37, N.Y. Giants 9

1942

EASTERN DIVISION

	W	L	T	Pct.	Pts.	OP
Washington	10	1	0	.909	227	102
Pittsburgh	7	4	0	.636	167	119
N.Y. Giants	5	5	1	.500	155	139
Brooklyn	3	8	0	.273	100	168
Philadelphia	2	9	0	.182	134	239

WESTERN DIVISION

	W	L	T	Pct.	Pts.	OP
Chi. Bears	11	0	0	1.000	376	84
Green Bay	8	2	1	.800	300	215
Cleveland	5	6	0	.455	150	207
Chi. Cardinals	3	8	0	.273	98	209
Detroit	0	11	0	.000	38	263

NFL Championship: Washington 14, Chicago Bears 6

1943

EASTERN DIVISION

	W	L	T	Pct.	Pts.	OP
Washington	6	3	1	.667	229	137
N.Y. Giants	6	3	1	.667	197	170
Phil-Pitt	5	4	1	.556	225	230
Brooklyn	2	8	0	.200	65	234

WESTERN DIVISION

	W	L	T	Pct.	Pts.	OP
Chi. Bears	8	1	1	.889	303	157
Green Bay	7	2	1	.778	264	172
Detroit	3	6	1	.333	178	218
Chi. Cardinals	0	10	0	.000	95	238

Eastern Division playoff: Washington 28, N.Y. Giants 0

NFL Championship: Chicago Bears 41, Washington 21

1944

EASTERN DIVISION

	W	L	T	Pct.	Pts.	OP
N.Y. Giants	8	1	1	.889	206	75
Philadelphia	7	1	2	.875	267	131
Washington	6	3	1	.667	169	180
Boston	2	8	0	.200	82	233
Brooklyn	0	10	0	.000	69	166

WESTERN DIVISION

	W	L	T	Pct.	Pts.	OP
Green Bay	8	2	0	.800	238	141
Chi. Bears	6	3	1	.667	258	172
Detroit	6	3	1	.667	216	151
Cleveland	4	6	0	.400	188	224
Card-Pitt	0	10	0	.000	108	328

NFL Championship: Green Bay 14, N.Y. Giants 7

1945

EASTERN DIVISION

	W	L	T	Pct.	Pts.	OP
Washington	8	2	0	.800	209	121
Philadelphia	7	3	0	.700	272	133
N.Y. Giants	3	6	1	.333	179	198
Boston	3	6	1	.333	123	211
Pittsburgh	2	8	0	.200	79	220

WESTERN DIVISION

	W	L	T	Pct.	Pts.	OP
Cleveland	9	1	0	.900	244	136
Detroit	7	3	0	.700	195	194
Green Bay	6	4	0	.600	258	173
Chi. Bears	3	7	0	.300	192	235
Chi. Cardinals	1	9	0	.100	98	228

NFL Championship: Cleveland 15, Washington 14

1946

EASTERN DIVISION

	W	L	T	Pct.	Pts.	OP
N.Y. Giants	7	3	1	.700	236	162
Philadelphia	6	5	0	.545	231	220
Washington	5	5	1	.500	171	191
Pittsburgh	5	5	1	.500	136	117
Boston	2	8	1	.200	189	273

WESTERN DIVISION

	W	L	T	Pct.	Pts.	OP
Chi. Bears	8	2	1	.800	289	193
Los Angeles	6	4	1	.600	277	257
Green Bay	6	5	0	.545	148	158
Chi. Cardinals	6	5	0	.545	260	198
Detroit	1	10	0	.091	142	310

NFL Championship: Chicago Bears 24, N.Y. Giants 14

1947

EASTERN DIVISION

	W	L	T	Pct.	Pts.	OP
Philadelphia	8	4	0	.667	308	242
Pittsburgh	8	4	0	.667	240	259
Boston	4	7	1	.364	168	256
Washington	4	8	0	.333	295	367
N.Y. Giants	2	8	2	.200	190	309

WESTERN DIVISION

	W	L	T	Pct.	Pts.	OP
Chi. Cardinals	9	3	0	.750	306	231
Chi. Bears	8	4	0	.667	363	241
Green Bay	6	5	1	.545	274	210
Los Angeles	6	6	0	.500	259	214
Detroit	3	9	0	.250	231	305

Eastern Division playoff: Philadelphia 21, Pittsburgh 0

NFL Championship: Chicago Cardinals 28, Philadelphia 21

1948

EASTERN DIVISION

	W	L	T	Pct.	Pts.	OP
Philadelphia	9	2	1	.818	376	156
Washington	7	5	0	.583	291	287
N.Y. Giants	4	8	0	.333	297	388
Pittsburgh	4	8	0	.333	200	243
Boston	3	9	0	.250	174	372

WESTERN DIVISION

	W	L	T	Pct.	Pts.	OP
Chi. Cardinals	11	1	0	.917	395	226
Chi. Bears	10	2	0	.833	375	151
Los Angeles	6	5	1	.545	327	269
Green Bay	3	9	0	.250	154	290
Detroit	2	10	0	.167	200	407

NFL Championship: Philadelphia 7, Chicago Cardinals 0

1949

EASTERN DIVISION

	W	L	T	Pct.	Pts.	OP
Philadelphia	11	1	0	.917	364	134
Pittsburgh	6	5	1	.545	224	214
N.Y. Giants	6	6	0	.500	287	298
Washington	4	7	1	.364	268	339
N.Y. Bulldogs	1	10	1	.091	153	368

WESTERN DIVISION

	W	L	T	Pct.	Pts.	OP
Los Angeles	8	2	2	.800	360	239
Chi. Bears	9	3	0	.750	332	218
Chi. Cardinals	6	5	1	.545	360	301
Detroit	4	8	0	.333	237	259
Green Bay	2	10	0	.167	114	329

NFL Championship: Philadelphia 14, Los Angeles 0

1950

AMERICAN CONFERENCE

	W	L	T	Pct.	Pts.	OP
Cleveland	10	2	0	.833	310	144
N.Y. Giants	10	2	0	.833	268	150
Philadelphia	6	6	0	.500	254	141
Pittsburgh	6	6	0	.500	180	195
Chi. Cardinals	5	7	0	.417	233	287
Washington	3	9	0	.250	232	326

NATIONAL CONFERENCE

	W	L	T	Pct.	Pts.	OP
Los Angeles	9	3	0	.750	466	309
Chi. Bears	9	3	0	.750	279	207
N.Y. Yanks	7	5	0	.583	366	367
Detroit	6	6	0	.500	321	285
Green Bay	3	9	0	.250	244	406
San Francisco	3	9	0	.250	213	300
Baltimore	1	11	0	.083	213	462

American Conference playoff: Cleveland 8, N.Y. Giants 3

National Conference playoff: Los Angeles 24, Chicago Bears 14

NFL Championship: Cleveland 30, Los Angeles 28

1951

AMERICAN CONFERENCE

	W	L	T	Pct.	Pts.	OP
Cleveland	11	1	0	.917	331	152
N.Y. Giants	9	2	1	.818	254	161
Washington	5	7	0	.417	183	296
Pittsburgh	4	7	1	.364	183	235
Philadelphia	4	8	0	.333	234	264
Chi. Cardinals	3	9	0	.250	210	287

NATIONAL CONFERENCE

	W	L	T	Pct.	Pts.	OP
Los Angeles	8	4	0	.667	392	261
Detroit	7	4	1	.636	336	259
San Francisco	7	4	1	.636	255	205
Chi. Bears	7	5	0	.583	286	282
Green Bay	3	9	0	.250	254	375
N.Y. Yanks	1	9	2	.100	241	382

NFL Championship: Los Angeles 24, Cleveland 17

1952

AMERICAN CONFERENCE

	W	L	T	Pct.	Pts.	OP
Cleveland	8	4	0	.667	310	213
N.Y. Giants	7	5	0	.583	234	231
Philadelphia	7	5	0	.583	252	271
Pittsburgh	5	7	0	.417	300	273
Chi. Cardinals	4	8	0	.333	172	221
Washington	4	8	0	.333	240	287

NATIONAL CONFERENCE

	W	L	T	Pct.	Pts.	OP
Detroit	9	3	0	.750	344	192
Los Angeles	9	3	0	.750	349	234
San Francisco	7	5	0	.583	285	221
Green Bay	6	6	0	.500	295	312
Chi. Bears	5	7	0	.417	245	326
Dallas	1	11	0	.083	182	427

National Conference playoff: Detroit 31, Los Angeles 21

NFL Championship: Detroit 17, Cleveland 7

1953

EASTERN CONFERENCE

	W	L	T	Pct.	Pts.	OP
Cleveland	11	1	0	.917	348	162
Philadelphia	7	4	1	.636	352	215
Washington	6	5	1	.545	208	215
Pittsburgh	6	6	0	.500	211	263
N.Y. Giants	3	9	0	.250	179	277
Chi. Cardinals	1	10	1	.091	190	337

WESTERN CONFERENCE

	W	L	T	Pct.	Pts.	OP
Detroit	10	2	0	.833	271	205
San Francisco	9	3	0	.750	372	237
Los Angeles	8	3	1	.727	366	236
Chi. Bears	3	8	1	.273	218	262
Baltimore	3	9	0	.250	182	350
Green Bay	2	9	1	.182	200	338

NFL Championship: Detroit 17, Cleveland 16

1954

EASTERN CONFERENCE

	W	L	T	Pct.	Pts.	OP
Cleveland	9	3	0	.750	336	162
Philadelphia	7	4	1	.636	284	230
N.Y. Giants	7	5	0	.583	293	184
Pittsburgh	5	7	0	.417	219	263
Washington	3	9	0	.250	207	432
Chi. Cardinals	2	10	0	.167	183	347

WESTERN CONFERENCE

	W	L	T	Pct.	Pts.	OP
Detroit	9	2	1	.818	337	189
Chi. Bears	8	4	0	.667	301	279
San Francisco	7	4	1	.636	313	251
Los Angeles	6	5	1	.545	314	285
Green Bay	4	8	0	.333	234	251
Baltimore	3	9	0	.250	131	279

NFL Championship: Cleveland 56, Detroit 10

1955

EASTERN CONFERENCE

	W	L	T	Pct.	Pts.	OP
Cleveland	9	2	1	.818	349	218
Washington	8	4	0	.667	246	222
N.Y. Giants	6	5	1	.545	267	223
Chi. Cardinals	4	7	1	.364	224	252
Philadelphia	4	7	1	.364	248	231
Pittsburgh	4	8	0	.333	195	285

WESTERN CONFERENCE

	W	L	T	Pct.	Pts.	OP
Los Angeles	8	3	1	.727	260	231
Chi. Bears	8	4	0	.667	294	251
Green Bay	6	6	0	.500	258	276
Baltimore	5	6	1	.455	214	239
San Francisco	4	8	0	.333	216	298
Detroit	3	9	0	.250	230	275

NFL Championship: Cleveland 38, Los Angeles 14

1956

EASTERN CONFERENCE

	W	L	T	Pct.	Pts.	OP
N.Y. Giants	8	3	1	.727	264	197
Chi. Cardinals	7	5	0	.583	240	182
Washington	6	6	0	.500	183	225
Cleveland	5	7	0	.417	167	177
Pittsburgh	5	7	0	.417	217	250
Philadelphia	3	8	1	.273	143	215

WESTERN CONFERENCE

	W	L	T	Pct.	Pts.	OP
Chi. Bears	9	2	1	.818	363	246
Detroit	9	3	0	.750	300	188
San Francisco	5	6	1	.455	233	284
Baltimore	5	7	0	.417	270	322
Green Bay	4	8	0	.333	264	342
Los Angeles	4	8	0	.333	291	307

NFL Championship: N.Y. Giants 47, Chicago Bears 7

1957

EASTERN CONFERENCE

	W	L	T	Pct.	Pts.	OP
Cleveland	9	2	1	.818	269	172
N.Y. Giants	7	5	0	.583	254	211
Pittsburgh	6	6	0	.500	161	178
Washington	5	6	1	.455	251	230
Philadelphia	4	8	0	.333	173	230
Chi. Cardinals	3	9	0	.250	200	299

WESTERN CONFERENCE

	W	L	T	Pct.	Pts.	OP
Detroit	8	4	0	.667	251	231
San Francisco	8	4	0	.667	260	264
Baltimore	7	5	0	.583	303	235
Los Angeles	6	6	0	.500	307	278
Chi. Bears	5	7	0	.417	203	211
Green Bay	3	9	0	.250	218	311

Western Conference playoff: Detroit 31, San Francisco 27

NFL Championship: Detroit 59, Cleveland 14

1958

EASTERN CONFERENCE

	W	L	T	Pct.	Pts.	OP
N.Y. Giants	9	3	0	.750	246	183
Cleveland	9	3	0	.750	302	217
Pittsburgh	7	4	1	.636	261	230
Washington	4	7	1	.364	214	268
Chi. Cardinals	2	9	1	.182	261	356
Philadelphia	2	9	1	.182	235	306

WESTERN CONFERENCE

	W	L	T	Pct.	Pts.	OP
Baltimore	9	3	0	.750	381	203
Chi. Bears	8	4	0	.667	298	230
Los Angeles	8	4	0	.667	344	278
San Francisco	6	6	0	.500	257	324
Detroit	4	7	1	.364	261	276
Green Bay	1	10	1	.091	193	382

Eastern Conference playoff: N.Y. Giants 10, Cleveland 0

NFL Championship: Baltimore 23, N.Y. Giants 17, sudden-death overtime

1959

EASTERN CONFERENCE

	W	L	T	Pct.	Pts.	OP
N.Y. Giants	10	2	0	.833	284	170
Cleveland	7	5	0	.583	270	214
Philadelphia	7	5	0	.583	268	278
Pittsburgh	6	5	1	.545	257	216
Washington	3	9	0	.250	185	350
Chi. Cardinals	2	10	0	.167	234	324

WESTERN CONFERENCE

	W	L	T	Pct.	Pts.	OP
Baltimore	9	3	0	.750	374	251
Chi. Bears	8	4	0	.667	252	196
Green Bay	7	5	0	.583	248	246
San Francisco	7	5	0	.583	255	237
Detroit	3	8	1	.273	203	275
Los Angeles	2	10	0	.167	242	315

NFL Championship: Baltimore 31, N.Y. Giants 16

1960 AFL

EASTERN DIVISION

	W	L	T	Pct.	Pts.	OP
Houston	10	4	0	.714	379	285
N.Y. Titans	7	7	0	.500	382	399
Buffalo	5	8	1	.385	296	303
Boston	5	9	0	.357	286	349

WESTERN DIVISION

	W	L	T	Pct.	Pts.	OP
L.A. Chargers	10	4	0	.714	373	336
Dall. Texans	8	6	0	.571	362	253
Oakland	6	8	0	.429	319	388
Denver	4	9	1	.308	309	393

AFL Championship: Houston 24, L.A. Chargers 16

1960 NFL

EASTERN CONFERENCE

	W	L	T	Pct.	Pts.	OP
Philadelphia	10	2	0	.833	321	246
Cleveland	8	3	1	.727	362	217
N.Y. Giants	6	4	2	.600	271	261
St. Louis	6	5	1	.545	288	230
Pittsburgh	5	6	1	.455	240	275
Washington	1	9	2	.100	178	309

WESTERN CONFERENCE

	W	L	T	Pct.	Pts.	OP
Green Bay	8	4	0	.667	332	209
Detroit	7	5	0	.583	239	212
San Francisco	7	5	0	.583	208	205
Baltimore	6	6	0	.500	288	234
Chicago	5	6	1	.455	194	299
L.A. Rams	4	7	1	.364	265	297
Dall. Cowboys	0	11	1	.000	177	369

NFL Championship: Philadelphia 17, Green Bay 13

1961 AFL

EASTERN DIVISION

	W	L	T	Pct.	Pts.	OP
Houston	10	3	1	.769	513	242
Boston	9	4	1	.692	413	313
N.Y. Titans	7	7	0	.500	301	390
Buffalo	6	8	0	.429	294	342

WESTERN DIVISION

	W	L	T	Pct.	Pts.	OP
San Diego	12	2	0	.857	396	219
Dall. Texans	6	8	0	.429	334	343
Denver	3	11	0	.214	251	432
Oakland	2	12	0	.143	237	458

AFL Championship: Houston 10, San Diego 3

1961 NFL

EASTERN CONFERENCE

	W	L	T	Pct.	Pts.	OP
N.Y. Giants	10	3	1	.769	368	220
Philadelphia	10	4	0	.714	361	297
Cleveland	8	5	1	.615	319	270
St. Louis	7	7	0	.500	279	267
Pittsburgh	6	8	0	.429	295	287
Dall. Cowboys	4	9	1	.308	236	380
Washington	1	12	1	.077	174	392

WESTERN CONFERENCE

	W	L	T	Pct.	Pts.	OP
Green Bay	11	3	0	.785	391	223
Detroit	8	5	1	.615	270	258
Baltimore	8	6	0	.571	302	307
Chicago	8	6	0	.571	326	302
San Francisco	7	6	1	.538	346	272
Los Angeles	4	10	0	.285	263	333
Minnesota	3	11	0	.214	285	407

NFL Championship: Green Bay 37, N.Y. Giants 0

1962 AFL

EASTERN DIVISION

	W	L	T	Pct.	Pts.	OP
Houston	11	3	0	.786	387	270
Boston	9	4	1	.692	346	295
Buffalo	7	6	1	.538	309	272
N.Y. Titans	5	9	0	.357	278	423

WESTERN DIVISION

	W	L	T	Pct.	Pts.	OP
Dall. Texans	11	3	0	.786	389	233
Denver	7	7	0	.500	353	334
San Diego	4	10	0	.286	314	392
Oakland	1	13	0	.071	213	370

AFL Championship: Dallas Texans 20, Houston 17, sudden-death overtime

1962 NFL

EASTERN CONFERENCE

	W	L	T	Pct.	Pts.	OP
N.Y. Giants	12	2	0	.857	398	283
Pittsburgh	9	5	0	.643	312	363
Cleveland	7	6	1	.538	291	257
Washington	5	7	2	.417	305	376
Dall. Cowboys	5	8	1	.385	398	402
St. Louis	4	9	1	.308	287	361
Philadelphia	3	10	1	.231	282	356

WESTERN CONFERENCE

	W	L	T	Pct.	Pts.	OP
Green Bay	13	1	0	.929	415	148
Detroit	11	3	0	.786	315	177
Chicago	9	5	0	.643	321	287
Baltimore	7	7	0	.500	293	288
San Francisco	6	8	0	.429	282	331
Minnesota	2	11	1	.154	254	410
Los Angeles	1	12	1	.077	220	334

NFL Championship: Green Bay 16, N.Y. Giants 7

1963 AFL

EASTERN DIVISION

	W	L	T	Pct.	Pts.	OP
Boston	7	6	1	.538	317	257
Buffalo	7	6	1	.538	304	291
Houston	6	8	0	.429	302	372
N.Y. Jets	5	8	1	.385	249	399

WESTERN DIVISION

	W	L	T	Pct.	Pts.	OP
San Diego	11	3	0	.786	399	255
Oakland	10	4	0	.714	363	282
Kansas City	5	7	2	.417	347	263
Denver	2	11	1	.154	301	473

Eastern Division playoff: Boston 26, Buffalo 8

AFL Championship: San Diego 51, Boston 10

1963 NFL

EASTERN CONFERENCE

	W	L	T	Pct.	Pts.	OP
N.Y. Giants	11	3	0	.786	448	280
Cleveland	10	4	0	.714	343	262
St. Louis	9	5	0	.643	341	283
Pittsburgh	7	4	3	.636	321	295
Dallas	4	10	0	.286	305	378
Washington	3	11	0	.214	279	398
Philadelphia	2	10	2	.167	242	381

WESTERN CONFERENCE

	W	L	T	Pct.	Pts.	OP
Chicago	11	1	2	.917	301	144
Green Bay	11	2	1	.846	369	206
Baltimore	8	6	0	.571	316	285
Detroit	5	8	1	.385	326	265
Minnesota	5	8	1	.335	309	390
Los Angeles	5	9	0	.357	210	350
San Francisco	2	12	0	.143	198	391

NFL Championship: Chicago 14, N.Y. Giants 10

1964 AFL

EASTERN DIVISION	W	L	T	Pct.	Pts.	OP
Buffalo	12	2	0	.857	400	242
Boston	10	3	1	.769	365	297
N.Y. Jets	5	8	1	.385	278	315
Houston	4	10	0	.286	310	355

WESTERN DIVISION	W	L	T	Pct.	Pts.	OP
San Diego	8	5	1	.615	341	300
Kansas City	7	7	0	.500	366	306
Oakland	5	7	2	.417	303	350
Denver	2	11	1	.154	240	438

AFL Championship: Buffalo 20, San Diego 7

1964 NFL

EASTERN CONFERENCE	W	L	T	Pct.	Pts.	OP
Cleveland	10	3	1	.769	415	293
St. Louis	9	3	2	.750	357	331
Philadelphia	6	8	0	.429	312	313
Washington	6	8	0	.429	307	305
Dallas	5	8	1	.385	250	289
Pittsburgh	5	9	0	.357	253	315
N.Y. Giants	2	10	2	.167	241	399

WESTERN CONFERENCE	W	L	T	Pct.	Pts.	OP
Baltimore	12	2	0	.857	428	225
Green Bay	8	5	1	.615	342	245
Minnesota	8	5	1	.615	355	296
Detroit	7	5	2	.583	280	260
Los Angeles	5	7	2	.417	283	339
Chicago	5	9	0	.357	260	379
San Francisco	4	10	0	.286	236	330

NFL Championship: Cleveland 27, Baltimore 0

1965 AFL

EASTERN DIVISION	W	L	T	Pct.	Pts.	OP
Buffalo	10	3	1	.769	313	226
N.Y. Jets	5	8	1	.385	285	303
Boston	4	8	2	.333	244	302
Houston	4	10	0	.286	298	429

WESTERN DIVISION	W	L	T	Pct.	Pts.	OP
San Diego	9	2	3	.818	340	227
Oakland	8	5	1	.615	298	239
Kansas City	7	5	2	.583	322	285
Denver	4	10	0	.286	303	392

AFL Championship: Buffalo 23, San Diego 0

1965 NFL

EASTERN CONFERENCE	W	L	T	Pct.	Pts.	OP
Cleveland	11	3	0	.786	363	325
Dallas	7	7	0	.500	325	280
N.Y. Giants	7	7	0	.500	270	338
Washington	6	8	0	.429	257	301
Philadelphia	5	9	0	.357	363	359
St. Louis	5	9	0	.357	296	309
Pittsburgh	2	12	0	.143	202	397

WESTERN CONFERENCE	W	L	T	Pct.	Pts.	OP
Green Bay	10	3	1	.769	316	224
Baltimore	10	3	1	.769	389	284
Chicago	9	5	0	.643	409	275
San Francisco	7	6	1	.538	421	402
Minnesota	7	7	0	.500	383	403
Detroit	6	7	1	.462	257	295
Los Angeles	4	10	0	.286	269	328

Western Conference playoff: Green Bay 13, Baltimore 10, sudden-death overtime

NFL Championship: Green Bay 23, Cleveland 12

1966 AFL

EASTERN DIVISION	W	L	T	Pct.	Pts.	OP
Buffalo	9	4	1	.692	358	255
Boston	8	4	2	.667	315	283
N.Y. Jets	6	6	2	.500	322	312
Houston	3	11	0	.214	335	396
Miami	3	11	0	.214	213	362

WESTERN DIVISION	W	L	T	Pct.	Pts.	OP
Kansas City	11	2	1	.846	448	276
Oakland	8	5	1	.615	315	288
San Diego	7	6	1	.538	335	284
Denver	4	10	0	.286	196	381

AFL Championship: Kansas City 31, Buffalo 7

1966 NFL

EASTERN CONFERENCE	W	L	T	Pct.	Pts.	OP
Dallas	10	3	1	.769	445	239
Cleveland	9	5	0	.643	403	259
Philadelphia	9	5	0	.643	326	340
St. Louis	8	5	1	.615	264	265
Washington	7	7	0	.500	351	355
Pittsburgh	5	8	1	.385	316	347
Atlanta	3	11	0	.214	204	437
N.Y. Giants	1	12	1	.077	263	501

WESTERN CONFERENCE	W	L	T	Pct.	Pts.	OP
Green Bay	12	2	0	.857	335	163
Baltimore	9	5	0	.643	314	226
Los Angeles	8	6	0	.571	289	212
San Francisco	6	6	2	.500	320	325
Chicago	5	7	2	.417	234	272
Detroit	4	9	1	.308	206	317
Minnesota	4	9	1	.308	292	304

NFL Championship: Green Bay 34, Dallas 27

Super Bowl I: Green Bay (NFL) 35, Kansas City (AFL) 10

1967 AFL

EASTERN DIVISION

	W	L	T	Pct.	Pts.	OP
Houston	9	4	1	.692	258	199
N.Y. Jets	8	5	1	.615	371	329
Buffalo	4	10	0	.286	237	285
Miami	4	10	0	.286	219	407
Boston	3	10	1	.231	280	389

WESTERN DIVISION

	W	L	T	Pct.	Pts.	OP
Oakland	13	1	0	.929	468	238
Kansas City	9	5	0	.643	408	254
San Diego	8	5	1	.615	360	352
Denver	3	11	0	.214	256	409

AFL Championship: Oakland 40, Houston 7

1967 NFL

EASTERN CONFERENCE

Capitol Division

	W	L	T	Pct.	Pts.	OP
Dallas	9	5	0	.643	342	268
Philadelphia	6	7	1	.462	351	409
Washington	5	6	3	.455	347	353
New Orleans	3	11	0	.214	233	379

Century Division

	W	L	T	Pct.	Pts.	OP
Cleveland	9	5	0	.643	334	297
N.Y. Giants	7	7	0	.500	369	379
St. Louis	6	7	1	.462	333	356
Pittsburgh	4	9	1	.308	281	320

WESTERN CONFERENCE

Coastal Division

	W	L	T	Pct.	Pts.	OP
Los Angeles	11	1	2	.917	398	196
Baltimore	11	1	2	.917	394	198
San Francisco	7	7	0	.500	273	337
Atlanta	1	12	1	.077	175	422

Central Division

	W	L	T	Pct.	Pts.	OP
Green Bay	9	4	1	.692	332	209
Chicago	7	6	1	.538	239	218
Detroit	5	7	2	.417	260	259
Minnesota	3	8	3	.273	233	294

Conference Championships: Dallas 52, Cleveland 14; Green Bay 28, Los Angeles 7
NFL Championship: Green Bay 21, Dallas 17
Super Bowl II: Green Bay (NFL) 33, Oakland (AFL) 14

1968 AFL

EASTERN DIVISION

	W	L	T	Pct.	Pts.	OP
N.Y. Jets	11	3	0	.786	419	280
Houston	7	7	0	.500	303	248
Miami	5	8	1	.385	276	355
Boston	4	10	0	.286	229	406
Buffalo	1	12	1	.077	199	367

WESTERN DIVISION

	W	L	T	Pct.	Pts.	OP
Oakland	12	2	0	.857	453	233
Kansas City	12	2	0	.857	371	170
San Diego	9	5	0	.643	382	310
Denver	5	9	0	.357	255	404
Cincinnati	3	11	0	.214	215	329

Western Division playoff: Oakland 41, Kansas City 6
AFL Championship: N.Y. Jets 27, Oakland 23

1968 NFL

EASTERN CONFERENCE

Capitol Division

	W	L	T	Pct.	Pts.	OP
Dallas	12	2	0	.857	431	186
N.Y. Giants	7	7	0	.500	294	325
Washington	5	9	0	.357	249	358
Philadelphia	2	12	0	.143	202	351

Century Division

	W	L	T	Pct.	Pts.	OP
Cleveland	10	4	0	.714	394	273
St. Louis	9	4	1	.692	325	289
New Orleans	4	9	1	.308	246	327
Pittsburgh	2	11	1	.154	244	397

WESTERN CONFERENCE

Coastal Division

	W	L	T	Pct.	Pts.	OP
Baltimore	13	1	0	.929	402	144
Los Angeles	10	3	1	.769	312	200
San Francisco	7	6	1	.538	303	310
Atlanta	2	12	0	.143	170	389

Central Division

	W	L	T	Pct.	Pts.	OP
Minnesota	8	6	0	.571	282	242
Chicago	7	7	0	.500	250	333
Green Bay	6	7	1	.462	281	227
Detroit	4	8	2	.333	207	241

Conference Championships: Cleveland 31, Dallas 20; Baltimore 24, Minnesota 14
NFL Championship: Baltimore 34, Cleveland 0
Super Bowl III: N.Y. Jets (AFL) 16, Baltimore (NFL) 7

1969 AFL

EASTERN DIVISION

	W	L	T	Pct.	Pts.	OP
N.Y. Jets	10	4	0	.714	353	269
Houston	6	6	2	.500	278	279
Boston	4	10	0	.286	266	316
Buffalo	4	10	0	.286	230	359
Miami	3	10	1	.231	233	332

WESTERN DIVISION

	W	L	T	Pct.	Pts.	OP
Oakland	12	1	1	.923	377	242
Kansas City	11	3	0	.786	359	177
San Diego	8	6	0	.571	288	276
Denver	5	8	1	.385	297	344
Cincinnati	4	9	1	.308	280	367

Divisional playoffs: Kansas City 13, N.Y. Jets 6; Oakland 56, Houston 7
AFL Championship: Kansas City 17, Oakland 7

1969 NFL

EASTERN CONFERENCE

Capitol Division

	W	L	T	Pct.	Pts.	OP
Dallas	11	2	1	.846	369	223
Washington	7	5	2	.583	307	319
New Orleans	5	9	0	.357	311	393
Philadelphia	4	9	1	.308	279	377

Century Division

	W	L	T	Pct.	Pts.	OP
Cleveland	10	3	1	.769	351	300
N.Y. Giants	6	8	0	.429	264	298
St. Louis	4	9	1	.308	314	389
Pittsburgh	1	13	0	.071	218	404

WESTERN CONFERENCE

Coastal Division

	W	L	T	Pct.	Pts.	OP
Los Angeles	11	3	0	.786	320	243
Baltimore	8	5	1	.615	279	268
Atlanta	6	8	0	.429	276	268
San Francisco	4	8	2	.333	277	319

Central Division

	W	L	T	Pct.	Pts.	OP
Minnesota	12	2	0	.857	379	133
Detroit	9	4	1	.692	259	188
Green Bay	8	6	0	.571	269	221
Chicago	1	13	0	.071	210	339

Conference Championships: Cleveland 38, Dallas 14; Minnesota 23, Los Angeles 20
NFL Championship: Minnesota 27, Cleveland 7
Super Bowl IV: Kansas City (AFL) 23, Minnesota (NFL) 7

1970

AMERICAN CONFERENCE

Eastern Division

	W	L	T	Pct.	Pts.	OP
Baltimore	11	2	1	.846	321	234
Miami*	10	4	0	.714	297	228
N.Y. Jets	4	10	0	.286	255	286
Buffalo	3	10	1	.231	204	337
Boston	2	12	0	.143	149	361

Central Division

	W	L	T	Pct.	Pts.	OP
Cincinnati	8	6	0	.571	312	255
Cleveland	7	7	0	.500	286	265
Pittsburgh	5	9	0	.357	210	272
Houston	3	10	1	.231	217	352

Western Division

	W	L	T	Pct.	Pts.	OP
Oakland	8	4	2	.667	300	293
Kansas City	7	5	2	.583	272	244
San Diego	5	6	3	.455	282	278
Denver	5	8	1	.385	253	264

NATIONAL CONFERENCE

Eastern Division

	W	L	T	Pct.	Pts.	OP
Dallas	10	4	0	.714	299	221
N.Y. Giants	9	5	0	.643	301	270
St. Louis	8	5	1	.615	325	228
Washington	6	8	0	.429	297	314
Philadelphia	3	10	1	.231	241	332

Central Division

	W	L	T	Pct.	Pts.	OP
Minnesota	12	2	0	.857	335	143
Detroit*	10	4	0	.714	347	202
Chicago	6	8	0	.429	256	261
Green Bay	6	8	0	.429	196	293

Western Division

	W	L	T	Pct.	Pts.	OP
San Francisco	10	3	1	.769	352	267
Los Angeles	9	4	1	.692	325	202
Atlanta	4	8	2	.333	206	261
New Orleans	2	11	1	.154	172	347

**Wild Card qualifier for playoffs*

Divisional playoffs: Baltimore 17, Cincinnati 0; Oakland 21, Miami 14
AFC Championship: Baltimore 27, Oakland 17
Divisional playoffs: Dallas 5, Detroit 0; San Francisco 17, Minnesota 14
NFC Championship: Dallas 17, San Francisco 10
Super Bowl V: Baltimore (AFC) 16, Dallas (NFC) 13

1971

AMERICAN CONFERENCE

Eastern Division

	W	L	T	Pct.	Pts.	OP
Miami	10	3	1	.769	315	174
Baltimore*	10	4	0	.714	313	140
New England	6	8	0	.429	238	325
N.Y. Jets	6	8	0	.429	212	299
Buffalo	1	13	0	.071	184	394

Central Division

	W	L	T	Pct.	Pts.	OP
Cleveland	9	5	0	.643	285	273
Pittsburgh	6	8	0	.429	246	292
Houston	4	9	1	.308	251	330
Cincinnati	4	10	0	.286	284	265

Western Division

	W	L	T	Pct.	Pts.	OP
Kansas City	10	3	1	.769	302	208
Oakland	8	4	2	.667	344	278
San Diego	6	8	0	.429	311	341
Denver	4	9	1	.308	203	275

NATIONAL CONFERENCE

Eastern Division

	W	L	T	Pct.	Pts.	OP
Dallas	11	3	0	.786	406	222
Washington*	9	4	1	.692	276	190
Philadelphia	6	7	1	.462	221	302
St. Louis	4	9	1	.308	231	279
N.Y. Giants	4	10	0	.286	228	362

Central Division

	W	L	T	Pct.	Pts.	OP
Minnesota	11	3	0	.786	245	139
Detroit	7	6	1	.538	341	286
Chicago	6	8	0	.429	185	276
Green Bay	4	8	2	.333	274	298

Western Division

	W	L	T	Pct.	Pts.	OP
San Francisco	9	5	0	.643	300	216
Los Angeles	8	5	1	.615	313	260
Atlanta	7	6	1	.538	274	277
New Orleans	4	8	2	.333	266	347

**Wild Card qualifier for playoffs*

Divisional playoffs: Miami 27, Kansas City 24, sudden-death overtime; Baltimore 20, Cleveland 3

AFC Championship: Miami 21, Baltimore 0

Divisional playoffs: Dallas 20, Minnesota 12; San Francisco 24, Washington 20

NFC Championship: Dallas 14, San Francisco 3

Super Bowl VI: Dallas (NFC) 24, Miami (AFC) 3

1972

AMERICAN CONFERENCE

Eastern Division

	W	L	T	Pct.	Pts.	OP
Miami	14	0	0	1.000	385	171
N.Y. Jets	7	7	0	.500	367	324
Baltimore	5	9	0	.357	235	252
Buffalo	4	9	1	.321	257	377
New England	3	11	0	.214	192	446

Central Division

	W	L	T	Pct.	Pts.	OP
Pittsburgh	11	3	0	.786	343	175
Cleveland*	10	4	0	.714	268	249
Cincinnati	8	6	0	.571	299	229
Houston	1	13	0	.071	164	380

Western Division

	W	L	T	Pct.	Pts.	OP
Oakland	10	3	1	.750	365	248
Kansas City	8	6	0	.571	287	254
Denver	5	9	0	.357	325	350
San Diego	4	9	1	.321	264	344

NATIONAL CONFERENCE

Eastern Division

	W	L	T	Pct.	Pts.	OP
Washington	11	3	0	.736	336	218
Dallas*	10	4	0	.714	319	240
N.Y. Giants	8	6	0	.571	331	247
St. Louis	4	9	1	.321	193	303
Philadelphia	2	11	1	.179	145	352

Central Division

	W	L	T	Pct.	Pts.	OP
Green Bay	10	4	0	.714	304	226
Detroit	8	5	1	.607	339	290
Minnesota	7	7	0	.500	301	252
Chicago	4	9	1	.321	225	275

Western Division

	W	L	T	Pct.	Pts.	OP
San Francisco	8	5	1	.607	353	249
Atlanta	7	7	0	.500	269	274
Los Angeles	6	7	1	.464	291	286
New Orleans	2	11	1	.179	215	361

**Wild Card qualifier for playoffs*

Divisional playoffs: Pittsburgh 13, Oakland 7; Miami 20, Cleveland 14

AFC Championship: Miami 21, Pittsburgh 17

Divisional playoffs: Dallas 30, San Francisco 28; Washington 16, Green Bay 3

NFC Championship: Washington 26, Dallas 3

Super Bowl VII: Miami (AFC) 14, Washington (NFC) 7

1973

AMERICAN CONFERENCE

Eastern Division

	W	L	T	Pct.	Pts.	OP
Miami	12	2	0	.857	343	150
Buffalo	9	5	0	.643	259	230
New England	5	9	0	.357	258	300
Baltimore	4	10	0	.286	226	341
N.Y. Jets	4	10	0	.286	240	306

Central Division

	W	L	T	Pct.	Pts.	OP
Cincinnati	10	4	0	.714	286	231
Pittsburgh*	10	4	0	.714	347	210
Cleveland	7	5	2	.571	234	255
Houston	1	13	0	.071	199	447

Western Division

	W	L	T	Pct.	Pts.	OP
Oakland	9	4	1	.679	292	175
Denver	7	5	2	.571	354	296
Kansas City	7	5	2	.571	231	192
San Diego	2	11	1	.179	188	386

NATIONAL CONFERENCE

Eastern Division

	W	L	T	Pct.	Pts.	OP
Dallas	10	4	0	.714	382	203
Washington*	10	4	0	.714	325	198
Philadelphia	5	8	1	.393	310	393
St. Louis	4	9	1	.321	286	365
N.Y. Giants	2	11	1	.179	226	362

Central Division

	W	L	T	Pct.	Pts.	OP
Minnesota	12	2	0	.857	296	168
Detroit	6	7	1	.464	271	247
Green Bay	5	7	2	.429	202	259
Chicago	3	11	0	.214	195	334

Western Division

	W	L	T	Pct.	Pts.	OP
Los Angeles	12	2	0	.857	388	178
Atlanta	9	5	0	.643	318	224
New Orleans	5	9	0	.357	163	312
San Francisco	5	9	0	.357	262	319

**Wild Card qualifier for playoffs*

Divisional playoffs: Oakland 33, Pittsburgh 14; Miami 34, Cincinnati 16
AFC Championship: Miami 27, Oakland 10
Divisional playoffs: Minnesota 27, Washington 20; Dallas 27, Los Angeles 16
NFC Championship: Minnesota 27, Dallas 10
Super Bowl VIII: Miami (AFC) 24, Minnesota (NFC) 7

1974

AMERICAN CONFERENCE

Eastern Division

	W	L	T	Pct.	Pts.	OP
Miami	11	3	0	.786	327	216
Buffalo*	9	5	0	.643	264	244
New England	7	7	0	.500	348	289
N.Y. Jets	7	7	0	.500	279	300
Baltimore	2	12	0	.143	190	329

Central Division

	W	L	T	Pct.	Pts.	OP
Pittsburgh	10	3	1	.750	305	189
Cincinnati	7	7	0	.500	283	259
Houston	7	7	0	.500	236	282
Cleveland	4	10	0	.286	251	344

Western Division

	W	L	T	Pct.	Pts.	OP
Oakland	12	2	0	.857	355	228
Denver	7	6	1	.536	302	294
Kansas City	5	9	0	.357	233	293
San Diego	5	9	0	.357	212	285

NATIONAL CONFERENCE

Eastern Division

	W	L	T	Pct.	Pts.	OP
St. Louis	10	4	0	.714	285	218
Washington*	10	4	0	.714	320	196
Dallas	8	6	0	.571	297	235
Philadelphia	7	7	0	.500	242	217
N.Y. Giants	2	12	0	.143	195	299

Central Division

	W	L	T	Pct.	Pts.	OP
Minnesota	10	4	0	.714	310	195
Detroit	7	7	0	.500	256	270
Green Bay	6	8	0	.429	210	206
Chicago	4	10	0	.286	152	279

Western Division

	W	L	T	Pct.	Pts.	OP
Los Angeles	10	4	0	.714	263	181
San Francisco	6	8	0	.429	226	236
New Orleans	5	9	0	.357	166	263
Atlanta	3	11	0	.214	111	271

**Wild Card qualifier for playoffs*

Divisional playoffs: Oakland 28, Miami 26; Pittsburgh 32, Buffalo 14
AFC Championship: Pittsburgh 24, Oakland 13
Divisional playoffs: Minnesota 30, St. Louis 14; Los Angeles 19, Washington 10
NFC Championship: Minnesota 14, Los Angeles 10
Super Bowl IX: Pittsburgh (AFC) 16, Minnesota (NFC) 6

1975

AMERICAN CONFERENCE

Eastern Division

	W	L	T	Pct.	Pts.	OP
Baltimore	10	4	0	.714	395	269
Miami	10	4	0	.714	357	222
Buffalo	8	6	0	.571	420	355
New England	3	11	0	.214	258	358
N.Y. Jets	3	11	0	.214	258	433

Central Division

	W	L	T	Pct.	Pts.	OP
Pittsburgh	12	2	0	.857	373	162
Cincinnati*	11	3	0	.786	340	246
Houston	10	4	0	.714	293	226
Cleveland	3	11	0	.214	218	372

Western Division

	W	L	T	Pct.	Pts.	OP
Oakland	11	3	0	.786	375	255
Denver	6	8	0	.429	254	307
Kansas City	5	9	0	.357	282	341
San Diego	2	12	0	.143	189	345

NATIONAL CONFERENCE

Eastern Division

	W	L	T	Pct.	Pts.	OP
St. Louis	11	3	0	.786	356	276
Dallas*	10	4	0	.714	350	268
Washington	8	6	0	.571	325	276
N.Y. Giants	5	9	0	.357	216	306
Philadelphia	4	10	0	.286	225	302

Central Division

	W	L	T	Pct.	Pts.	OP
Minnesota	12	2	0	.857	377	180
Detroit	7	7	0	.500	245	262
Chicago	4	10	0	.286	191	379
Green Bay	4	10	0	.286	226	285

Western Division

	W	L	T	Pct.	Pts.	OP
Los Angeles	12	2	0	.857	312	135
San Francisco	5	9	0	.357	255	286
Atlanta	4	10	0	.286	240	289
New Orleans	2	12	0	.143	165	360

Wild Card qualifier for playoffs

Divisional playoffs: Pittsburgh 28, Baltimore 10; Oakland 31, Cincinnati 28
AFC Championship: Pittsburgh 16, Oakland 10
Divisional playoffs: Los Angeles 35, St. Louis 23; Dallas 17, Minnesota 14
NFC Championship: Dallas 37, Los Angeles 7
Super Bowl X: Pittsburgh (AFC) 21, Dallas (NFC) 17

1976

AMERICAN CONFERENCE

Eastern Division

	W	L	T	Pct.	Pts.	OP
Baltimore	11	3	0	.786	417	246
New England*	11	3	0	.786	376	236
Miami	6	8	0	.429	263	264
N.Y. Jets	3	11	0	.214	169	383
Buffalo	2	12	0	.143	245	363

Central Division

	W	L	T	Pct.	Pts.	OP
Pittsburgh	10	4	0	.714	342	138
Cincinnati	10	4	0	.714	335	210
Cleveland	9	5	0	.643	267	287
Houston	5	9	0	.357	222	273

Western Division

	W	L	T	Pct.	Pts.	OP
Oakland	13	1	0	.929	350	237
Denver	9	5	0	.643	315	206
San Diego	6	8	0	.429	248	285
Kansas City	5	9	0	.357	290	376
Tampa Bay	0	14	0	.000	125	412

NATIONAL CONFERENCE

Eastern Division

	W	L	T	Pct.	Pts.	OP
Dallas	11	3	0	.786	296	194
Washington*	10	4	0	.714	291	217
St. Louis	10	4	0	.714	309	267
Philadelphia	4	10	0	.286	165	286
N.Y. Giants	3	11	0	.214	170	250

Central Division

	W	L	T	Pct.	Pts.	OP
Minnesota	11	2	1	.821	305	176
Chicago	7	7	0	.500	253	216
Detroit	6	8	0	.429	262	220
Green Bay	5	9	0	.357	218	299

Western Division

	W	L	T	Pct.	Pts.	OP
Los Angeles	10	3	1	.750	351	190
San Francisco	8	6	0	.571	270	190
Atlanta	4	10	0	.286	172	312
New Orleans	4	10	0	.286	253	346
Seattle	2	12	0	.143	229	429

Wild Card qualifier for playoffs

Divisional playoffs: Oakland 24, New England 21; Pittsburgh 40, Baltimore 14
AFC Championship: Oakland 24, Pittsburgh 7
Divisional playoffs: Minnesota 35, Washington 20; Los Angeles 14, Dallas 12
NFC Championship: Minnesota 24, Los Angeles 13
Super Bowl XI: Oakland (AFC) 32, Minnesota (NFC) 14

1977

AMERICAN CONFERENCE

Eastern Division

	W	L	T	Pct.	Pts.	OP
Baltimore	10	4	0	.714	295	221
Miami	10	4	0	.714	313	197
New England	9	5	0	.643	278	217
N.Y. Jets	3	11	0	.214	191	300
Buffalo	3	11	0	.214	160	313

Central Division

	W	L	T	Pct.	Pts.	OP
Pittsburgh	9	5	0	.643	283	243
Houston	8	6	0	.571	299	230
Cincinnati	8	6	0	.571	238	235
Cleveland	6	8	0	.429	269	267

Western Division

	W	L	T	Pct.	Pts.	OP
Denver	12	2	0	.857	274	148
Oakland*	11	3	0	.786	351	230
San Diego	7	7	0	.500	222	205
Seattle	5	9	0	.357	282	373
Kansas City	2	12	0	.143	225	349

NATIONAL CONFERENCE

Eastern Division

	W	L	T	Pct.	Pts.	OP
Dallas	12	2	0	.857	345	212
Washington	9	5	0	.643	196	189
St. Louis	7	7	0	.500	272	287
Philadelphia	5	9	0	.357	220	207
N.Y. Giants	5	9	0	.357	181	265

Central Division

	W	L	T	Pct.	Pts.	OP
Minnesota	9	5	0	.643	231	227
Chicago*	9	5	0	.643	255	253
Detroit	6	8	0	.429	183	252
Green Bay	4	10	0	.286	134	219
Tampa Bay	2	12	0	.143	103	223

Western Division

	W	L	T	Pct.	Pts.	OP
Los Angeles	10	4	0	.714	302	146
Atlanta	7	7	0	.500	179	129
San Francisco	5	9	0	.357	220	260
New Orleans	3	11	0	.214	232	336

**Wild Card qualifier for playoffs*

Divisional playoffs: Denver 34, Pittsburgh 21; Oakland 37, Baltimore 31, sudden-death overtime

AFC Championship: Denver 20, Oakland 17

Divisional playoffs: Dallas 37, Chicago 7; Minnesota 14, Los Angeles 7

NFC Championship: Dallas 23, Minnesota 6

Super Bowl XII: Dallas (NFC) 27, Denver (AFC) 10

1978

AMERICAN CONFERENCE

Eastern Division

	W	L	T	Pct.	Pts.	OP
New England	11	5	0	.688	358	286
Miami*	11	5	0	.688	372	254
N.Y. Jets	8	8	0	.500	359	364
Buffalo	5	11	0	.313	302	354
Baltimore	5	11	0	.313	239	421

Central Division

	W	L	T	Pct.	Pts.	OP
Pittsburgh	14	2	0	.875	356	195
Houston*	10	6	0	.625	283	298
Cleveland	8	8	0	.500	334	356
Cincinnati	4	12	0	.250	252	284

Western Division

	W	L	T	Pct.	Pts.	OP
Denver	10	6	0	.625	282	198
Oakland	9	7	0	.563	311	283
Seattle	9	7	0	.563	345	358
San Diego	9	7	0	.563	355	309
Kansas City	4	12	0	.250	243	327

NATIONAL CONFERENCE

Eastern Division

	W	L	T	Pct.	Pts.	OP
Dallas	12	4	0	.750	384	208
Philadelphia*	9	7	0	.563	270	250
Washington	8	8	0	.500	273	283
St. Louis	6	10	0	.375	248	296
N.Y. Giants	6	10	0	.375	264	298

Central Division

	W	L	T	Pct.	Pts.	OP
Minnesota	8	7	1	.531	294	306
Green Bay	8	7	1	.531	249	269
Detroit	7	9	0	.438	290	300
Chicago	7	9	0	.438	253	274
Tampa Bay	5	11	0	.313	241	259

Western Division

	W	L	T	Pct.	Pts.	OP
Los Angeles	12	4	0	.750	316	245
Atlanta*	9	7	0	.563	240	290
New Orleans	7	9	0	.438	281	298
San Francisco	2	14	0	.125	219	350

**Wild Card qualifier for playoffs*

First-round playoff: Houston 17, Miami 9

Divisional playoffs: Houston 31, New England 14; Pittsburgh 33, Denver 10

AFC Championship: Pittsburgh 34, Houston 5

First-round playoff: Atlanta 14, Philadelphia 13

Divisional playoffs: Dallas 27, Atlanta 20; Los Angeles 34, Minnesota 10

NFC Championship: Dallas 28, Los Angeles 0

Super Bowl XIII: Pittsburgh (AFC) 35, Dallas (NFC) 31

1979

AMERICAN CONFERENCE

Eastern Division

	W	L	T	Pct.	Pts.	OP
Miami	10	6	0	.625	341	257
New England	9	7	0	.563	411	326
N.Y. Jets	8	8	0	.500	337	383
Buffalo	7	9	0	.438	268	279
Baltimore	5	11	0	.313	271	351

Central Division

	W	L	T	Pct.	Pts.	OP
Pittsburgh	12	4	0	.750	416	262
Houston*	11	5	0	.688	362	331
Cleveland	9	7	0	.563	359	352
Cincinnati	4	12	0	.250	337	421

Western Division

	W	L	T	Pct.	Pts.	OP
San Diego	12	4	0	.750	411	246
Denver*	10	6	0	.625	289	262
Seattle	9	7	0	.563	378	372
Oakland	9	7	0	.563	365	337
Kansas City	7	9	0	.438	238	262

NATIONAL CONFERENCE

Eastern Division

	W	L	T	Pct.	Pts.	OP
Dallas	11	5	0	.688	371	313
Philadelphia*	11	5	0	.688	339	282
Washington	10	6	0	.625	348	295
N.Y. Giants	6	10	0	.375	237	323
St. Louis	5	11	0	.313	307	358

Central Division

	W	L	T	Pct.	Pts.	OP
Tampa Bay	10	6	0	.625	273	237
Chicago*	10	6	0	.625	306	249
Minnesota	7	9	0	.438	259	337
Green Bay	5	11	0	.313	246	316
Detroit	2	14	0	.125	219	365

Western Division

	W	L	T	Pct.	Pts.	OP
Los Angeles	9	7	0	.563	323	309
New Orleans	8	8	0	.500	370	360
Atlanta	6	10	0	.375	300	388
San Francisco	2	14	0	.125	308	416

**Wild Card qualifier for playoffs*

First-round playoff: Houston 13, Denver 7
Divisional playoffs: Houston 17, San Diego 14; Pittsburgh 34, Miami 14
AFC Championship: Pittsburgh 27, Houston 13
First-round playoff: Philadelphia 27, Chicago 17
Divisional playoffs: Tampa Bay 24, Philadelphia 17; Los Angeles 21, Dallas 19
NFC Championship: Los Angeles 9, Tampa Bay 0
Super Bowl XIV: Pittsburgh (AFC) 31, Los Angeles (NFC) 19

1980

AMERICAN CONFERENCE

Eastern Division

	W	L	T	Pct.	Pts.	OP
Buffalo	11	5	0	.688	320	260
New England	10	6	0	.625	441	325
Miami	8	8	0	.500	266	305
Baltimore	7	9	0	.438	355	387
N.Y. Jets	4	12	0	.250	302	395

Central Division

	W	L	T	Pct.	Pts.	OP
Cleveland	11	5	0	.688	357	310
Houston*	11	5	0	.688	295	251
Pittsburgh	9	7	0	.563	352	313
Cincinnati	6	10	0	.375	244	312

Western Division

	W	L	T	Pct.	Pts.	OP
San Diego	11	5	0	.688	418	327
Oakland*	11	5	0	.688	364	306
Kansas City	8	8	0	.500	319	336
Denver	8	8	0	.500	310	323
Seattle	4	12	0	.250	291	408

NATIONAL CONFERENCE

Eastern Division

	W	L	T	Pct.	Pts.	OP
Philadelphia	12	4	0	.750	384	222
Dallas*	12	4	0	.750	454	311
Washington	6	10	0	.375	261	293
St. Louis	5	11	0	.313	299	350
N.Y. Giants	4	12	0	.250	249	425

Central Division

	W	L	T	Pct.	Pts.	OP
Minnesota	9	7	0	.563	317	308
Detroit	9	7	0	.563	334	272
Chicago	7	9	0	.437	304	264
Tampa Bay	5	10	1	.343	271	341
Green Bay	5	10	1	.343	231	371

Western Division

	W	L	T	Pct.	Pts.	OP
Atlanta	12	4	0	.750	405	272
Los Angeles*	11	5	0	.688	424	289
San Francisco	6	10	0	.375	320	415
New Orleans	1	15	0	.063	291	487

**Wild Card qualifier for playoffs*

First-round playoff: Oakland 27, Houston 7
Divisional playoffs: San Diego 20, Buffalo 14; Oakland 14, Cleveland 12
AFC Championship: Oakland 34, San Diego 27
First-round playoff: Dallas 34, Los Angeles 13
Divisional playoffs: Philadelphia 31, Minnesota 16; Dallas 30, Atlanta 27
NFC Championship: Philadelphia 20, Dallas 7
Super Bowl XV: Oakland (AFC) 27, Philadelphia (NFC) 10

1981

AMERICAN CONFERENCE

Eastern Division

	W	L	T	Pct.	Pts.	OP
Miami	11	4	1	.719	345	275
N.Y. Jets*	10	5	1	.656	355	287
Buffalo*	10	6	0	.625	311	276
Baltimore	2	14	0	.125	259	533
New England	2	14	0	.125	322	370

Central Division

	W	L	T	Pct.	Pts.	OP
Cincinnati	12	4	0	.750	421	304
Pittsburgh	8	8	0	.500	356	297
Houston	7	9	0	.438	281	355
Cleveland	5	11	0	.313	276	375

Western Division

	W	L	T	Pct.	Pts.	OP
San Diego	10	6	0	.625	478	390
Denver	10	6	0	.625	321	289
Kansas City	9	7	0	.563	343	290
Oakland	7	9	0	.438	273	343
Seattle	6	10	0	.375	322	388

NATIONAL CONFERENCE

Eastern Division

	W	L	T	Pct.	Pts.	OP
Dallas	12	4	0	.750	367	277
Philadelphia*	10	6	0	.625	368	221
N.Y. Giants*	9	7	0	.563	295	257
Washington	8	8	0	.500	347	349
St. Louis	7	9	0	.438	315	408

Central Division

	W	L	T	Pct.	Pts.	OP
Tampa Bay	9	7	0	.563	315	268
Detroit	8	8	0	.500	397	322
Green Bay	8	8	0	.500	324	361
Minnesota	7	9	0	.438	325	369
Chicago	6	10	0	.375	253	324

Western Division

	W	L	T	Pct.	Pts.	OP
San Francisco	13	3	0	.813	357	250
Atlanta	7	9	0	.438	426	355
Los Angeles	6	10	0	.375	303	351
New Orleans	4	12	0	.250	207	378

**Wild card qualifier for playoffs*

First-round playoff: Buffalo 31, N.Y. Jets 27
Divisional playoffs: San Diego 41, Miami 38 (OT); Cincinnati 28, Buffalo 21
AFC Championship: Cincinnati 27, San Diego 7
First-round playoff: N.Y. Giants 27, Philadelphia 21
Divisional playoffs: Dallas 38, Tampa Bay 0; San Francisco 38, N.Y. Giants 24
NFC Championship: San Francisco 28, Dallas 27
Super Bowl XVI: San Francisco (NFC) 26, Cincinnati (AFC) 21

*1982

AMERICAN CONFERENCE

	W	L	T	Pct.	Pts.	OP
L.A. Raiders	8	1	0	.889	260	200
Miami	7	2	0	.778	198	131
Cincinnati	7	2	0	.778	232	177
Pittsburgh	6	3	0	.667	204	146
San Diego	6	3	0	.667	288	221
N.Y. Jets	6	3	0	.667	245	166
New England	5	4	0	.556	143	157
Cleveland	4	5	0	.444	140	182
Buffalo	4	5	0	.444	150	154
Seattle	4	5	0	.444	127	147
Kansas City	3	6	0	.333	176	184
Denver	2	7	0	.222	148	226
Houston	1	8	0	.111	136	245
Baltimore	0	8	1	.063	113	236

NATIONAL CONFERENCE

	W	L	T	Pct.	Pts.	OP
Washington	8	1	0	.889	190	128
Dallas	6	3	0	.667	226	145
Green Bay	5	3	1	.611	226	169
Minnesota	5	4	0	.556	187	198
Atlanta	5	4	0	.556	183	199
St. Louis	5	4	0	.556	135	170
Tampa Bay	5	4	0	.556	158	178
Detroit	4	5	0	.444	181	176
New Orleans	4	5	0	.444	129	160
N.Y. Giants	4	5	0	.444	164	160
San Francisco	3	6	0	.333	209	206
Chicago	3	6	0	.333	141	174
Philadelphia	3	6	0	.333	191	195
L.A. Rams	2	7	0	.222	200	250

**Top eight teams in each Conference qualified for playoffs under format necessitated by strike-shortened season*

First-round playoffs: Miami 28, New England 13; L.A. Raiders 27, Cleveland 10; N.Y. Jets 44, Cincinnati 17; San Diego 31, Pittsburgh 28
Second-round playoffs: N.Y. Jets 17, L.A. Raiders 14; Miami 34, San Diego 13
AFC Championship: Miami 14, N.Y. Jets 0
First-round playoffs: Green Bay 41, St. Louis 16; Washington 31, Detroit 7; Minnesota 30, Atlanta 24; Dallas 30, Tampa Bay 17
Second-round playoffs: Washington 21, Minnesota 7; Dallas 37, Green Bay 26
NFC Championship: Washington 31, Dallas 17
Super Bowl XVII: Washington 27, Miami 17

1983

AMERICAN CONFERENCE

Eastern Division

	W	L	T	Pct.	Pts.	OP
Miami	12	4	0	.750	389	250
New England	8	8	0	.500	274	289
Buffalo	8	8	0	.500	283	351
Baltimore	7	9	0	.438	264	354
N.Y. Jets	7	9	0	.438	313	331

Central Division

	W	L	T	Pct.	Pts.	OP
Pittsburgh	10	6	0	.625	355	303
Cleveland	9	7	0	.562	356	342
Cincinnati	7	9	0	.438	346	302
Houston	2	14	0	.125	288	460

Western Division

	W	L	T	Pct.	Pts.	OP
L.A. Raiders	12	4	0	.750	442	338
Seattle*	9	7	0	.562	403	397
Denver*	9	7	0	.562	302	327
San Diego	6	10	0	.375	358	462
Kansas City	6	10	0	.375	386	367

NATIONAL CONFERENCE

Eastern Division

	W	L	T	Pct.	Pts.	OP
Washington	14	2	0	.875	541	332
Dallas*	12	4	0	.750	479	360
St. Louis	8	7	1	.531	374	428
Philadelphia	5	11	0	.313	233	322
N.Y. Giants	3	12	1	.219	267	347

Central Division

	W	L	T	Pct.	Pts.	OP
Detroit	9	7	0	.562	347	286
Green Bay	8	8	0	.500	429	439
Chicago	8	8	0	.500	311	301
Minnesota	8	8	0	.500	316	348
Tampa Bay	2	14	0	.125	241	380

Western Division

	W	L	T	Pct.	Pts.	OP
San Francisco	10	6	0	.625	432	293
L.A. Rams*	9	7	0	.562	361	344
New Orleans	8	8	0	.500	319	337
Atlanta	7	9	0	.438	370	389

**Wild card qualifier for playoffs*

First-round playoff: Seattle 31, Denver 7

Divisional playoffs: Seattle 27, Miami 20; L.A. Raiders 38, Pittsburgh 10

AFC Championship: L.A. Raiders 30, Seattle 14

First-round playoff: L.A. Rams 24, Dallas 17

Divisional playoffs: San Francisco 24, Detroit 23; Washington 51, L.A. Rams 7

NFC Championship: Washington 24, San Francisco 21

Super Bowl XVIII: L.A. Raiders 38, Washington 9

1984

NATIONAL CONFERENCE

Eastern Division

	W	L	T	Pct.	Pts.	OP
Washington	11	5	0	.688	426	310
N.Y. Giants*	9	7	0	.563	299	301
St. Louis	9	7	0	.563	423	345
Dallas	9	7	0	.563	308	308
Philadelphia	6	9	1	.406	278	320

Central Division

	W	L	T	Pct.	Pts.	OP
Chicago	10	6	0	.625	325	248
Green Bay	8	8	0	.500	390	309
Tampa Bay	6	10	0	.375	335	380
Detroit	4	11	1	.281	283	408
Minnesota	3	13	0	.188	276	484

Western Division

	W	L	T	Pct.	Pts.	OP
San Francisco	15	1	0	.939	475	227
L.A. Rams*	10	6	0	.625	346	316
New Orleans	7	9	0	.438	298	361
Atlanta	4	12	0	.250	281	382

AMERICAN CONFERENCE

Eastern Division

	W	L	T	Pct.	Pts.	OP
Miami	14	2	0	.875	513	298
New England	9	7	0	.563	362	352
N.Y. Jets	7	9	0	.438	332	364
Indianapolis	4	12	0	.250	239	414
Buffalo	2	14	0	.125	250	454

Central Division

	W	L	T	Pct.	Pts.	OP
Pittsburgh	9	7	0	.563	387	310
Cincinnati	8	8	0	.500	339	339
Cleveland	5	11	0	.313	250	297
Houston	3	13	0	.188	240	437

Western Division

	W	L	T	Pct.	Pts.	OP
Denver	13	3	0	.813	353	241
Seattle*	12	4	0	.750	418	282
L.A. Raiders*	11	5	0	.688	368	278
Kansas City	8	8	0	.500	314	324
San Diego	7	9	0	.438	394	413

**Wild card qualifier for playoffs*

Wild Card Game: N.Y. Giants 16, L.A. Rams 13

NFC Divisional playoffs: San Francisco 21, N.Y. Giants 10; Chicago 23, Washington 19

NFC Championship: San Francisco 23, Chicago 0

Wild Card Game: Seattle 13, L.A. Raiders 7

AFC Divisional playoffs: Miami 31, Seattle 10; Pittsburgh 24, Denver 17

AFC Championship: Miami 45, Pittsburgh 28

Super Bowl XIX: San Francisco 38, Miami 16

1985

AMERICAN CONFERENCE

Eastern Division

	W	L	T	Pct.	Pts.	OP
Miami	12	4	0	.750	428	320
N.Y. Jets	11	5	0	.688	393	264
New England	11	5	0	.688	362	290
Indianapolis	5	11	0	.313	320	386
Buffalo	2	14	0	.125	200	381

CENTRAL DIVISION

	W	L	T	Pct.	Pts.	OP
Cleveland	8	8	0	.500	287	294
Cincinnati	7	9	0	.438	441	437
Pittsburgh	7	9	0	.438	379	355
Houston	5	11	0	.313	284	412

WESTERN DIVISION

	W	L	T	Pct.	Pts.	OP
L.A. Raiders	12	4	0	.750	354	308
Denver	11	5	0	.688	380	329
Seattle	8	8	0	.500	349	303
San Diego	8	8	0	.500	467	435
Kansas City	6	10	0	.375	327	360

NATIONAL CONFERENCE

Eastern Division

	W	L	T	Pct.	Pts.	OP
Dallas	10	6	0	.625	357	333
N.Y. Giants	10	6	0	.625	399	283
Washington	10	6	0	.625	298	313
Philadelphia	7	9	0	.438	286	310
St. Louis	5	11	0	.313	279	415

CENTRAL DIVISION

	W	L	T	Pct.	Pts.	OP
Chicago	15	1	0	.938	456	198
Green Bay	8	8	0	.500	337	355
Minnesota	7	9	0	.438	346	359
Detroit	7	9	0	.438	307	366
Tampa Bay	2	14	0	.125	294	448

WESTERN DIVISION

	W	L	T	Pct.	Pts.	OP
L.A. Rams	11	5	0	.688	340	287
San Francisco	10	6	0	.625	411	263
New Orleans	5	11	0	.313	294	401
Atlanta	4	12	0	.250	282	452

Wild Card Game: New England 26, N.Y. Jets 14
AFC Divisional playoffs: Miami 24, Cleveland 21; New England 27, L.A. Raiders 20
AFC Championship: New England 31, Miami 14
Wild Card Game: N.Y. Giants 17, San Francisco 3
NFC Divisional playoffs: L.A. Rams 20, Dallas 0; Chicago 21, N.Y. Giants 0
NFC Championship: Chicago 24, L.A. Rams 0
Super Bowl XX: Chicago 46, New England 10

1986

AMERICAN CONFERENCE

Eastern Division

	W	L	T	Pct.	Pts.	OP
N.Y. Giants	14	2	0	.875	371	236
Washington	12	4	0	.750	368	296
Dallas	7	9	0	.438	346	337
Philadelphia	5	10	1	.344	256	312
St. Louis	4	11	1	.281	218	351

Central Division

	W	L	T	Pct.	Pts.	OP
Chicago	14	2	0	.875	352	187
Minnesota	9	7	0	.563	398	273
Detroit	5	11	0	.313	277	326
Green Bay	4	12	0	.250	254	418
Tampa Bay	2	14	0	.125	239	473

Western Division

	W	L	T	Pct.	Pts.	OP
San Francisco	10	5	1	.656	374	247
L.A. Rams	10	6	0	.625	309	267
Atlanta	7	8	1	.469	280	280
New Orleans	7	9	0	.438	288	287

NATIONAL CONFERENCE

Eastern Division

	W	L	T	Pct.	Pts.	OP
New England	11	5	0	.688	412	307
N.Y. Jets	10	6	0	.625	364	386
Miami	8	8	0	.500	430	405
Buffalo	4	12	0	.250	287	348
Indianapolis	3	13	0	.188	229	400

Central Division

	W	L	T	Pct.	Pts.	OP
Cleveland	12	4	0	.750	391	310
Cincinnati	10	6	0	.625	409	394
Pittsburgh	6	10	0	.375	307	336
Houston	5	11	0	.313	274	329

Western Division

	W	L	T	Pct.	Pts.	OP
Denver	11	5	0	.688	378	327
Kansas City	10	6	0	.625	358	326
Seattle	10	6	0	.625	366	293
L.A. Raiders	8	8	0	.500	323	346
San Diego	4	12	0	.250	335	396

NFC Wild Card Game: Washington 19, L.A. Rams 7
NFC Divisional playoffs: Washington 27, Chicago 13; N.Y. Giants 49, San Francisco 3
NFC Championship: N.Y. Giants 17, Washington 0
AFC Wild Card Game: N.Y. Jets 35, Kansas City 15
AFC Divisional playoffs: Cleveland 23, N.Y. Jets 20 (2 OT); Denver 22, New England 17
AFC Championship: Denver 23, Cleveland 20 (OT)
Super Bowl XXI: N.Y. Giants 39, Denver 20

1987

NATIONAL CONFERENCE

Eastern Division

	W	L	T	Pct.	Pts.	OP
Washington	11	4	0	.733	379	285
St. Louis	7	8	0	.467	362	368
Dallas	7	8	0	.467	340	348
Philadelphia	7	8	0	.467	337	380
N.Y. Giants	6	9	0	.400	280	312

Central Division

	W	L	T	Pct.	Pts.	OP
Chicago	11	4	0	.733	356	282
Minnesota	8	7	0	.533	336	335
Green Bay	5	9	1	.367	255	300
Tampa Bay	4	11	0	.267	286	360
Detroit	4	11	0	.267	269	384

Western Division

	W	L	T	Pct.	Pts.	OP
San Francisco	13	2	0	.867	459	253
New Orleans	12	3	0	.800	422	283
L.A. Rams	6	9	0	.400	317	361
Atlanta	3	12	0	.200	205	436

AMERICAN CONFERENCE

Eastern Division

	W	L	T	Pct.	Pts.	OP
Indianapolis	9	6	0	.600	300	238
New England	8	7	0	.533	320	293
Miami	8	7	0	.533	362	335
Buffalo	7	8	0	.467	270	305
N.Y. Jets	6	9	0	.400	334	360

Central Division

	W	L	T	Pct.	Pts.	OP
Cleveland	10	5	0	.667	390	239
Houston	9	6	0	.600	345	349
Pittsburgh	8	7	0	.533	285	299
Cincinnati	4	11	0	.267	285	370

Western Division

	W	L	T	Pct.	Pts.	OP
Denver	10	4	1	.700	379	288
Seattle	9	6	0	.600	371	314
San Diego	8	7	0	.533	253	317
L.A. Raiders	5	10	0	.333	301	289
Kansas City	4	11	0	.267	273	388

NFC Wild Card Game: Minnesota 44, New Orleans 10
NFC Divisional playoffs: Minnesota 36, San Francisco 24; Wash. 21, Chicago 17
NFC Championship: Washington 17, Minnesota 10
AFC Wild Card Game: Houston 23, Seattle 20 (OT)
AFC Divisional playoffs: Cleveland 38, Indianapolis 21; Denver 34, Houston 10
AFC Championship: Denver 38, Cleveland 33
Super Bowl XXII: Washington 42, Denver 10

1988

AMERICAN CONFERENCE

Eastern Division

	W	L	T	Pct.	Pts.	OP
Buffalo	12	4	0	.750	329	237
Indianapolis	9	7	0	.563	354	315
New England	9	7	0	.563	250	284
N.Y. Jets	8	7	1	.531	372	354
Miami	6	10	0	.375	319	380

Central Division

	W	L	T	Pct.	Pts.	OP
Cincinnati	12	4	0	.750	448	329
Cleveland	10	6	0	.625	304	288
Houston	10	6	0	.625	424	365
Pittsburgh	5	11	0	.313	336	421

Western Division

	W	L	T	Pct.	Pts.	OP
Seattle	9	7	0	.563	339	329
Denver	8	8	0	.500	327	352
L.A. Raiders	7	9	0	.438	325	369
San Diego	6	10	0	.375	231	332
Kansas City	4	11	1	.281	254	320

NATIONAL CONFERENCE

Eastern Division

	W	L	T	Pct.	Pts.	OP
Philadelphia	10	6	0	.625	379	319
N.Y. Giants	10	6	0	.625	359	304
Washington	7	9	0	.438	345	387
Phoenix	7	9	0	.438	344	398
Dallas	3	13	0	.188	265	381

Central Division

	W	L	T	Pct.	Pts.	OP
Chicago	12	4	0	.750	312	215
Minnesota	11	5	0	.688	406	233
Tampa Bay	5	11	0	.313	261	350
Detroit	4	12	0	.250	220	313
Green Bay	4	12	0	.250	240	315

Western Division

	W	L	T	Pct.	Pts.	OP
San Francisco	10	6	0	.625	369	294
L.A. Rams	10	6	0	.625	407	293
New Orleans	10	6	0	.625	312	283
Atlanta	5	11	0	.313	244	315

AFC Wild Card Game: Houston 24, Cleveland 23
AFC Divisional playoffs: Cincinnati 21, Seattle 13; Buffalo 17, Houston 10
AFC Championship: Cincinnati 21, Buffalo 10
NFC Wild Card Game: Minnesota 28, L.A. Rams 17
NFC Divisional playoffs: Chicago 20, Philadelphia 12, San Francisco 34, Minnesota 9
NFC Championship: San Francisco 28, Chicago 3
Super Bowl XXIII: San Francisco 20, Cincinnati 16

Giants' Jeff Hostetler was super in Super Bowl XXV.

1989

AMERICAN CONFERENCE

Eastern Division

	W	L	T	Pct.	Pts.	OP
Buffalo	9	7	0	.563	409	317
Indianapolis	8	8	0	.500	298	301
Miami	8	8	0	.500	331	379
New England	5	11	0	.313	297	391
N.Y. Jets	4	12	0	.250	253	411

Central Division

	W	L	T	Pct.	Pts.	OP
Cleveland	9	6	1	.594	334	254
Houston	9	7	0	.563	365	412
Pittsburgh	9	7	0	.563	265	326
Cincinnati	8	8	0	.500	404	285

Western Division

	W	L	T	Pct.	Pts.	OP
Denver	11	5	0	.688	362	226
Kansas City	8	7	1	.531	318	286
L.A. Raiders	8	8	0	.500	315	297
Seattle	7	9	0	.438	241	327
San Diego	6	10	0	.375	266	290

NATIONAL CONFERENCE

Eastern Division

	W	L	T	Pct.	Pts.	OP
N.Y. Giants	12	4	0	.750	348	252
Philadelphia	11	5	0	.688	342	274
Washington	10	6	0	.625	386	308
Phoenix	5	11	0	.313	258	377
Dallas	1	15	0	.063	204	393

Central Division

	W	L	T	Pct.	Pts.	OP
Minnesota	10	6	0	.625	351	275
Green Bay	10	6	0	.625	362	356
Detroit	7	9	0	.438	312	364
Chicago	6	10	0	.375	358	377
Tampa Bay	5	11	0	.313	320	419

Western Division

	W	L	T	Pct.	Pts.	OP
San Francisco	14	2	0	.875	442	253
L.A. Rams	11	5	0	.688	426	344
New Orleans	9	7	0	.563	386	301
Atlanta	3	13	0	.188	279	437

AFC Wild Card Game: Pittsburgh 26, Houston 23 (OT)
AFC Divisional playoffs: Cleveland 34, Buffalo 30; Denver 24, Pittsburgh 23
AFC Championship: Denver 37, Cleveland 21
NFC Wild Card Game: L.A. Rams 21, Philadelphia 7
NFC Divisional playoffs: L.A. Rams 19, N.Y. Giants 13 (OT); San Francisco 41, Minnesota 13
NFC Championship: San Francisco 30, L.A. Rams 3
Super Bowl XXIV: San Francisco 55, Denver 10

1990

AMERICAN CONFERENCE

Eastern Division

	W	L	T	Pct.	Pts.	OP
Buffalo	13	3	0	.813	428	263
Miami	12	4	0	.750	336	242
Indianapolis	7	9	0	.438	281	353
N.Y. Jets	6	10	0	.375	295	345
New England	1	15	0	.063	181	446

Central Division

	W	L	T	Pct.	Pts.	OP
Cincinnati	9	7	0	.563	360	352
Houston	9	7	0	.563	405	307
Pittsburgh	9	7	0	.563	292	240
Cleveland	3	13	0	.188	228	462

Western Division

	W	L	T	Pct.	Pts.	OP
L.A. Raiders	12	4	0	.750	337	268
Kansas City	11	5	0	.688	369	257
Seattle	9	7	0	.563	306	286
San Diego	6	10	0	.375	315	281
Denver	5	11	0	.313	331	374

NATIONAL CONFERENCE

Eastern Division

	W	L	T	Pct.	Pts.	OP
N.Y. Giants	13	3	0	.813	335	211
Philadelphia	10	6	0	.625	396	299
Washington	10	6	0	.625	381	301
Dallas	7	9	0	.438	244	308
Phoenix	5	11	0	.313	268	396

Central Division

	W	L	T	Pct.	Pts.	OP
Chicago	11	5	0	.688	348	280
Tampa Bay	6	10	0	.375	264	367
Detroit	6	10	0	.375	373	413
Green Bay	6	10	0	.375	271	347
Minnesota	6	10	0	.375	351	326

Western Division

	W	L	T	Pct.	Pts.	OP
San Francisco	14	2	0	.875	353	239
New Orleans	8	8	0	.500	274	275
L.A. Rams	5	11	0	.313	345	412
Atlanta	5	11	0	.313	348	365

AFC First round: Miami 17, Kansas City 16; Cincinnati 41, Houston 14
AFC Divisional playoffs: Buffalo 44, Miami 34; L.A. Raiders 20, Cincinnati 10
AFC Championship: Buffalo 51, L.A. Raiders 3
NFC First round: Washington 20, Philadelphia 6; Chicago 16, New Orleans 6
NFC Divisional playoffs: San Francisco 28, Washington 10; N.Y. Giants 31, Chicago 3
NFC Championship: N.Y. Giants 15, San Francisco 13
Super Bowl XXV: N.Y. Giants 20, Buffalo 19

1991 NFL DRAFT

*Underclassman

Player	Order No.	Pos.	College	Club	Round
Agee, Mel	152	DT	Illinois	Indianapolis	6
Alexander, Zeno	318	LB	Arizona	Detroit	12
Alsbury, Paul	303	P	SW Texas State	New England	11
Amsler, Greg	198	RB	Tennessee	Phoenix	8
Anderson, Herbie	255	DB	Texas A&I	Phoenix	10
Andrews, Richie	151	K	Florida State	Detroit	6
Arthur, Mike	130	C	Texas A&M	Cincinnati	5
Austin, Elijah	308	NT	North Carolina State	Cleveland	12
Austin, Randy	199	TE	UCLA	Atlanta	8
Backes, Tom	272	DE	Oklahoma	Chicago	10
Bagsby, Terry	120	LB	East Texas State	Tampa Bay	5
Bailey, Robert	107	DB	Miami	Los Angeles Rams	4
Baker, Al	261	RB	Kentucky	New York Jets	10
*Baldwin, Randy	92	RB	Mississippi	Minnesota	4
Barnett, Tim	77	WR	Jackson State	Kansas City	3
Barrett, Reggie	58	WR	Texas-El Paso	Detroit	3
Beauford, Terry	192	G	Florida A&M	San Diego	7
Beavers, Darrell	327	DB	Morehead State	Philadelphia	12
Bell, Charles	243	DB	Baylor	Washington	9
Bell, Nick	43	RB	Iowa	Los Angeles Raiders	2
Bennett, Antoine	322	DB	Florida A&M	Cincinnati	12
Bethel, Randy	251	TE	Miami	New England	10
Bieniemy, Eric	39	RB	Colorado	San Diego	2
Blevins, Frank	169	LB	Oklahoma	Green Bay	7
Boatswain, Harry	137	T	New Haven	San Francisco	5
Boles, Tony	291	RB	Michigan	Dallas	11
Bouldin, Jerry	250	WR	Mississippi State	New York Giants	9
Bowles, Scott	165	T	North Texas State	San Francisco	6
Bradley, James	181	WR	Michigan State	Indianapolis	7
Brady, Jeff	323	LB	Kentucky	Pittsburgh	12
Bridewell, Jeff	309	QB	Cal-Davis	Phoenix	12
Brown, Gary	214	RB	Penn State	Houston	8
Brown, Ivory Lee	171	RB	Arkansas-Pine Bluff	Phoenix	7
Brown, Larry	320	DB	Texas Christian	Dallas	12
Brownlow, Darrick	132	LB	Illinois	Dallas	5
Brunson, Joe	331	DT	Tenn.-Chattanooga	Miami	12
Bruton, Tim	208	TE	Missouri	Indianapolis	8
Bryant, Blaise	148	RB	Iowa State	New York Jets	6
Bunch, Jarrod	27	RB	Michigan	New York Giants	1
Burnette, Reggie	176	LB	Houston	Green Bay	7
Caesar, Ivan	286	LB	Boston College	Minnesota	11
*Campbell, Jesse	48	DB	North Carolina State	Philadelphia	2
Canley, Sheldon	193	RB	San Jose State	San Francisco	7
*Carpenter, Rob	109	WR	Syracuse	Cincinnati	4
Carroll, Wesley	42	WR	Miami	New Orleans	2
Carter, Marty	207	DB	Middle Tennessee	Tampa Bay	8
Carter, Simmie	195	DB	So. Mississippi	New York Giants	7
Cash, Keith	188	WR	Texas	Washington	7
Cash, Kerry	125	TE	Texas	Indianapolis	5
Chamblee, Al	314	LB	Virginia Tech	Tampa Bay	12
Christian, Bob	310	RB	Northwestern	Atlanta	12
Clark, Stephen	333	TE	Texas	Buffalo	12

Cowboys tabbed Miami DT Russell Maryland as No. 1 overall.

UCLA safety Eric Turner, second pick, landed in Cleveland.

Player	Order No.	Pos.	College	Club	Round
Clark, Vinnie	19	DB	Ohio State	Green Bay	1
*Coates, Ben	124	TE	Livingstone	New England	5
Collins, Linzy	316	WR	Missouri	Green Bay	12
Colon, Harry	196	DB	Missouri	New England	8
Confer, Cliff	332	DE	Michigan State	San Francisco	12
Conover, Frank	197	DT	Syracuse	Cleveland	8
Conover, Scott	118	G	Purdue	Detroit	5
Cook, John	328	DT	Washington	Chicago	12
Cooper, Adrian	103	TE	Oklahoma	Pittsburgh	4
Covington, Tony	93	DB	Virginia	Tampa Bay	4
Cox, Bryan	113	LB	Western Illinois	Miami	5
Crafts, Jerry	292	T	Louisville	Indianapolis	11
Craver, Aaron	60	RB	Fresno State	Miami	3
Crews, Terry	281	LB	Western Michigan	Los Angeles Rams	11
Cristobal, Luis	278	G	Miami	New York Giants	10
Croel, Mike	4	LB	Nebraska	Denver	1
Curry, Shane	40	DE	Miami	Indianapolis	2
Dahl, Bob	72	DT	Notre Dame	Cincinnati	3

Rams went for Notre Dame's Todd Lyght as No. 5.

Eagles chose Tennessee tackle Antone Davis No. 8.

Player	Order No.	Pos.	College	Club	Round
*Daniels, David	74	WR	Penn State	Seattle	3
Davey, Don	67	DE	Wisconsin	Green Bay	3
Davis, Antone	8	T	Tennessee	Philadelphia	1
*Davis, Dexter	86	DB	Clemson	Phoenix	4
Davis, Harlan	128	DB	Tennessee	Seattle	5
Dawsey, Lawrence	66	WR	Florida State	Tampa Bay	3
De Lorenzo, Tony	277	G	New Mexico State	Buffalo	10
Dean, Walter	149	RB	Grambling	Green Bay	6
Dingle, Mike	211	RB	South Carolina	Cincinnati	8
Dingman, Dean	212	G	Michigan	Pittsburgh	8
Dohring, Tom	218	T	Michigan	Kansas City	8
Donahue, Mitch	95	LB	Wyoming	San Francisco	4
Donnalley, Kevin	79	T	North Carolina	Houston	3
Drabczak, Mark	321	G	Minnesota	New Orleans	12
Dumas, Mike	28	DB	Indiana	Houston	2
Edwards, Dixon	37	LB	Michigan State	Dallas	2
Edwards, Tim	307	DT	Delta State	New England	12
Ellison, Bernard	189	DB	Nevada-Reno	Kansas City	7
Erickson, Craig	131	QB	Miami	Philadelphia	5
Ervins, Ricky	76	RB	Southern California	Washington	3
Evans, Jerry	204	TE	Toledo	Phoenix	8
Evans, Scott	209	DT	Oklahoma	Phoenix	8
Fain, Richard	157	DB	Florida	Cincinnati	6

Arizona State RB Leonard Russell became a Patriot.

Player	Order No.	Pos.	College	Club	Round
Favre, Brett	33	QB	So. Mississippi	Atlanta	2
Fields, Floyd	127	DB	Arizona State	San Diego	5
Fields, Jeff	228	NT	Arkansas State	Los Angeles Rams	9
Fite, Jeff	135	P	Memphis State	Green Bay	5
Flannery, John	44	C	Syracuse	Houston	2
Flores, Mike	298	DE	Louisville	Philadelphia	11
Fort, Neal	143	T	Brigham Young	Los Angeles Rams	6
Freeman, Kyle	183	LB	Angelo State	Houston	7
Gardner, Moe	87	NT	Illinois	Atlanta	4
*Gardocki, Chris	78	P-K	Clemson	Chicago	3
Garrett, Shane	241	WR	Texas A&M	Cincinnati	9
Garten, Joe	164	C	Colorado	Green Bay	6
Giannetti, Frank	263	DE	Penn State	Indianapolis	10
Gibson, Don	227	NT	Southern California	Denver	9
Glenn, O'Neil	224	G	Maryland	New England	9
Glonek, Paul	234	DT	Arizona	New York Jets	9
Glover, Andrew	274	TE	Grambling	Los Angeles Raiders	10
Goode, James	114	LB	Oklahoma	Atlanta	5
Graham, Jeff	46	WR	Ohio State	Pittsburgh	2
Green, Chris	191	DB	Illinois	Miami	7
Greenfield, Brian	252	P	Pittsburgh	Cleveland	10
Griffith, Howard	236	RB	Illinois	Indianapolis	9
Gulledge, David	299	DB	Jacksonville State	Washington	11

Lions caged Virginia WR Herman Moore with 10th pick.

Player	Order No.	Pos.	College	Club	Round
Gunn, Mark	94	DT	Pittsburgh	New York Jets	4
Hall, Rhett	147	DT	California	Tampa Bay	6
Hamilton, Millard	166	WR	Clark	Buffalo	6
Hammond, Vance	117	DT	Clemson	Phoenix	5
Hanks, Merton	122	DB	Iowa	San Francisco	5
Hansen, Phil	54	DE	North Dakota State	Buffalo	2
Hargain, Tony	221	WR	Oregon	San Francisco	8
Harlow, Pat	11	T	Southern California	New England	1
Harmon, Andy	156	DE	Kent State	Philadelphia	6
Harmon, Eric	271	G	Clemson	Philadelphia	10
Harper, Alvin	12	WR	Tennessee	Dallas	1
Harris, Ike	324	G	South Carolina	Seattle	12
Harris, Kevin	110	DE	Texas Southern	Dallas	4
Harrison, Nolan	146	DT	Indiana	Los Angeles Raiders	6
Hayes, Mark	315	T	Arizona State	New York Jets	12
Haynes, Hayward	182	G	Florida State	New Orleans	7

Player	Order No.	Pos.	College	Club	Round
Heldt, Mike	257	C	Notre Dame	San Diego	10
Henderson, Jerome	41	DB	Clemson	New England	2
Hickson, Hyland	265	RB	Michigan State	Tampa Bay	10
Hill, Randal	23	WR	Miami	Miami	1
Hill, Tony	108	DE	Tenn.-Chattanooga	Dallas	4
Holdbrooks, Byron	276	NT	Alabama	San Francisco	10
Hollas, Donald	99	QB	Rice	Cincinnati	4
Horton, Larry	217	DB	Texas A&M	Chicago	8
Hudson, Gerald	232	RB	Oklahoma State	Minnesota	9
Hughes, Darren	313	WR	Carson-Newman	Minnesota	12
Irvin, Raymond	225	DB	Central Florida	Cleveland	9
*Ismail, Raghib	100	WR	Notre Dame	Los Angeles Raiders	4
Jackson, Cedric	205	RB	Texas Christian	Detroit	8
Jackson, Michael	141	WR	So. Mississippi	Cleveland	6
Jackson, Steve	71	DB	Purdue	Houston	3
James, Tim	202	DB	Colorado	New York Jets	8
Jefferson, Shawn	240	WR	Central Florida	Houston	9
Jenkins, Carlos	65	LB	Michigan State	Minnesota	3
Johnson, Alex	325	WR	Miami	Houston	12
Johnson, Dennis	330	WR	Winston-Salem	Los Angeles Raiders	12
Johnson, Joe	105	DB	North Carolina State	Chicago	4
Johnson, John	53	LB	Clemson	San Francisco	2
Johnson, Reggie	30	TE	Florida State	Denver	2
Johnson, Reggie	206	DE	Arizona	Minnesota	8
Jones, Andre	185	LB	Notre Dame	Pittsburgh	7
Jones, Brian	213	LB	Texas	Los Angeles Raiders	8
Jones, Clarence	111	T	Maryland	New York Giants	4
Jones, David	177	WR	Delaware State	San Diego	7
Jones, Henry	26	DB	Illinois	Buffalo	1
Jones, James	57	NT	Northern Iowa	Cleveland	3
Jones, Mike	32	DE	North Carolina State	Phoenix	2
*Jones, Reginald	126	DB	Memphis State	New Orleans	5
Jones, Todd	280	G	Henderson (Ark.)	Cleveland	11
Joseph, James	187	RB	Auburn	Philadelphia	7
Justin, Paul	190	QB	Arizona State	Chicago	7
Kasay, John	98	K	Georgia	Seattle	4
Katoa, Andy	230	LB	Southern Oregon	San Diego	9
Keen, Robbie	244	K	California	Kansas City	9
Keeton, Rocen	288	LB	UCLA	New York Jets	11
Key, David	140	DB	Michigan	New England	6
*King, Ed	29	G	Auburn	Cleveland	2
Kirkland, Dean	305	G	Washington	Buffalo	11
Kowalkowski, Scott	216	LB	Notre Dame	Philadelphia	8
La Duke, Nathan	282	DB	Arizona State	Phoenix	11
Laister, Jimmy	150	T	Oregon Tech	San Diego	6
Lamb, Brad	222	WR	Anderson (Ind.)	Buffalo	8
Lavin, Jim	268	G	Georgia Tech	Cincinnati	10
Lett, Leon	173	DT	Emporia State	Dallas	7
Lewis, Darren	161	RB	Texas A&M	Chicago	6
Lewis, Darryl	38	DB	Arizona	Houston	2
Lewis, Greg	115	RB	Washington	Denver	5
Lewis, Morris	63	LB	Georgia	New York Jets	3
Lewis, Tahaun	247	DB	Nebraska	Los Angeles Raiders	9
Logan, Ernie	226	DE	East Carolina	Atlanta	9
Long, Stacy	301	G	Clemson	Chicago	11
*Love, Sean	264	G	Penn State	Dallas	10
*Lucas, Pete	258	T	Stevens Point (Wis.)	Atlanta	10
Luedeke, Rob	319	C	Penn State	Indianapolis	12
Lyght, Todd	5	DB	Notre Dame	Los Angeles Rams	1
Maddox, Mark	249	LB	Northern Michigan	Buffalo	9

Player	Order No.	Pos.	College	Club	Round
Malone, Darrell	162	DB	Jacksonville State	Kansas City	6
*Marinovich, Todd	24	QB	Southern California	Los Angeles Raiders	1
Maryland, Russell	1	DT	Miami	Dallas	1
Mayfield, Curtis	253	WR	Oklahoma State	Denver	10
Mays, Damon	235	WR	Missouri	Dallas	9
McAfee, Fred	154	RB	Mississippi College	New Orleans	6
McCaffrey, Ed	83	WR	Stanford	New York Giants	3
McCardell, Keenan	326	WR	Nevada-Las Vegas	Washington	12
McCloughan, Dave	69	DB	Colorado	Indianapolis	3
McGhee, Kanavis	55	LB	Colorado	New York Giants	2
McGonnigal, Bruce	238	TE	Virginia	Pittsburgh	9
McGriggs, Lamar	223	DB	Western Illinois	New York Giants	8
McGwire, Dan	16	QB	San Diego State	Seattle	1
McRae, Charles	7	T	Tennessee	Tampa Bay	1
Milburn, Darryl	231	DE	Grambling	Detroit	9
Miller, Blake	168	C	Louisiana State	New England	7
Miller, Corey	167	LB	South Carolina	New York Giants	6
Miller, Scott	246	WR	UCLA	Miami	9
Mills, Ernie	73	WR	Florida	Pittsburgh	3
Mincy, Charles	133	DB	Washington	Kansas City	5
Mitchell, Brian	172	DB	Brigham Young	Atlanta	7
Moore, Curtis	267	LB	Kansas	Houston	10
*Moore, Herman	10	WR	Virginia	Detroit	1
Moore, Shawn	284	QB	Virginia	Denver	11
Moore, Vince	279	WR	Tennessee	New England	11
Morgan, Anthony	134	WR	Tennessee	Chicago	5
Moss, Anthony	139	LB	Florida State	New York Giants	5
Moten, Eric	47	G	Michigan State	San Diego	2
Musgrave, Bill	106	QB	Oregon	Dallas	4
Myles, Godfrey	62	LB	Florida	Dallas	3
Nagle, Browning	34	QB	Louisville	New York Jets	2
O'Hara, Pat	260	QB	Southern California	Tampa Bay	10
Olive, Bobby	300	WR	Ohio State	Kansas City	11
Pahukoa, Jeff	311	T	Washington	Los Angeles Rams	12
Parrish, Doug	175	DB	San Francisco State	New York Jets	7
Pegram, Erric	145	RB	North Texas State	Atlanta	6
Phifer, Roman	31	LB	UCLA	Los Angeles Rams	2
Pickens, Bruce	3	DB	Nebraska	Atlanta	1
Pierce, Brady	259	T	Wisconsin	Minnesota	10
Poles, Roland	254	RB	Tennessee	San Diego	10
Popson, Ted	306	TE	Portland State	New York Giants	11
Porter, Rapier	262	TE	Arkansas-Pine Bluff	Green Bay	10
Pritchard, Mike	13	WR	Colorado	Atlanta	1
#Pritchett, Kelvin	20	DT	Mississippi	Dallas	1
Ramsey, Eric	273	DB	Auburn	Kansas City	10
Ransom, Dennis	159	TE	Texas A&M	Washington	6
Rasul, Amir	194	RB	Florida A&M	Buffalo	7
Reagan, Scotty	179	DT	Humboldt State	Minnesota	7
Reed, Jake	68	WR	Grambling	Minnesota	3
Richard, Stanley	9	DB	Texas	San Diego	1
*Richards, Curvin	97	RB	Pittsburgh	Dallas	4
Richards, James	64	G	California	Dallas	3
Richardson, Huey	15	DE	Florida	Pittsburgh	1
Riddick, Louis	248	DB	Pittsburgh	San Francisco	9
Riley, Mike	160	DB	Tulane	New York Jets	6
Ringoen, Erik	266	LB	Hofstra	Seattle	10
Robertson, Marcus	102	DB	Iowa State	Houston	4
Rocker, David	101	DT	Auburn	Houston	4

Traded to Detroit

Raiders made Canada-bound ND's "Rocket" Ismail No. 100.

Player	Order No.	Pos.	College	Club	Round
Rogers, Ernie	302	G	California	Miami	11
Rogers, Lamar	52	DT	Auburn	Cincinnati	2
Ross, Scott	293	LB	Southern California	New Orleans	11
Russell, Derek	89	WR	Arkansas	Denver	4
Russell, Leonard	14	RB	Arizona State	New England	1
Ryan, Tim	136	G	Notre Dame	Tampa Bay	5
Sagapolutele, Pio	85	NT	San Diego State	Cleveland	4
Samuels, Chris	317	RB	Texas	San Diego	12
Scott, Kevin	91	DB	Stanford	Detroit	4
Scott, Todd	163	DB	SW Louisiana	Minnesota	6
Selby, Rob	75	T	Auburn	Philadelphia	3
Shale, Cris	270	P	Bowling Green	Washington	10
Shelton, Tyrone	170	RB	William & Mary	Los Angeles Rams	7
Shipley, Ron	329	G	New Mexico	Kansas City	12
Sims, Joe	283	NT	Nebraska	Atlanta	11
Sinclair, Mike	155	DE	Eastern New Mexico	Seattle	6
Slaughter, Bobby	304	WR	Louisiana Tech	San Francisco	11
Smith, Chris	295	TE	Brigham Young	Cincinnati	11
Smith, James	294	DB	Richmond	Houston	11
Smith, Roland	220	DB	Miami	Miami	8
Solomon, Ariel	269	T	Colorado	Pittsburgh	10
Spencer, Jimmy	215	DB	Florida	Washington	8
Stephens, Calvin	56	G	South Carolina	New England	3
Stewart, Tony	297	RB	Iowa	Seattle	11

Player	Order No.	Pos.	College	Club	Round
Stonebreaker, Mike	245	LB	Notre Dame	Chicago	9
Subis, Nick	142	T	San Diego State	Denver	6
Sullivan, Mike	153	G	Miami	Dallas	6
Sunvold, Mike	287	DT	Minnesota	Tampa Bay	11
Sutton, Walter	256	WR	SW Minnesota	Atlanta	10
*Swann, Eric	6	DE	New Orleans College	Phoenix	1
Taylor, Treamelle	233	WR	Nevada-Reno	Tampa Bay	9
Thigpen, Yancey	90	WR	Winston-Salem	San Diego	4
Thomas, Doug	51	WR	Clemson	Seattle	2
Thomas, Efrum	296	DB	Alabama	Pittsburgh	11
Thomas, Franklin	178	TE	Grambling	Detroit	7
Thomas, Stan	22	T	Texas	Chicago	1
Thomas, William	104	LB	Texas A&M	Philadelphia	4
Thome, Chris	119	C	Minnesota	Minnesota	5
*Thompson, Ernie	312	RB	Indiana	Los Angeles Rams	12
Thompson, Leroy	158	RB	Penn State	Pittsburgh	6
Thornton, George	36	DT	Alabama	San Diego	2
Tiggle, Calvin	174	LB	Georgia Tech	Tampa Bay	7
Titley, Michael	275	TE	Iowa	Miami	10
Traylor, Keith	61	LB	Central State (Okla.)	Denver	3
Tuaolo, Esera	35	NT	Oregon State	Green Bay	2
Tucker, Mark	186	C	Southern California	Atlanta	7
Turner, Eric	2	DB	UCLA	Cleveland	1
Tyrance, Pat	201	LB	Nebraska	Los Angeles Rams	8
Valerio, Joe	50	T	Pennsylvania	Kansas City	2
Vander Poel, Mark	96	T	Colorado	Indianapolis	4
*Vaughn, Jon	112	RB	Michigan	New England	5
Vega, Eduardo	144	T	Memphis State	Phoenix	6
Vinson, Fernandus	184	DB	North Carolina State	Cincinnati	7
Wainright, Frank	210	TE	Northern Colorado	New Orleans	8
Walker, Johnny	203	WR	Texas	Green Bay	8
Walker, Kenny	200	DE	Nebraska	Denver	8
*Walker, Sammy	88	DB	Texas Tech	Pittsburgh	4
Wallace, Anthony	237	RB	California	New Orleans	9
Wanke, Larry	334	QB	John Carroll	New York Giants	12
Washington, Ted	25	DT	Louisville	San Francisco	1
Watkins, Slip	285	KR	Louisiana State	Detroit	11
Watters, Ricky	45	RB	Notre Dame	San Francisco	2
Weatherspoon, Chuck	242	RB	Houston	Philadelphia	9
*Webb, Chuck	81	RB	Tennessee	Green Bay	3
Weinberg, Joaquim	290	WR	Johnson C. Smith	San Diego	11
Welborne, Tripp	180	DB	Michigan	Minnesota	7
Wellman, Gary	129	WR	Southern California	Houston	5
Wierenga, J. J.	289	DE	Central Michigan	Green Bay	11
Wiggins, Shawn	239	WR	Wyoming	Cleveland	9
Wilbourn, Shawn	138	DB	Cal State-Long Beach	Buffalo	5
Williams, Aeneas	59	DB	Southern U.	Phoenix	3
Williams, Alfred	18	LB	Colorado	Cincinnati	1
Williams, Eric	70	T	Central State (Ohio)	Dallas	3
Williams, Gene	121	G	Iowa State	Miami	5
Williams, Harvey	21	RB	Louisiana State	Kansas City	1
Wilson, Bobby	17	DT	Michigan State	Washington	1
Wilson, Robert	80	RB	Texas A&M	Tampa Bay	3
Witkowski, Dean	229	LB	North Dakota	Green Bay	9
Woulard, Todd	219	LB	Alabama A&M	Los Angeles Raiders	8
Wren, Darryl	82	DB	Pittsburgh (Kan.)	Buffalo	3
Young, Duane	123	TE	Michigan State	San Diego	5
Young, Robert	116	DE	Mississippi State	Los Angeles Rams	5
Zolak, Scott	84	QB	Maryland	New England	4
Zorich, Chris	49	DT	Notre Dame	Chicago	2

Huey Richardson, Florida LB
Steelers (No. 15)

Charles McRae, Tennessee T
Buccaneers (No. 7)

Giants made Michigan RB Jarrod Bunch their No. 1.

1991 NFL SCHEDULE

***NIGHT GAME**

SUNDAY, SEPT. 1
Atlanta at Kansas City
Cincinnati at Denver
Dallas at Cleveland
Los Angeles Raiders at Houston
Miami at Buffalo
Minnesota at Chicago
New England at Indianapolis
Philadelphia at Green Bay
Phoenix at Los Angeles Rams
San Diego at Pittsburgh
Seattle at New Orleans
Tampa Bay at New York Jets
*Detroit at Washington

MONDAY, SEPT. 2
*San Francisco at New York Giants

SUNDAY, SEPT. 8
Chicago at Tampa Bay
Cleveland at New England
Denver at Los Angeles Raiders
Green Bay at Detroit
Indianapolis at Miami
Los Angeles Rams at New York Giants
Minnesota at Atlanta
New Orleans at Kansas City
New York Jets at Seattle
Phoenix at Philadelphia
Pittsburgh at Buffalo
San Diego at San Francisco
*Houston at Cincinnati

MONDAY, SEPT. 9
*Washington at Dallas

SUNDAY, SEPT. 15
Atlanta at San Diego
Buffalo at New York Jets
Cincinnati at Cleveland
Indianapolis at Los Angeles Raiders
Miami at Detroit
New England at Pittsburgh
New York Giants at Chicago
Philadelphia at Dallas
Phoenix at Washington
San Francisco at Minnesota
Seattle at Denver
Tampa Bay at Green Bay
*Los Angeles Rams at New Orleans

MONDAY, SEPT. 16
*Kansas City at Houston

SUNDAY, SEPT. 22
Buffalo at Tampa Bay
Cleveland at New York Giants
Detroit at Indianapolis
Green Bay at Miami
Houston at New England
Los Angeles Raiders at Atlanta
Los Angeles Rams at San Francisco
Minnesota at New Orleans
Pittsburgh at Philadelphia
San Diego at Denver
Seattle at Kansas City
Washington at Cincinnati
*Dallas at Phoenix

MONDAY, SEPT. 23
*New York Jets at Chicago

SUNDAY, SEPT. 29
Chicago at Buffalo
Green Bay at Los Angeles Rams
Indianapolis at Seattle
Kansas City at San Diego
Miami at New York Jets
New England at Phoenix
New Orleans at Atlanta
New York Giants at Dallas
San Francisco at Los Angeles Raiders
Tampa Bay at Detroit
*Denver at Minnesota

Steelers' Bubby Brister hit for career-high 20 TDs.

MONDAY, SEPT. 30
*Philadelphia at Washington

SUNDAY, OCT. 6
Dallas vs. Green Bay at Milwaukee
Denver at Houston
Miami at New England
Minnesota at Detroit
New York Jets at Cleveland
Philadelphia at Tampa Bay
Phoenix at New York Giants
San Diego at Los Angeles Raiders
Seattle at Cincinnati
Washington at Chicago
*Pittsburgh at Indianapolis

MONDAY, OCT. 7
*Buffalo at Kansas City

SUNDAY, OCT. 13
Cincinnati at Dallas
Cleveland at Washington
Houston at New York Jets
Indianapolis at Buffalo

Miami at Kansas City
New Orleans at Philadelphia
Phoenix at Minnesota
San Diego at Los Angeles Rams
San Francisco at Atlanta
*Los Angeles Raiders at Seattle

MONDAY, OCT. 14
*New York Giants at Pittsburgh

THURSDAY, OCT. 17
*Chicago at Green Bay

SUNDAY, OCT. 20
Atlanta at Phoenix
Cleveland at San Diego
Detroit at San Francisco
Houston at Miami
Kansas City at Denver
Los Angeles Rams at Los Angeles Raiders
Minnesota at New England
New York Jets at Indianapolis
Seattle at Pittsburgh
Tampa Bay at New Orleans

MONDAY, OCT. 21
*Cincinnati at Buffalo

SUNDAY, OCT. 27
Chicago at New Orleans
Cincinnati at Houston
Dallas at Detroit
Denver at New England
Green Bay at Tampa Bay
Los Angeles Rams at Atlanta
Minnesota at Phoenix
Pittsburgh at Cleveland
San Diego at Seattle
San Francisco at Philadelphia
*Washington at New York Giants

MONDAY, OCT. 28
*Los Angeles Raiders at Kansas City

SUNDAY, NOV. 3
Atlanta at San Francisco
Cleveland at Cincinnati
Detroit at Chicago
Green Bay at New York Jets
Houston at Washington
Miami at Indianapolis
New England at Buffalo
New Orleans at Los Angeles Rams
Phoenix at Dallas
Tampa Bay at Minnesota
*Pittsburgh at Denver

MONDAY, NOV. 4
*New York Giants at Philadelphia

SUNDAY, NOV. 10
Atlanta at Washington
Buffalo vs. Green Bay at Milwaukee
Dallas at Houston
Detroit at Tampa Bay
Indianapolis at New York Jets
Kansas City at Los Angeles Rams
Los Angeles Raiders at Denver
New York Giants at Phoenix
Philadelphia at Cleveland
Pittsburgh at Cincinnati
San Francisco at New Orleans
Seattle at San Diego
*New England at Miami

MONDAY, NOV. 11
*Chicago at Minnesota

SUNDAY, NOV. 17
Chicago at Indianapolis
Cincinnati at Philadelphia
Dallas at New York Giants
Denver at Kansas City
Los Angeles Rams at Detroit
Minnesota at Green Bay
New Orleans at San Diego
New York Jets at New England
Phoenix at San Francisco
Seattle at Los Angeles Raiders
Tampa Bay at Atlanta
Washington at Pittsburgh
*Cleveland at Houston

MONDAY, NOV. 18
*Buffalo at Miami

SUNDAY, NOV. 24
Buffalo at New England
Dallas at Washington
Denver at Seattle

Detroit at Minnesota
Houston at Pittsburgh
Indianapolis vs. Green Bay at Milwaukee
Kansas City at Cleveland
Los Angeles Raiders at Cincinnati
Miami at Chicago
New York Giants at Tampa Bay
Philadelphia at Phoenix
San Diego at New York Jets
*Atlanta at New Orleans

MONDAY, NOV. 25
*San Francisco at Los Angeles Rams

THURSDAY, NOV. 28
Chicago at Detroit
Pittsburgh at Dallas

SUNDAY, DEC. 1
Cleveland at Indianapolis
Green Bay at Atlanta
Kansas City at Seattle
New England at Denver
New Orleans at San Francisco
New York Giants at Cincinnati
New York Jets at Buffalo
Tampa Bay at Miami
Washington at Los Angeles Rams
*Los Angeles Raiders at San Diego

MONDAY, DEC. 2
*Philadelphia at Houston

SUNDAY, DEC. 8
Atlanta at Los Angeles Rams
Buffalo at Los Angeles Raiders
Denver at Cleveland
Green Bay at Chicago
Indianapolis at New England
New Orleans at Dallas
New York Jets at Detroit
Philadelphia at New York Giants
Pittsburgh at Houston
San Diego at Kansas City
San Francisco at Seattle
Washington at Phoenix
*Minnesota at Tampa Bay

MONDAY, DEC. 9
*Cincinnati at Miami

SATURDAY, DEC. 14
Kansas City at San Francisco
Tampa Bay at Chicago

SUNDAY, DEC. 15
Cincinnati at Pittsburgh
Dallas at Philadelphia
Detroit at Green Bay
Houston at Cleveland
Los Angeles Rams at Minnesota
Miami at San Diego
New England at New York Jets
New York Giants at Washington
Phoenix at Denver
Seattle at Atlanta
*Buffalo at Indianapolis

MONDAY, DEC. 16
*Los Angeles Raiders at New Orleans

SATURDAY, DEC. 21
Green Bay at Minnesota
Houston at New York Giants

SUNDAY, DEC. 22
Atlanta at Dallas
Cleveland at Pittsburgh
Denver at San Diego
Detroit at Buffalo
Indianapolis at Tampa Bay
Kansas City at Los Angeles Raiders
New England at Cincinnati
New Orleans at Phoenix
New York Jets at Miami
Washington at Philadelphia
*Los Angeles Rams at Seattle

MONDAY, DECEMBER 23
*Chicago at San Francisco

Nationally Televised Games

REGULAR SEASON

Sunday, Sept. 1—Minnesota at Chicago (day, CBS)
Detroit at Washington (night, TNT)
Monday, Sept. 2—San Francisco at New York Giants (night, ABC)
Sunday, Sept. 8—Denver at Los Angeles Raiders (day, NBC)
Houston at Cincinnati (night, TNT)
Monday, Sept. 9—Washington at Dallas (night, ABC)
Sunday, Sept. 15—Indianapolis at Los Angeles Raiders (day, NBC)
Los Angeles Rams at New Orleans (night, TNT)
Monday, Sept. 16—Kansas City at Houston (night, ABC)
Sunday, Sept. 22—Los Angeles Rams at San Francisco (day, CBS)
Dallas at Phoenix (night, TNT)
Monday, Sept. 23—New York Jets at Chicago (night, ABC)
Sunday, Sept. 29—San Francisco at Los Angeles Raiders (day, CBS)
Denver at Minnesota (night, TNT)
Monday, Sept. 30—Philadelphia at Washington (night, ABC)
Sunday, Oct. 6—San Diego at Los Angeles Raiders (day, NBC)
Pittsburgh at Indianapolis (night, TNT)
Monday, Oct. 7—Buffalo at Kansas City (night, ABC)
Sunday, Oct. 13—Miami at Kansas City (day, NBC)
Los Angeles Raiders at Seattle (night, TNT)
Monday, Oct. 14—New York Giants at Pittsburgh (night, ABC)
Sunday, Oct. 20—Los Angeles Rams at Los Angeles Raiders (day, CBS)
Chicago at Green Bay (night, TNT)
Monday, Oct. 21—Cincinnati at Buffalo (night, ABC)
Sunday Oct. 27—San Diego at Seattle (day, NBC)
Washington at New York Giants (night, ESPN)
Monday, Oct. 28—Los Angeles Raiders at Kansas City (night, ABC)
Sunday, Nov. 3—New Orleans at Los Angeles Rams (day, CBS)
Pittsburgh at Denver (night, ESPN)
Monday, Nov. 4—New York Giants at Philadelphia (night, ABC)
Sunday, Nov. 10—Kansas City at Los Angeles Rams (day, NBC)
New England at Miami (night, ESPN)
Monday, Nov. 11—Chicago at Minnesota (night, ABC)
Sunday, Nov. 17—Dallas at New York Giants (day, CBS)
Cleveland at Houston (night, ESPN)
Monday, Nov. 18—Buffalo at Miami (night, ABC)
Sunday, Nov. 24—Denver at Seattle (day, NBC)
Atlanta at New Orleans (night, ESPN)
Monday, Nov. 25—San Francisco at Los Angeles Rams (night, ABC)
Thursday, Nov. 28—Chicago at Detroit (day, CBS)
Pittsburgh at Dallas (day, NBC)
Sunday, Dec. 1—Washington at Los Angeles Rams (day, CBS)
Los Angeles Raiders at San Diego (night, ESPN)
Monday, Dec. 2—Philadelphia at Houston (night, ABC)

Tim McDonald continues as Cardinals' top tackler.

Sunday, Dec. 8—Buffalo at Los Angeles Raiders (day, NBC)
Minnesota at Tampa Bay (night, ESPN)
Monday, Dec. 9—Cincinnati at Miami (night, ABC)
Saturday, Dec. 14—Tampa Bay at Chicago (day, CBS)
Kansas City at San Francisco (day, NBC)
Sunday, Dec. 15—New York Giants at Washington (day, CBS)
Buffalo at Indianapolis (night, ESPN)
Monday, Dec. 16—Los Angeles Raiders at New Orleans (night, ABC)
Saturday, Dec. 21—Houston at New York Giants (day, NBC)
Green Bay at Minnesota (day, CBS)
Sunday, Dec. 22—Kansas City at Los Angeles Raiders (day, NBC)
Los Angeles Rams at Seattle (night, ESPN)
Monday, Dec. 23—Chicago at San Francisco (night, ABC)

POSTSEASON

Saturday, Dec. 28—AFC and NFC Wild-Card Playoffs (ABC)
Sunday, Dec. 29—AFC and NFC Wild-Card Playoffs (NBC and CBS)
Saturday, Jan. 4—AFC and NFC Divisional Playoffs (NBC and CBS)
Sunday, Jan. 5—AFC and NFC Divisional Playoffs (NBC and CBS)
Sunday, Jan. 12—AFC and NFC Championship Games (NBC and CBS)
Sunday, Jan. 26—Super Bowl XXVI at Metrodome, Minnesota (CBS)
Sunday, Feb. 2—AFC-NFC Pro Bowl, Honolulu (ESPN)